Courtesy of the National Portrait Gallery

HUGH LATIMER
APOSTLE to the ENGLISH

by

ALLAN G. CHESTER

"I will speak of thy testimonies also before kings and will not be ashamed."   *Psalm* 119:46

PHILADELPHIA

UNIVERSITY OF PENNSYLVANIA PRESS

1954

Published in Great Britain, India, and Pakistan
by Geoffrey Cumberlege: Oxford University Press
London, Bombay, and Karachi

To Florence

NOTE BY THE PUBLISHER

Allan G. Chester was born in Philadelphia on January 13, 1900. He was graduated from the University of Pennsylvania with the degree of Bachelor of Arts in 1922. He received the degrees of Master of Arts and Doctor of Philosophy from the same university in 1924 and 1930. He has been a member of the Department of English of the University of Pennsylvania since 1923.

He is the author of Thomas May, Man of Letters *(Philadelphia, 1932) and the editor of* The Bible: Selections from the Old and New Testaments *(Rinehart Editions, New York, 1952.) Among his more recent articles in scholarly journals are "Richard Johnson's Golden Garland,"* Modern Language Quarterly, *X (1949), 61-67; "Robert Barnes and the Burning of the Books,"* Huntington Library Quarterly, *XIV (1951), 211-21; "Hugh Latimer at Cambridge,"* Crozer Quarterly, *XXVIII (1951), 306-18; "Milton, Latimer, and the Lord Admiral,"* Modern Language Quarterly, *XIV (1953), 15-20. Since 1936 he has been one of the compilers of the "American Bibliography" of English studies published annually in the* Publications of the Modern Language Association.

PREFACE

Hugh Latimer was the most influential preacher of that phase of the English Reformation which began shortly after 1517 with the impact of Lutheranism and ended in 1553 with the accession of Queen Mary. During these years England was separated from obedience to Rome, English monasticism was destroyed, the established economic order was overthrown, and—not least—the English Bible was wrought. In all of these radical changes Latimer played a conspicuous part. Now that the four-hundredth anniversary of his martyrdom is approaching, it may be appropriate to attempt a fresh evaluation of his services to the first English revolution.

There can be no doubt of Latimer's influence upon his own time. The ambassador of Charles V, writing in 1535, declared that Latimer had made more heretics than Luther. The statement is hyperbolic, since Latimer's work was purely insular, but the general force of the remark is accurate enough. It is difficult, however, to assess his work precisely, since it was exercised principally by means of the spoken word, in sermons preached at court, at Paul's Cross, in cathedrals and abbeys and village churches throughout the land. His importance to his age was certainly not that of a speculative thinker. His sermons reflected rather than formulated the advanced religious opinions of the time. But it may safely be said that for every man whose mind was convinced by the theology of a Cranmer or a Ridley, there were a hundred whose consciences were touched by the voice of Latimer.

Since he spoke out vigorously and often incautiously on hotly controversial issues, it is not surprising that Hugh Latimer was idolized by some of his contemporaries and abhorred by others. His admirers hailed him as the apostle to the English, the only prophet in England. His enemies called him a knave bishop and said they trusted to see him burned. These rival attitudes broke out afresh in the nineteenth century. During the heat of the Oxford Movement, John Henry Newman called down anathema upon the "whole tribe of Cranmers, Latimers, Ridleys." But James Anthony Froude, for whom the enchantments of the Oxford Movement faded early, wrote of Latimer as "the one man in England whose conduct was, perhaps, absolutely straightforward, upright, and untainted with the alloy of base metal."

Amidst this factional vehemence, ancient and modern, it is not always easy to be sure that one has discovered the truth. The problem is the more difficult because, in matters of religious controversy, it is impossible to escape one's own ingrained assumptions. But the effort to see a man like Latimer as he really was is rewarding. He was neither a knave nor a saint. He was a fundamentally honest man who tried always to move in the direction of what he believed to be the truth. Sometimes he hesitated because of inner uncertainty; sometimes, but not often, he swerved a little from his course, when the powerful emotions of fear or ambition took control, as they can do with the best of men. His martyr's death is the authoritative witness to the ultimate intensity and sincerity of his convictions.

It will be apparent that the present essay was written by one who gladly subscribes to the words of Sir John Cheke: "I have an ear for other preachers, but I have a heart for Latimer." But it is to be hoped that the reader will feel that the study has not been written in the spirit of factionalism. It does not seek to prove Latimer right and his opponents wrong. It seeks merely to present, as truthfully and accurately as may be, the facts about an interesting human being whose life and work were significant in his own age, and of far greater import for ours than is commonly supposed.

I am happy to acknowledge my special debt to three of those writers on Latimer whose work is listed in my notes and bibliography. The first of these is John Foxe the martyrologist, through whose regard for Latimer were preserved many biographical details of importance, as well as the substance of the "Sermons on the Card" and the texts of a number of letters. Anyone who works with Foxe's great *Acts and Monuments* learns to move warily through the mists of its propaganda, but at the same time he acquires a high regard for Foxe as a researcher, particularly as a digger in the archives. The second is Robert Demaus, whose *Hugh Latimer,* first published in 1869, was a pioneering work which any serious student must respect. Although at some points I differ sharply from Demaus in matters of interpretation, I confess that in matters of factual detail I have gleaned where he reaped. The third is Canon Corrie, who edited Latimer's sermons and other remains for the Parker Society.

I wish also to express my gratitude to all those who have aided me directly in the preparation of this book. The Committee on the Advancement of Research of the University of Pennsylvania has generously supplied me with several grants-in-aid for photographic materials and clerical assistance. Miss Nellie O'Farrell has transcribed materials relating to Latimer in the Public Record Office. The Rev. J. F. Mozley, Professor Conyers Read, and Mr. Charles C. Butterworth have given generously of their wide knowledge of Tudor history and Tudor literature. Professor Read and Mr. Butterworth have read the manuscript and made suggestions for revision which I have been glad to adopt. My wife has read and criticized the manuscript at every stage and has helped with the index and the proof. She has also, in ways known only to her, removed the obstacles which stood in the way of the completion of the book.

Allan G. Chester

Narberth, Pennsylvania
May 15, 1953

CONTENTS

Note

Since my purpose is not textual, all quotations from Latimer's sermons are in the modernized form used in the Parker Society edition of Latimer's Works. However, I have checked all quotations against the original documents or earliest printed texts; where necessary I have corrected the Parker Society text. For the convenience of readers who may wish to follow up any of the references, my citations of the sermons are likewise to the Parker Society text rather than to the original editions, which can be consulted only in a few libraries or on troublesome reels of microfilm.

It should be noted also that all dates have been modernized. Any date between January 1 and March 24 which in the sources is given according to the old practice of dating the New Year from March 25 has been translated—e.g. February 1, 1530, becomes February 1, 1531.

ABOUT THE NOTES

The notes will be found on pages 219-243. In the text, referential notes are indicated by superior numbers in roman type; discussion notes by superior numbers in italics. In the note section, at the upper right-hand corner of each recto page and the upper left-hand corner of each verso page, will be found numbers indicating the pages of the text to which the notes on these two pages refer.

CHAPTER ONE

STUDENT AND PRIEST

On March 8, 1549, Hugh Latimer preached before King Edward VI and his court at Westminster. The chapel royal was too small to accommodate all those who wanted to hear the most eloquent preacher in England, and a pulpit had been erected especially for him the year before in the private gardens of Westminster Palace. A crude woodcut in John Foxe's celebrated *Acts and Monuments* helps us to visualize the scene. Latimer, an elderly man in square cap and black gown, is mounted upon the high wooden pulpit. A dozen or so privileged personages stand on the platform beside him. A feminine devotee, seated on the steps leading up to the pulpit, takes notes of the sermon. The garden is thronged with folk whose costumes indicate their rank—ministers of state, courtiers, prelates, civic dignitaries of London and Westminster. From a window in the gallery of the palace the boy King, not yet twelve years old, listens gravely. Beside him sits the bearded figure of his uncle, Edward Seymour, the Lord Protector Somerset. Latimer, preaching with the relaxed assurance born of thirty years' experience, raises his right hand in an admonitory gesture towards the King. In his left hand he holds a Bible.

The scene reveals Latimer at the zenith of his career as the "apostle to the English." But it may justly stand at the beginning of a study of his life, for it was in the sermon preached on that occasion that Latimer spoke the famous words which tell us virtually all that we know of his origins. Frankness was one of his most engaging qualities; it was characteristic that he spoke freely of his humble beginnings even before that distinguished audience. He was illustrating the plight of the English yeoman:

My father was a yeoman, and had no lands of his own, only he had a farm of three or four pound by year at the uttermost, and hereupon he tilled so much as kept half a dozen men. He had walk for a hundred sheep; and my mother milked thirty kine. He was able, and did find the king a harness, with himself and his horse, while he came to the place that he should receive the king's wages. I can remember that I buckled his harness when he went unto Blackheath Field [where the Cornish rebels were crushed in June, 1497]. He kept me to school, or else I had not been able to have preached before the king's majesty now. He married my sisters with five pounds or twenty nobles apiece; so that he brought them up in godliness and fear of God. He kept hospitality for his poor neighbors, and some alms he gave to the poor. And all this he did of the said farm, where he that now hath it payeth sixteen pound by year, or more, and is not able to do anything for his prince, for himself nor for his children, or give a cup of drink to the poor.[1]

The passing of more than fifty years may have mellowed the preacher's recollection. But it is clear that he looked back with pleasure to the days when there had been bread enough and to spare, and that he never lost his pride in the class from which he was sprung. He was quite aware of the fact that by mid-century it had produced many of the leaders in the government and most of those in the church. In the same sermon he dwelt upon the topic a little further:

> For if ye bring it to pass that the yeomanry be not able to put their sons to school . . . and that they be not able to marry their daughters to the avoiding of whoredom, I say that ye pluck salvation from the people and utterly destroy the realm. For by yeomen's sons the faith of Christ is and hath been maintained chiefly. Is this realm taught by rich men's sons? No, no; read the chronicles: ye shall find sometime noblemen's sons which have been unpreaching bishops and prelates, but ye shall find none of them learned men.[2]

All that is known of Latimer's family can be set down in one short page. Nothing is discoverable of his remoter ancestors. He himself would have been quite untroubled by the failure of his biographers to discover the names of his grandparents, who lived long before the parish register was instituted to record the short and simple annals of the humble poor. Certainly he would have chuckled at the misdirected efforts of some writers to establish a connection between his family and the wealthy and powerful Latimers of Yorkshire. It is possible, however, to amplify a little Latimer's statement about his father,[3] who was also named Hugh. The few acres he farmed were in or near Thurcaston, a tiny village about five miles north by west of the town of Leicester, in the valley of the Soar. Probably the little farm was part of the manor of Thurcaston.[4] Hugh Latimer's own words indicate that his father was the yearly tenant of the land which he farmed. He thus belonged to a class which enjoyed a moderate prosperity in the latter years of the fifteenth century. But it was a class which, from 1500 onwards, suffered grievously from enclosures for pasturage and from rising rents. The freeholder was protected against increased rents by his fee simple, and the copyholder was partially protected by manorial custom. But the yearly tenant was at the mercy of his landlord. We have Latimer's word for it that within half a century the rents of the yearly tenant had quadrupled. If the elder Latimer lived on until about 1520, it is likely that in his last years he knew the chill touch of penury. The name of Latimer's mother—she who sturdily supervised the milking of thirty cows—has not been preserved. Foxe tells us that she bore her husband several sons, of whom only Hugh lived to maturity, and six daughters.[5] Of these daughters nothing is known save the baptismal names of two of their daughters, Hugh Latimer's nieces. One of these, named Elizabeth, became the wife of Dr. Thomas Sampson, a puritan divine well known in the reign of Queen Elizabeth.[6] The other, Mary, was married first to Robert Glover, who was burned as a heretic at Coventry in 1555, second to a Master Watt, who survived her and composed a lugubrious ballad to her memory.[7] Mary and her first husband were particularly devoted to her uncle and named a son for him.[8] We shall hear more of them later.

Hugh Latimer's birthplace, then, was Thurcaston, in Leicestershire. Unfortunately we cannot be equally certain of the date of his birth. Augustine Bernher, Latimer's close friend in later years, asserted that at some time during the reign of Edward VI Latimer was "above three-score and seven years of age." [9] This statement, which was repeated by John Foxe,[10] would seem to place the great preacher's birth at some time between 1480 and 1486. A date close to the earlier of these limits is suggested by the legend on the portrait which is reproduced as the frontispiece to this book—"1555. Æt. 74." But there is a difficulty with this range of dates. Latimer entered Cambridge in 1506 or 1507.[11] If he had been born between 1480 and 1486, he would have been at least twenty and perhaps as much as twenty-seven years old when he matriculated—and this in a period when the average matriculate was about fourteen. We are helped out of the difficulty by Foxe and by Latimer himself. Speaking of Latimer's early years, Foxe (to whose contradictions one becomes accustomed) said that Latimer entered the university at the age of fourteen [12]; and Latimer said that he was about thirty when he was "converted," [13] an event which can be dated precisely in the year 1524. Together, these statements put Latimer's birth between 1492 and 1494. This dating seems the more probable. Until more conclusive evidence is discovered, let us settle for the year 1492, a date easy to bear in mind. In that case, he would have been twenty-four when he was ordained to the priesthood, forty-three when he was consecrated a bishop, and sixty-three at the time of his death—quite old enough, in terms of the sixteenth century, to merit the designation "Old Latimer" which was so frequently applied to him in his later years.[14]

Foxe asserts that Latimer was of such quickness of wit that at the age of four he was sent to the "common schools of his own country" to be trained up in "erudition and good literature." [15] The latter phrase refers merely to the study of Latin grammar and such passages of Latin literature as were included in the standard textbooks of the time. That Latimer began to study his Latin at the age of four need not (in spite of Foxe) be taken as a sign of precocity; he was doing no more than was normally expected of the bright sons of ambitious parents. What Foxe meant by common schools is less certain. Perhaps Latimer received part of his early training in one of the grammar schools which were then springing up. But it is more probable that, like his great friend Archbishop Cranmer, he "learned his grammar of a rude parish clerk of that barbarous time." [16]

As a matter of fact, the only certain information about Latimer's boyhood has to do with sport rather than letters. He once recalled that as a boy he had been instructed by his father in the use of the bow. "He taught me how to draw, how to lay my body in my bow, and not to draw with strength of arms, as other nations do, but with strength of body; I had my bows bought me, according to my age and strength; as I increased in them, so my bows were made bigger and bigger." [17] This pleasant picture suggests that the elder Latimer was a good citizen who obeyed the law which required all Englishmen to have some training in archery. It also suggests that the preacher may have been reading *Toxophilus*, by his young friend Roger Ascham. Characteristically, he contrasted this wholesome exercise of his youth with the "gulling and whoring within the towns" which he imputed to a younger generation.

That is all we know of Latimer's boyhood. The piety of his parents and a genuine vocation on his own part settled the matter of his life's work. He would become a priest. Reasonable ambition, and the means to promote it, determined that he should go to one of the universities, the most certain avenue to preferment in the church. Accordingly, he next

3

appears at Cambridge, where he seems to have been in residence more or less continuously for a quarter of a century.

Today the exterior charm of Cambridge rests in the Jacobean grace of a dozen colleges, the Gothic magnificence of the chapel of King's, and the quiet beauty of the "Backs," where arched bridges span the Cam to connect highly civilized lawns with meadow and playing field. No such graciousness or splendor attached to Cambridge at the turn of the sixteenth century. The streets of the town were narrow lanes with shops and dwellings huddled on either side. The most distinguished architectural features of the place were the parish churches—St. Mary's the Great, St. Edward's, half a dozen others. Work on King's College Chapel had been started a few years before, but had bogged down when royal support lagged. The climate was damp and unhealthy by reason of the proximity of the fenlands.

The university itself was small and, as compared to Oxford, provincial. Its masters and fellows were, for the most part, nonentities. In 1500 Cambridge had had no Grocyn, no Linacre, no Colet to make it a center of the new scholarship. Within a generation all this was to be changed. Sons of Cambridge were to play a distinguished part in the religious, social, and economic revolution of the sixteenth century and to raise their *alma mater* to a status of equality with the older university—an equality now so immemorially established that it is perhaps rash to recall that it has not existed from the beginning.

Since Latimer proceeded B.A. in 1510, it is likely that he matriculated at Cambridge in 1506. He had neither exhibition nor scholarship; the conclusion from his own words is that his father found the means to maintain him during the years which elapsed before he proceeded master of arts.[18] He has left us no comment upon the outward circumstances of his life during those years. Unquestionably he suffered from the austerities commonly complained of by Tudor students—the dank sleeping cubicle, the coarse monotonous diet, the dreary lectures before dawn. But the tedium and discomfort were relieved from time to time by the recurrent pageantry of religious and academic ceremonial and by the occasional excitement of a town-and-gown brawl.

Latimer spent seven years in the study of what remained, at the close of the middle ages, of the ancient disciplines of the *trivium* and the *quadrivium*.[19] His name first appears in the official records of the university during the academic year 1509-10, when he became a *questionist*—so called because the candidate for the bachelor's degree was required to go through the formality of answering a question put to him by the "father" of his college. Evidently this ceremony, in Latimer's time, was a mere formality, for if a disputation developed, the beadle was required to make sufficient noise to drown out the voices of the disputants. Subsequently he paid his "caution," or deposit, of 13*s.* 4*d.,* pledging that he would proceed to the degree.[20] Finally, the Grace Books record in full the "grace" by virtue of

which, early in 1510, the B.A. was conferred upon him; from this grace
we can glean the fact, but not the reason for it, that an exception to
the statute was granted in Latimer's case, and that he was permitted to
"respond to the question" after only eleven terms of study.[21]

It is sometimes asserted [22] that Latimer's first college was Peterhouse,
the oldest of the Cambridge foundations. The evidence for this is tenuous.[23]
When he proceeded B.A. he was almost certainly a member of Clare Hall,
for at the Feast of the Purification (February 2), 1510, while he was
still a questionist, he was elected a fellow of Clare.[24] Apparently he remained at Clare for more than twenty years—at least there is no record
of his resignation or deprivation—and in the annals of Cambridge it is
with that house that his name is quite properly associated. Indeed, Bishop
Ridley regarded Latimer as one of Clare's chief ornaments. In 1549,
when Clare had fallen on evil times and it was proposed to unite it to
Trinity, Ridley wrote to Somerset, the Lord Protector, in opposition to
the plan:

> I consider not only what learned men may be brought up there in time to
> come, but also how many hath been already, some such as I think it is hard for
> the whole University to match them with the like. I will speak now but of one.
> I mean Master Latimer, which is, as I do think, a man appointed of God, and
> endued with excellent gifts of grace to set forth God's Word, to whom in my
> judgment not only the King's majesty and his honorable council, but also the
> whole realm is much bound . . . . Alexander, as I do rightly remember the his-
> tory, in the victorious course of the conquest did spare a city for the memory
> of the famous poet Homer's sake. Latimer far passeth that poet, and the King's
> highness by your grace's advice shall also excel that gentle prince in all kind
> of mercy and clemency.[25]

If the concluding sentiments of this letter suggest that Ridley had drunk
more deeply of Jordan than of the springs of Helicon, they still testify
to Clare Hall's right to venerate Latimer as one of its most distinguished
members.[26]

According to the ancient statutes of Clare Hall, one of the fellows
might be a student of medicine, another might be a civilian, two might be
canonists, but the rest were required to be students of theology or the
liberal arts.[27] At the time of his election to a fellowship Latimer was one
of the "artists." He would have been chosen by the master, with the approval of the fellows, on the basis of his "conversation, condition, morals,
knowledge, poverty, and aptitude." He was provided with a room which
he shared with another fellow of the hall—only the master had a room
to himself—and with an allowance of one shilling per week for commons,
plus a little extra on holy days. There was also an annual stipend. For
the master this was 60s.; the stipend of the other fellows is not specified.[28]
Small as it must have been, it would surely have provided Latimer with
a welcome addition to his paternal subvention.

When Latimer was elected a fellow of Clare he was just about to
begin the second part of the usual program in the liberal arts,[29] in which
course of study he continued for nine more terms. One golden opportunity
he did not seize. This was the period of Erasmus' second and longer stay
at Cambridge.[30] The great humanist's lectures on Greek grammar attracted a few of the zealous, but Hugh Latimer was not among them.
By his own confession he was at this time apathetic, if not actively hostile,

5

to any academic innovation, as were also Dr. Edmund Natares, the master of Clare, and the other fellows of that hall. Indeed, Erasmus was reduced to a deep melancholy by the general opposition and indifference to his teaching. He had been living for months in his rooms at Queen's, like a snail in a shell, he wrote, poring over the texts of the New Testament and of St. Jerome. Meanwhile, his handful of students failed to pay their fees—a form of neglect to which the Dutch scholar was particularly sensitive. Finally, fear of the plague and the dank prospect of another fenland winter proved unendurable, and in the winter of 1513-14 Erasmus fled from Cambridge, never to return. Thus Latimer, declining the opportunity to sit at the feet of Europe's finest scholar, proceeded M.A. in Easter term, 1514. The "grace" for the degree records that he had kept his nine terms, and had made the required disputations and responsions.[31] The Proctors' accounts add the detail that he deposited with the authorities a silver cup, in lieu of the usual "caution" of 13s. 4d.[32]

It is pleasant to be able to escape briefly from this arid record of responsions and degrees to repeat an anecdote of a more personal nature. Probably every young scholar has had his fledgling wings clipped by some member of his family who remains unimpressed by his claims to erudition. The yeoman's son from Thurcaston did not escape the experience. In his later years he told the story on himself, surely with a chuckle.

I was once called to one of my kinsfolk (it was at that time when I had taken degree at Cambridge, and was made master of art) I was called, I say, to one of my kinsfolk, which was very sick, and died immediately after my coming. Now there was an old cousin of mine, which, after the man was dead, gave me a wax candle in my hand, and commanded me to make certain crosses over him that was dead; for she thought the devil would run away by and by. Now I took the candle, but I could not cross him as she would have me to do; for I had never seen it afore. Now she, perceiving that I could not do it, with a great anger took the candle out of my hand, saying, "It is pity that thy father spendeth so much upon thee," and so she took the candle, and crossed and blessed him, so that he was sure enough.[33]

Hugh Latimer received deacon's orders at Lincoln, the episcopal seat of the diocese in which he had been born, on April 7, 1515. He was ordained a priest on the following July 15.[34] The ordaining bishop would have been William Atwater, bishop of Lincoln, or one of his suffragans. Although the record of Latimer's life for the next seven years is blank,[35] it is possible to reconstruct its broad outline. In the year between his M.A. and his ordination he would have served his required term as regent master at Cambridge. For the period of his regency he was bound to lecture, to participate in disputations, and to attend all congregations and convocations. Meanwhile he retained his fellowship at Clare and began the more advanced program in divinity. The university statutes stipulated a period of not less than five years of study for the B.D., but a much longer period of residence was by no means unusual. In Latimer's case it was ten years. Into the study of medieval divinity he seems to have entered zealously, for it is recorded of him that he was most apt in "the labyrinth of the school doctors, as in Tho. of Aquine, Hugo de Victore, with such like." [36]

The veil of obscurity lifts a little in 1522, when Latimer was appointed one of the twelve university preachers.[37] The post was a modest one. Nevertheless it represented a minor success, for those appointed to it had been winnowed out from the mass of incipient theologians. Later in the same year, a much greater honor was bestowed upon Latimer, in the form of his appointment as cross-keeper to the university. This office was abolished in 1568, and for centuries its nature was forgotten.[38] Hence it has been usually and understandably assumed that Latimer became, with this appointment, merely a kind of superior crucifer whose function was to carry the great university cross on memorable occasions.[39] Actually, the cross-keeper was also the chaplain of the university's New Chapel, a post involving varied and important responsibilities. Bishop Ridley, one of Latimer's successors as chaplain, regarded it as one of the chief honors which Cambridge had bestowed upon him.[40]

As cross-keeper, the holder of this office was charged with responsibility for the great university cross, a magnificent silver crucifix which was sold during the reign of Edward VI, when such objects had come to be regarded as idolatrous, for its 336 ounces of silver.[41] The crucifix was elaborately ornamented. Above the staff, in two tiers, were the figures of various bishops and saints; above these was the scene of the coronation of the Virgin; surmounting all was the crucifix proper, with the figures of the Blessed Mother and St. John on either side the Christ. The *custos crucis* was responsible for the maintenance of this handsome object and for its presence on ceremonial occasions. At the greatest of these he may have carried it himself, but ordinarily the task was delegated to a recently incepted master in grammar. So much for the cross-keeper as such. As chaplain, his primary duty was to say the anniversary masses for the souls of the university's dead benefactors. In addition, the chaplain and cross-keeper had certain fiscal responsibilities. He collected the rents from the local properties which had been bequeathed to the university by some of its benefactors, and he supervised the expenditures for the maintenance of those properties; his accounting of the funds was subject to a yearly audit. He was also custodian of the building housing the public schools— that is, the university, as distinguished from the college, lecture rooms. Finally, he was keeper of the small but growing collection of books in the university library.

To this office, with its manifold duties and perquisites, Hugh Latimer was appointed in 1522.[42] It is not known to whom he owed his preferment. According to a contemporary, he was "for his gravity and years preferred to the keeping of the University Cross, which no man had to do withal but such an one as in sanctimony of life excelled another." [43] The actual records of his conduct of the office are few, but no fewer than those of other holders of the post. Thus we read of his activities in 1522 in supervising the expenditure of considerable sums of money for repairs to buildings. [44] His accounts were audited in 1523, 1526, and 1528, and proved to be in good order. [45] There are several records of payments for bearing the cross on important ceremonial occasions. In 1522, for instance, the "clerk of the schools" (that is, Latimer in his capacity as custodian of university buildings) was paid a total of 16*d.* for bearing the cross four times—twice during Henry VIII's visit to Cambridge in that year, once in Advent, and once at the "Great Cessation." [46] The details of the King's visit must have kept him busy, for the cross was refurbished and the chapel spruced up in honor of the occasion. Indeed, as the records abundantly testify, the presence of the royal visitor put the whole university to a great deal of trouble and expense. [47]

It is difficult to arrive at any precise statement of Latimer's income from his varied functions as chaplain and cross-bearer, but some estimate may still be made. In 1534, shortly after Latimer's time, the annual stipend of the chaplain *qua* chaplain was £1. 8s. 10d. [48]; presumably it was about the same during Latimer's tenure of the office. This salary covered the chaplain's function as obit keeper for the benefactors, and as custodian of the New Chapel and its ornaments. There were additional fees for special masses on saints' days and at commencements. He also had a salary as keeper of the public school buildings and of the books in the university library. The amount of this additional salary is nowhere specified, but in 1525, 1527, and 1528 the Proctor's records show payments of 40 shillings to Latimer "pro salario suo," probably for these latter services. [49] To these sums were added the annual fee of 3s. 4d. for his services as rent-collector, and the occasional payments for his services as cross-keeper. [50] An additional perquisite of the chaplain was a small fee from each supplicant for the bachelor's degree in arts, apparently for the use of the books in the library. From this source the chaplain seems to have averaged about 4d. at each congregation or commencement. [51] The gross income from all these sources would come to about £5, roughly £250 in the money of today. From this total the chaplain was probably required to pay part of the salary of the servant who tended the school buildings and the fees of the actual *portator crucis* when that function was not performed by the chaplain himself.

Latimer continued to perform these offices until 1529. His successor was Nicholas Heath, likewise a fellow of Clare. Heath was followed by Nicholas Ridley. In all this there is a certain irony, for in 1543 Heath became bishop of Worcester, [52] Latimer's former diocese, and at the time of the Oxford martyrdom he was archbishop of York and lord chancellor of England. In the latter capacity he signed the death warrant for Archbishop Cranmer.

It is clear that from 1522 on Latimer was in a position of some prominence and influence at Cambridge. As university preacher his voice was often heard on public occasions, and as university chaplain he had a small but clearly defined part in university affairs. He knew what was going on, and he was in a position to make his opinion felt. Meanwhile he continued his studies in divinity, chiefly in the old learning of the medieval church. He did indeed pay some attention to the new views coming out of Germany, but only to refute them, for his disputation for the B.D. was directed against the doctrines of Philip Melanchthon. Although the "grace" for the degree was not formally recorded, it is certain that Latimer proceeded B.D. in 1524, for in that year his name appears in the Proctors' Books among those who had graduated B.D. without being required to pay the usual fees. [53]

As far as the records indicate, this was his final degree. There has been much debate as to whether he was ever created doctor of divinity. In the deed for restoring the temporalities of the see of Worcester when Latimer assumed the bishopric, he is described as "Magistrem Hugonem Latymer sacrae theologiae professorem," and there is ample authority for translating "professor" as "doctor." [54] On the other hand, as late as 1535, when he was bishop-elect of Worcester, he is referred to specifically in the Proctors' Books as bachelor of theology.[55] Moreover, during the heresy proceedings at Oxford in 1555, Latimer was treated with less ceremony than Ridley because, according to the record, he was not a doctor. The weight of the evidence seems to support the negative. The fact that in his later years the great preacher was often called "Dr. Latimer" is of little significance. In both academic and ecclesiastical circles many a worthy elder finds himself a doctor *honoris causa* by popular rather than official dispensation.

CHAPTER TWO

THE CAMBRIDGE REFORMERS

For almost a century—since, in fact, the publication of Frederic Seebohm's *Oxford Reformers* and J. R. Green's *Short History of the English People*—scholars have customarily applied the phrase "the new learning" to the new scholarship inaugurated at Oxford by Grocyn, Linacre, Colet, More, and Erasmus. Historically it is more correct to use the term "revival of learning," or better still "revival of classical learning," to designate the academic innovations for which these men were responsible—the resuscitation of Ciceronian prose, the introduction of the study of Greek and, in the cases of Erasmus and Colet, the application of the techniques of sound scholarship to biblical exegesis. In the age of Erasmus and Sir Thomas More, the "new learning" meant something quite different. When the Duke of Norfolk exclaimed, "It was a merry England before this new learning came up," [1] his hearers understood perfectly well that he was not alluding to the scholarly activities of the Oxford reformers. He was attacking the new doctrines, the new *teaching*—since grammarians had not yet decreed a distinction between "learn" and "teach"—of Martin Luther and the great German's increasing insistence upon the paramount authority of Scripture.*

In England, the first academic habitation of the "new learning" in this primary sense was Cambridge, not Oxford. The Oxford reformers, to be sure, had sniffed the presence of dry rot in the church of the later

*Throughout the present work the term *new learning* is used in its primary sense of "new doctrines."

Middle Ages. The strictures of More and Erasmus upon the aridity of scholastic theology, and upon the abuses associated with pilgrimages and the veneration of relics, were no less severe than those of the later protestant reformers. They, or their disciples, might have been expected to become the intellectual pioneers of the English reformation. But More and Erasmus drew back; whether they were wise or merely timid is still an unanswered question. It would not be exact to extend the famous metaphor about Erasmus and Luther and say that Oxford laid the eggs which Cambridge hatched. The shade of William Tyndale, an Oxford man, would rebuke the jester. It is true, however, that for a decade or so Cambridge took the lead from Oxford in the matter which was to prove critical for almost two centuries—the question of the reformation of religion and all the vital issues of church and state with which that question was inextricably involved.

In the period between 1515 and 1530 Cambridge was a breeding ground for young radicals who subsequently became bishops of the Anglican communion. Thomas Cranmer and Hugh Latimer both proceeded B.A. in 1510, and probably at the same convocation. Of about the same vintage were Nicholas Shaxton and Miles Coverdale. Somewhat younger were Nicholas Ridley, who suffered with Latimer in 1555; Matthew Parker, the future archbishop; and William Barlow, upon the validity of whose episcopal orders depend the validity of Parker's and, according to the strict constructionists, the apostolic claims of Anglicanism itself. Of those who fell short of episcopal preferment but were none the less distinguished pioneers of the English reformation, there were, to name only a few, Robert Barnes, John Frith, George Joye, Edward Crome, George Stafford, and Thomas Bilney. It is a distinguished roll call. Until 1525 or thereabouts these men were either unknown or insignificant. No one of them was as yet the author of any book; no one of them had made his voice heard beyond the Cam. Yet within a decade many of them were famous in England and beyond the narrow seas. Cranmer, Latimer, Shaxton, and Barlow had respectively the sees of Canterbury, Worcester, Salisbury, and St. Asaph's. Coverdale had completed his first Bible. With one or two exceptions the others had achieved some measure of celebrity.

It is significant that none of these men, as far as can be discovered, was directly infected with the Lollard or popular tradition of reform. From the time of Wyclif that tradition had run strong and deep, in London, in various rural pockets of heresy, particularly in the midland and eastern counties, and even (although this is debatable) at Oxford itself. But it seems not to have touched Cambridge; and there is no evidence that, before they came to Cambridge, any of those named above were connected with Lollardy or the older popular tradition of reform. It is within Cambridge, then, that we must search for the springs of their thought and conduct.

A page or so back a distinction was made between the new learning and the new scholarship. There were times, however, when the two movements were contiguous. One such occasion was the publication of

Erasmus' Greek text of the New Testament, particularly the second edition of 1519. By its publication we can date almost precisely the beginnings of the new learning at Cambridge.

We have already caught a glimpse of Erasmus fleeing away from Cambridge late in 1513, depressed by the climate, his illness, and a sense of failure. During most of his three years there he had held the Lady Margaret Readership in Divinity. He had attracted few students to his lectures on Greek and divinity; of those whose names are known none later achieved great distinction or influence.[2] It often happens in academic circles, however, that scholarly output is in inverse ratio to the teaching load. In his room at Queen's, Erasmus had leisure for the study of his beloved early Greek Fathers, whom he greatly preferred to the Latin Fathers, and for the preparation of the edition of the Greek New Testament upon which his title to enduring fame most surely rests.

The first edition, called the *Novum Instrumentum,* was published at Basle on March 1, 1516, twenty-seven months after Erasmus had left Cambridge. In it the familiar version of the Vulgate was printed side by side with the Greek text. Early in 1519 a second edition appeared. The title was changed to *Novum Testamentum,* and the traditional Vulgate text was emended and revised more drastically than in the edition of 1516. The conception underlying the work was daring, and the application of the principles of textual and historical criticism to the divine page was revolutionary. Inevitably, as the full implication of the work was realized, the conservatives gave tongue. The schoolmen saw, or thought they saw, Erasmus' audacious scholarship pulling down the whole vast superstructure of ancient and medieval commentary, to the study of which they had dedicated their lives, and upon which their authority and indeed their livelihood depended. At Cambridge their cries were no less anguished than at Oxford or Paris or Rome.

A few young men, however, found the *Novum Testamentum* exciting in quite a different way. For none did it have graver consequences than for Thomas Bilney,[3] a student at Trinity. In 1519 Bilney, a Norfolk man, was probably about twenty-five years old. He was a small man— Latimer was fond of calling him "little Bilney"—and of great sweetness of character. Said Latimer years later, "I have known hitherto few such, so prompt and ready to do every man good after his power, both friend and foe . . . a very simple good soul, nothing fit or meet for this wretched world."[4] His friends attest his zeal in study and devotion, and in ministering to the sick and the comfortless of Cambridge. To this sweetness of disposition was added a rigid asceticism, a more than monastic austerity of life. He despised music, ecclesiastical as well as secular, and was particularly plagued by the tyro performance upon the recorders of Thomas Thirlby (later a distinguished member of the episcopal bench), who occupied the room below Bilney's. It is further proof of sweetness of temper that when Thirlby played, Bilney resorted to nothing more violent than prayer.

Bilney was ordained a priest at Ely on June 18, 1519, before he had taken any degree.[5] It must have been about this time or a little earlier that he bought a copy of Erasmus' New Testament. Apparently Bilney could not read Greek; he was particularly attracted by Erasmus' alterations in the Vulgate. Ten years later, when he was about to stand trial on charges of heresy, Bilney addressed to Cuthbert Tunstall a letter in which he described the impact of the *Novum Testamentum* upon him. Here is the passage, in Foxe's translation of the Latin original:

> But at last I heard speak of Jesus, even then when the New Testament was first set forth by Erasmus; which when I understood to be eloquently done by him, being allured rather by the Latin than by the word of God (for at that time I knew not what it meant), I bought it even by the providence of God, as I do now well understand and perceive: and at the first reading (as I well remember) I chanced upon this sentence of St. Paul (O most sweet and comfortable sentence to my soul!) in 1 Tim. i., 'It is a true saying, and worthy of all men to be embraced, that Christ Jesus came into the world to save sinners; of whom I am the chief and principal.' This one sentence, through God's instruction and inward working, which I did not then perceive, did so exhilarate my heart, being before wounded with the guilt of my sins, and being almost in despair, that even immediately I seemed unto myself inwardly to feel a marvellous comfort and quietness, insomuch that 'my bruised bones leaped for joy.'
>
> After this, the Scripture began to be more pleasant unto me than the honey or the honey-comb; wherein I learned, that all my travails, all my fasting and watching, all the redemption of masses and pardons, being done without trust in Christ, who only saveth his people from their sins; these, I say, I learned to be nothing else but even (as St. Augustine saith) a hasty and swift running out of the right way . . . .[6]

Probably no words uttered by an English reformer of the sixteenth century have been quoted more often than these. Probably none strike a clearer or stronger note of sincerity.

Erasmus' New Testament had an equally profound, if less dramatic, effect upon George Stafford of Pembroke, of whom little is known save the few records of the Grace Books and some passing notices in Foxe.[7] Stafford, a native of Durham, proceeded B.A. in 1515. It is likely that he was one of Erasmus' unnamed pupils, since he was learned in both Greek and Hebrew. He was ordained deacon at Ely in 1517, and presumably was advanced to priest's orders shortly thereafter. In 1523 he was proctor and university preacher, and he proceeded B.D. in 1524. He died of the plague in 1529.[8]

Stafford must have been distinguished for his learning, for in 1524 he was appointed reader in divinity at Pembroke, a post which he is said to have held for four years. Before this, however, he had become devoted to the study of the Scriptures; it is probable that his zeal for the New Testament antedated Bilney's, since Stafford had the competence to read Erasmus' Greek text. When he began to lecture, he startled his audience by expounding the New Testament instead of the traditional *Sentences* of Peter Lombard. Apparently he was the first lecturer on divinity to do so at Cambridge, and the effect was profound. By 1524 the new learning had made much headway at Cambridge, and there is evidence to suggest that Stafford attracted enthusiastic followers. He was also, as we shall see, the object of virulent attack. While his teaching did not come under official censure, he was reported to Wolsey for having expressed some unorthodox opinions regarding the epistle to the Romans. According to a not entirely reliable witness,[9] he profited on this occasion from his friendship with Stephen Gardiner, by this time one of Wolsey's secretaries and a rising man, who warned Stafford to moderate his utterances.

Of Stafford's personal qualities we know nothing. Death removed him early from the developing drama, and he left no writing behind him. It seems clear that he was more intellectual, or at least more learned, than Bilney; he appears also to have been less emotional. Of his influence there can be no doubt. A generation later Thomas Becon could write of Stafford as one of the most potent forces at Cambridge in the 1520's. Had he lived longer, Stafford's true importance might have been remembered; as it is, he is all but forgotten.

It would be inaccurate to think of Bilney and Stafford as being exclusively responsible for the dissemination of the new learning at Cambridge from 1520 onward. No doubt others were also won to the New Testament directly by a study of Erasmus' text. Yet the more closely one meditates upon the facts, the more one is convinced that these two men, above all others, were the means by which the seeds of the protestant revolt were sown at Cambridge. Both were zealous proselytizers. Foxe tells us that Stafford met his death through his concern for the soul of a superstitious priest, called Sir Henry the Conjurer. The priest lay dying of the plague, and Stafford, "seeing the horrible danger his soul was in, was so moved in conscience to help the dangerous case of the priest, that he, neglecting his own bodily death, to recover the other from eternal damnation, came unto him, exhorted, and so laboured him, that he would not leave him before he had converted him, and saw his conjuring books burned before his face." [10] Immediately thereafter Stafford himself sickened and died. The story is not without its note of Foxean hyperbole, but in this case the martyrologist could adduce the testimony of two bishops of London to support his statement. [11] As for Bilney, we have his own word, in the letter to Tunstall already quoted, that after his own eyes were opened he "desired nothing more than that . . . [he] might teach the wicked His ways, which are mercy and truth; and that the wicked might be converted unto Him . . . ." In their proselytizing both Bilney and Stafford seem to have been remarkably successful. Within a short time they had gathered about them a group of eager young men. [12] Among their earlier converts were Thomas Arthur, William Paget, and Richard Smith, all of Trinity, Bilney's own college; Thomas Farman, Nicholas Shaxton, and John Thixtell, all Norfolk-born and presumably of Bilney's close acquaintance. To this group were added, as time passed, men whose names were later to be more distinguished: George Joye, Robert Barnes, Miles Coverdale, Hugh Latimer, Matthew Parker. Which of these were won to the new learning by Bilney, which by Stafford, is by no means clear. What is clear is the fact that for a few years Bilney and Stafford were the center about which the others revolved.

To the ferment caused by the study of the New Testament were added, almost from the beginning, the even headier doctrines of Martin Luther. Within a few months of that fateful October 31, 1517, when Luther nailed his famous Theses to the door of Castle Church at Wittenberg, a copy of that momentous document had been sent by Erasmus to Colet and More in England, just as copies had been widely disseminated on the continent. Thereafter few theologians could take their ease in Zion, and in the universities of Europe the debate became increasingly heated and acrimonious as Luther's writings continued to pour from the printing presses of Germany. In 1520 the flood of Luther's literary output reached a high-water mark with the publication of three of the great reformer's most celebrated works—*An den christlichen Adel deutscher Nation* (*An address to the Christian Nobility of the German Nation*), *De Captivitate Babylonica* (*The Babylonian Captivity of the Church*), and *Von der Freiheit eines Christenmenscher* (*The Freedom of a Christian*). In these volumes Luther's basic ideas reached their final crystallization—the insistence upon the primacy of Scripture, the rejection of the sacraments as a sufficient means of grace, the formulation of the Lutheran implication of the Pauline doctrine of justification by faith, the denial of transubstantiation, and the administration of the communion in both kinds to the laity.

To these works were added a host of pamphlets and broadsides which served as outriders for Luther's own works. There is considerable vagueness of detail as to the way in which these books were first circulated in England. It is a matter of record, however, that throughout the year 1520 an Oxford bookseller carried on a flourishing trade in Lutheran books and pamphlets.[13] Thereafter the circulation of such books became a matter of official concern. After Luther defiantly burnt the bull *Exsurge Domine* and the volumes of the canon law at Wittenberg on December 10, 1520, Cardinal Wolsey reluctantly summoned a group of learned divines to London to sit in judgment upon the heretical books. Accordingly Lutheran books were ceremoniously burned at Paul's Cross on May 12, 1521, with John Fisher, the learned and devout bishop of Rochester, preaching a sermon appropriate to the occasion.[14] Two months later royalty itself stepped into the arena; Henry VIII caused to be published, under his own name, the famous *Assertio septem sacramentorum* which won for him the title *Fidei Defensor* he so greatly cherished.

At Cambridge the Lutheran books were avidly read by Bilney and his associates. As the force of Lutheranism was added to the influence of Erasmus' New Testament, and the feeling about Lutheranism became more intense, both pro and con, Bilney and his followers fell into the practice (or so Foxe says) of meeting at the White Horse Inn for talk of Luther and his doctrines.[15] Among Cambridge antiquaries there is a good deal of uncertainty about the White Horse, but the general opinion seems to be that it stood near the site of the later Bull Inn, and that it was the property of St. Catherine's Hall. According to tradition, the lane known as Mill Street passed behind the building and provided access to a back door through which the eager young men might enter unobserved.[16] Since the talk was all of Lutheranism, the White Horse came to be known facetiously as "Germany" and its frequenters as "Germans." Later tradition has probably made too much of Foxe's picturesque detail; certainly a distinguished modern historian [17] who sees the White Horse as a kind of heretics' club has overshot the mark. None the less, in students' rooms and even in the divinity schools, as well as at the White Horse, there was enough traffic with heresy to worry the authorities.

No one was more apprehensive than the chancellor of the university, John Fisher, bishop of Rochester, whose long devotion to Cambridge had found frequent and varied expression.[18] Although he was to die a martyr for the old faith, Fisher was in many respects a liberal. He had supported the new scholarship of Grocyn and Colet and More, the so-called Oxford reformers. He had been instrumental in establishing the Lady Margaret Professorship in Divinity, and had had a main finger if not a whole hand in formulating the rules of that foundation. He had approved the appointment of Erasmus as the second occupant of the chair (Fisher himself was the first) and had apparently felt no misgivings when the Dutch scholar chose to expound Greek and the Greek Fathers rather than the traditional theology. He had encouraged Erasmus in his work on the *Novum Instrumentum.* Moreover, Fisher's care for the welfare of the church had found direct expression in his zeal for preaching. He had helped in the foundation of the Lady Margaret preachership, along with the professorship, with the design that evangelical sermons in the vernacular might be brought to the laity. He had urged Erasmus to write a treatise on preaching. In an age of unpreaching prelates, Fisher was himself an earnest and indefatigable preacher and a stern critic of abuse. On at least one occasion he had spoken out vehemently against the worldliness of the bishops, particularly—with a long glance at Wolsey, who was present—those who neglected their cure of souls for political careers.

Liberal though he might be in educational matters, in doctrine Fisher was a conservative. No churchman of his day was a more vigorous opponent of the teachings of Martin Luther. He had certainly had some part in the preparation of Henry VIII's *Assertio,* if he was not indeed the ghost writer of that celebrated document. He had gladly accepted the assignment to preach at the burning of the books at Paul's Cross on May 12, 1521. But the burning of books does not destroy ideas, as Fisher very well knew, and in 1523 he joined with other bishops in urging upon Wolsey an episcopal visitation of Cambridge, with a view to stamping out heresy. Wolsey declined. Although it is doubtful that such a visitation would have been of great effect, Wolsey's refusal formed the substance of one of the long list of accusations brought against him after his fall.[19]

So, from about 1520 onward, the winds of the new doctrines blew about Latimer's Cambridge, and about Oxford, and about humbler places. The reformers were in the minority, and at first they were not in positions of much influence. Arrayed against them at Cambridge were virtually all the heads of houses, an undistinguished but collectively formidable party of opposition. One wonders whether the reformers had any real concept of the forces they had unleashed, or of the uses to which those forces would be put. Temperate men of all parties must have shared the apprehension of the unknown writer of a letter addressed to the Earl of Surrey: "I do tremble to remember the end of all these high and new enterprises. For oftentimes it hath been seen, that to a new enterprise, there followeth a new manner and a strange sequel. God of His mercy send His grace unto such fashion, that it may be for the best." [20]

CHAPTER THREE

CONVERT

When Bilney and his friends began to sow the seeds of the new doctrines at Cambridge, Hugh Latimer was a man in his late twenties. No description of him as he was in those days has survived. It appears that he was ever a lean man; so he is in the portrait painted in his old age and preserved in the National Portrait Gallery, and so he was, according to Foxe, at the time of his execution. The portrait emphasizes his angular features, especially the large, beak-like nose. The eyes are penetrating, but tired; eye-glasses are suspended from a cord about the neck. Perhaps the description will serve also for a younger Latimer. He seems never to have been entirely robust. From the age of forty onward he complained frequently of illness, and of the pains, such as toothache, for which the medical science of the period provided no relief.

From the beginning of his career he must have been a compelling preacher. He was quick rather than profound, impulsive, given to vigorous and sometimes rash speech. He had the qualities which make the successful orator, but not the subtle theologian. When he ascended the pulpit his hearers were assured of a skillful performance. He kept his eye on them, not on his manuscript, and he knew both their capacities and their prejudices. The method, a shrewd admixture of invective and moral indignation, was in the direct tradition of the preaching of the medieval friars, as Owst has pointed out.[1] It was calculated to arouse enthusiasm or intense hostility, depending upon the theological complexion of the audience.

Until 1524, these considerable talents were marshaled in opposition to the new learning. By his own account no one was more vehement in denunciation of Lutheranism. In the time of his "blindness," as he was fond of calling the period of his adherence to the old religion, he was in his own words, "as obstinate a papist as any was in England." "I have thought in times past," he wrote, "that the Pope, Christ's vicar, hath been lord of all the world, as Christ is: so that if he had deprived the king of his crown . . . it had been enough; for he could do no wrong."[2] His gift for mordant and satiric utterance made him a formidable champion of the faith. His position as university preacher provided him with abundant opportunity for exercising his talent. He was licensed to preach throughout the kingdom, and it is possible that his voice was heard beyond the narrow limits of Cambridge and its environs.

Outside the pulpit, too, Latimer attacked the new doctrines. An anonymous contemporary records the bluntness of his controversy with the young men whose radicalism was infecting the Schools:

. . . he of purpose (perceiving the youth of the university inclined to the reading of the scriptures, leaving off those tedious authors and kinds of study [the schoolmen] . . .) came into the Sophany school among the youth, there gathered together of daily custom to keep sophanies and disputations: and there most eloquently made to them an oration, dissuading them from this new fangled kind of study of the scriptures, and vehemently persuaded them to the study of school-author . . . .[3]

Against George Stafford especially did Latimer breathe out threatenings and slaughter. The two men were contemporaries, or nearly so; they took their B.D.'s at the same time; both were university preachers. But Stafford, as reader in divinity, had deserted the Doctors for the New Testament, and to Latimer he was clearly an apostate. Foxe records an episode of this period: "Master Latimer, being yet a fervent and zealous papist, standing in the schools when Master Stafford read, bade the scholars not to hear him; and also preaching against him, exhorted the people not to believe him . . . ." [4] The reader, accustomed to the decorum of the modern lecture room, may see in Latimer's attack on Stafford some want of tact and good manners. Indeed, Stafford himself may have found it so, for Foxe's somewhat ambiguous narrative indicates that hard feelings remained between the two men even after Latimer's conversion. But it is pleasant to repeat Foxe's assurances that, upon Latimer's suing for forgiveness, peace was made between them before Stafford's death in 1529.[5]

Thus, until 1524, preached the man of whom it was later said that he had disseminated more heresies than Luther. His change of heart and opinion—the "conversion" which was to turn him into the foremost preacher and perhaps the foremost popularizer of the reformation in England—seems to have come suddenly. The agent was that intense little man, Thomas Bilney. No doubt Bilney had been aware of Latimer's fulminations against the new doctrines long before he determined that here was a man worth working upon. Perhaps Latimer's assurance had already been shaken a little by one of Stafford's lectures in the Schools, for an obscure contemporary reference suggests that Stafford was partly an instrument in the great change.[6] However that may be, we have Latimer's word for it that Bilney was the principal agent. The occasion was Latimer's disputation for the degree of B.D.

In that disputation Latimer chose to attack the doctrines of Philip Melanchthon. Recently William Paget had been lecturing on Melanchthon's *Rhetoric*,[7] and it may have been Latimer's intention to wing two modernists with one disputation. No doubt many listened with delight; and Dr. Edmund Natares, the master of Clare and a leader of the conservatives, must have rejoiced that in Latimer, chaplain of the university and one of Clare's most distinguished fellows, there was no shadow of unsound doctrine.

Sitting quietly in the Divinity School as Latimer undertook to refute the opinions of Melanchthon was Thomas Bilney. He knew Latimer well, and he took no pleasure in the day's performance. Surely there could have been nothing in the disputant's words to suggest that he was ripe for the new doctrine. But in matters such as these Bilney seems to have had a

17

special sensitivity; perhaps in the very violence of Latimer's utterances Bilney detected a lack of inner assurance. Then and there he resolved to win Latimer to the cause.

Bilney was a man of subtle mind. He was well aware that Latimer, an emotional man, was not to be won by public debate; if opposed by argument, he would maintain his own views all the more stubbornly. Emotionally, however, he was vulnerable, if only Bilney could probe the inner uncertainty. Accordingly Bilney sought out Latimer privately, in his room at Clare, and begged him, as a priest, to hear his, Bilney's, confession. Here is the story in Latimer's own words:

> Here I have occasion to tell you a story which happened at Cambridge. Master Bilney, or rather Saint Bilney, that suffered death for God's word sake; the same Bilney was the instrument whereby God called me to knowledge; for I may thank him, next to God, for that knowledge that I have in the word of God. For I was as obstinate a papist as any was in England, insomuch that when I should be made bachelor of divinity, my whole oration went against Philip Melanchthon and against his opinions. Bilney heard me at that time, and perceived that I was zealous without knowledge; and he came to me afterward in my study, and desired me, for God's sake, to hear his confession. I did so; and to say the truth, by his confession I learned more than before in many years. So from that time forward I began to smell the word of God, and forsook the school-doctors and such fooleries.[8]

Thus, tersely for him, Latimer tells the story of the crucial event of his life—the event which led to the episcopal palace at Worcester, to the pulpits at Windsor and Westminster, and to the fires at Oxford. There is a temptation to embroider upon Latimer's narrative, but it is really self-sufficient. It is enough to add that Latimer ever afterwards regarded Bilney's memory with special tenderness, and that because of the circumstances of his conversion he could never bring himself to reject entirely a belief in the efficacy of auricular confession.[9] In sermons preached twenty-five years later, when the cause for which Bilney had died seemed to be reaching its happy fruition, Latimer spoke of him repeatedly in terms of closest affection.

Although Latimer does not provide us with the exact date of this critical moment in his life, it is possible to set the time within reasonable limits. His degree in divinity is mentioned in the University Grace Book for the academic year between Michaelmas, 1523, and Michaelmas, 1524.[10] July was the customary season for disputations, and the degrees were conferred immediately thereafter. July, 1524, was therefore the probable date of Latimer's disputation; the celebrated interview with Bilney probably belongs to the latter half of the same year. Allowing for a few weeks or even months for his new views to develop, we may safely conclude that Latimer was firmly settled in his acceptance of the new doctrines by the end of 1524.

More important than the date of Latimer's conversion, however, are the motives, external or internal, which underlay it. It might be possible to explain his conversion, at least in part, in terms of economics. He was sprung from a class which in some quarters had become hostile to the vested interests of the church, particularly those of the monastic foundations. Towards the monks, who were landlords and rent collectors, the yeoman at times felt the same antagonism which he directed towards the squire and the lord of the manor. Towards the friars, who by the rule of their order were, in theory at least, impoverished wanderers and beggars, the yeoman felt the scorn which the self-supporting poor ever manifest towards those who are neither landed nor guilded. Many of the reformers were of yeoman stock, and it is not impossible that Latimer's conversion was partly conditioned by the economic prejudices of his class. But all this is speculation upon the flimsiest of evidence, and there is much to suggest in opposition to it. For one thing, at the very time of his conversion, Latimer, as university chaplain, was making at least a moderate living from the vested interests of the church. For another, we shall see that when the monasteries were being suppressed, Latimer, as bishop of Worcester, was far more considerate of the regular clergy than were Henry VIII's visitors and others, both clergy and laity, who stood to profit from the suppression.

It may be true, as most modern historians insist, that at the reformation religion and economics were so inextricably intertwined that few men took their stand on a basis of religion pure and undefiled. But a few did so. Luther's fear of hell, and his apprehensiveness that the sacraments were inadequate to keep him out of it, had for him a reality beside which the misery of the German peasant was quite insignificant. Such a man, or his ideas, may be used by baser men for their own ends. But to a Luther, or a Bilney, the determining factor is the need for assurance that the Redeemer liveth, and that he will stand at the latter day.

In his own measure, and at his own level, Hugh Latimer was of this chosen few. He was a man of intense religious feeling, but like Bilney he found little peace in the outward observances of his religion. For a while he had hoped that certainty would come through intensification of his external duties. In one of his sermons of 1549 he said, "I remember how scrupulous I was in my time of blindness and ignorance: when I should say mass, I have put in water twice or thrice for failing; insomuch that when I have been at my *memento,* I have had a grudge in my conscience, fearing I had not put in water enough." [11] Years earlier, he had written to Sir Edward Baynton, "I have thought in times past, that if I had been a friar and in a cowl, I could not have been damned, nor afraid of death; and by occasion of the same, I have been minded many times to have been a friar, namely when I was sore sick and diseased . . . ." [12]

These words are sufficient to suggest Latimer's religious psychology. He was one of those whose souls stand in need of certainty, and he was also one of those, like Luther and Bilney, whose need the sacramental system in itself had failed to satisfy. With the winds of doctrine blowing strongly about Cambridge, the New Testament and the Lutheran version of justification provided him with the assurance he needed. To these, and to the doctrinal and administrative changes which were their consequences, Latimer devoted his not inconsiderable abilities for the next thirty years. Sometimes he wavered, as did all but Tyndale among the first generation of English reformers. Sometimes, as his fame increased, he found himself in the strange company of politicians who used the principles of the reformation for their own ends. But in general, from the time of his conversion onward, Latimer followed a straight line.

It is difficult to be precise about the extent of Latimer's conversion in 1524 and the nature of his views at that time. His earliest recorded utterances belong to the year 1529, by which time, presumably, his opinions had undergone considerable development. We do have, however, his own statement, quoted above, that at the time of his conversion he accepted the Holy Scriptures as the sole authority in matters of faith and doctrine, and that he thenceforward rejected the authority of the vast accumulation of scholastic literature upon which the church of the Middle Ages had come to depend. It is also probable that from 1524 onward Latimer accepted the Lutheran emphasis upon justification by faith, although not all of its implications were immediately clear to him and, like Bilney, he remained perfectly orthodox in the matter of the sacraments for many years.

It is needless to be more precise at this time. The study of Latimer's career will reveal the development of his thought in doctrinal matters. But it is perhaps important to emphasize again that the development was a gradual one. History has painted Latimer as one of the most reckless and precipitous of the reformers. Actually, his progress was slow, and often he seems to have waited for the guidance of minds more profound than his own. Often, too, his gift for emphatic utterance led his hearers to believe that his views were more extreme than they actually were. It is one thing to condemn the abuse of a practice; it is quite another to deny the validity of the practice itself. Many of Latimer's admirers were simple-minded zealots unable to make such a distinction, and more than one of them found himself in trouble for having run ahead of the preacher's own thought. Protestant historians have sometimes fallen into the same error.

For a year or so after Latimer's conversion to the new learning the theological controversies between the conservatives and the radicals at Cambridge remained purely local and perhaps personal; at any rate, nothing that the party of reform did or said between the end of 1524 and the end of 1525 became a matter of official record. For Latimer, it was probably a period of intellectual and emotional turmoil, as zeal for the New Testament gradually shook loose the deposit of traditional theology which he had absorbed through years of devoted study.

During this year the most significant factor in Latimer's life was the ripening of his friendship with Thomas Bilney. The two were in constant association. In some ways they were an ill-assorted pair. But Bilney, quiet, thoughtful, deeply spiritual, admirably complemented the more vigorous, out-giving Latimer. Each must have had much to gain from the other. They appear to have developed a custom of daily walks on Castle Hill, which from this association was known for years as Heretics' Hill.[13] For a time Latimer was the pupil, as Bilney gradually expounded the ideas which had been ripening in his own mind for five years or more. As they talked together, they experienced a deepening and a widening of their hostility toward abuses growing out of the sale of indulgences, the excessive reliance of the ignorant upon devotion to the saints, and the laxity of church discipline. More than anything else, they must have talked of the light which the New Testament shed upon these problems, and beyond a doubt they awaited impatiently the publication of William Tyndale's English translation. Tyndale, although an Oxford man, had been at Cambridge for a few years prior to 1521; both he and his proposed translation were well known to Bilney and Latimer.[14]

Meanwhile, Latimer's new way of thought would have brought him into frequent association with the other adherents of the new learning. The group was growing rapidly. Latimer was not the only distinguished convert of the year 1524. In that same year the party of reform at Cambridge was strengthened—or so it must have seemed at the time—by the conversion to the cause of Robert Barnes, prior of the Cambridge house of the Austin Friars.[15] Barnes had been educated partly at Louvain, where he acquired some distinction as a humanist. In the early 1520's his lectures on Terence, Plautus, and Cicero had made his Cambridge priory a little center of humanistic studies. Among his pupils was no less a person than Miles Coverdale. Barnes' conversion to the new doctrines, like Latimer's, grew out of a disputation for a degree in divinity. In this case, it was the candidate who converted the doctor. The candidate was George Stafford; Barnes, one of the examiners, was so moved by Stafford's arguments that he forsook his purely humanistic pursuits for the more stimulating and more dangerous study of the New Testament and of Luther. Barnes was a man of mercurial temperament. Latimer was given to forceful and sometimes rash speech. With their addition to the ranks of the "Germans," the discussions at the White Horse must have become livelier if not weightier.

How soon after his conversion did Latimer become a public advocate of the new doctrines? Foxe and another writer of whom we shall hear more in the next chapter both assert that he began to proclaim his new views immediately after his change of heart, and there is no reason to doubt their joint testimony. Says the latter, ". . . so he mightily, tracting no time, preached daily in the university of Cambridge, both in English and *ad clerum,* to the great admiration [i.e., wonder] of all men that aforetime had known him of a contrary severe opinion." [16] And Foxe: "After his winning to Christ, he was not satisfied with his own conversion only, but, like a true disciple of the blessed Samaritan, pitied the misery of others, and therefore he became both a public preacher and also a private instructor, to the rest of his brethren within the University, by the space of two years, spending his time partly in the Latin tongue among the learned, and partly amongst the simple people in his natural and vulgar language." [17]

Latimer was ever a forthright man, and it is likely that he began to give expression to his new views before the end of 1524. At first, however, his opinions were no more radical than those which the university had come to expect from Bilney and Stafford, and the "admiration" of the conservatives was not so much at the views themselves as it was at the sudden conversion of a man who had hitherto been known as one of the stanchest of the conservatives. Latimer had strayed into new pastures, to the consternation of those who had counted him as secure within their own fold. No doubt Dr. Natares, the ultra-conservative master of Clare Hall, was distressed at what he could only regard as the apostasy of one of the most distinguished fellows of his house, as was Dr. Henry Bullock, of Queen's, a learned humanist who none the less had no tolerance of Lutheranism and whose attacks on Latimer are recorded by Foxe.[18] No doubt there were many others to whom Latimer's conversion was a bitter pill.

CHAPTER FOUR

LATIMER, BISHOP WEST, AND CARDINAL WOLSEY: A CHAPTER OF PROBLEMS

For more than a year after Latimer's conversion to the new doctrines the Cambridge reformers were content to promote their cause quietly. But on Christmas Eve, 1525, Prior Robert Barnes preached at St. Edward's an inflammatory sermon which got him into serious trouble; Bilney may have been involved at least to the extent of having encouraged Barnes; and it is probable that the watchful eye of authority was focussed more sharply upon the radical group. There is some indication that Latimer was also in trouble for his new views at the same time. The evidence for this is murky, however, and the probability is that Latimer escaped official censure at this time.

The first witness is Foxe. In the reliable first edition of the *Acts and Monuments,* Foxe tells a straightforward story; Latimer, he says, was converted by Bilney, preached his new doctrines for two years, then was cited before Wolsey for heresy and renounced his objectionable opinions.[1] In his second edition, Foxe altered *two years* to *three years,* and this is probably correct; Latimer, as we shall see, was certainly before the Cardinal early in 1528. But in the second edition Foxe also added a note to the effect that Nicholas West, bishop of Ely, preached against Latimer at Barnwell Abbey (the house of the Augustinian Canons near Cambridge), and at some time before Barnes' sermon of Christmas Eve, 1525, forbade Latimer to preach within the churches of the University. Because of this inhibition, says Foxe, Barnes offered Latimer the pulpit of the Augustinian Church, which was exempt from West's jurisdiction; and Latimer preached there on Christmas Eve, while Barnes was preaching at St. Edward's.[2]

In the matter of the exchange of pulpits there is nothing fundamentally improbable. But in the rest of the story there is much to question.

First there is the matter of date. The statement that West silenced Latimer before December 24, 1525, would seem to contradict Foxe's other statement that for three years after his conversion Latimer preached without interference. For another thing, Foxe's statement is out of place; he interpolated it, in the edition of 1570, after his account of the Sermons on the Card, which Latimer preached at Christmastide, 1529. It almost looks as if Foxe had telescoped the event of two Christmas seasons; in any case, it is clear that he was by no means confident of his chronology.

There is, moreover, the question of the character of Bishop West.[3] West was a political bishop, a statesman and a diplomat. In 1525 he was not yet a hunter of heretics. As late as the summer of that year he issued to Bilney a license to preach anywhere in the diocese of Ely, although by that time Bilney's views were well known. Furthermore, West was so ill during the early part of 1525 that Wolsey was momentarily expecting his death and had offered the succession to the see of Ely to Cuthbert Tunstall, who declined.[4] It seems unlikely that in the autumn or winter of 1525 West's state of health would have permitted him to be personally active in searching out heresy, even if his temperament had inclined him to do so.

There is also the question of jurisdiction. West might indeed have inhibited Latimer from preaching in certain churches of Cambridge and elsewhere in the diocese of Ely, although there is no record of such an inhibition in the Ely registers, which for this period are remarkably complete. But the two churches in which Latimer was most likely to have preached were St. Mary's and St. Edward's; the former was the so-called "University Church" and the latter served as the chapel for the students of Clare and Christ's. St. Mary's was a "peculiar" of Trinity and St. Edward's was a "peculiar" of Christ's, and the pulpits of both would have been open to Latimer in spite of a prohibition by West. Moreover, the vice-chancellor, not the bishop of Ely, was ordinary of the university clergy who did not hold benefices elsewhere, and it is not likely that West would have risked a clash with the university over the matter of jurisdiction. As recently as April, 1525, when Wolsey was levying outrageous assessments against the clergy in the interests of his foreign policy, West had written to the Cardinal expressing the hope that Wolsey himself would deal with Cambridge in the matter, because the colleges were extremely jealous of their prerogatives and would not recognize West's authority.[5]

But what of Foxe's specific statement that West preached against Latimer at Barnwell Abbey? Here again it is probable that this occurred, if at all, at a later date. At a synod of the diocese of Ely held at Barnwell in June, 1528, West did attack the new learning [6]—specifically the *biblia secundum novam interpretationem* (that is, Tyndale's translations)—and it is possible that he also preached against Latimer, who by that time was speaking out vigorously. It seems much more likely that West's attacks on Latimer belong to that occasion rather than to the year 1525, as Foxe suggests.

All things considered, Foxe's note falls down under careful scrutiny. It has the marks of a bit of hearsay which Foxe added uncertainly to his revised work. In any case, there is nothing in the record, beyond the suggestion of an exchange of pulpits, to lead us to assume, as so many writers have done, that Latimer was implicated in the troubles of Robert Barnes. The Barnes affair was a *cause célèbre.*[7] It involved a long row at the university, after which Barnes was examined by Wolsey and by an ecclesiastical commission. In the end the unlucky Prior recanted, and bore his fagot at a spectacular ceremony at Paul's Cross. But neither Barnes' own prolix account [8] of the affair nor the accounts given by any of the chroniclers indicate that Latimer was in any way involved.

Foxe's troublesome note is not the only piece of evidence which suggests that Latimer had a dangerous antagonist in Bishop West. Indeed, Foxe may have taken a hint from the story of an encounter of Latimer with West and Wolsey which is told in six pages (folios 84-86) of Harleian MS 422. This manuscript, a collection of documents relating to the English reformation, was once the property of Foxe. Some of its materials he incorporated into the *Acts and Monuments,* but he did not include the narrative with which we are here concerned. The story is picturesque.[9]

Briefly, it tells that when Bishop West learned of Latimer's "new conversion" he determined to hear for himself what manner of doctrine the university cross-bearer was disseminating. Accordingly, on a day when Latimer was preaching *ad clerum* at St. Mary's, West came without announcement from Ely and entered the church abruptly after the sermon was begun. Latimer paused until the Bishop and his attendants were placed. Then, declaring that a new audience required a new theme, the preacher gave out a new text—*Christus existens pontifex futurorum bonorum, etc.*—and this he expounded in such a way as to contrast the high calling of a bishop with the character and performance of the episcopal bench as then constituted. West, an astute prelate, heard the sermon quietly, and after it was over called Latimer to him.

"Master Latimer," said the bishop, "I heartily thank you for your good sermon. If you will do one thing at my request, I will kneel down and kiss your feet for the good admonition that I have received of your sermon."

"What is your lordship's pleasure that I should do for you?" asked Latimer.

"Marry," said the bishop, "that you will preach me in this place one sermon against Martin Luther and his doctrine."

Latimer was not to be caught. "My lord, I am not acquainted with the doctrine of Luther; nor we are not permitted here to read his works; and therefore it were but a vain thing for me to refute his doctrine, not understanding what he hath written, nor what opinion he holdeth. I have preached before you this day no man's doctrine, but only the doctrine of God out of the Scriptures. And if Luther do none otherwise than I have done, there needeth no confutation of his doctrine."

"Well, well, Master Latimer," replied the bishop, "I perceive that you somewhat smell of the pan. You will repent this gear one day." And from that day forward he sought means to put Latimer to silence.

Some time later (the narrative is vague as to the time interval) some enemies of Latimer within the university—the writer mentions one Tyrell,[10] who had also been active against Barnes—complained of him to Wolsey, and he was summoned to York Place. After cooling his heels for a time in an outer room, he was ushered into the presence of the Cardinal-archbishop.

"Is your name Latimer?" asked Wolsey.

"Yea, forsooth."

"You seem that you are of good years nor no babe, but one that should wisely and soberly use yourself in all your doings; yet it is reported to me of you that you are much infected with this new fantastical doctrine of Luther and such like heretics, and that you do much harm among the young and light-headed."

Said Latimer, "Your grace is misinformed, for I have studied the doctors in my time, and I ought not to be so simply reported of."

The answer pleased Wolsey, who ordered two of his chaplains, Dr. Capon and Dr. Marshall, to quiz Latimer on Duns Scotus. In the disputation which followed Latimer confounded the doctors, corrected their citations, and in general showed himself more than their match in the traditional theology.

Finally the Cardinal intervened. He rebuked his chaplains for bringing such a man before him, and inquired of Latimer why West and the others were so hot against him. Whereupon Latimer told him the whole story of the St. Mary's sermon. West, he said, had finally found the means to inhibit him both in the diocese and in the university.

"Did you not preach any other doctrine than you have rehearsed?" asked Wolsey.

"No, surely."

"Then if the bishop of Ely cannot abide such doctrine as you have here repeated, you shall have my license, and shall preach it into his beard, let him say what he will."

So Latimer, to the amazement of both friends and enemies, returned to Cambridge with the Cardinal's license to preach anywhere in England. Not long after this Wolsey fell from power, and it was reported that Latimer's license was no longer valid. But from the pulpit Latimer declared otherwise. "Where ye think that my license decayeth with my lord Cardinal's temporal fall, I take it nothing so. For he being, I trust, reconciled to God from his pomp and vanities, I now set more by his license than ever I did before, when he was in his most felicity."

So runs the story. Every admirer of Latimer would like to believe in its truth. But a candid analysis arouses suspicion. The actors are out of character, and the episodes smell of the pan, as Bishop West himself might have said. Latimer, as far as can be known, was never remarkable for suavity or erudition. But here he deftly outwits Nicholas West, a political churchman, trained in courtliness and diplomacy. In the sequel, he faces up to Wolsey with calmness and assurance. He easily gets the better of Wolsey's chaplains; yet Dr. Capon was the master of Jesus

College and in 1528 was chosen by Wolsey to be dean of the short-lived college at Ipswich, and Dr. Marshall was a distinguished canonist.

A further doubt arises when we consider the history of the manuscript. According to Strype,[11] it is in the handwriting of Ralph Morice, Archbishop Cranmer's secretary. Morice, a Cambridge contemporary and a life-long friend of Latimer, was certainly in a position to know the facts. But it is by no means certain that the handwriting is Morice's.[12] If it is, then Latimer's friend was guilty of a lapse of memory at the very beginning of his reminiscences, for in the first paragraph (not included in the foregoing summary) he attributes Latimer's conversion to George Stafford, although Latimer himself repeatedly attributed it to Bilney. Perhaps Morice's memory was at fault; perhaps he shared Foxe's propensity to embroider. In this instance even Foxe must have been skeptical, else he would have enthusiastically repeated a story which exalted one of his heroes.

Such subjective criticism as this is dangerous. Granted that Latimer was not quite so deft as the story indicates in his handling of West and Wolsey, still the narrative has in it certain circumstantialities which make it hazardous to reject it in its entirety on such grounds. Suppose we reduce it to its lowest terms, and assume merely that at some time or other West did make an effort to silence Latimer and that Latimer was summoned before Cardinal Wolsey. When are these events most likely to have occurred?

It is at once evident that in the matter of dates the narrative itself is confusing. The writer indicates that the St. Mary's sermon was preached shortly after Latimer's conversion—some time in 1525, perhaps, but certainly not later than the close of 1526. But he says also that the appearance before Wolsey took place shortly before the Cardinal's fall from power, which ocurred in October, 1529. We must therefore conclude either that three or four years elapsed between the two episodes, or that one of them is misdated. The first alternative is improbable, since it requires us to believe that shortly before October, 1529, Latimer was summoned to answer for a sermon which he had preached several years earlier. On the other hand, it is difficult to bring the two episodes into closer proximity. If we move the appearance before Wolsey backward to a period roughly in 1525-26, we invalidate the circumstantial account of Latimer's remarks after Wolsey's fall. If we move the St. Mary's sermon forward and keep the interview with Wolsey in 1529, we are confronted with the difficulty, inherent in the story from the beginning, of believing that at any time after 1527 Wolsey would have treated Latimer so light-heartedly and genially as the narrative suggests.

On the whole, it seems clear that the narrative in Harleian 422 has little evidential value. It is probably best regarded as part of the not inconsiderable hagiographical literature associated with the uncanonized saints of English protestantism.

The arguments here advanced for believing that for several years after his conversion Latimer preached his new doctrines without interruption or serious censure are supported by the fact that his career at Cambridge suffered no interruption whatever. He retained his fellowship at Clare, although his new views must have alarmed the conservative Dr. Natares. He continued to perform the manifold duties of cross-keeper and chaplain, and to receive the stipends and emoluments associated with those offices. He seems to have acquired an increasing influence in university affairs.

His earliest extant letter,[13] dated October 14, 1524, belongs to a period immediately after his change of heart. In it we find him reporting to Dr. Thomas Greene, the Vice-Chancellor of that year, upon rather delicate negotiations which he had undertaken upon behalf of the university. By reason of the death of Sir Thomas Lovell, the office of high steward of the university was vacant, and Latimer had been despatched to sound out Richard Wingfield, chancellor of the Duchy of Lancaster, from whose residence at Kimbolton Castle the letter is dated. Latimer had talked with Wingfield's friends, and presumably with Sir Richard himself, and he was able to report that Wingfield was eager for the post. A slight difficulty arose from the fact that the stewardship had been half-promised to Sir Thomas More, whom Latimer cordially disliked. But the King, Latimer assured Greene, had intervened on Wingfield's behalf and had persuaded More to withdraw his candidacy. Wingfield had the confidence and ear of the King; in the office of steward, as Latimer pointed out, he would be both an ornament to the university and a useful friend at Court. The whole tone of the letter is acute and persuasive. Its conclusion is characteristic: "Farewell, your worship. I write this late at night, after equinoctial rain, and after being well nigh suffocated and out of my wits with the heat of the sun, the fumes of victuals, and the excessive feasting besides." Clearly the affair was ticklish. The man who conducted the negotiations, although a recent convert to the new learning, was certainly of the inner circle in university politics. It is clear also that he was using his position to support the cause of a candidate who might be expected to show more tolerance towards the new doctrines than Sir Thomas More would have done. Latimer's negotiations were successful. The appointment was given to Wingfield, but his death in the following year made it possible for the university to redeem its broken promise to More.

The accounts of the university proctors likewise attest the fact that Latimer's career suffered no interruption by reason of his activities on behalf of the new learning. The payment of his annual stipend of 40s. as cross-keeper and chaplain is recorded for the years 1524-25, 1526-27, and 1527-28.[14] There are also frequent notations of special payments to the cross-keeper, the most interesting of which has to do with the bearing of the cross in the procession which honored the papal nuncio who visited Cambridge in September, 1524, just about the time of Latimer's conversion.[15]

Twice between 1526 and 1528 audits were made of the Barrow trust funds, of which Latimer, as chaplain, was the treasurer. Dr. Natares was one of the auditors in 1526; Thomas Cranmer was among those for 1528.[16]

Perhaps even more significant than these entries dealing with routine affairs is the appearance of Latimer's name as a member of two committees,
as we would call them, which were charged with looking into and adjust-
ing certain financial matters. In 1526-27, the Vice-Chancellor appointed
a committee consisting of Drs. Crome, Cranmer, and Imar, and Masters
Latimer, Stafford, Middleton, and Aldrich to systematize and regulate
the methods of accounting of certain trust funds.[17] Crome, Stafford, and
Latimer were all known to be active in the party of reform. (It ought to be
pointed out also that this entry in the proctors' accounts is the earliest
document to bring together the names of Latimer and Cranmer, although
by this time the two men, later to be so closely associated, must have been
old acquaintances if not friends.) Two years later, Latimer was appointed
to still another committee, the purpose in this instance being to adjust the
stipend of one Master Day.[18]

Here, then, is a picture which is at first glance confusing. A convert
to the new learning has been preaching doctrines which are distasteful to
the constituted ecclesiastical and academic authorities. Yet at the same time
he is permitted to retain his post as chaplain and cross-keeper. He represents the university in negotiations involving one of its honorary func-
tionaries. Together with other known reformers, he serves on committees
which must have been regarded as of some importance, if for no other
reason than that they were concerned with money. What can we conclude?
Two things, surely: that Latimer's career in the new doctrines was less
precipitous than has usually been supposed, and that we today are able to
perceive more clearly the explosive potential in the troubles with which
Cambridge was beset in 1525-26 than were the participants in those troubles.
If these conclusions are correct, then there is nothing fundamentally in-
congruous in the picture of Hugh Latimer continuing to say masses for
the repose of the souls of dead benefactors of the university, or of his
appointment by a succession of conservative vice-chancellors to a share in
the management of Cambridge affairs. It is important to bear in mind that
as yet the church was not constricted by the definitions of Trent, and that
if the earlier reformers were not fully aware of all the implications of
their new doctrines, neither were the conservatives, who were not without
hope of keeping all the sheep within one fold.

CHAPTER FIVE

THE TESTING OF LITTLE BILNEY

The year following Robert Barnes' recantation in February 1526 was one of comparative quiet among the Cambridge reformers. Some of them were busy in London about the distribution of Tyndale's New Testament and the inflammatory tracts which were coming out of Germany. No doubt also they were in constant communication with John Frith and their other colleagues who had accepted Wolsey's invitation to remove to Oxford and were energetically sowing the seeds of the reformation in the Cardinal's new college in that ancient university. No doubt the authorities at Cambridge were keeping a watchful eye on the activities of Bilney, Stafford, Latimer, Crome, and the other reformers. Under the circumstances, until the turmoil stirred up by the Barnes sermon had subsided, the apostles of the new learning were content for a time to restrain their public utterances.

In the end, it was Bilney who broke silence. The first of the Cambridge men to espouse the cause of reform, he had been satisfied for a half-dozen years to disseminate his convictions by private rather than public means. It was thus that he had converted Latimer and the rest of his numerous followers. Although licensed to preach anywhere within the diocese of Ely,[1] he seems not to have done so in any way which gave concern to the authorities. He had perhaps been before the Cardinal in connection with the Barnes case, but not because of any recorded public utterances. We may conclude that he was by nature not much inclined to preaching. Now, however, Barnes had been silenced and was in confinement, and it was Bilney who had urged Barnes to speak out. The little man was not one to urge upon others risks which he himself was unwilling to take. Accordingly, in the summer of 1527, Bilney left Cambridge to undertake a kind of preaching mission in some of the smaller towns and then in London itself.

If we turn briefly from Cambridge to glance at affairs in London, it becomes possible to make a guess concerning another motive underlying Bilney's hazardous enterprise. The supporters of religious reform in London were a miscellaneous group. Some of them were Lollards in the Wycliffite tradition. Some were Germans, Hanseatic merchants of the Steelyard, who were so far infected with Lutheranism that they had abolished the sacrifice of the mass from their parish church of Allhallows. Others were of academic background, like Dr. Thomas Farman, sometime of Queen's College and now the rector of All Saints, Honey Lane. All of them had for the past two years been reading Tyndale's New Testament, which had been published in 1526, and many of them had been engaged in the circulation of the English tracts which were coming off the printing presses of Germany to be smuggled into England for the dissemination of Lutheranism.

Over the diocese of London in which all this ferment was working presided Cuthbert Tunstall.[2] Tunstall was not by nature a persecutor of heretics. As bishop of Durham, in later years, he tolerated the presence of John Knox within his diocese, and even John Foxe confessed that he was "no great bloody persecutor." [3] Tunstall had appointed Sir Thomas More as his official refuter of heresy. Left to himself, he might have taken no sterner measure. But by this time Wolsey was determined to deal sharply with the Lutherans, and there is little doubt that it was the Cardinal who stirred the Bishop to more vigorous activity. Accordingly, in protestant histories of the period Tunstall is remembered chiefly for his spirited but unavailing attempts to suppress Tyndale's New Testament, which he truly believed to be erroneous and pernicious.

Thus the year 1527 was one of peril for the London reformers. Early in the year Tunstall and his vicar-general began a visitation of the diocese with the particular purpose of detecting heretics and heretical books. In the city and in Essex, particularly at Colchester, they sat judicially in their ecclesiastical courts and heard the confessions of upwards of fifty men and women, some of whom confessed only to having owned and read the New Testament in English, others of whom had gone so far as to deny the presence of Christ in the sacrament of the altar. A few of the offenders were priests with cures of souls; the great majority were humble men and women, artisans, small tradesmen, and housewives. Under examination most of them abjured their heresies. None suffered extreme penalties.[4]

It is not too fanciful to suppose that Bilney, aware that the teachings of the Cambridge reformers had had some influence, however indirect, in shaping the views of these humbly placed folk, felt it his solemn duty to speak to these people who were now in grave jeopardy, that their views might be confirmed and strengthened by the open expression of his own deep-seated convictions. Although he might not share their more radical opinions with respect to the sacraments, he was heart and soul behind them in their devotion to the Bible in English, so recently made available to them by the work of Tyndale, and so recently as the autumn of 1526 made the center of Tunstall's book-burning at Paul's Cross.

Bilney's mission took him first into Suffolk.[5] At Ipswich and other towns he preached against the worldliness of the clergy, against the idolatry involved in the veneration of the saints, against the palpable hoaxes and chicanery practiced at such celebrated shrines as that at Walsingham. Apparently he urged also that children should be taught the Paternoster in English, and that at mass the Gospel and Epistle should be read in the vernacular. Foxe seems to imply that Bilney also spoke directly in criticism of the Lord Cardinal, but on this point the martyrologist's narrative is cloudy. Finally, Bilney's itinerant preaching took him toward London. He preached at Willesden, Kensington, Chelsea, and Newington in the suburbs, then at St. Helen's and St. Magnus' London Bridge in the city itself. The influence of his sermons must have been great, for John Pykas of Colchester, one of the most troublesome of the heretics examined by Tunstall, confessed that it was Bilney's preaching at Ipswich which confirmed him in his heretical opinions.[6]

The sermon which finally brought Bilney before authority was one preached during Whitsun Week, 1527, at St. Magnus', where a new rood had been erected and was in process of being gilded. Bilney improved the occasion by denouncing the rood as idolatrous, and repeating his customary condemnation of pilgrimages and prayers to the saints. Once again he declared in favor of the Scriptures in English. He may have uttered even more dangerous sentiments, for some of the opinions later charged against him savored more nearly of genuine heresy than these. It seems to be true also that at St. Magnus' Bilney preached without the Bishop's license. All things considered, it is evident that Bilney left Tunstall little choice but to proceed against him.

Although Bilney was cited for heresy not long after the offending sermon, he was not tried until the end of November. During some of the intervening months he must have been at liberty, for it was later charged that between his citation and his trial he had again rashly preached in churches of the diocese of London without the Bishop's license. During this period Bilney seems to have hoped that if he could get the ear of Tunstall, a mild man, the charges against him might be dropped. But Tunstall denied his importunities for a private audience, perhaps, it has been suggested, because Tunstall was wary of Bilney's special powers of making converts in private sessions.[7] Failing in his hope of an audience, Bilney composed five letters which he despatched to the Bishop. Three of them are preserved by Foxe. The first begins with a dignified and sincere tribute to Tunstall's learning and justice, continues with the eloquent account of Bilney's conversion to the new learning, and begs that he may be tried before the Cardinal, to whom he would rather look for mercy than to his representatives. The other letters are carefully documented statements of some of his opinions. They may have helped Bilney's case to the extent of making Tunstall patient with Bilney after his conviction.

On November 27, 1527, Bilney was brought before the Cardinal and an ecclesiastical commission in the chapter house at Westminster. Thomas Arthur, another Cambridge man, who had been proclaiming the freedom of any man, priest or layman, to preach the Gospel without episcopal license, was called before the same tribunal at the same time. Among the bishops present, in addition to Tunstall, were Warham of Canterbury, Fisher of Rochester, Nix of Norwich, West of Ely. The chapter house was thronged with a crowd of divines and lawyers, including Sir Thomas More, who were professionally interested in the case. At the first session, the Cardinal presided and took the lead in questioning both Bilney and Arthur. Of Bilney, Wolsey inquired particularly whether he had not on a former occasion taken an oath not to preach the opinions of Luther. No doubt the Cardinal was alluding to Bilney's appearance before him during the Barnes affair. Bilney replied that he had taken such an oath, but not judicially—that is, not during a formal process such as the present one. To us it may seem that Bilney was equivocating. But the point was technical and legal, and Bilney's answer seems to have satisfied the bishops, for in the sequel Bilney was not treated as a relapsed heretic. After taking the testimony of witnesses, Wolsey adjourned the hearing and himself withdrew from further participation in the proceedings. On the following day additional testimony was taken against Arthur.

The hearing of the two Cambridge men was not resumed until December 2, when, with Tunstall presiding, Bilney and Arthur were examined jointly upon thirty-four questions. In addition, Bilney's utterances at St. Magnus' were separately charged against him, including the accusation that he had said that for five centuries there had been no good pope, and that there had been no more than fifty good popes in the church's whole history. Bilney's answers to about half the charges were entirely satisfactory, including his admission that many of Luther's opinions were heretical. His answers to the others were qualified or equivocal. Though it is possible that some accusations were brought against him falsely, certain things are clear. He had said that the church could err, though not in matters of faith. He had denounced the superstitious worship of images and the practice of praying to the saints. He had preached that the Scriptures, or at least part of them, should be rendered into English, and that at mass the Gospel and Epistle should be read in English. He had denounced pardons and indulgences. His answers to the more strictly theological questions leave some doubt as to his exact position. One point, however, should be noticed. It was not charged against Bilney, as it was against Arthur, that he had denied the presence of the very Body of Christ in the sacrament of the altar. In the matter of the sacraments, Bilney remained orthodox to the end. According to post-Tridentine standards Bilney's utterances were not heretical, although some of them were dangerous. But according to the standards of 1527, and of the court which tried him, Bilney's admitted opinions were sufficient to convict him of heretical pravity.

When Bilney was again brought before the bishops, he was formally urged to abjure his erroneous views. He replied that he would stand upon his conscience, and permitted himself to become rhapsodical as he quoted Scripture. Whereupon Tunstall put off his cap, made the sign of the cross, and pronounced Bilney to be convicted of heresy. Sentence was postponed until the next day. When he appeared for sentence, Bilney asked permission to call additional witnesses. The request was denied on the legally correct ground that the verdict had already been rendered. Once again the judges urged Bilney to abjure in order that he might be restored to the Church and his life spared. Once again Bilney refused, but Tunstall, with great forbearance, granted him until 9 A.M. of the following day to consider his case, to pray, and to consult with his friends.

In the end, after thirty-six hours of anguished conference with his friends, Bilney gave in. When he appeared before the tribunal on the Saturday, he read a complete abjuration of his heresies and submitted himself to the mercy of the court. For a penance, he was required next day to go before the procession at St. Paul's, bare-headed and carrying a fagot on his shoulder, and to stand before the preacher at the Cross during the whole of the sermon. Bilney never recovered from the disgrace, nor from his own bitter sense of having betrayed his conscience. If ever a man yearned for martyrdom, it was Bilney from this time forward. He spent the next year or so in the Tower, awaiting the Cardinal's pleasure. When, at the end of 1528, he was permitted to return to Cambridge, he was a man of a broken and contrite heart.

Latimer, his closest friend, found it impossible to console him. Listen to Latimer's own words:

> Little Bilney, that blessed martyr of God, what time he had borne his fagot and was come again to Cambridge, had such conflicts within himself, beholding this image of death, that his friends were afraid to let him alone. They were fain to be with him day and night and comforted him as they could, but no comforts would serve. As for the comfortable places of Scripture, to bring them unto him it was as though a man would run him through the heart with a sword.[8]

As yet Latimer had not been overtaken by a zeal for martyrdom, and it is quite possible that his failure to console Bilney was due to a deficiency, not of sympathy, but of comprehension. For two years more Bilney bore his burden of anguish and shame.

In one way, however, it was possible for Latimer to distract Bilney from his melancholia. The works of mercy which both men regarded as so much more important than voluntary works became more frequent. The lazar-cots and the prison of Cambridge were once more the scene of their humanitarian visitation. Years later, Latimer told of an experience which grew out of these prison visits, apparently towards the close of 1529.[9] One of the prisoners was a woman who had been convicted of murdering her own child. The charge had been lodged against her by her husband, who wanted to be rid of her, but Latimer and Bilney were persuaded that the child had in fact died accidentally. The woman was again pregnant and execution was being postponed until after the birth of the infant. About this time Latimer was summoned to preach at Windsor. He told the King of the woman's predicament, and went back to Cambridge with a royal pardon for her in his pocket. Latimer and Bilney said nothing of the pardon, however, but continually exhorted the woman to confess the truth. Her child was born, Latimer standing as godfather at the christening. Still the exhortations continued. Then, on the very eve of the execution, the two clerics discovered that the only burden on the woman's conscience was the fear that she would be damned if she died without "purification" after childbirth. Satisfied that she was innocent of murder, they were able to assure her that the ceremony of the churching of women had nothing to do with salvation. Then they showed her the King's pardon and let her go.

The latter part of this episode may arouse little sympathy for Bilney and Latimer in the mind of the modern reader. Certainly our hearts go out to the poor woman in her uncertainty and anguish during the days or weeks while two earnest divines satisfied themselves of her soul's health. Such humanitarian considerations, however, belong to a more recent, less theological age, which has minimized the importance anciently attached to souls. Seen in the light of its own day, the episode speaks eloquently of the zeal of Latimer and Bilney for the eternal welfare of those to whom they ministered.

CHAPTER SIX

THE ENGLISH BIBLE

No sermon or other reliable attestation of Latimer's opinions can be dated earlier than the close of 1529. It is therefore difficult to generalize about the extent or intensity of his convictions during the first five years following his "conversion." His practical mind was never much bent toward speculation upon doctrinal matters. From the record of his later career it appears that his acceptance of the purely doctrinal elements in Luther's teaching was gradual and even halting. But of his support of the more practical side of Luther's program there can be no doubt. He fully assented to the Lutheran condemnation of the penitential system as it was practiced in the later Middle Ages, and to the criticism of laxity and venality among the clergy. Uppermost in his thought, however, was the view that the Bible must be regarded as the primal foundation of the Christian faith.[1]

A corollary of the latter opinion, when it rubs elbows with the doctrine that only faith justifies, is that the Bible must be made available to Christians in their own languages. To this end Luther had prepared his German Bible, and Tyndale had translated the New Testament into English. But Tyndale's translation was a forbidden book. In spite of the prohibition, many earnest souls had undertaken the dangerous work of distributing copies surreptitiously. Such underground activities could result only in a tightening of the legal restrictions. What was needed was an effective propaganda, not directly in support of Tyndale's translation but rather on behalf of the principle of an authorized English version of the Bible. Such work might be less dangerous than the secret distribution of New Testaments, but in the end it would have more important results. For the dissemination of such propaganda some of the university men were strategically situated, and none more so than Latimer, who as cross-keeper, chaplain, and university preacher was in a position of some influence at Cambridge. Accordingly, early in his career as a reformer, Latimer began to preach openly on behalf of the Bible in English. He continued to do so, with unswerving devotion to the cause, until an English translation was licensed in 1537. It may fairly be claimed for him that his work on behalf of the English Bible ranks below only that of Cranmer and the translators themselves.

It cannot now be discovered when he first spoke out, but there is some evidence that he preached a series of daring sermons on this topic early in the year 1528. The evidence is slight; we shall have to attempt an archaeological reconstruction from a few scattered fragments. The first hint is to be found in Foxe's report of the famous Sermons on the Card, which Latimer preached during the Christmas season of 1529. Foxe says that Master Latimer "also" preached a series of sermons advocating the

Bible in English which have not been preserved,[2] but the statement is so garbled that it is impossible to know whether Foxe is alluding to a separate series of sermons or to the Sermons on the Card themselves. Similarly vague is the testimony of William Turner, at this period a student at Cambridge. In 1551, when he was dean of Wells, Turner published a controversial tract called *A preservative or treacle against the poison of Pelagius,* which he dedicated to Latimer. In that dedication Turner speaks of the influence exerted by Latimer upon the Cambridge youth of "about twenty years ago." He mentions sermons denouncing "will-works" (one of the principal topics of the Sermons on the Card) and he seems to refer also to other sermons in which Latimer spoke at length on the necessity of reading and studying the word of God.[3]

More specific is the testimony of Thomas Becon, a student at St. John's who proceeded B.A. in 1530 and in later years was the author of numerous tracts in support of the reformed religion. In one of these, *The Jewel of Joy,* printed in the reign of Edward VI, he pays eloquent tribute to Latimer:

I was sometime a poor scholar at Cambridge, very desirous to have the knowledge of good letters; and in the time of my being there, this godly man [Latimer] preached many learned and Christian sermons both in the Latin and in the English tongue, at the which all I for most part was present; and, although at that time I was but a child of sixteen years, yet I noted his doctrine so well as I could, partly reposing it in my memory, partly commending it to letters, as most faithful treasures unto memory.

I was present when, with manifest authorities of God's word and arguments invincible, besides the allegations of doctors, he proved in his sermons, that the holy scriptures ought to be read in the English tongue of all Christian people, whether they were priests or laymen, as they be called; which thing divers drowsy duncers, with certain false flying flattering friars, could not abide, but openly in their unsavoury sermons resisted his godly purpose, even as Alexander the coppersmith, and Elymas the sorcerer, with many other, resisted blessed Paul and his godly doctrine; notwithstanding, he (yea, rather God in him, whose cause he handled) gat the victory; and it came to pass according to his teaching. Neither was I absent when he inveighed against temple-works, good intents, blind zeal, superstitious devotion, etc.; as the painting of tabernacles, gilding of images, setting up of candles, running on pilgrimage, and such other idle inventions of men, whereby the glory of God was obscured, and the works of mercy the less regarded.[4]

Clearly, from the way in which the foregoing passage is ordered, Becon had in mind two groups of sermons, one series advocating the Bible in English, the other denouncing will-works. On this point his testimony is identical with that of Turner. But Becon tells us more. The sermons were preached when Becon was a lad of sixteen. Now Becon was born in 1512, and he would have been sixteen sometime in 1528. It would be unsafe to press the point too far, since Becon was writing some twenty years later, but it seems not unlikely that Latimer preached a series of sermons on the Bible in that year.

Like Bilney a year earlier, Latimer had chosen a singularly dangerous time to speak out on behalf of the Scriptures in English or on any other topic associated with the Lutheran ideology. Wolsey, after a period of slackness, was bearing down upon Lutheranism in the universities in genuine earnest, with the result that for the reformers the years 1527 and 1528 were marked by terror and alarm. At Cambridge, many besides Bilney were in trouble. Oxford also felt the weight of Wolsey's severity. The newly established Cardinal College had been discovered to be a hotbed of heresy, some of it imported from Cambridge. As a consequence John Frith and other canons of the college were imprisoned for a period of several months. Before the year was out, many of the Cambridge and Oxford men were forced to sign articles abjuring their Lutheran opinions. Indeed, so many recanted that one unsympathetic historian has contended that lying, perjury, and insincere abjuration were all part of a settled program among the reformers.[5]

Becon's remarks sufficiently attest the outcry provoked by Latimer's sermons of 1528 among the "drowsy duncers" and other conservative members of Cambridge university. It may be, too, that these were the same sermons which brought Latimer to the unfavorable notice of Bishop West. It has already been pointed out that on June 9, 1528, at a diocesan synod held at Barnwell Abbey, West attacked Tyndale's New Testament and forbade the clergy of his diocese to read it.[6] It is possible that West's action was in some way related to Latimer's preaching, and indeed may have been directly excited by teachings so opposite to his own views. Perhaps, as has been suggested, we may associate with these sermons of 1528 Foxe's vexatious statement that West preached against Latimer at Barnwell and forbade him to preach within the churches of the university.[7]

Bishop West's part in the affair must remain a matter of speculation. But there can be no doubt that as a result of his preaching in the early months of 1528 Latimer was called before Wolsey, probably for the first time. Foxe's clear statement that Latimer was examined by Wolsey about three years after his conversion fits well enough with this period, and it is supported by two independent bits of evidence. The first is an entry in the Grace Books recording the fact that in 1528, probably during Lent, a servant of the Cardinal came to Cambridge with a summons bearing the King's seal for Master Latimer and others.[8] The second is the testimony of the man who probably brought the summons, Ralph Moryson. Writing in 1533, Moryson asserted that five years earlier he had been sent to Cambridge by the Cardinal to look into Latimer's case.[9] There is every likelihood that Foxe, Moryson, and the entry in the Grace Book all refer to the same episode.

Who were the others named with Latimer in the Cardinal's summons, and what was their offense? A Foxean manuscript, now lost but fortunately summarized by Strype[10] before its disappearance, provides some clues to an answer. According to this document, Rodolph Bradford, a fellow of King's and a pious gospeller (he was later one of Latimer's chaplains at Worcester), had been busy about the distribution of English New Testaments. In London he had met Geoffrey Lome, another ardent reformer, who had once been an usher at St. Anthony's school but was now servant to Dr. Farman, the rector of All Saints, Honey Lane. The two went from London to Reading to distribute Testaments among the monks of the abbey there, some of whom had already been infected with heretical literature by the agency of Thomas Garrett (or Gerard) of Corpus Christi, Oxford, an indefatigable disseminator of Tyndale's work,[11] who also later became one of Bishop Latimer's chaplains. At Reading, however, something went awry, and a monk who had been involved in the transaction was detected and arrested. During his examination he implicated Bradford and those from whom he had had the Testaments. Letters were then sent to the Vice-Chancellor [12] of Cambridge to arrest Bradford, Dr. Richard Smith of Trinity Hall, Simon Smith of Caius, Sygar Nicholson (sometime of Gonville Hall, and latterly a Cambridge stationer who on several occasions was in trouble over the possession of Lutheran books), and Hugh Latimer. Strype's narrative closes with the statement that Bradford fled with an Austin friar to Ireland, where he was arrested and imprisoned for two years, after which time he returned to Cambridge.

Here, then, are the probable names of the others who, along with Latimer, were summoned before Wolsey by the authority of the document cited in the Grace Book. The nature of their offenses seems clear. Latimer had been preaching on behalf of the English Bible; some of the others, probably all of them, had been distributing copies of Tyndale's New Testament. Unfortunately, Strype does not date the episode, but the subsequent history of most of the actors places it certainly in the year 1528. Bradford lost his fellowship at King's in that year, an inevitable consequence of his flight to Ireland. Richard Smith of Trinity, called "Doctor" by Strype, did not become a D.D. until 1528; he died in 1529. From other sources we know that Sygar Nicholson was cited for heresy and abjured in 1528; so did Geoffrey Lome, although Lome, not being of the university, was not included in the summons sent to the Vice-Chancellor. About this time Simon Smith fled to Antwerp, where he remained until 1530 or 1531.[13]

There is a strong temptation to associate Latimer's appearance before the Cardinal on this occasion with the story, already related, of his confounding Wolsey's chaplains. Unfortunately the apocryphal elements in that story require that the temptation be sternly resisted.[14] This occasion was too serious, the times were too dangerous, for cleverness and a prevailing air of geniality and good will. The fact that no record survives of Latimer's examination by Wolsey must not blind us to the danger for Latimer. Had he been guilty of violating the law or of preaching genuine heresy, he would have been tried judicially. From such a trial he would have emerged a convicted heretic, for in such cases the guilt of the accused was never in doubt. The only questions at issue were the degree of guilt and the nature of the punishment, the latter depending upon the pertinacity with which the accused persisted in his errors. Even if Latimer had abjured, he would have stood in peril of his life upon any future occasion when he might have been accused of a relapse. Indeed (this is to anticipate) his career would certainly have come to an untimely end five years later, when he was summoned to give an account of himself before Convocation.

As it turned out, Latimer got off lightly. He was content, Foxe says, to subscribe to the articles put to him by Wolsey. In so doing, he no doubt disclaimed any irregular views concerning the authority of the church and the nature and efficacy of the sacraments. No judicial proceedings were instituted against him, and he was let off with an admonition.[15] As contrasted with the treatment meted out to Barnes and Bilney, his punishment was mild indeed. One reason must have been that he was not personally involved in the distribution of forbidden New Testaments, the

37

point on which Bradford and the others had collided with the law. Nor, it is certain, had he launched a personal attack upon Wolsey's malfeasance; such attacks always proved disastrous to those who ventured them. Probably his sermons had been limited to a plea for the legalizing of the Scriptures in English. This was daring, even dangerous, but in a strict sense it was neither heretical nor illegal. Wolsey, a fair man so long as his personal vanity was not touched, was satisfied to dismiss him with a rebuke and a warning.

It is probable, however, that upon his return to Cambridge Latimer found that a local reprisal had been arranged. Such at least may be the interpretation to be placed upon the fact that about this time he ceased to be cross-keeper and university chaplain, both of which offices were transferred to Nicholas Heath. The incumbent could no doubt have been removed at the instigation of the Chancellor, Bishop Fisher, who was no admirer of Latimer and certainly was ill disposed towards the translation of the Bible into English. But it would be unwise to push too strongly the suggestion that Latimer was removed punitively, for the precise date of Heath's succession is not clear. Shortly after these events Latimer moved into a larger arena, and it may be that he resigned his office voluntarily. In any case, his career as university preacher suffered little or no interruption. From the Grace Books we learn that in the autumn of 1528—specifically on September 23 and 30—he was again preaching *ad clerum* at St. Mary's, the university church.[16]

CHAPTER SEVEN

THE SERMONS ON THE CARD

The year following Latimer's appearance before Wolsey was one of increasing tension; and the summer and autumn of the year 1529 were critical. Two years had passed since King Henry had first seen the "gospel-light" in Anne Boleyn's eyes, and the first round of his long struggle for the annulment of his marriage to Queen Catherine had ended in defeat. In July, Cardinal Campeggio adjourned the legatine court which had been hearing the evidence, and shortly thereafter it was learned that the case would after all be referred to Rome, with the certainty of long delay and the probability of a decision adverse to Henry. In a dudgeon the King retired to Waltham.

The second round began almost immediately. On October 16, 1529, Wolsey was removed from the chancellorship and began the period of re-

tirement and disgrace which ended in his death a year later. The seals of
office were transferred to Sir Thomas More. Two weeks later the King
convoked Parliament for the first time in years. This Parliament sat inter-
mittently for seven years. Because of its drastic measures for the correction of the church, it is commonly called the Reformation Parliament.

The first session of the Reformation Parliament served as a kind of
warning that if the Pope and the Roman Curia persisted in refusing to
annul the King's marriage a way would be found to separate England
from obedience to Rome. The Commons, under crown guidance, were
permitted free discussion of ecclesiastical abuses, and corrective measures
were proposed. In the upper house, the bishops' opposition to these measures was vigorous and alarmed. In the end, the King so checked the Commons and so intimidated the bishops as to secure the passage of three bills.
The first imposed a restriction on mortuary fees—the hateful exaction of
a "gift" from the estate of a deceased person, even when there was no
estate and the demand worked genuine hardship upon the survivors. The
second limited the fees which the ecclesiastical courts might charge for
probating wills. The third attempted to correct the grossest abuses of
pluralism and the non-residence of beneficed clergy. This third bill included an adroit warning to the Pope in the form of a clause which made
it a penal offense to appeal to Rome for a dispensation from the provisions
of the act. It is clear that if Henry had not already determined to break
with Rome, he had at least concluded that the papal claims, as far as they
extended to England, might be limited by act of Parliament.

Among historians there has been much debate as to the extent to
which these measures reflected public opinion. It has been charged, with
strong presumption of truth, that many members of the Commons were
hand-picked to do the King's bidding, and it is entirely true that the bills
were largely drafted by the King or his agents. On the other hand, the
measures struck at the very abuses which had for years been the object of
attack by both lay and clerical reformers.[1] They were well calculated to
secure a considerable measure of popular support for the King and his
cause. Certainly they met with the approval of reforming preachers like
Hugh Latimer and encouraged them, perhaps unduly, to speak out more
freely than heretofore. It was against this background that Latimer dared
to preach his famous Sermons on the Card.

By the autumn of 1529 Latimer had assumed the lead among the
Cambridge reformers. It would be rewarding to know more of the gathering intensity of feeling within the university at this time. Foxe is disappointingly silent, except for the asseveration that "as Satan never sleepeth
when he seeth his kingdom begin to decay, so likewise now, seeing that this
worthy member of Christ [Latimer] would be a shrewd shaker thereof,
he raised up his impious imps to molest and trouble him." [2] Further than
this, we must be content with Thomas Becon's assertion that for years
afterwards there was a famous saying referring to this period—"When

Master Stafford read and Master Latimer preached then was Cambridge blessed." [3]

Our authority for the Sermons on the Card is Foxe,[4] whose summaries provide us with our only knowledge of the sermons themselves and the circumstances under which they were preached. Here again, as for all these Cambridge matters, Foxe's testimony is confused, and the story must be told in terms of probabilities. It appears that shortly before Christmas, 1529, Latimer preached a sermon which gave great offense to some of the conservatives. The sermon has not been preserved, but the sequel indicates that Latimer touched upon two inflammatory topics—the need for the Bible in English and the folly of such "voluntary works" as pilgrimages and devotions to the saints. This sermon provoked an attack upon Latimer by Dr. John Venutus, a Benedictine, who in 1529 was deputy vice-chancellor. Venutus was a foreigner, from his name presumably a Venetian, who had received the B.D. in 1514-15 and the D.D. in 1518.[5] He was evidently a person of some consideration within the university. To Foxe, of course, he was but a railing friar who raged against Latimer, "calling him a mad and brainless man, and willing the people not to believe him." The first of the two recorded Sermons on the Card is palpably a rejoinder to this attack.

The time was December 19, the Sunday before Christmas, the place St. Edward's church. According to custom, the bell was rung to summon the people to a sermon, and when the congregation had assembled the preacher gave out his text. It was from the gospel for the day—the words *tu quis es?* quoted in John 1:19 as having been addressed by the Pharisees to the Baptist. In his introduction, Latimer developed the point that the Christian need not answer this question by saying, "I am a lump of sin, the just inheritor of hell." By the mercy of Christ in the waters of baptism, he may say instead, "I am a Christian man, the child of everlasting joy, through the merits of the bitter passion of Christ."

But Christ requires that a Christian should follow Christ's rule. What is Christ's rule? Here Latimer entered upon the principal theme of his sermon. Here also he startled his congregation by drawing out of the sleeve of his gown a pack of cards, and declaring his intention of following the custom of playing cards at Christmas. Owst has pointed out that the use of playing-cards to illustrate a sermon was by no means original.[6] Latimer's originality lay in his application to a learned congregation of a trick designed by the friars to captivate village audiences. Apart from the question of taste, it was a daring stunt, one which could be carried off successfully only by a masterful speaker. Latimer quelled the murmurs. These were Christ's cards, he declared, with which he intended to play the game called "triumph" (a kind of primitive bridge), but it would be God's triumph, in which not only the dealer, but all the other players and the onlookers as well would win.

Latimer picked up the first card, examined its face, and declared it to be a trump to win all the other cards. What was it? Why, one of the first rules for a Christian man, a card that was made and spoken by Christ. "You have heard what was spoken to men of the old law, 'Thou shalt not kill; whosoever shall kill shall be in danger of the judgment'; but I say unto you, of the new law, saith Christ, that whosoever is angry with his neighbor, shall be in danger of judgment; and whosoever shall say unto his neighbor, *Raca,* that is to say brainless, or any other like word of rebuking, shall be in danger of council; and whosoever shall say unto his neighbor, *Fool,* shall be in danger of hell-fire."

With his eye on Venutus, who had called him mad and brainless, Latimer proceeded to the division of his text. According to the old law, the commandment might be kept if a man did not kill his enemy's body with a dagger. But under the new dispensation a man who is angry with his brother and calls him brainless or a fool kills his own soul. As for degrees of punishment, judgment is less in degree than council, and signifies the lesser pain in hell for him who is angry but conceals his anger. Council and hell-fire were reserved for those who expressed their anger with various degrees of vigor. Probably most of his hearers were as familiar as Latimer with the traditional gloss on *council, judgment,* and *hell-fire;* but Latimer was careful that Dr. Venutus should not miss the point.

A man, Latimer continued, may kill himself spiritually by being angry with another. But there are other ways of killing. Parents kill themselves spiritually by their sins, and they kill their children by the bad example which they set for them. So also masters kill themselves and their servants and their apprentices. They kill also by their silence, by their failure to admonish children and servants, and by their readiness to condone offenses without correction.

Only by repentance (Latimer does not use the word, but it is clear that he means *penitence,* not *penance*) can a man's sins be forgiven. The Magdalene is the perfect example of the repentant sinner; the arrogant Pharisee, Simon, is the perfect example of pride which knows no repentance. Sitting in the stalls of St. Edward's, said Latimer, there were many Simons, perking and presuming to sit by Christ in the church. But there is more forgiveness for the poor Magdalene hidden away in the belfry than for the pharisaical masters and doctors in their stalls.

This much of the sermon Foxe gives us probably from notes supplied by someone who had heard the sermon and reconstructed it imperfectly from memory. But there was more to it than this. In the part not reported, as the violent retorts of his opponents indicate, Latimer repeated his now favorite preachment that the Bible is the only means of knowing the truth and of being assured that one would indeed answer "I am a Christian man" to the question "Who are you?" Since every man must answer the question for himself, it is obvious that he should be enabled to read and study the Bible for himself, in his own language.

Latimer ended his sermon on an equally daring note by referring his audience to the fifth chapter of the Book of Wisdom. Out of that chapter, says Foxe, he demonstrated "how the true servants and preachers of God in this world commonly are scorned and reviled by the proud enemies of God's word, which count them here as mad-men, fools, brainless, and drunken; so did they in the Scripture call them which most purely preached and set forth the glory of God's word. But (said he) what will be the end of these jolly fellows, or what will they say in the end?

Nos insensati, nos insensati. We madmen, we mad fools. We, we ourselves. And that will be their end except they repent."

Foxe concludes his account of the first Sermon on the Card with the assertion that poor Dr. Venutus was so confounded that he was driven not only out of countenance but also clean out of the university. This is Foxean hyperbole; Venutus was still at Cambridge in 1530 and served as a member of the commission appointed to pass upon the matter of the King's divorce. The direct reply to Latimer's sermon came not from Venutus but from Dr. Robert Buckenham, prior of the Dominican house at Cambridge, who had proceeded B.D. in 1524 and was thus a contemporary of Latimer. He is remembered also for his connection with the arrest of Tyndale in 1535.[7]

Buckenham chose to reply with a "Sermon on the Dice." Mounting the pulpit a few days after Latimer's sermon, he drew from the sleeve of his gown a pair of dice. With great cunning he cast "cinque and quater," expounded the signification of his dice as Latimer had expounded his cards. The four stood for the Four Doctors, by whom he would prove that it was not expedient to have the Scriptures in English. The five signified five places in Scripture which proved that reading of Scripture might tempt workingmen to abandon their labor. "As for example the plowman when he heareth this in the Gospel, 'No man that layeth his hand on the plow and looketh back is meet for the kingdom of God,' might peradventure hearing this cease from his plow. Likewise the baker when he heareth that a little leaven corrupteth a whole lump of dough, may percase leave our bread unleavened, and so our bodies shall be unseasoned. Also the simple man, when he heareth in the gospel, 'If thine eye offend thee, pluck it out, and cast it from thee,' may make himself blind, and so fill the world full of beggars. These with other more this clerkly friar brought out to the number of five, to prove his purpose."

In his first edition Foxe says merely that Latimer replied briefly to Buckenham's attack, but in later editions he is more ample. Latimer, he says, resolved at once to answer the prior, and in the afternoon of the same day or "shortly after" he appeared once more in the pulpit at St. Edward's. Evidently his intention had been heralded by more advance publicity than the customary ringing of the church bell, for a great crowd had gathered to hear him, "as well of the university as of the town, both doctors and other graduates." Immediately beneath the pulpit, with his Blackfriar's cowl about his shoulders, sat Dr. Buckenham.

Point by point Latimer sought to refute Buckenham's fears concerning the plowman, the baker, and the simpleton. Then he turned to deal with the Prior more directly. The Scriptures, he said, were not difficult of comprehension. Even those pasasges which require allegorical interpretation were no more esoteric than the metaphors of speech or than the allegorical pictures of which painters are so fond. "As for example (saith he, looking toward the friar that sat over against him) when they paint a fox preaching out of a friar's cowl, none is so mad as to take this to be a fox that preacheth, but know well enough the meaning of the matter, which is to point out unto us what hypocrisy, craft and subtle dissimulation lieth hid many times in these friars' cowls, willing us thereby to beware of them."

So, according to the not impartial testimony of Foxe, Latimer demolished poor Prior Buckenham, who "with this sermon was so dashed that never after he durst peep out of the pulpit against Master Latimer." As in the case of Dr. Venutus, we must be skeptical of Foxe's assertion concerning the ignominy suffered by Latimer's opponent. Buckenham remained for some years a consequential personage within the university.

It is difficult to fit the sermon which Foxe calls the Second Sermon on the Card into the sequence of indecorous controversy with which we have just been concerned. From its context it might have come either before or after Buckenham's attack. In any case we must examine it closely, for its attack upon voluntary works is characteristic of the thought of both the English and the Continental reformers.

His text—his card—for this second sermon was Matthew 5: 23-24, which he rendered: "When thou makest thine oblation at mine altar, and there dost remember that thy neighbor has anything against thee, lay down there thine oblation, and go first and reconcile thy neighbor, and then come and offer thy oblation." This "card" was spoken by Christ against those who presume by prayers, alms-deeds, or any work of charity to make oblation unto God without first being reconciled to their neighbors whom they had offended and in whom they had thus induced the mortal sin of anger. Without such reconciliation—such *repentance*—oblations to God are vain.

In this matter, Latimer continued, a Christian must be the Master's true servant. He must effect a true reconciliation with his neighbor. It will not be sufficient for him to attempt to mollify his neighbor by offering him a pennyworth of ale or a banquet. The offended man may smile and speak fair, yet still carry in his bosom a rusty bag of malice twenty years old. Nor will it do to say, "I will be reconciled with my neighbor provided it costs me neither sacrifice nor pain." Christ, although it lay within His power to work our salvation without sacrifice of Himself, chose nevertheless the anguish of the cross. He who enjoined us to take up His cross will permit us no easy evasion of the costs of our sin.

So the first meaning of this card is that one must be reconciled with his neighbor. But Latimer emphasized two further points. First, even though a man be reconciled with his neighbor, God will not accept his oblation if the money which pays for it has been procured by extortion, the mismanagement of other men's estates, or any other manner of dishonesty. Second, God will refuse an oblation, even though the money which pays for it has been honestly procured, if the offerer has failed to relieve the sufferings of the poor. For in the latter event Christ will say, "Depart from me, ye cursed, for I was an hungered and ye gave me no meat; I was thirsty and ye gave me no drink; I was a stranger, and ye took me not in."

Wherefore, Latimer concludes, it follows that one should bestow the greater part of his goods in works of mercy, the lesser part in voluntary works. As if to an audience of children, Latimer spelled out the three kinds of works. Necessary works are the presentation of tithes at the four offering-days. Works of mercy consist of visiting and relieving the poor. Voluntary works are setting up candles, gilding and painting images, going on pilgrimages. Necessary works and works of mercy are of the commandments; voluntary works are not. The peroration of the sermon concedes that voluntary works are meritorious, but only in so far as they testify that a man has provided God with a glorious place in his heart.

The Sermons on the Card provide us with a summary glimpse of Latimer's opinions as of the close of 1529, approximately five years after his conversion. While the tone of the sermons is distinctly Lutheran, the theology, what there is of it, is not clearly so. The passages on total depravity and the inefficacy of good works have Lutheran implications, but the juxtaposed passages on the sacraments as the channels of grace have not. The anomaly need not surprise us. In adopting the views of Luther and others, Latimer was eclectic rather than consistent. We shall find that theologically he was disposed to follow the lead of the moderate English thinkers. Cranmer, rather than Tyndale, was the filter through which he received the Continental theology. Like Cranmer, Latimer moved slowly and with great caution towards a change of opinion in the fundamental matters of the sacraments and the nature of grace.

As a preacher and an apostle of righteousness, Latimer was captivated less by Luther's theology than by the subsidiary practicalities of the Lutheran program. These practicalities were all adumbrated in the fragmentary Sermons on the Card, and they became the core of Latimer's preaching during the next five years. They were, not necessarily in the order of importance: the insistence upon the authority of Scripture and the corollary insistence upon the translation of Scripture into the vernacular; the demand for reform of abuses which had developed in the cult of the saints and in the penitential system generally; finally, the insistence upon righteousness, manifested in love and service to fellow human beings, as the necessary mark of the Christian, layman and priest alike. These are the matters upon which Latimer at this stage had made up his mind, and about which he cared greatly and preached vehemently. It would be a mistake, of course, to insist upon an exclusively Lutheran origin for this program. Much of it can be found in medieval preaching and in the writings of Catholic humanists like More and Erasmus. But considered in their entirety, Latimer's views in 1529 must be regarded as primarily Lutheran, and the intensity with which he girded himself for the attack was entirely so.

On one other matter Latimer had almost certainly made up his mind when he preached the Sermons on the Card. This was the question of the papal supremacy. It is said that as early as 1525 Thomas Cranmer was praying that England might be relieved of obedience to Rome. Latimer's acceptance of this view would not have been long delayed. He does not touch upon the subject in the Sermons on the Card, but within a few weeks, as we shall see, he took a leading part in supporting King Henry against the papal claims in the matter of the divorce. There is no reason to believe that he did so against his conscience.

The Sermons on the Card provide us also with our first opportunity to sample Latimer's style of pulpit oratory. Here is a key passage from the peroration of the "second" sermon:

> And I promise you, if you build a hundred churches, give as much as you can make to gilding of saints, and honoring of the church; and if thou go as many pilgrimages as the body can well suffer, and offer as great candles as oaks; if thou leave the works of mercy and the commandments undone, these works shall nothing avail thee . . . . Again, if you list to gild and paint Christ in your churches, and honor him in vestments, see that before your eyes the poor people die not for lack of meat, drink, and clothing. Then do you deck the very true temple of God, and honor him in rich vestures that will never be worn, and so forth use yourselves according unto the commandments: and then, finally, set up your candles, and they will report what a glorious light remaineth in your hearts; for it is not fitting to see a dead man light candles. Then, I say, go your pilgrimages, build your material churches, do all your voluntary works; and they will then represent you unto God, and testify with you, that you have provided him a glorious place in your hearts.[8]

We are indebted once again to Mr. Owst for pointing out that the ideas in this and related passages are all to be found in the preaching of the friars.[9] But we are here concerned with style. If the words are Latimer's own (remember that these sermons survive only in Foxe's summary, and he speaks of them as having been "summarized" by a reporter) then we may well claim for him a command of the language superior to that of many of his contemporaries who enjoy a greater reputation in the world of letters. There is little to match it for clarity or cadence in the English writing of Sir Thomas More or in the writing of William Tyndale outside his translation of Scripture.

The tone of the passage just quoted is remarkably moderate. But the moderation was not characteristic of the sermon as a whole. Latimer was ever gifted with a talent for extreme utterance, and he often expressed his views more sharply than he intended. Other parts of the sermons were raucous enough. It is not surprising that they gave great offense to those who were personally attacked, and also to the conservatives who on principle opposed the Bible in English and to those who scented in Latimer's remarks upon voluntary works a threat to the vested interests. It was not only Friar Venutus and Prior Buckenham who snapped back at Latimer. Foxe names five heads of houses who preached against him— Natares of Clare, Watson of Christ's, Metcalfe of St. John's (who was also archdeacon of Rochester and chaplain to Bishop Fisher), Blithe of King's, and Palmes of St. Nicholas' Hostel.[10] Attacks came also from William Filey, vice-master of Michaelhouse, Robert Cliff of Clement's Hostel and chancellor of the diocese of Ely, Geoffrey Downes of Jesus, and four fellows of St. John's—Ralph Baynes, Thomas Greenwood, John Brygenden, and one Rud. Concerning the attacks upon Latimer by such men as Watson, Natares, and the other masters we have no information; subsequent events indicate that they were speaking in their private rather than their official capacities. With respect to the four fellows of St. John's, however, the record is not so barren. Their outcries against Latimer were so loud and so protracted that the whole affair finally became the object of official action. First, a word about the four men. Rud I have not been able to identify; his name does not appear in the Grace Books or in the list of Cambridge alumni. Brygenden had been junior proctor in 1523-24, during which time he was involved, it would appear innocently, in an affair resulting in the death of a townsman; otherwise he too is unknown to fame.[11] Greenwood later achieved a kind of distinction by refusing to acknowledge the royal supremacy, for which refusal he was imprisoned. He died during his imprisonment; whether he was executed or not is not clear.[12] Of the four, only Ralph Baynes achieved prominence in later life. He became a learned Hebraist, was the author of a Hebrew grammar and a commentary on Proverbs, and was for a while professor of Hebrew at Paris. During the reign of Mary he became bishop of Lichfield and Coventry, in which capacity he was a zealous searcher-out of Protestant heresy. At the accession of Elizabeth he was deprived of his bishopric and was imprisoned. He died November 18, 1559, and was buried in St. Dunstan's-in-the-West.[13]

These four—Rud, Brygenden, Greenwood, and Baynes—were the most vocal of Latimer's critics. Their attacks continued for the better part of a month. Latimer did not keep silence; his own expressions became more and more extreme, and his enemies prepared formal articles of heresy against him. In the end, the controversy threatened the peace and good name of the university. News of the disturbance spread far beyond Cambridge, and at last the King intervened through his almoner Edward Fox, who was also provost of King's. On January 24, 1530, Fox despatched a letter to William Buckmaster, of King's Hall, who was then Vice-chancellor, warning him that the controversy must be stopped.

Mr. Vice-chancellor, I heartily commend me unto you, advertising the same that it hath been greatly complained unto the king's highness of the shameful contentions used now of late in sermons made between Mr. Latimer and certain of St. John's College, insomuch his grace intendeth to set some order therein which should not be greatly to yours and other the heads of the university's worship. Wherefore I pray you to use all your wisdom and authority ye can to appease the same, so that no further complaints be made thereof. It is not unlikely but that they of St. John's proceedeth of some private malice towards Mr. Latimer and that also they be animated so to do by their master Mr. Watson [a mistake—Watson was Master of Christ's. The Master of St. John's was Metcalfe] and such other my lord of Rochester's friends. Which malice also peradventure cometh partly for that Mr. Latimer favoreth the king's cause and I assure you it is so reported to the king. And contrary peradventure Mr. Latimer being by them exasperated is more vehement than becometh the very evangelist of Christ and *de industria* speaketh in his sermons certain *paradoxa* to offend and slander the people, which I assure you in my mind is neither wisely done *ut nunc sunt tempora* neither like a good evangelist. You shall therefore in my opinion do well to command both of them to silence; and that neither of them from henceforth preach until you know farther of the king's pleasure or else by some other ways to reduce them in concordance. The ways how to order the same I remit to your wisdom and Mr. Edmunds', to whom I pray you have me heartily commended, trusting to see you shortly. At London the xxiiii day of January.

Your loving friend,
Edward Fox.[14]

Unfortunately we cannot take the whole of this letter at its face value. It would be pleasant to think that Latimer's original sermons were inoffensive, and that the increasing vehemence of his utterances was due to the provocation of his opponents. But it is obvious that Edward Fox, inspired by the King, is not adjudicating the case solely upon its merits. The "king's great matter"—the divorce from Queen Catherine—was approaching a critical stage. We may accept as true Fox's statement that by this time Latimer was known to favor the King's cause. We may also accept the statement that Metcalfe, who was Fisher's chaplain, and the fellows of St. John's were inspired to attack Latimer by Bishop Fisher, who from the start had opposed the King's scheme. Insofar as the tone of the letter is sympathetic towards Latimer we must conclude that Fox was writing in the interests of the King's matter. Henry had already discerned how the reformers might be useful, and among the Cambridge reformers Latimer was the chief. Under the guise of disinterestedness, Fox's letter is a warning to the university that the attacks on Latimer must be stopped.

Dr. Buckmaster, the vice-chancellor, and Dr. Edmunds, his immediate predecessor in that office, were not slow to take the hint. Normally, apart from their personal sympathies, they would have favored Latimer's opponents, since the latter had the backing of Bishop Fisher, the chancellor of the university. But Fox represented a yet higher authority. Accordingly Buckmaster, acting as ordinary of the university, immediately summoned Latimer, and was easily satisfied by his answers to the articles of heresy and malice which had been charged against him. Baynes, Greenwood, Brygenden, and Rud were likewise summoned; but either because they knew their charges would not hold water, or because they knew the case had been prejudged, they failed to appear. Accordingly on January 29 Buckmaster convened the senate of the university and handed down his formal disposition of the case. His formal address to the senate, in the customary Latin, has not been preserved. Fortunately there survives at Cambridge Buckmaster's own minute, in English, of what he said—"These words or such other like did I speak." The vice-chancellor first reviewed the facts. Then he addressed the combatants directly:

Mr. Latimer first. I command you, *sub poena excommunicationis,* that henceforth ye touch no such things in the pulpit as hath been in controversy betwixt you and other, and whereupon contention hath risen. Moreover, I command you that ye be circumspect and discreet in your sermons and that ye speak no such thing which may be occasion of offense unto your audience in any wise.

Now unto you Masters Baynes, Brygenden, Greenwood and Mr. Proctor [perhaps a mistake for "Prior"—i.e., Buckenham]. Under the same pain of excommunication I charge and command you that here in time to come ye touch no such matters as hath been in controversy nor to inveigh or cry out in the pulpit as ye have done in times past, for this hath caused the slanderous bruit which runneth of us in every place to our shame and rebuke. Ye know and remember certain articles which were imputed unto Mr. Latimer and that they were slanderously and suspiciously spoken. Ye know what satisfaction he hath made in the same. Ye know what declaration he hath made concerning the said articles. As I am informed he hath declared them so plainly and so openly that now no manner of man being indifferent or yet well affected towards him can be offended with him or yet think that he hath not on this behalf made due satisfaction. In case he hath not satisfied every man, he is ready and shall be at all times (that known) to satisfy them unto his power and learning. This being true as it is indeed methinks every man ought to be contented.

And again, forasmuch as I appointed you a day if ye had anything to lay unto Mr. Latimer's charge ye should come in before me and ye should be heard according unto equity and justice and then ye came not in, now if ye would accuse him it might be thought to be done more of malice and of some evil passion, than of charity or any good zeal towards the faith of Christ. But much more it should be thought and judged to be misdone if ye should persevere in crying out in the pulpit as ye have done tofore. In case that Mr. Latimer shall hereafter offend you or affirm anything that is contrary unto the catholic faith, then come ye unto me and show me of it and I shall so advertise the matter by due correction and justice that ye shall be contented withal. This seemeth unto me a better way, that I should first examine the matter before that ye pass upon the same. For in case he said amiss and will be reformed, who shall better make amends than himself? Unto whom shall more credence be given of the audience, to him or to you? In case he will be reformed, have ye not then won your brother? In case himself will revoke that thing that hath been evil spoken and declare his faith unto his audience according unto the truth, what can ye or ought ye desire more? If ye be not thus satisfied and contented, but still inveigh and cry out in the pulpit as ye have been accustomed, what shall men say upon you but think ye be malicious, contentious, and froward, seeking nothing the correction of your brother, but to satisfy your own naughty affections? What peace and tranquility shall we trust of, since ye shall so exasperate your brother by that ungoodly manner that he must needs defend himself and so retaliate his injury upon you? If ye persevere as ye have begun, how and by what means shall we bring down this slanderous bruit which is risen upon us almost in every place to our utter rebuke and shame? Let us regard our good name. It is not a little to be esteemed. If it shall be famed that we be thus at contention still amongst ourselves, what credence shall be given unto our preachings when we shall come abroad? Oh, what prejudice shall this be to God's word? What hindrance and what hurt? Every man shall be brought unto such a doubt and perplexity by this manner that they shall not know whom to believe.[15]

Considered apart from its historical context, this is a noble document. It is a plea for fair play, for truth rather than faction, for peace and good order within the university. Unfortunately, Edward Fox's letter will not permit us to regard it so. The fair exterior imperfectly conceals Henry's ugly purpose with respect to Catherine.

Thus ended the episode of the Sermons on the Card. Latimer had got off lightly, with a warning that was scarcely a warning. His enemies had been put to flight. Latimer's own comment upon the episode, and his defense of any lack of restraint of which he may have been guilty, is probably to be found in his reply to a letter from John Redman, a conservative theologian who was also something of a humanist. Redman's letter, probably but not certainly written in connection with the Sermons on the Card, rebukes Latimer for insolent overconfidence in his own opinions. Latimer's reply indicates no lack of confidence. "Reverend Master Redman, it is even enough for me that Christ's sheep hear no man's voice but Christ's; and as for you, you have no voice of Christ against me, whereas, for my part, I have a heart that is ready to hearken to any voice of Christ that you can bring me. Thus fare you well, and trouble me no more from the talking with the Lord my God." [16]

CHAPTER EIGHT

THE KING'S GREAT MATTER

In the summer of 1529, as we have seen, King Henry was at Waltham, brooding over Wolsey's failure to achieve the annulment of the marriage to Catherine. Henry was attended by two of his ablest advisers—Edward Fox, the King's almoner and newly elected provost of King's College, and Stephen Gardiner, now the King's secretary, master of Trinity Hall, and shortly to be bishop of Winchester.[1] In the preceding year these two had unsuccessfully represented Henry's case to the Pope; the failure of their mission was in no way due to deficiency of ability or zeal on their part. At Waltham they were quartered in the house of a man named Cressy, where it chanced that in that summer another Cambridge man was also resident. Up until this time, the figure of Thomas Cranmer had been relatively obscure.[2] A contemporary of Latimer and the other Cambridge reformers, he was not quite of their number. A certain scholarly caution seems to have dissuaded him from any direct religious avowal of the kind that Bilney, Barnes, and Latimer had already made. Yet he was entirely sympathetic to the new learning. He was a careful, dedicated student of the Scriptures. He was no friend of the papacy; it is reported that as early as 1525 he was praying that England might be separated from the Roman obedience. At Cambridge his career had been interrupted by an imprudent marriage which resulted in the loss of his fellowship at Jesus. After the early death of his wife, he was restored to his fellowship and was ordained. The Grace Books reveal that throughout the decade from 1520 to 1530 he was an active if inconspicuous figure in Cambridge affairs.

In the summer of 1529 Cranmer was serving as tutor to two of the Cressy boys in the house at Waltham. He was well known to Gardiner and Fox, his more prominent contemporaries, and they were glad to listen to his opinions concerning the divorce. Cranmer was convinced that Henry's marriage might be annulled on canonical grounds. But he was impatient of the law's delays in this matter for which, he believed, there was both spiritual and political urgency. To Gardiner and Fox he made his famous suggestion that the matter of the divorce should be referred to the faculties of the principal universities of Europe. A decision favorable to the King might not influence the Pope's judgment, but it would furnish Henry with righteous and learned ammunition in support of whatever action he might subsequently feel compelled to take.

Highly impressed, Gardiner and Fox lost no time in conveying the suggestion to the King. Thus began Cranmer's spectacular rise. In November, after the fall of Wolsey, Cranmer was summoned to Greenwich to enlarge upon his scheme. Installed at Durham Place, the home of Thomas Boleyn, now the Earl of Wiltshire, he was engaged, during the months of December and January, in preparing a book on the divorce. The book seems never to have been printed, but it circulated in manuscript, and some authorities believe that the text of the work is identical with a treatise on the divorce which is preserved among the Cotton manuscripts.[3]

The appeal to the universities was quickly made, with results that are well known. First Cambridge, then Oxford, decided in the King's favor. Paris, Orléans, Bourges, Toulouse, Ferrara, Bologna, and Padua followed. Henry's critics have charged that the favorable verdicts were paid for; his defenders have countered by saying that he merely paid the costs of investigating the case. Alcala, Salamanca, Poitiers, and Vicenza were subject to the influence of the Emperor, Charles V, Catherine's nephew, and voted for Catherine. At Angers no agreement could be reached. The German universities, mindful of Henry's attack on Luther and not willing to add to their difficulties with Charles V, refused to consider the question.

We are concerned only with Cambridge's handling of the case and of Hugh Latimer's share in the deliberations. From the beginning it was clear to Henry and his agents that Cambridge would be more amenable to the King's will than Oxford, partly because it was known that the strong party of reform at Cambridge would support the King, partly because Cranmer's book on the divorce had been widely read in Cambridge and had won adherents to the King's cause. At any rate Henry did not find it necessary to send to Cambridge such threatening letters as he thrice addressed to Oxford. Towards the end of February, 1530, Gardiner and Fox carried to Cambridge a letter [4] addressed "to our trusty and well-beloved the vice-chancellor, doctors, and other regents and non-regents of our university of Cambridge." The university was enjoined to debate and answer the question *utrum ducere uxorem fratris mortui sine liberis sit prohibitum jure divino et naturali*—whether the laws of God and of nature forbid a man to marry the childless widow of his deceased brother. The tone of the letter indicated that there could be no doubt that such a marriage was illegal and should be annulled. Doctor Gardiner and Master Fox were to be present to answer questions and resolve doubts. The proper decision, sealed with the seal of "our university," was to be sent to the King. "In doing whereof ye shall deserve our especial thanks and give us cause to increase our favor towards you as we shall not fail to do accordingly."

As it turned out, the affair did not go off so smoothly as had been expected. There survives a letter [5] written by Gardiner to the King which reports that on "Saturday last past"—probably February 26—he and Fox had arrived at Cambridge and immediately had gone into conference with Dr. William Buckmaster, the vice-chancellor, and Dr. John Edmunds, the master of Peterhouse. Buckmaster, as we know, was a conservative, and there can be no doubt of his private opinion. But now, as he had been in the Latimer case only a few weeks earlier, he was amenable to the King's will. Gardiner reported that he and Edmunds were well disposed and labored diligently to round up supporters for the King's cause. But the party of the opposition was equally active—"there was much done by others for the let and impeachment of the same; and as we assembled, they assembled, as we made friends they made friends . . . wherein the first day they were the superiors, for they had put in the ears of them by whose voices such things do pass *multas fabulas* too tedious to write unto your grace."

Such a conflict of opinion was of course to be expected. The divorce had become inextricably involved with the question of papal authority. Although the formal question was merely concerned with the legality of the marriage and made no mention of the question of the Pope's power to dispense, the latter was uppermost in the minds of everyone. Almost automatically party lines were drawn. Men like Latimer, Shaxton, Crome, and Bilney were instinctively on the King's side. Men like Watson, Baynes, Rud, and the others who had tried to howl Latimer down a few weeks before were in opposition. But these were not the key men. The key men were those like the Vice-Chancellor, men like Goodrich and Heath, who, while devoted to the most conservative doctrine in matters of religion, were still neutral or even hostile towards the papal authority, and who could therefore be won to the support of the King's cause on purely political grounds.

On Sunday afternoon, the usual time for such gatherings, the Vice-Chancellor convened a full 'congregation' of the university and to them he read the King's letter and the proposition to be voted upon. There was no intention, however, of following the naïve procedure of allowing the whole congregation to vote upon the proposition. The doctors, who were entitled to be heard first, were called into separate consultation. There was great difference of opinion. After they had talked themselves out, Buckmaster proposed to them the procedure which Gardiner and Fox had worked out in advance.

He suggested that the question be referred to a committee which would be empowered to act for the whole university. Buckmaster and Gardiner had already determined the membership of the committee, and the doctors, while agreeing in general to the suggested procedure, objected at once to the inclusion of certain persons who, it was charged, had been brought to Cambridge for the specific purpose of voting for the King, and to others who were known to have read and approved Cranmer's book on the divorce. "We said thereunto," writes Gardiner, "that by that reason they might except against all; for it was lightly [likely?] that in a question so notable as this, every man learned hath said to his friend as he thinketh in it for the time; but we ought not to judge of any man, that he setteth more to defend that which he hath once said, than truth afterward known." In the end enough pressure was put upon the doctors to force them to agree to the procedure proposed.

It was late afternoon when Buckmaster reconvened the whole congregation. He proposed that a committee be appointed to consider the proposition that it is unlawful for a man to marry his brother's childless widow; that if a majority of the committee approved, the action of the committee would be regarded as representing the consensus of the university; and that the opinion would then be transmitted to the King, sealed with the seal of the university. But the congregation would have none of it; tempers were frayed; the conservatives were suspicious, and wanted the opportunity to debate the main question. When a secret vote was taken it was found that the Vice-Chancellor's proposal had been defeated. Accordingly Buckmaster adjourned the meeting until 1 P.M. the following day.

Overnight, Gardiner, Fox, and Buckmaster went to work on a new resolution which was presented on Monday to the reconvened senate. The Latin resolution, or "grace" as it was called, begins with the names of the members of the proposed committee; and it proposes that a two-thirds vote, instead of a simple majority, be required for the approval of the King's proposition, and that the meetings of the committee be held publicly so that members of the university might hear the debate and, in a few privileged cases, present their views.

These concessions were reported to the King by Gardiner, who added cheerfully that he had no doubt of the happy outcome of the committee's deliberations. Indeed, the committee had been chosen with such care as to insure Gardiner's confidence. We know of its composition not only from the formal grace, but also from a list enclosed in Gardiner's letter to the King, on which list he labeled those favorable to the King's cause with the letter "A", presumably for "Anne." Although it was a packed group, the conservative party was represented by such stalwarts as Dr. Watson, Dr. Touson, Dr. Downes, and Master Baynes, of whom we have already heard as opponents of Latimer over the Sermons on the Card, as well as such lesser lights as Masters Middleton, Nicols, Hutton, and Day. Those known to be favorable to the King's cause were the Vice-Chancellor and the two proctors, Drs. Capon alias Salcot, Rugg alias Reppes, Edmunds, Crome, Wigan, and Boston; Masters Latimer, Heynes, Shaxton, Simon, Skip, Goodrich, and Heath. Four others—Dr. Venutus, and Masters Mylsent, Longford, and Hadway—were of uncertain position and after their names Gardiner added the note, "de isto bene speratur." Gardiner's analysis of the situation was optimistic: "In the schedule which we send unto your grace herewith, containing the names of those who shall determine your grace's question, all marked with A. be already of your grace's opinion; by which we trust, and with other good means, to induce and attain a great part of the rest . . . . Your highness may perceive by the notes, that we be sure of as many as be requisite, wanting only three; and we have good hope of four; of which four if we get two, and obtain of another to be absent, it is sufficient for our purpose." Gardiner adds piously, "Thus we beseech Almighty God to preserve your most noble and royal estate."

Concerning the deliberations of the committee there is no record. We do not know how often they met. Their decision, however, was not submitted to the whole university until March 9, so that their deliberations must have extended over a week, and possibly two. Nor do we know how animated were their discussions. We do know, of course, the canonical points which were involved. Was the famous text from Leviticus 18:16 binding upon Christians—"Thou shalt not uncover the nakedness of thy brother's wife: it is thy brother's nakedness"? If this was the divine law, did the Pope have the power to dispense from it? Or had the passage from Leviticus been nullified by the contradictory passage from Deuteronomy 25:5—"If brethren dwell together, and one of them die, and have no child, the wife of the dead shall not marry without unto a stranger: her husband's brother shall go in unto her, and take her to him to wife, and perform the duty of a husband's brother unto her"? The King's party argued that the canon from Leviticus was absolute; that the injunction from Deuteronomy had no sanction in the practice of either the Jewish or the Christian world; and that the marriage of the King was therefore invalid. The conservatives reversed the argument.

Fortunately, a safe two-thirds voted for Leviticus as against Deuteronomy. But the conservatives had a minor triumph which in a large measure nullified the main proposition. They managed to add to the resolution the qualification that marriage with a brother's widow was forbidden *provided* that the first marriage had been consummated. Since Catherine was vehemently affirming that the marriage with Prince Arthur had *not* been consummated, the resolution as finally passed was tantamount to saying, "If Catherine is telling the truth, we are on her side."

We have no sure way of knowing how large or how important a part Hugh Latimer played in the deliberations of this committee. In the formal grace approved by the university senate his name appears only as one of the twenty-nine doctors and masters appointed to act. Nevertheless, it seems likely that he took a leading part—had indeed acted as whip for the group of radical theologians who were counted upon to provide the main support for the King's cause. Indeed, in view of the close relationship between Latimer and Cranmer from this time forward, it is safe to suppose that Latimer was the spokesman for Cranmer's point of view. Probably Dr. Crome provided able support. Cranmer was not himself a member of the commission. Since he had already written and circulated a treatise strongly supporting the divorce, it would have been a tactical blunder to include him. It was presumably important to preserve the fiction that the commission was composed of judges rather than advocates. Still, Cranmer's was the official opinion. It was necessary that it be presented to the group. Who is more likely than Hugh Latimer to have presented it? In any event, what he did was sufficiently notable to be reported to the King, with the result, as we shall see, that Latimer was invited to preach before the King at Windsor, and did so on the Sunday next after the final passage of the resolution. Only Dr. Crome was similarly honored.

On Wednesday, March 9, 1530, Dr. Buckmaster made his report to the whole senate of the university.[6] Since it had been previously decided that the resolution as passed by the committee would be regarded as the opinion of the whole university, there was no further debate and no need for a confirming vote. But there was much murmuring and grumbling, and at least one outburst of violence. Dr. John Dakyn, or Dakers, of St. Nicholas' Hostel, was so outraged by the action of the university that he inflicted physical injuries upon one Christopher, Gardiner's servant. When Buckmaster undertook to discipline him for bearing arms and disturbing the peace, both Dakyn and the principal of St. Nicholas' defied Buckmaster's authority, and the matter was settled only after much agitation and with great difficulty.[7]

The episode may stand as a kind of symbol of Buckmaster's position in these proceedings. He was a conservative, and probably not in sympathy with the proposed divorce. He yielded to pressure, and was in the unhappy position of having to give public support to a measure of which he privately disapproved, and to steer it through the deliberations of a largely antagonistic senate. When it was all over, he had alienated many of his former friends and had acquired no new ones. The university, he secretly felt, had suffered disgrace in submitting to the King's will. "All the world," he wrote privately to Dr. Edmunds, "almost cryeth out of Cambridge for this act, and specially on me. But I must bear it as well as I may. I have lost a benefice by it which I should have had within this ten days, for there hath one fallen in Mr. Throckmeter's gift which he hath faithfully promised to me many a time, but now his mind is turned and alienate from me." [8] His was the common fate of the timeserver. He had neither public applause nor private satisfaction. As we shall see, when he delivered the university's resolution to the King, he was submitted to further indignities.

Whatever Latimer's share in the debates on the divorce may have been, there is no doubt that his speeches made a considerable impression upon one influential member of the university who probably was present with a kind of watching brief from the King. This was Sir William Butts, the King's physician.[9] Butts was a B.A. of Gonville Hall, had proceeded M.D. in 1518, and for many years was the trusted physician and friend of the King and his children. He seems early to have developed an interest in Lutheranism, and since he maintained a residence in Cambridge he may have heard with approval Latimer's Christmas sermons in 1529. Indeed, John Foxe says that it was "by the means of Dr. Butts" that Latimer was of the commission that "labored in the cause of the King's supremacy." [10] If Foxe meant "divorce" rather than "supremacy," there is nothing improbable in the story. It is more likely, however, that it was *because* of Latimer's labors for the divorce that Butts recommended to the King that Latimer be rewarded by an invitation to preach before the court at Windsor.

Henry, as everyone knows, fancied himself as a theologian. He greatly enjoyed the opportunities for discussion and criticism provided by the court sermons. Indeed, he seems to have taken delight in having clerics of differing views preach before him on successive Sundays, or even on the same Sunday, so that he might correct their errors, adjudicate their differences, and set them both in the way of orthodoxy once more. Up to this point, however, none of the reformers suspected of the taint of Lutheranism had been invited to preach at court. But now Henry had perceived how the radical theologians could be of use to him in his quarrel with the papacy. It would do no harm to reward one of their leaders with the coveted appointment as court preacher. If the sermon savored of the Lutheran heresy, Henry himself, as defender of the faith, would set the preacher right.

Accordingly Latimer was invited to preach at Windsor on the second Sunday in Lent, March 13, 1530.[11] The preacher for the first Sunday was an unnamed "Black Monk"; for the third Sunday, Rowland Philips, prebendary of St. Paul's and vicar of Croydon.[12] Philips, a fine priest and famous preacher, was of unswerving loyalty to the old religion.[13] Probably the "Black Monk" was of the same theological complexion, so that Latimer's sermon would have been well cushioned on both sides by traditional orthodoxy.

It is impossible to overestimate the importance of the opportunity which was thus presented to the leader of the Cambridge reformers. His fame was already known to the King, and the King had made use of him and of his followers. But the King was no favorer of doctrinal irregularities; his feeling toward Latimer must have been an admixture of gratitude and suspicion. If Latimer had fumbled at this juncture, it would have meant the end of his career and, more importantly, the end of his usefulness to the cause of reform.

Latimer did not fumble. We do not know for certain what his topic was or how he handled it. But it would be unsafe to assume, as did one of Latimer's idolators, that it was "some plain honest exposition of Christian duty, with special reference to the peculiar duty devolving upon kings."[14] On this occasion Latimer was politic. It seems almost certain that his topic was closely related to the King's divorce, of course on its doctrinal rather than its political side. Whatever it was, it gave great pleasure to the King and, perhaps of even greater importance, to Ann Boleyn, who was present and who from this time forward was Latimer's stanchest advocate at court.

It would be gratifying to have some record of the conversation which must have taken place at this first meeting between Latimer and Anne, and to know his private opinion of this strange, amoral woman who became his patroness. Were her known Lutheran sympathies sufficient to make him disregard the lightness of her character and conduct? Did he in some measure succumb to her charm? Was he able to accept calmly the fact that she was already installed at court as Queen Catherine's successor? His only recorded opinion of her belongs to the period after her death, at which time he praised her modesty, prudence, and gravity, and her zeal to promote "the Gospel." [15]

To return to matters of fact. The best evidence that the King approved of Latimer's sermon is the record of the payment for it. It would appear that the usual honorarium for a court sermon was one pound. The records of Brian Tuke, treasurer of the chamber, for March, 1530, duly record that this sum (easily the equivalent of £50 in our money) was paid to the unnamed Black Monk, to Latimer, and to the vicar of Croydon for preaching before the King the first three Sundays in Lent.[16] But the Privy Purse accounts record that on March 16 Latimer received an additional gift of £5—a truly princely sum.[17] It would be a mistake to regard this gift as merely a manifestation of the King's generosity toward a preacher whose sermon had pleased him. It was also payment—generous, to be sure—for yeoman service done at Cambridge in the cause of the King's divorce.

Less fiscal, perhaps less important, but certainly more dramatic is the account of the King's reaction to Latimer's sermon given by the unfortunate Dr. Buckmaster in that same letter to Dr. Edmunds which has already been quoted.[18] Poor Buckmaster, bearing the formal statement of the university's decision on the divorce, arrived at Windsor on Sunday, March 13, in time to hear Latimer's sermon, which was delivered just before vespers. After vespers he was granted an audience in the chamber of presence, and, after making an obsequious little speech, duly presented the document to the King, who read it quickly, expressed his thanks, and commented upon the wisdom and discretion of the university. All this was courteous enough. But after the audience was ended, the King made a point of speaking, in Buckmaster's hearing, in praise of Latimer's sermon. Then, still audibly, the King said to the Duke of Norfolk, "This displeaseth greatly Master Vice-Chancellor yonder. Yon same is Master Vice-Chancellor of Cambridge." Then the King and the Duke whispered together.

Greater humiliation was to follow. The next day, after dinner, Buckmaster and the proctor who had accompanied him were again received by the King. When they arrived at the King's gallery they found Gardiner, Fox, *and Latimer* already with the King. The King, it appeared, was not so completely pleased with the Cambridge resolution as had first appeared. He was not troubled by the fact that the university had inserted the qualification concerning the question of the consummation of Catherine's marriage to Arthur. But he was distinctly annoyed that the university had not denied the Pope's right to dispense from the prohibition against a marriage with the wife of a deceased brother. He was annoyed with Gardiner and Fox for not having included a consideration of the dispensation in the question originally proposed to the university. Apparently he was annoyed with Buckmaster for not having himself had the foresight to include the question. Only Latimer, it appears, had escaped the royal disapproval. Buckmaster had every right to feel aggrieved. In vain did he protest that the commission would never have approved a resolution denying the Pope's right to dispense. For two hours the King scolded, and threatened that after Easter he would require the university to decide *An Papa possit dispensare cum jure divino.*

Buckmaster's humiliation was complete. He had done all that was asked of him, and it had not been enough. Latimer, whose views he despised, was obviously in the ascendancy. It was small comfort that Gardiner and Fox had likewise incurred the King's displeasure. To make matters worse, a coldness developed also in that quarter; and when Buckmaster departed the court Gardiner and Fox did not invite him to drink with them. Some reward he did have. From the Privy Purse he was given a gift of twenty nobles (£ 6.13.4); the proctor got five marks (£ 3.6.8).[19]

CHAPTER NINE

OF HERETICAL BOOKS

Little or nothing is known of Latimer's private affairs during the year 1530. According to Vice-chancellor Buckmaster he was back in Cambridge shortly after his appearance at court, preaching with undiminished fervor *"quod emuli ejus graviter ferunt"* [1] [so that his opponents are outraged]. John Foxe says, presumably of this year, "Then went he to court, where he remained a certain time in the said Dr. Butt's chamber, preaching then in London very often." [2] By "the court" in this context Foxe apparently means Westminster or Greenwich, and it may well be that Latimer was invited on more than one occasion to preach before the King, and that he took advantage of his sojourns at court, and of his license as university preacher, to preach in some of the churches of London. But of all this there is no record except Foxe's vague statement. There seems to be no basis for the assertion of many historians that at this time Latimer served as court chaplain. Certainly he had no official appointment of that kind. In the absence of other records, our knowledge of his doings is limited to his participation in public affairs.

It is well known that on every occasion when Henry VIII clipped the temporal wings of the church, he forthwith, in some manner or other, gave public expression of his personal zeal for orthodoxy. So it was in the spring of 1530. At the close of 1529 the Reformation Parliament had enacted measures designed to correct and curtail the venality of the clergy. Conservatives like Fisher and Richard Nix,[3] bishop of Norwich, had actively opposed these measures; and while Henry was angered by their opposition he had no wish, at present, to alienate such men entirely. In one matter he could placate them. Rumors were circulating that the King was now a favorer of heresy and was willing that Tyndale's New Testament should be read freely. Actually Henry shared to the limit the conservative disapproval of much of Tyndale's work. The King realized that by taking active measures against heretical books he could demonstrate his unwavering orthodoxy and relieve the anxieties of the conservatives.

In May, 1530, therefore, Henry undertook the suppression of these pernicious books. But he had no intention of issuing an unsupported ukase. The universities had been useful to him in the matter of the divorce; he saw how they could also be useful to him in this matter of heresy. This time, however, he did not refer the question to the universities as a whole. Instead his plan called for an ecclesiastical commission to be made up of a nucleus of his own appointees and twelve delegates each from Oxford and Cambridge.

Buckmaster carefully preserved the King's letter summoning the delegates from Cambridge. Dated from Enfield on Wednesday, May 4,

1530, it is addressed to "our trusty and well-beloved the vice-chancellor of our University of Cambridge." It reports that the King has been informed that certain English books containing erroneous and pestiferous opinions are current in the realm, that he is mindful of his duty as God's deputy in England to preserve the unity of the faith, and that he is therefore summoning a council to determine, fairly and without prejudgment, whether the books are indeed heretical as alleged. Wherefore, the King continues, I "pray you that of the best learned men in divinity within that our university of Cambridge you will choose out and appoint the number of twelve, willing and commanding them to resort to London so as they may be there by Tuesday at night at the farthest. At what time there shall also convene a like number of our university at Oxford . . . ." [4]

Buckmaster had recently learned by bitter experience the way in which these things were managed. He had seen that the debate on the canonical questions involved in the King's divorce was but an empty show of things, designed to cover up the fact that the result had been carefully predetermined. He knew perfectly well what the outcome of the deliberations in London would be. The books would be condemned as heretical, and all the members of the commission would probably be required to subscribe to that opinion. With his usual care Buckmaster added to the foot of the King's letter a list of "the names of them which I did appoint." Eight of his delegates were conservative stalwarts. But it must have been with a touch of malice that he included the names of four reformers—Crome, Shaxton, Thixtel, and Latimer. Especially Latimer, who had supported the divorce and had since been riding the crest of the wave. Buckmaster had recently experienced the humiliation of being required to subscribe to opinions which contravened his mind and conscience. Now it would be Latimer's turn.

The commission, presided over by Archbishop Warham, sat from May 11 until May 24. Its procedure followed the familiar pattern. The official point of view was represented by Cuthbert Tunstall, who as bishop of London had presided over the burning of Tyndale's New Testaments in 1526 and had just now been translated from London to Durham; by Sir Thomas More, now lord chancellor, who had been Tunstall's official censor and was the author of what may be regarded as the official *critiques* of Tyndale's work; and by Stephen Gardiner, the King's secretary. A glance at the names of the other members of the commission will indicate that from the beginning there was a safe majority of conservatives. But the minority was vigorous, if not numerically strong. The chronicler Hall [5] reports that there was "long debating," and Latimer himself says there were "three or four" who were vigorous in opposition, "yet it happened there, as it is ever more seen, that the most part overcometh the better." There can be little doubt that Latimer's "better" part included Crome, Shaxton, Thixtel, and himself. At the end of the sessions, Warham was careful to announce that every man had been free to express his opinion, as his learning and conscience dictated, without fear of reprisal; and that in the end they were in unanimous agreement. The unanimity, however, was of that fictional variety, well known to all who have served on committees, which obtains when the majority has thoroughly browbeaten the minority and the latter, from motives of fear or favor, does not dare to bring in an independent report.

From the "public instrument"—that is, the formal decisions of the commission—preserved in Warham's register[6] we learn of the books which the commission examined and of the verdicts upon them. In the *Primer* and the *Kalendar of the Primer* (this was probably the first English primer, possibly by George Joye, of which no copy is known to be extant) five errors were found;[7] in Simon Fish's *Supplication for the Beggars,* one; and in his *The Sum of the Scripture,* ninety-three; in John Frith's *Revelation of Antichrist* forty-nine; in an *Exposition* on 1 Corinthians 7, translated from Luther probably by William Roy, forty-seven. Two works of Tyndale, in addition to his translation of Scripture, were the subjects of special consideration. In his *Parable of the Wicked Mammon,* on the thesis that faith only justifies, the commission found thirty-one heresies or errors. They discovered a like number in *The Obedience of a Christian Man,* which was singled out especially because it was an answer to the charges of the prelates that the reformers were teaching disobedience to princes. There is no need to examine the separate errors or heresies detected in these books. But a sampling of those cited from Tyndale's *Wicked Mammon* may be suggestive: this book, it was found, taught that faith only justifies; that even Christ in all his *deeds* did not deserve heaven; that the saints cannot help us to gain heaven; that the ceremonies of the church had alienated the world from God; and that churches are for preaching only, and not for the uses to which they are now put.

It is interesting to note that while the commission examined and condemned Tyndale's translation of Scripture, it did not specify the errors that were discovered therein. Hall says that "it was alleged that the translation of Tyndale and Joye were not truly translated, and also that in them were prologues and prefaces which sounded to heresy and railed against the bishops uncharitably . . . ."[8] But the "public instrument" contains merely a generalized condemnation of "the translation of Scripture corrupted by William Tyndale, as well in the Old Testament as in the New." Nevertheless, it is clear from the statements of Hall and Latimer that it was the question of the Scriptures which provoked the hottest debate in the sessions of the commission.

On Tuesday, May 24, 1530, the commission made its formal report to the King. The scene was St. Edward's chapel, "set on the east side of the Parliament chamber," in the palace of Westminster. Present were More, Warham, Tunstall, Gardiner, Latimer, Crome, and a host of others. Presumably it was Warham who read the "public instrument," which took the form of a proclamation to be issued in Warham's name as primate. The "pestiferous" books are listed in order, with their several heresies and errors carefully analyzed. There follows a "bill in English to be published by the preachers" which sets forth at length that it is the duty of the preacher to warn his flock to beware of false prophets; that the King's commission has determined that the books cited contain false doctrine; and that the preachers are therefore to enjoin any of their hearers who possess these books to deliver them up at once to their spiritual superiors. Above all, the bill concludes, the preachers are to emphasize the fact that the learned have advised the King that the clamorings of those who insist that it is the King's duty to have the Bible translated are without foundation, and that Christian men need only to take heed of such lessons as the clergy teach them. For the present, while heresy is rampant, it is better that the Scriptures be not translated. Later, when heresy has abated, the King may request the learned to prepare a translation.

No doubt Henry was duly gratified that the judgment of the commission coincided so precisely with his own views. He accepted their recommendations *in toto*. The chronicler Hall says that on this occasion the King went so far as to command the bishops to arrange for a new translation, to be made by the "best learned men" of the two universities.[9] Hall's statement is probably inaccurate, for when in June the King's formal proclamation on the subject was printed by Thomas Berthelet, its terms were precisely those of the commission's recommendations.[10]

I have already indicated my belief that Latimer was among the minority who, in the sittings of the commission, opposed the wholesale condemnation of these books, especially Tyndale's translation of the Scriptures. I have also indicated my belief that Warham's statement concerning the unanimity of the commission's judgment was one of those fictions which are familiar to all who have any experience of the way in which legislative decisions are arrived at. Nevertheless, Latimer's participation in the work of this commission has been troublesome to all his biographers. It is known that he held some of the views which were condemned. He had already given public utterance to some of them; in the next few years he would give expression to many more. Friendly writers have tried to make as sympathetic an explanation of his conduct as they can manage: the time was not yet ripe, Latimer was not yet settled in his convictions, and so on. Unfriendly writers, on the other hand, have charged him with utter craft or cowardice.

As it happens, however, both groups of critics have made an error in fact which nullifies both their apologetics and their condemnation. The error is their oft-reiterated statement that Latimer indicated his agreement with the official opinion of the commission, and thus formally forswore his genuine convictions, by signing his name to the "public instrument" in which that opinion was embodied. He did not. The mistake has arisen from the fact that the "public instrument" contains a list of the names of those who were *present* when the document was presented to the King; Hugh Latimer is there listed among the bachelors of divinity. All previous writers except one [11] have concluded that these men signed the instrument. But a glance at the document as it is preserved in Archbishop Warham's register, and as it has been reprinted in several places, reveals that it was signed only by Warham and three notaries, who attested it in the customary legal Latin.

It is possible, as has been suggested, that Vice-chancellor Buckmaster, in appointing Latimer as one of the Cambridge delegates, had hoped that Latimer would be required to sign away his convictions. It is even possible that Latimer would have signed the document if the procedure of requiring all the members of the commission to sign had been adopted. But that procedure was not adopted, Latimer did not sign, and, on this occasion at least, he was not forsworn. There is nothing in the record to preclude the assumption that throughout the deliberations of the committee Latimer was one of the small minority who honorably opposed the opinions which finally prevailed. According to modern practice, Latimer, Shaxton, Crome, and a few others might have brought in a minority report. But it is simply naïve to believe that they might or should have done so in the year 1530.

One further point must be made about Latimer's share in this affair. Although he had preached at court, he as yet occupied no important post; he was not the master of a college and he had no benefice of any kind. It might therefore be concluded that he was an inconsequential member of the commission and his share in its deliberations of no great importance. On the contrary, however, there is evidence that he was regarded in some quarters as the most important, or at least the most prominent, of the Cambridge delegates. Each of the twelve was paid a mark (13s. 4d.) for his expenses. The money seems to have been advanced by Edward Fox, as King's almoner. When, in September, Fox was reimbursed, the privy purse accounts record that £8. was paid to Fox "for money laid out to Mr. Latimer and other scholars of Cambridge, for their costs to London and back." [12] It is not without significance, surely, that only Latimer is mentioned by name. As for the amount of the compensation, it was just about enough to cover expenses for two weeks in London. In this instance, evidently, the King felt that the services rendered had not been such as to require any particular expression of his munificence.

On June 22, 1530, the King's proclamation against heretical books was promulgated. As might have been expected, it proved of little effect. The old books continued to circulate; new ones, like Tyndale's *Practice of Prelates* and his *Answer to More's Dialogue* and George Joye's *Hortulus Animae* (a primer of Lutheran bias) [13] were published on the Continent and promptly smuggled into England, where they were read eagerly. A few humble folk were apprehended and punished for possessing and reading the offending volumes. Meanwhile, as the year wore on, it became evident that the King and the bishops had no intention of relaxing the prohibition against the English Bible. Accordingly, on December 1, 1530, a long letter, famous in the history of the reformation, was addressed to the King. It is a stirring and subtle plea for the Scriptures in English, and it contains a good many references to the work, during the preceding spring, of the King's commission on heretical books. Foxe, who was the first to print the letter, asserts without qualification that Latimer was its author. Although two distinguished modern historians have questioned this attribution, there is every reason to believe that the traditional view is correct.

Four versions of the letter survive. Two of them are manuscripts preserved in the Public Record Office. [14] The two manuscripts are without date and without indication of authorship. One of them is fragmentary, lacking the first quarter of the letter. The other two versions are those printed by Foxe, from copies not now known to be extant. The first Foxe text appears in the first (1563) edition of the *Acts and Monuments*,[15] where it is headed, "The letter of maister Latimer written to King Henry, answering to the foresaid inhibition of the Byshops." For this text Foxe used a copy of the letter of which the last page or so was missing; the letter breaks off some three hundred words short of the end with the note, "More of this letter came not to our handes (gentle reader): and yet we would not defraud thee of that we had, considering the pithiness thereof." Before his edition of 1570 went to press, Foxe had managed to procure a complete copy of the letter.[16] This is headed, "The letter of Maister Latymer written to Kyng Henry, for the restoryng agayne the free liberty of readyng the holy scripture." It contains the conclusion missing from Foxe's first text, and supplies us, at the end, with the date of the letter—December 1, 1530—not to be found in any of the other copies. From Foxe's text, it appears that this copy was also unsigned. It would be interesting to know whether Foxe devised the headings which he used or whether he took them from his copies.

No two copies of the letter agree in all particulars. Apart from the missing beginning in one of the Record Office copies and the missing ending in one of Foxe's copies, there are also verbal discrepancies. None of these is of any great significance.[17] In a few instances the manuscripts provide readings which seem superior to Foxe's, but on the whole it appears that Foxe's second text is the best of the four.

It seems evident that this letter was one of those popular documents—many other examples might be adduced—which circulated in manuscript among the reformers, somewhat after the manner in which the primitive churches circulated the Pauline epistles. It was not unusual for the reformers to address long letters to each other with the request that a copy be made for a third person, or for a group to preserve and cherish a letter of advice or encouragement from one of their leaders. I think this letter addressed to the King was such a treasured document. Probably there were more copies than the four of which we now have record. The letter begins in that apostolic vein which Sir Thomas More objected to in the writings of the reformers—"To the most mighty prince, King of England, Henry the Eighth, grace, mercy, and peace from God the Father by our Lord Jesus Christ." The letter is far too long to quote in its entirety, but it may be summarized as follows:

The writer has read in St. Augustine that anyone who conceals the truth for fear of any power provokes the wrath of God upon himself, in that he fears man more than God. Therefore, lest he be a traitor to the truth and a very Judas to Christ who is the cause of all truth, the writer must set forth what he believes to be true. Alas, that bishops and counsellors will not do the same, even though they profess to know the Holy Scriptures, in which the truth is to be found. They will neither show forth the word of God themselves nor suffer others to do so, and in this course they have attempted to gain the support of all the kings to Christendom. Here in England they have made it treason against the King to have the Scriptures in English.

The writer confesses his boldness in thus addressing the king, since there is as great a difference between the King and him as there is between God and man. Indeed, the King is in God's stead. Still, the King is mortal and, having the corruption of Adam, is in danger of sin. So the King, no less than his subjects, has need of Christ's passion. All are members of Christ's mystical body; although the King is the higher member, he must not disdain the lower members. Realizing these things, and knowing the King's gentle nature, the writer is bold to indite this rude and homely letter.

Let the King consider the rule of Christ, "The tree is known by the fruit" (Matt. 7:16), that from it he may learn who are the true teachers of Christ's Gospel and who are not. Christ lived in poverty, and his true followers do not esteem the riches of the world. But consider the monks and the friars and the prelates, who have professed poverty, yet live like lords and will stick at nothing to preserve their wealth. To be sure, not all the spiritualty are corrupt with worldly ambition, yet many of them have tried to evade the restrictions imposed upon their superfluities by the recent parliament. To correct these evils, the King need not take away the goods of the church; he need only take away all evil persons from the goods and set better in their place.

This rule, "The tree is known by its fruit," is clearly set forth in the Gospel. So are the other truths of Christ. But these worldly persecutors, whose fruits are naught, dare not let these truths be known abroad. They oppose therefore an English translation of the Scriptures, arguing that such a translation will promote heresy and insurrection. Thus they presume to gather figs from thistles: they call light darkness, and darkness light.

In his last proclamation the King promised to allow the Scriptures in English. Let it be done at once—today, not tomorrow. The King's counsellors will argue that the followers of the Gospel will be guilty of heresy and disobedience. They may cite the cases of those who lately in London were found guilty of keeping prohibited books. They may say that such persons will violate other statutes and ordinances. But the argument is false. These people know that the late proclamation, so far as it touched the New Testament, was opposed by a minority on the commission, but that the majority forced it through. They do not believe that the proclamation represents the King's will, but that it was merely set forth in his name. The same thing has been done before, to the trouble of the realm. It is known that some of the prelates, on their own authority, have forbidden the English Scriptures in their dioceses. Probably they have now over-persuaded the King to extend the prohibition to the whole realm.

As for the argument that reading the Scriptures will promote civil disobedience, what has been the cause of disobedience in this realm? Why are there so many thieves, extortioners, murderers? Is it not because of the reckless sale of pardons and indulgences? Are not all these malefactors haters of the Gospel? On the other hand, can it be shown that any of those who defied the proclamation against the New Testament have violated any other ordinance than this? If there are any such, can it be shown that their reading of the Scriptures was the cause of their other offenses?

The letter concludes:

Wherefore, gracious King, remember yourself, have pity upon your soul; and think that the day is even at hand when you shall give account of your office, and of the blood which hath been shed with your sword. In the which day that your grace may stand steadfastly, and not be ashamed, but be clear and ready in your reckoning, and to have (as they say) your *quietus est* sealed with the blood of our Saviour Christ, which only serveth at that day, is my daily prayer to Him that suffered death for our sins, which also prayeth to His Father for grace for us continually. To whom be all honor and praise forever, Amen. The Spirit of God preserve your grace.—Anno Domini 1530. Prim. die Decembris.

Was Foxe correct in attributing this famous and splendid letter to Latimer? The attribution has been accepted by all of Latimer's biographers and by such historians of the English reformation as Froude [18] and Canon Dixon.[19] But some modern writers [20] have denied Latimer's authorship, on the ground that the two copies in the Public Record Office are unsigned and, presumably, that Latimer's authorship cannot be reconciled with the supposed fact that in May Latimer "signed" the public instrument condemning the English Bible. One writer adds the diverting thought that if Latimer wrote this letter he stands condemned as a liar, since the author professes to believe that the proclamation was issued in the King's name but without the King's assent.[21]

The last objection may be dismissed as representing failure to recognize the satiric thrust of much of the letter. The writer does not say that he himself doubts the King's assent to the proclamation; he says that humble folk, unacquainted with the facts, may doubt the King's assent. It is a neat point. But the other objections must be reckoned with, and it is for that reason that in the preceding section emphasis was placed upon the fact that the judgment of the commission of May, 1530, was *not* unanimous, except in a fictional sense, and that Latimer did *not* sign the document condemning the Bible in English. If in May he had weakly acquiesced to the majority opinion and had affixed his signature to that opinion, and if in December he had written the letter here under consideration, Latimer could indeed be accused of cowardice or hypocrisy or both. If, on the other hand, as seems likely, Latimer was a member, perhaps the leader, of his majesty's loyal opposition in the commission which examined the books alleged to be mischievous, and if, as is perfectly clear, Latimer was not required to sign the public instrument, then there is no inconsistency whatever between Latimer's conduct as a member of the commission and his conduct in writing the letter to the King.

The objection that the extant manuscript copies are unsigned, and that apparently Foxe's copies were also unsigned, likewise vanishes, and other difficulties are cleared up, if we assume, as I believe we must, that the letter was from the beginning anonymous. It was not intended to be a letter in the ordinary sense. Indeed, there is no evidence that it was actually delivered to Henry. It is not, as its author pretends, a simple, homely letter. It has wit, satire, a combination of flattery and criticism, all of which mark the carefully studied composition. It is not the work of an uninformed layman, but of one who knew intimately the details of the deliberations of the King's commission. But its author deliberately conceals his identity and the fact that he had himself sat on that commission. "And so as concerning your last proclamation, prohibiting such books, the very true cause of it and chief counsellors (*as men say, and of likelihood it should be*) were they whose evil living and cloaked hypocrisy these books uttered and disclosed. And howbeit that there were three or four that would have had the scripture to go forth in English, yet it happened there, as it is evermore seen, that the most part overcometh the better." [22] Even Foxe was fooled. He quite obviously was unaware that Latimer had been a member of the commission, and he glosses Latimer's "three or four" with the note, "He meaneth of Cranmer, Cromwell, and one or two more, against whom the bishop of Winchester and his faction did prevail." [23] Neither Cromwell nor Cranmer was on the commission.

On all counts, then, the objections to Latimer's authorship of this letter are shaky. The fact remains that Foxe *did* attribute it to Latimer. Foxe had sources of information lost to modern scholarship, and he has never been convicted of deliberate falsification of records. In this case, as against modern scholarship, the testimony of Foxe must prevail. In support of it, moreover, may be brought the evidence from style. To be sure, such evidence is likely to be tenuous. But consider the following short passage. Does it not have, making due allowance for the fact that the words are addressed to the King, the vigor, the turn of phrase, the muscular quality which are always quite properly associated with Latimer?

But here mark their shameless boldness, which be not ashamed, contrary to Christ's doctrine, to gather figs of thorns and grapes of bushes, and to call light darkness, and darkness light, sweet sour, and sour sweet, good evil, and evil good, and to say that that which teacheth all obedience should cause dissension and strife. But such is their belly-wisdom, wherewith they judge and measure everything, to hold and keep still this wicked mammon, the goods of this world, which is their God, and hath so blinded the eyes of their hearts, that they cannot see the clear light of the sacred scripture, though they babble never so much of it.[24]

In one respect, however, Foxe was mistaken about this letter. He praises Latimer for his reckless courage, at the risk of his career and perhaps even of his life, in daring to admonish the King.[25] But the letter was anonymous, and in writing it Latimer ran no great risk.

CHAPTER TEN

WEST KINGTON

Early in the year 1531, the King generously rewarded the services of several of the Cambridge men who had promoted the cause of the divorce. Cranmer, for whom much greater things were in store, was appointed Archdeacon of Taunton, a sinecure which left him free for further service to the King. To Latimer went the rectory of West Kington in Chippenham hundred in Wiltshire, which had recently been made vacant by the death of William Dowdyng. The living was in the gift of the bishop of Salisbury, but Latimer's appointment to it came from the Crown.[1] The parish was on the remote borders of a remote county, and the income was modest. Acording to a survey of ecclesiastical incomes compiled in 1535, it carried an annual stipend of £ 17.1s.,[2] the equivalent of about £ 850 in the money of today. The parish was in the diocese of Salisbury, the register of which records that on Januay 14, 1531, Latimer was formally instituted as rector of West Kington by Richard Hilley, vicar-general of the diocese, acting for Campeggio, the absentee bishop.[3]

According to Foxe, Latimer by this time had grown weary of the court and was eager to escape from its intrigues and artificialities. Foxe also indicates that Latimer accepted the living of West Kington over the protests of Dr. Butts, whose hopes for Latimer ran to something better than a country parish.[4] All this may be true enough. But it is partly contradicted by Foxe's own statement that Butts was instrumental in securing Latimer's appointment. Moreover, it ignores the fact that promotion to a benefice was an important step upward in the ecclesiastical world. A vast professional and social gulf has always separated the beneficed from the unbeneficed priest.

The little parish church of West Kington is dedicated to St. Mary. It is of early English style, in the form of a Greek cross. Local tradition kept the memory of Latimer's association with the church alive for two hundred years; late in the seventeenth century John Aubrey wrote, "In the walk at the Parsonage House is a little scrubbed hollow oak called 'Latimer's Oak' where he used to sit."[5] The oak is gone, but when the church was "restored" in the middle of the nineteenth century, a memorial window to Latimer was installed on the south side of the chancel to remind parishioners and visitors of the great man who once served there.[6]

From the first, Latimer was a faithful parish priest. His correspondence for this period abundantly testifies to his pleasure in the daily round of parish duty—the regular celebration of the mass, the christenings, the marriages. When his examination by Convocation detained him in London for several months, he professed great anxiety that he was kept from his cure of souls during Lent, when his parishioners had most need of him.[7] He was fond also of the village festivities. In one letter he wrote, ". . . if I be not prevented shortly, I intend to make merry with my parishioners this Christmas . . . I have heard say that a doe is as good in winter as a buck in summer."[8] Probably he found the life not unlike that which he had known as a youth in Leicestershire, and relished it all the more on that account. It was a busy career, and he pursued it diligently. It seems to have taken some toll of his health; at any rate, it is at this period that he begins to speak of his long bouts with headache and pain in the side, as well as the colic and the "stone" with which he is newly afflicted.[9] The burden was the greater because, at least during part of his tenure at West Kington, he performed his parochial duties unassisted.[10]

Latimer's appointment to West Kington came just between two events of great significance to the development of the English Reformation. Wolsey had died on November 30, 1530. In December, King Henry thoroughly alarmed his clergy, especially his bishops, by charging that in acknowledging the authority of the Cardinal as legate *a latere* of the Pope they had put themselves under obedience to a foreign power. Even for Henry, this was an unprecedented piece of hypocrisy, but the helpless clergy, threatened with prosecution under the ancient statute of provisors and *praemunire,* were glad to compound for their offense by voting substantial money grants to the King—£ 100,000 from the province of Canterbury, £ 18,840 from the province of York. Then on February 11, 1531, Convocation was required to acknowledge the King as "the sole protector and supreme head of the Church and clergy of England." This declaration of independence from the Roman obedience, so necessary to Henry's plan for making Anne Boleyn his queen, was bitterly opposed by honorable conservatives like Bishop Fisher and Sir Thomas More. But the utmost concession they could win was the addition of the qualification "so far as the law of Christ allows" to the title proposed for himself by the King. Taken literally, the qualification was important; to Henry it signified nothing.

Depressing as these events were to the conservatives, they gave new hope and confidence to the reformers. The bishops had suffered grievous limitation of their powers; the bishop of Rome had been put upon notice. Since opposition to the Roman obedience was a cardinal point with the reformers, perhaps their other objectives—the legalizing of the English Bible and the reform of abuses—might now be within their grasp. So it was that the Cambridge men began to preach with increased daring.

Of them all, Bilney risked the most.[11] He had been convicted of heretical pravity; he had abjured and had been absolved. Another conviction would condemn him as a relapsed heretic, with the flames at the end of the road. Despite the danger, Bilney felt the need to expiate the weakness of his abjuration in 1527. Late in 1530 or early in 1531, he solemnly informed his Cambridge friends that he "must go up to Jerusalem" (the expression has been considered arrogant by unsympathetic writers). He went into his native Norfolk, preaching his old opinions in the fields and distributing forbidden New Testaments so openly that detection and arrest were inevitable.

At about the same time, Dr. Crome began to preach more daringly than he had ever done before. Crome is a shadowy figure from the past,[12] and the bare facts of his career reveal a record of vacillation which makes it difficult to see in him a man of strong convictions. Intellectually, however, he was a convinced friend of the new doctrines, and his moments of weakness need not obscure the fact that he had also moments of courage. Such a moment came to him in the early months of 1531.

Over in the west, where the cause of reform had as yet made very little progress indeed, Hugh Latimer began to preach with apostolic zeal. He writes that he was preaching daily, in his own church and in surrounding parishes.[13] There is no adequate record of his activity in this period, but from extant letters we learn of the substance of his sermons and of the controversy which they provoked.

Shortly after his installation at West Kington, he preached a sermon at nearby Marshfield, a town about eleven miles east of Bristol. The sermon gave great offense to one Dr. William Sherwood, otherwise unknown to fame, who undertook to rebuke the preacher for disseminating the doctrines of Luther, Oecolampadius, and Melanchthon.[14] The reply was in Latimer's characteristic vein. In place of the usual apostolic greeting, it began with some uncomplimentary reflections on Dr. Sherwood's shortcomings in matters of sobriety and Christian charity, and continued with a point-by-point consideration of Sherwood's charges. The text of the sermon to which Sherwood objected had been John 10:1—"He that entereth not by the door into the sheepfold, but climbeth up some other way, the same is a thief and a robber." Latimer had applied the text to nonpreaching prelates who battened upon the people. He had said further that the church consisted not of ecclesiastics alone, but of all people who know and confess the truth. (In his reply to Sherwood, Latimer is careful to point out that this is not Lutheran doctrine, but has the support of such doctors as Jerome, Chrysostom, Augustine, and Nicholas of Lyra.) It followed that it was not sufficient for the Christian merely to affirm, supinely, that he believes what the church believes. It was necessary for the Christian to believe the truth, and that he might know the truth it was necessary that he be instructed by a preaching and teaching clergy who were themselves adequately grounded in God's word.

These innocent but basic utterances, says Latimer, Sherwood had wilfully distorted to make it appear that the preacher had said that all the bishops were thieves (Sherwood quotes Latimer as having said that there was insufficient hemp in England to hang them all), that all Christians were priests, and that therefore the alleged power of the keys was a deception. Sherwood replied to Latimer's letter,[15] saying that the preacher's version of the sermon was indeed different from that which had been reported to him. He had been particularly concerned, he said, with the report that Latimer had deprecated the use of the "Hail Mary" as a prayer. He, Sherwood, had warned his people against such doctrine, and that was the extent of his "abuse" of Latimer. He was now satisfied that Latimer had preached no false doctrine.

Probably Latimer's own summary of his sermon is a reliable statement of its content. If so, it was free from any shadows of heresy. On the other hand, Sherwood's letters are restrained, Latimer's is satiric, witty, at times malicious—"may God make you of a better spirit, or keep you as far away as possible from my preaching," it ends—and it is impossible to escape the conclusion that Latimer's sermon had been extreme in its manner, if not in its matter. It was a fault to which he confessed abjectly a year or so later.

More interesting, because it indicates his unrelenting advocacy of the Scriptures in English, is another letter which Latimer wrote about this time.[16] The letter, in Latimer's own handwriting, is addressed to William Hubberdin, a divine of whom we shall soon hear more. Hubberdin had preached, somewhere in the neighborhood of West Kington, a bitter attack on the new learning, which was not God's truth, he said, because its professors lived naughtily and persecuted the priests. Latimer's letter undertakes to set him straight. The charge of naughtiness against the men of the new learning, Latimer writes, is too preposterous to need confutation. As for persecution, it is the favorers of the new learning who are imprisoned for the faith; the priests of the old learning who are in prison are there for whoredom, theft, and murder, "with such their common practices." But it is not such scurrility as this which makes the letter interesting. Rather, it is Latimer's contrast between the terms "old learning" and "new learning," a contrast that amounts to the earliest definition we have of those terms as they are properly applied to the thought of this period. The following passages are representative:

For to begin withal: ye call the Scripture the new learning, which I am sure is older than any learning which ye wot to be the old. But if ye will say, that it is not the Scripture that ye call new, but other books lately put in English, I answer that the Scripture was the first which you and your fautors condemned; besides that those other, for the most, teach nothing but that which is manifest in the Scripture, and also plain in the ancient doctors. I speak not of your old doctors, Duns and St. Thomas, Halcot, Bright, and others, but of Augustine, Jerome, Chrysostom, Ambrose, Hilary, and such other, which, in like manner be called new doctors, as the scripture new learning; and as Tully, new Latin; as the text of Aristotle, new philosophy; and likewise of all sciences.

And so in this appeareth your first lie, that ye call the Scripture new doctrine; except that ye would call it new, either because it makes the receivers of it new men, or else that it was now newly received into the world, for the condemnation of them that reject it, and the salvation of the receivers; of which newness I am sure ye spake not. . . .

But you will say that you condemn not the Scripture, but Tyndale's translation. Therein ye show yourselves contrary to your words; for ye have condemned it in all other common tongues, wherein they be approved in other countries. So that it is plain, that it is the Scripture, and not the translation, that ye bark against, calling it new learning. And this much for the first lie."

It is a forceful letter; like many such, it made no impression whatever upon its recipient.

If the reformers had felt that recent developments in Parliament and Convocation were the prelude to any official relaxation of Catholic orthodoxy, they were soon made aware that they had miscalculated. The bishops, having been required to pay tremendous money fines and to subscribe to the royal supremacy, were in no mood to make further concessions. Moreover, there was a newcomer among them who, in Foxe's interpretation (which has become the classical protestant view of his character), was to prove a mighty hammer of the heretics. This was Dr. John Stokesley,[18] who in July, 1530, had been nominated to the see of London, in succession to Cuthbert Tunstall, lately translated to Durham. Now fifty-five years old, Stokesley was an Oxford man; he had been successively fellow and vice-president of Magdalen College and principal of Magdalen Hall. While at Oxford he had achieved some reputation as a humanist, and had been praised by Erasmus as the compeer of More and Colet. More recently he had been dean of the Chapel Royal, Westminster. Of all the conservatives who supported the divorce, he was probably the one most genuinely convinced of its rightness. He was the co-author of a treatise in its support, and had been Henry's envoy to the Italian universities on its behalf. He had also been active in promoting the supremacy, and later on he was to prove useful in suppressing the monasteries within his diocese. The bishopric of London was just reward for services well rendered. In spite of his youthful humanism, however, and his willingness to reject the Roman obedience, Stokesley was staunchly conservative in all matters pertaining to doctrine. It is possible that, as in the case of Gardiner, his zeal for the purity of the faith was partly a compensation for his compliance with the King's politics.

As early as March 8, 1531, Convocation, probably at the instigation of Stokesley, turned its attention to Bilney, Crome, and Latimer. On that day it was proposed that the three Cambridge reformers be interrogated;

the suggestion was repeated on the eighteenth; but formal action was postponed until a later time.[19] No reason is given for the postponement. But almost immediately Crome was called up for examination, and shortly thereafter Bilney was apprehended and put on his trial before the bishop of Norwich. For the time being, Latimer was left untroubled.

Bilney's last agony began in the summer of 1531. His preaching and his distributing of heretical books in and about his native Norwich left the authorities of that diocese with no choice but to proceed against him. Richard Nix, the bishop of Norwich, was one of the most intransigent of the old-school bishops; Bilney had little to hope for in his court. But even so, Bilney had sealed his own fate; he was an abjured heretic, and he had now violated the law, if he had not preached heresy. After a long process, he was declared a relapsed heretic and handed over to the secular arm. On August 19, 1531, in the Lollards' Pit at Norwich, he went to the flames, the first of the Cambridge men to suffer martyrdom. After his death, it was given out by Sir Thomas More, on the testimony of some eye-witnesses to the execution, that at the last moment Bilney recanted. But the story has been abundantly proved a canard, and More himself, at best, the gullible victim of unscrupulous informants.[20]

A short time later, Latimer paid the first of his many tributes to Bilney's memory. Denying that he had publicly defended Bilney and attacked his judges, he yet attested to Bilney's saintliness of character. It had been charged that Bilney had behaved badly at his trial and at his death. Wrote Latimer: "How he ordered or misordered himself in judgment, I cannot tell, nor I will meddle withal; God knoweth, whose judgments I will not judge. But I cannot but wonder, if a man living so mercifully, so charitably, so patiently, so continently, so studiously and virtuously, and killing his old Adam (that is to say, mortifying his evil affections and blind motions of his heart so diligently), should die an evil death, there is no more, but 'Let him that standeth, beware that he fall not': for if such as he shall die evil, what shall become of me, such a wretch as I am?" [21]

If Bilney courted martyrdom, Dr. Crome did not. In his preaching, he had doubted purgatory and the efficacy of prayers for the dead. He had said that there was small efficacy in pilgrimages or in devotions to the saints. He had even denied that the sacraments were the exclusive channels of grace. When he was called before Stokesley at York Place he was required to sign articles which made it appear that he had renounced these views, and to affirm further that he did not believe that it was necessary for the lay folk to have the Bible in English.[22] To make his humiliation more complete, the bishops published his articles and forced him to read them from the pulpit. To Crome it was a mortifying experience; to some of his devoted followers, it was heart-breaking.

During the remainder of the year 1531, heresy and the traffic in forbidden books were handled with unusual severity in the diocese of London, and in December the fires of Smithfield burned with renewed vigor. In the autumn, Richard Bayfield, priest and sometime monk of the Benedictine abbey of Bury St. Edmunds, who had been engaged in smuggling prohibited books into England, was apprehended in Mark

Lane. He was sentenced as a relapsed heretic by Stokesley, and on December 4 was committed to the flames.[23] He was followed on December 29 by John Tewkesbury,[24] leather dealer of the parish of St. Michael in the Quern, whose case remains an unerased black mark in the record of Sir Thomas More.[25]

Until the close of this period of terror and alarm, Hugh Latimer was unmolested. The suggestion of the preceding March that he be summoned before Convocation had not been carried out. One reason may have been that, in the west of England, he was out of range. A more likely explanation is that his utterances were more moderate than those of the others who were apprehended at this time and that he had not engaged in, at any rate he had not been detected in, the traffic in prohibited literature. When he was finally called to account early in 1532, it was on the technicality that he had preached in London without the bishop's license.

CHAPTER ELEVEN

THE SERMON AT ST. MARY ABCHURCH

In the autumn of 1531 Latimer was able to leave his parish for a time. His inclination drew him to the center of things, and after preaching in Kent without incident he went up to London. In the city, certain merchants besought him to preach at St. Mary Abchurch, in Abchurch Lane, Cannon Street.[1] They seemed to be zealous seekers of the Word, and professed that great numbers of people were eager to hear him preach. Latimer was inclined to oblige them. Stokesley's severities of recent months, however, made him wary. He put the merchants off several times, on the ground that he did not have license from the bishop to preach in the diocese of London, although, to be sure, his license as university preacher legally entitled him to preach in any diocese in the kingdom.[2]

Some of the merchants suggested that Abchurch was a "peculiar"—that is, not subject to the bishop's jurisdiction—but Latimer, quite correctly as it turned out, was not convinced that this was the case. Finally the merchants persuaded him that the rector, Thomas Clark, and his curate were eager to have him preach. After assuring himself that the parson and curate were aware of his identity, Latimer consented. Later, looking back on these negotiations, Latimer was inclined to believe that the whole affair was a put-up job to bring him into Stokesley's hands.[3]

For this sermon, Latimer took as his text the words of St. Paul in Romans 6:14—"For ye are not under the law, but under grace."[4] The passage was part of the Epistle for the day, and it suited the preacher's purposes excellently. He discoursed upon his favorite theme that holiness and righteousness were more pleasing to God and more efficacious for salvation than pilgrimages, devotions to the saints, and the like. He may have been incautious in his observations concerning purgatory. One of his auditors thought he had denied transubstantiation, but this he certainly did not do, else his later difficulties would have been far greater than they actually were. The nub of his sermon, however, and that which gave greatest offense, was an attack upon the bishops for their reliance upon informants in the prosecution of cases of alleged heresies. He charged that in most cases, if not all, the informants were either adversaries of the accused or ignorant men incapable of reporting accurately what they had heard. In judging such cases, Latimer admonished, the bishops ought not to insist upon the rigors of the law; rather they should be guided by principles of equity and charity.[5] Later, Latimer insisted that he had made no allusion to Bilney nor to the court which condemned him, but it is clear that the burning of the little zealot in the Lollard's pit at Norwich would have been uppermost in the minds of the congregation as they listened to Latimer's words.

Soon after preaching this sermon, Latimer returned to West Kington and resumed his usual parochial duties. Then, just before Christmas, he was made aware of Stokesley's long arm. Dr. Richard Hilley, chancellor of the diocese of Salisbury, had received letters from Stokesley demanding that Latimer be sent up to London to answer to the charge of having preached at St. Mary Abchurch without the bishop's license, and of having uttered certain opinions suspected of being heretical.[6] Stokesley was particularly annoyed by Latimer's apparent defiance of his episcopal authority, and by the supposed allusions to Bilney, of which the Bishop had already complained to the King. There can be no doubt that Latimer was thoroughly alarmed; the recent humiliation of Crome and the burning of Bayfield did not encourage him to think he would get off lightly. Since he had not previously been condemned, he was in no danger of the flames, but at the least he would be subjected to the same fate as had overtaken Dr. Crome.

Latimer tried to escape by a technicality. Stokesley was not his ordinary; Hilley, in the absence of Campeggio, was. Latimer admitted that Hilley had the authority to send him up to London, and agreed to go if Hilley insisted. But he argued that Hilley was under no compulsion to obey the bishop of London. He, Latimer, would gladly submit to Hilley, and be reformed by him if it should be proved that his words and conduct had been censurable. He pleaded further the expense of the journey to London and the rigors of such a journey in the depths of winter, ill as he was with headache, backache, colic, and the stone. Hilley was so far moved by Latimer's arguments that he agreed to transmit them to Stokesley.[7] But the chancellor of the diocese of Salisbury had no intention of defying the bishop of London, and he held out very little encouragement.

Just after his interview with Hilley, Latimer received from Sir Edward Baynton, who held the lordship of the manor of Bromham, near West Kington, a letter requesting an explanation or defense of the Abchurch sermon. This letter has not been preserved, and it is not clear why Baynton wrote. Baynton was Queen Anne's chamberlain, and he was presumably sympathetic to the new learning. Perhaps he wrote at the suggestion of the King or the Queen.[8] He seems also to have been egged on by some of the local clergy who were hostile to Latimer. Whatever his motives, his letter provoked an interesting correspondence, which was preserved by Foxe.

Latimer's reply to Baynton's first letter is concerned exclusively with the Abchurch sermon and Bishop Stokesley's hostility. After setting forth the facts as reported in the beginning of this chapter, Latimer launches into a spirited attack upon those who have misunderstood his words. He denies Baynton's assertion that plain words will be plainly understood. St. Paul was misunderstood; Christ himself was misunderstood when He spoke of rebuilding the temple within three days.[9] The sermon on the text "For ye are not under the law, but under grace" must be rightly understood. He had attacked the abuse of their office by the bishops, and he had attacked voluntary works. But he had not preached defiance of the law. Everything he had said was according to Scriptures and the Fathers. He had not mentioned Bilney.

As for his preaching without Stokesley's license, he had had no intention of defying the Bishop. He would gladly have had Stokesley's license, but he had thought his Cambridge license sufficient, especially as the King had recently reaffirmed, in the presence of the bishops, the validity of the licenses of the university preachers. It would be a fault, says Latimer, for him to defy the Bishop, but is it not equally a fault for Stokesley to defy the King? He suggests that Stokesley might take a lesson from St. Paul, who was willing that some men should preach in envy of him, so long as they preached Christ.[10]

Throughout the letter, Latimer is merry at Stokesley's expense. He chides him for being an unpreaching prelate, marvels that so busy a man has time to trouble himself over so trifling affair as the Abchurch sermon, invites him to preach at West Kington.[11] He wonders how Stokesley would have dealt with St. Paul:

> If my said lord would have heard St. Paul declare his own mind of his own words, then he should have escaped, and the false apostles have been put to rebuke: if he would have rigorously followed *utcunque allegata et probata,* and have given sentence after relation of the accusers, then good St. Paul must have borne a fagot at Paul's Cross, my lord of London being his judge. Oh, it had been a godly sight, to have seen St. Paul with a fagot on his back, even at Paul's Cross, my lord of London, bishop of the same, sitting under the cross.[12]

The most interesting parts of the letter, however, are not the attacks upon Stokesley, but the statement of Latimer's opinions as of the year 1531. He believes the three creeds, and all of Holy Writ. "Yet I am ignorant in things which I trust hereafter to know, as I do now know things in which I have been ignorant heretofore: ever to learn and ever to be learned [i.e., taught]; to profit with learning, with ignorance not to annoy." [13] He had formerly thought the pope was lord of all the world; now he could believe otherwise. He had accepted the pope's approval of pluralities and absences from benefices; now he might be entreated to think otherwise. He had thought the pope had power to deliver souls from purgatory; now learning might persuade him otherwise. He had thought that if he had been a friar, he could not have been damned; now he abhors his superstition. He had thought that "images of saints" could deliver men from their diseases; now he grieves that the bishop of London can suffer the people to be deceived in such matters. The passage concludes with a Parthian glance at Stokesley, who in times past had thought a man might marry his brother's widow, but now dares think and say the contrary.[14]

It is clear, if we accept Latimer's statements at their face value, that he was yet a long way from heresy in the strict sense. But the letter was indiscreet, in places impudent. Obviously it was written in the belief that Baynton was a friend who could be relied upon. But Baynton was not satisfied with it. A second letter from Baynton disclosed the fact that he had shown the letter to some of his clerical friends, whose verdict was that Latimer was too sure of the correctness of his own opinions, too reckless in the exercise of private judgment, and that he spoke through zeal, but not according to knowledge. Baynton protested that he himself was not qualified to express an opinion in matters of doctrine, but he feared that, apart from such matters, Latimer's pulpit manner had been provocative and overaggressive.[15]

Latimer's reply is quite different from his first letter to Baynton. It is a serious defense of his right to interpret the Scriptures as it is given him to understand them. It is an earnest refutation of the charge that his preaching is disruptive of the unity of the church. It is, in every sense, a spirited *apologia pro vita sua.*

God alone, says Latimer, knows the truth. But every man must seek to understand the truth according to his capacity. If he is uncertain of his understanding, let him keep silence; if he is certain, he must preach what he believes. The certainty of faith is the most certain of all knowledge. True, there are those who have more zeal than knowledge. But worse are those who have knowledge without zeal and those who have lost the knowledge of faith through failure to practice it or teach it.[16]

If a preacher waits for certain knowledge of all things, says Latimer, he will ever halt between two opinions, and will teach and preach nothing. Many things in the Scriptures elude our comprehension. When we find ourselves in such deep waters, it is best to return to the safety of the shore as quickly as possible. To linger is to be caught in a whirlpool of subtleties which serve the devil by weakening the faith. The argument against overconfidence in private judgment may be valid against those preachers who debate such questions as whether we should have had stock-fish in Iceland if Adam had not sinned. It cannot be valid against one who preaches the simple duty of every man to do the good works which God has prepared him to do, every man in his office or calling, as the word of God appoints.[17]

As for the charge that his preaching is rending the seamless robe of Christ, Latimer replies that he is teaching only the truth of Scripture as received and agreed upon by the holy fathers of the church. The contention of Baynton's friends that any teaching which causes dissension is not of God is proved false by the whole history of the church. Paul's epistle caused dissension among the Galatians. The prologue to Jerome's canonical epistles indicates that the teaching of that great doctor had disrupted the unity of the Christian congregation. Erasmus' commentary upon First Corinthians, in the Paraphrase, had disrupted the peace not only in lonely cloisters, but also at Paul's Cross and St. Mary Spital.[18]

Furthermore, Latimer insists, the Christian congregation, whose unity is so earnestly desired, does not consist of all those who have been baptized. Rather it is made up of those baptized persons who have renounced Satan and all his works and pomps. In the creed men say that they accept "one Lord," "one faith," "one baptism." But it is necessary to remember also the Scriptures—"Not every one who saith, Lord, Lord, shall enter into the kingdom of heaven," and "Show me thy faith without thy works, and I will show thee my faith by my works." These utterances were directed, not at the unbaptized, but at those who, having been baptized, answer not to their baptism.[19]

The people, the letter continues, need to hear the truth. But suppose there are no preachers of the truth. St. Jerome, in his commentary on Nahum 3, says that in such case the people must themselves go up into the mountain of the Old and New Testaments, the prophets, the apostles, the evangelists. In the light of Jerome's words, how can there be objection to the lay people's having the Scriptures? The curates have lulled the laity to sleep for a great while. But now the folk have been awakened, and those who have awakened them are put in jeopardy.[20]

The curates, Latimer insists, must learn that they are not the masters of the people but the servants of Christ, whose doctrines they must teach. Even if they live evilly, they are to be obeyed as long as they preach the word of God and duly administer the sacraments, for God's ordinances are fruitful whatever the minister may be of himself. But it is required of the congregation that they be careful that the curates preach God's word and administer God's sacraments, and not their own doctrines and ordinances, "lest peradventure we take chalk for cheese, which will edge our teeth and hinder our digestion." [21]

It is better, Latimer argues, to have disunity than that no one should preach the truth. It is better to have disunity than that the people should continue in superstition and idolatry, in their ignorance doing those things which they need not do, leaving undone those things which they ought to do. What ought the curates to do? Only what He taught who said, "Peter, lovest thou me? Feed my lambs. Feed, feed." But that injunction is now set aside, as if to love Him were nothing except to wear rings, mitres, and rochets. Meanwhile, as long as their curates care only for gain and for ceremonies, the people cannot but fall into error.[22]

Even as he wrote the last words of this letter, Latimer learned that his plea to the chancellor of the diocese of Salisbury had failed.

Sir, I had made an end of this scribbling, and was beginning to write it again more truly and more distinctly, and to correct it; but there came a man of my lord of Farley [the prior of Monkton Farley], with the citation to appear before my lord of London in haste, to be punished for such excesses as I committed at my last being there; so that I could not perform my purpose: I doubt whether ye can read it as it is. If ye can, well be it: if not, I pray you send it me again, and that you so do, whether you can read it or not. Jesu mercy, what a world is this, that I shall be put to so great labor and pains, besides great costs, above my power, for preaching of a poor simple sermon.[23]

CHAPTER TWELVE

BEFORE CONVOCATION

The citation issued by Hilley on January 10, 1532, summoned Latimer to appear before Stokesley in St. Paul's Cathedral on Monday, January 29, to answer to charges of crimes and excesses committed or uttered by him in the diocese of London.[1] In all such cases, the guilt of the accused had already been determined; in no case was there a verdict of acquital. The only questions at issue were the degree of guilt and the nature of the punishment. Latimer went up to London with full knowledge of what was in store for him, and with no intention of making a martyr of himself. "And I look not to escape better than Dr. Crome," he wrote at the close of his second letter to Baynton; "but when I have opened my mind never so much, yet I shall be reported to deny my preaching, of them that have belied my preaching, as he was . . . . I shall have need of great patience to bear the false reports of the malignant church." [2]

If the proceedings began on schedule, Latimer was under examination for the better part of three months; his case was not finally disposed of until April 22. During much of this period, he was questioned three times a week—a wearisome business for all concerned. Quite early in the process Latimer was surprised and alarmed by a change of venue. The first hearings took place, as specified in the citation, in Stokesley's court. But they were subsequently transferred to the chapter house at Westminster, where Latimer found himself before a commission of the upper house of Convocation. There his judges, besides Stokesley, were Warham, the archbishop of Canterbury; Edward Lee, who had succeeded Wolsey as archbishop of York; Stephen Gardiner, newly created bishop of Winchester; the aged John Fisher, bishop of Rochester; John Veysey, bishop of Exeter; and two or three others of lesser rank. It was a formidable array. Warham, as it happened, was kept by illness from regular attendance (he died the following August); Stokesley seems to have presided at most of the sessions.

Unfortunately the original records of Convocation are no longer extant, and our knowledge of the formal proceedings must largely rest upon fragmentary and not very accurate excerpts made by the antiquaries Heyleyn and Wilkins before the disappearance of the originals. From Latimer himself we also glean a few details. During some twenty sessions he was quizzed about his opinions. Day after day he reiterated his assertion that he had not condemned catholic doctrines or practices, but had merely condemned abuses. Although he had no doubt about the outcome of the affair, by his own account he put up a game fight, skilfully evading the theological and legal pitfalls which were prepared for him. Twenty years later, in a sermon at Stamford, he described one of the traps:

I was once in examination before five or six bishops, where I had much tur-
moiling. Every week thrice I came to examinations, and many snares and traps
were laid to get something. Now God knoweth I was ignorant of the law; but
that God gave me answer and wisdom what I should speak. It was God indeed,
for else I had never escaped them. At the last I was brought forth to be examined
into a chamber hanged with arras, where I was before wont to be examined,
but now at this time the chamber was somewhat altered; for whereas before
there was wont ever to be a fire in the chimney, now the fire was taken away,
and an arras hanging hanged over the chimney, and the table stood near the
chimney's end; so that I stood between the table and the chimney's end. There
was among these bishops that examined me, one with whom I have been very
familiar, and took him for my friend, an aged man [this must have been either
Fisher or Veysey, probably the former, although it is difficult to understand how
Latimer could have thought that Fisher was friendly to him], and he sat next
the table end. Then among all other questions, he put forth one, a very subtle
and crafty one; and such one indeed as I could not think so great danger in.
And when I should make answer, "I pray you, Master Latimer," said he, "speak
out; I am very thick of hearing, and here be many that sit far off." I marvelled
at this, that I was bidden speak out, and began to misdeem, and gave an ear
to the chimney. And, Sir, there I heard a pen walking in the chimney behind
the cloth. They had appointed one there to write all mine answers: for they
made sure work that I should not start from them; there was no starting from
them. God was my good Lord, and gave me answer; I could never else have
escaped it. The question was this: "Master Latimer, do you not think on your conscience, that you have been suspected of heresy?" A subtle question, a very
subtle question. There was no holding of peace would serve. To hold my peace
had been to grant myself faulty. To answer it was every way full of danger.
But God, which alway hath given me answer, helped me, or else I could never
have escaped it; and delivered me from their hands.[3]

We must regret that Latimer has not left a record of his answer to
the bishop's "very subtle and crafty question."

At length, after many weary sessions, articles were prepared for his
subscription.[4] They were sixteen in number, and required him to affirm
his unqualified acceptance of the following: that there is a place of purgation for souls after this life, that the souls in purgatory are helped by
masses, prayers, and alms; that the holy apostles and martyrs in heaven
pray as mediators for us, that invocations to them are profitable, and that
pilgrimages and oblations to their shrines and relics are meritorious; that
men, by alms-deed, prayer, and other good work, may merit at God's
hand; that vows of chastity may not be broken without the dispensation
of the pope; that the keys given to Peter remain with the bishops, even
though they live evilly, and are never committed to a layman; that men
forbidden to preach ought not to do so until they have purged themselves
of suspicion and been lawfully restored by their superiors; that Lent and
fast days are to be kept; that God's grace is in all the seven sacraments;
that consecrations, sanctifications, and benedictions received in the church
are laudable and profitable; that it is laudable and profitable to have the
crucifix and the images of the saints in churches, to deck and trim them,
and to burn candles before them. These articles were similar to those administered the year before to Dr. Crome except for one significant omission.[5] Latimer's articles did not require him to affirm that it was unnecessary to have the Scriptures in the vernacular.

Most of the articles were patently centered about those "voluntary"
works the abuses of which Latimer had been denouncing for several years.
As phrased, the articles represented sound Catholic doctrine and practice

77

with which he was still in accord. To subscribe to them might have done no violence to his conscience if he had only to consider his private opinions. But he had to consider his public utterances as well. To subscribe to the articles without qualification would make it appear to those unversed in the niceties of legal and theological terminology that he not only accepted the doctrines but also condoned the excesses connected with them.

From Wilkins' excerpts from the register of Convocation, it appears that the articles were presented to Latimer on March 11, and that on that day he thrice refused to subscribe. Whereupon the Archbishop, with the consent of his colleagues, declared him contumacious, handed down a sentence of excommunication, and remanded him to custody in the episcopal palace at Lambeth.[6]

It must have been immediately after this that Latimer addressed a letter,[7] in Latin, to the Archbishop, for in it he speaks as if he were now for the first time in close custody. It is one of his most attractive letters, earnest, dignified, with none of his characteristic satire or invective. He speaks of his illness; he protests at the way in which the process has been protracted and at the efforts of his examiners to trap him. He repeats his now familiar theme of the distinction between necessary works and voluntary works:

> It is lawful, I own, to make use of images; it is lawful to go on pilgrimage; it is lawful to pray to saints; it is lawful to be mindful of souls abiding in purgatory: but these things, which are voluntary, are so to be moderated, that God's commandments of necessary obligation, which bring eternal life to those that keep them, and eternal death to those who neglect them, be not deprived of their just value . . . .[8]

No one can deny, he says, that in connection with pilgrimages and devotion to the saints there has been much ignorant superstition on the part of the people, much venality on the part of the clergy. It is against these things that he has been preaching; this is the work to which he has been called. "For these reasons I dare not, most reverend father, subscribe the bare propositions [*nudis sententiis*] which you require of me; being unwilling, as far as I may, to be the author of any longer continuance of the superstition of the people; and that I may not be also at the same time the author of my own damnation." [9]

From this point on the record is tangled. On March 21 Latimer was again brought before the commission. On that date, according to an entry in Stokesley's London register, he subscribed to all sixteen of the articles.[10] But Wilkins' extracts [11] from the register of Convocation tell a different story. There it is reported that on March 21 the deliberations of the commission were interrupted by the arrival of the prolocutor (the presiding officer of the lower house of Convocation), who entered into a long colloquy with Stokesley, presiding, and the other bishops. As a result of that conference it was decreed that Latimer would be absolved from the sentence of excommunication provided that he would confess that he had preached indiscreetly and would agree to subscribe to articles 11 and 14.

This was a startling, indeed a dramatic, reduction of Convocation's demands.

A point must be made about the two articles to which Latimer was asked to subscribe. As Englished by Foxe in his later editions, the articles are fifteen in number. So they have been reprinted by later writers. From this list, it has been made to appear that the two articles were those which affirmed that Lent and fast days ought to be kept, and that it is laudable and profitable to have the crucifix and images of the saints in churches. It would be difficult to explain why those particular articles were retained. But these are *not* the articles to which Latimer was asked to subscribe. A more authoritative list, in Latin, is preserved in the London registers, and was printed by Foxe in his first edition.[12] Here the articles are sixteen in number. Article 11 is that which affirms that anyone who has been forbidden by the bishops ought not to preach until he has been purged by his superiors and lawfully restored. Article 14 is that which affirms that consecrations, sanctifications, and benedictions received in the church are laudable and useful.

When it is rightly understood which articles Latimer was asked to subscribe to, the full implications of the action of Convocation become clear. All the articles having to do with pilgrimages, purgatory, shrines, invocations to the saints, the power of the keys—all those which Latimer could not have subscribed to without appearing to forswear himself— had been eliminated. There remained the relatively innocuous article concerning benedictions and consecrations and the article dealing with the authority of the bishops to license preaching within their respective dioceses. The latter was probably kept in order to mollify Stokesley who, if he was indeed the heresy-hunter which history has represented him to be, may be presumed to have felt some indignation that Latimer was being let off so easily.

If Wilkins' extract is to be trusted, it is clear that some powerful force had intervened on Latimer's behalf. Perhaps it was Warham, moved by the dignified appeal of Latimer's letter. More likely it was the King. Indeed, it is to be wondered that Henry, who had reason to value Latimer's usefulness, had not interfered before. He had additional reason to do so in the fact that one of the articles (Number 8) in the list proposed to Latimer required him to acknowledge the pope's power to dispense from vows of chastity. The pope's power to dispense from anything was at the moment a sore point with Henry, and according to Latimer this was one of the articles to which he had been most reluctant to subscribe.[13]

At any rate, Convocation had backed down so completely that Latimer must have felt considerable relief, not to say exultation. He came to terms at once. On his knees, he made formal submission to the bishops, in words carefully chosen to exclude any confession that he had preached false doctrine:

My lords, I do confess that I have misordered myself very far, in that I have so presumptuously and boldly preached, reproving certain things, by which the people that were infirm [in the faith] hath taken occasion of ill. Wherefore I ask forgiveness of my misbehavior; I will be glad to make amends; and I have spoken indiscreetly in vehemence of speaking, and have erred in some things, and in manner have been in a wrong way (as thus) lacking discretion in many things.[14]

Then he humbly petitioned to be absolved from the sentence of excommunication.

It might have been expected that articles 11 and 14 would have been administered at once. That may be the sense of the entry in Stokesley's register. But Wilkins' extracts (in Latin which is obviously garbled) from the Convocation register expressly state that Stokesley postponed the signing of the articles until April 10, when Latimer was to appear before the Archbishop or his representative to hear the sentence of the court.[15] One wonders why Stokesley wanted to delay for three weeks. Perhaps, in view of the gravity of the case, he felt that judgment should be handed down by Warham, whose illness continued. Possibly also Convocation was dissatisfied with the turn which events had taken, and hoped that some new development would enable it to deal with Latimer more severely. If the latter was the case, Convocation's hopes were gratified, for Latimer promptly committed a fresh indiscretion.

It will be recalled that in the controversy following the Sermons on the Card, one of his most vigorous opponents was Thomas Greenwood, a fellow of St. John's.[16] At the very time when Convocation relaxed its demands, Greenwood was spreading reports that Latimer had made a complete submission. Latimer lost his temper and his head. He wrote Greenwood an indignant letter,[17] admitting that he had preached indiscreetly, but denying that he had preached false doctrine or that he had made any public confession of error. He added, defiantly, that he would in the future preach with more consideration of his hearers' capacity, but he would in no way alter the substance of his teaching. The letter was, in effect, a foolish expression of exultation over the bishops. It was turned over to them so promptly that one suspects some kind of collusion between them and Greenwood.[18]

Accordingly, when Latimer appeared before the commission on April 10, he learned that he was not to get off as lightly as he had hoped. The garbled record seems to indicate that the bishops now demanded that he subscribe to all the articles, instead of the two to which he had formerly agreed. Obviously something had occurred to strengthen the position of the bishops, and to take the fight out of Latimer. We can only suppose that the King had learned of the Greenwood letter and agreed with the bishops that Latimer's submission did not represent any genuine repentance of his contumacy. We must conclude also that Latimer realized how seriously he had weakened his hand. Meekly he subscribed, was absolved of the sentence of excommunication, and was required to appear again on April 15 to answer to a further process relating to the letter to Greenwood.[19]

One wonders why the matter was handled in just this way. Why, since Latimer had made a full submission, was the Greenwood letter made the subject of a separate process? Why was absolution granted at this time? One can only hazard the guess that the commission hoped that the device of closing one process and starting another would enable them to deal with Latimer as a relapsed heretic and thus put him in a position of extreme danger.

On April 15 formal charges growing out of the Greenwood letter were preferred. Fortunately Latimer was given until the nineteenth to prepare his answers. During the four-day breathing spell, he hit upon a daring and astute plan. On the nineteenth he announced that he had appealed from Convocation to the King, and upon this appeal he wished to stand.[20] It was, as far as I know, an unprecedented move—the first instance of a person accused of heresy taking advantage of the fact that the King was now "supreme head" of the church. Moreover, it was beautifully timed. Only a month before, Parliament had sent to the King the famous "Supplication of the Commons against the Ordinaries," protesting against the power of the ecclesiastical courts. To be sure, mistreatment of suspected heretics was not included in the list of complaints, and the actual "submission of the clergy" was still a month in the future. Nevertheless, the commission did not dare to deny the King's right of jurisdiction in Latimer's case. They adjourned until April 22 to await the King's pleasure.

Unfortunately, the appeal to the supreme head met with only partial success. If Henry had already intervened once on Latimer's behalf, he probably felt that the Greenwood letter warranted a severer rebuke than that already administered. However that may be, it was subsequently reported (by an unfriendly witness) that the King warned Latimer to submit to the bishops and do penance as he deserved; otherwise the King would not intervene on his behalf.[21] At the same time, through the bishop of Winchester, he indicated his wishes to Convocation.

When the bishops reconvened on April 22 they were informed by Gardiner that the King had remitted to them the disposition of the case. This pleasant fiction enabled them to extract from Latimer a submission far more damaging to his position than the first one. On his knees he was required to affirm:

That where he had aforetime confessed, that he hath heretofore erred, and that he meant then it was only error of discretion, he hath since better seen of his own acts, and searched them more deeply, and doth knowledge, that he hath not erred only in discretion, but also in doctrine; and said that he was not called afore the said lords, but upon good and just ground, and hath been by them charitably and favorably intreated. And where he had aforetime misreported of the lords, he knowledgeth, that he hath done ill in it, and desired them humbly on his knees to forgive him: and where he is not of ability to make them recompense, he said, he would pray for them.[22]

The submission was galling enough. But so far, and no farther, the bishops were allowed to go in humiliating Latimer. The confession of erroneous opinions was kept in general terms. No further articles were prepared against him. There was no further sentence of excommunication. "At the special request of our lord the king," Stokesley, again presiding, pronounced the absolution from heretical pravity. The bishops preserved the appearance of independence by adding two riders—that in the event of relapse Latimer should be referred to them, and that this kind of submission (presumably a submission without the requirement of subscription to specific articles) should not be extended to other cases.[23]

It would be idle to speculate whether the form of Latimer's submission constituted apostasy in any real sense of that term. His confession that he had erred in matters of doctrine has been generally regarded as a very black mark on his record. Unfriendly critics have denounced his action as a piece of unscrupulous cynicism. Friendly writers have regarded it as an act of weakness for which he suffered the extremes of remorse. Probably it was neither. In Henry VIII's time all of the academic reformers who were called up on charges of heresy recanted at least once. Bilney, Barnes, Bayfield, Frith, Crome, Latimer—all abjured; the heroic exception is Tyndale, whose case belongs to another category. The explanation is to be found, not in cowardice or a settled policy of evasion, but in the fact that the issues were not yet clearly defined, the battle not definitely joined.

The plain fact is that Latimer, unlike Bilney, as yet felt no immortal longings. Such is the conclusion from the sentence in the Baynton letter quoted at the beginning of this chapter. Such, I think, is also the conclusion to be drawn from a conversation which Latimer is reported to have had, just after his trial was concluded, with James Bainham while the latter awaited execution as a relapsed heretic at Smithfield.

While Latimer was before the bishops, Bainham, [24] a man of very different quality, was under examination by Stokesley's vicar-general. Bainham was a member of the Middle Temple, a lawyer of some substance, who had become infected with Lutheran doctrine and had married the widow of Simon Fish (the author of the proscribed *Supplication for the Beggars*). In the fall of 1531, he was apprehended for disseminating heretical books and was accused of heresy to Sir Thomas More, who ordered him to be flogged; afterwards he was sent to the Tower and racked. During his examination he asserted that of all the preachers he had heard, only Latimer and Crome had preached the Gospel truly (from which it may be concluded that he was one of the "infirm" of faith who had been misled by the vehemence of Latimer's preaching), and he commented sharply upon Crome's recantation. In February, 1532, he abjured his heresies, carried a fagot at St. Paul's, and paid a fine of £ 20. A month later, he created a disturbance in St. Austin's church by publicly reasserting his old opinions. He was sentenced as a relapsed heretic, and burned at Smithfield on April 30, 1532.

The story of Latimer's interview with Bainham is to be found in a manuscript [25] written by the same hand which wrote the account, discussed in a previous chapter, of Latimer's interviews with Bishop West and Cardinal Wolsey. This document also was once the property of John Foxe, but he did not include the story in his *Acts and Monuments*.

The manuscript records that on the eve of Bainham's execution, Latimer, with Edward Isaac and William and Ralph Morice, went to the deep dungeon of Newgate, where they found Bainham sitting on a couch of straw and reading the Bible by the light of a candle. In the ensuing conversation Latimer took the lead. Urging the condemned man to be sure that he was dying in a just cause and to beware of vainglory, Latimer asked upon what articles Bainham had been convicted. Bainham replied that the first charge against him was that he had said that Thomas à Becket was a traitor to his prince and had instigated foreign invasions of the realm.

Then said Master Latimer, "Where read you this?"
Quoth Master Bainham, "I read it in an old history."
"Well," said Master Latimer, "this is no cause at all worthy for a man to

take his death upon, for it may be a lie, as well as a true tale, and in such a doubtful matter it were mere madness for a man to jeopard his life. But what else is laid to your charge?"

"The truth is," said Bainham, "I spake against purgatory, that there was no such thing, but that it picked men's purses; and against satisfactory masses. Which I defended by the authority of the Scriptures."

"Marry," said Master Latimer, "in these articles your conscience may be so stayed that you may seem rather to die in the defense thereof than to recant both against your conscience and the scriptures also. But yet beware of vainglory, for the devil will be ready now to infect you therewith, when you shall come into the multitude of the people." And then Master Latimer did animate him to take his death quietly and patiently.

Bainham thanked him heartily therefore. "And I likewise," said Bainham, "do exhort you to stand to the defense of the truth, for you that shall be left behind had need of comfort also, the world being so dangerous as it is." And so spake many comfortable words to Master Latimer.

When Latimer inquired if Bainham had a wife, the poor man fell a-weeping. Not only would his wife and children be left unprovided for, he said, but they would be scorned and ostracized because of his heresy. But Latimer rebuked his lack of trust, and in the end persuaded him that God was "able to be a husband to your wife and a father to your children if you commit them to Him with a strong faith."

In spite of its circumstantiality, several points in this narrative are of doubtful accuracy. It seems unlikely that Latimer and his friends could have been ignorant of Bainham and his activities before their visit. Yet the story clearly implies that they were. Also, Bainham's own statement of the articles upon which he had been condemned does not square with the known facts. The principal reasons for his conviction were that he had distributed heretical books and had denied the sacrament of the altar, but of these critical matters his reported statement says nothing. His concern for his wife, to whom he had been married less than a year (the children, if any, must have been by a former marriage) is understandable in all respects save his fear that she would become a figure of scorn. She had already acquired, in her own right and as the wife of the late Simon Fish, a considerable reputation as a trafficker in heretical books. All things considered, the story has a hagiographical quality which renders it suspect.

If, however, without scrutinizing the details too closely, we accept the narrative as substantively true, it is implicit in the first part of the conversation that Latimer regarded Bainham as a fanatic whose death was a needless sacrifice. His fear that Bainham, when brought before the crowd at Smithfield, would make a noisy scene, instead of taking his death quietly and patiently, proved well founded, if Foxe's account of Bainham's martyrdom is to be trusted. How far Latimer's reflections upon vainglory represent self-examination, no one can tell. The interview between Latimer and Bainham, if it ever took place, must have occurred within a week of Latimer's recantation. Of all the implications of that fact the moralist and the ironist must make what they will.

CHAPTER THIRTEEN

LATIMER AT BRISTOL

Nothing is discoverable of Latimer's activities for a year after his submission. Presumably he returned to West Kington and the regular performance of his parochial duties. Some evidence from local tradition indicates that he occasionally preached in neighboring parishes, but for the time being he evidently found it expedient to curb both the matter and the manner of his speaking. Another citation would have placed him in the position of a relapsed heretic; he was not yet prepared to take the risk.

During this year, however, events on the national scene were promoting his interests. On May 15, 1532, came the "submission of the clergy," whereby Convocation was deprived of the power of independent action and the church was made completely subject to the state. On the following day, Sir Thomas More resigned his chancellorship. On August 22 Warham died. By the autumn it was known that Thomas Cranmer, Latimer's good friend, had been nominated by the King to the see of Canterbury, although he was not actually consecrated until the following March. About the same time as Cranmer's nomination came the promotion of Thomas Cromwell,[1] an unscrupulous and self-interested friend of the reformation, to the chancellorship of the exchequer. By this time also there could be no doubt of the ultimate triumph of Latimer's other influential friend at court. For by January of 1532 it was known that Anne Boleyn was installed in the queen's apartment at court with a retinue comparable to that which had attended Catherine. In September, she was created Marchioness of Pembroke. By the end of the year she was pregnant. On or about January 25, 1533, although the matter of the divorce was not yet settled, Anne and Henry were secretly married.

It was therefore with a reasonable expectation of immunity from official interference that in March, 1533, Latimer dared to preach even more emphatically than he had done at Abchurch a year earlier. The scene was Bristol, just a few miles from West Kington, where Lollardy had long flourished, and where a large and influential faction was ready to hear Latimer's kind of preaching with enthusiasm.

On the second Sunday in Lent, March 9, 1533, Latimer preached in the church of St. Nicholas at Bristol in the forenoon, at the church of the Blackfriars in the afternoon. The next day he preached at St. Thomas's. According to his own account,[2] he preached by invitation of some of the clergy, who at the time received his sermons with approbation but subsequently used them to inform against him. This corresponds closely to his account of what had happened in London the preceding year. The sermons themselves have not been preserved; but it is possible, from his letters and from other documents relating to the episode, to reconstruct his own version of them.[3]

He began with his now familiar denunciation of the excessive veneration of the saints. Common folk, he said, were unable to distinguish between the saint in heaven and the image of the saint in the church. The statue should be the "layman's book," a reminder of the holy life of the saint departed.[4] It should neither be prayed to, nor richly decorated, nor have candles lighted before it. It is a "book"; a book need not be richly bound, and a man who is not blind may read it in the daytime without the light of many candles. As for the saints in heaven, they are our mediators by way of intercession, not of redemption. It is not according to Scripture (and here he was more positive than in any of his earlier utterances) that we pray to them. They intercede for us constantly, whether we spur them on or not. They became saints, not by praying to the saints, but by believing in Him that made them saints. Pilgrimages to their shrines should never be *required*. A pilgrimage, if made in the proper spirit and under proper circumstances, is meritorious; but in pilgrimages as now practiced there is much idolatry, and "much scurf must be pared away."

He turned next to a specific attack upon excessive devotion to Our Lady. This was a topic upon which he had probably touched in the preceding year, but in the Bristol sermons we have his first extended utterances on the subject. He wished, he said, no disrespect to the Virgin, but at Bristol her cultus had got out of bounds. In the churches of that city they sang an anthem hailing her as *"Salvatrix ac redemptrix."* He wished merely to prove that Christ was the Savior of the whole world, and therefore Mary's Savior. As to whether she was a sinner or not, the church had not ruled; a majority of the doctors held that she was not; since this was the general opinion, he accepted it, as every man ought to do. In either case, it did not matter; if she was a sinner, she was redeemed by Christ; if she was not, she was spared by Christ.

But now (Latimer is still speaking) she is regarded as a "Savioress." This the doctors had never taught. She was not impeccable; she was a creature preserved from sin by the goodness of God. To call her *salvatrix* is an offense to her Son. She should be called *"Salvatoris ac Redemptoris Mater."* Therefore "I will give as little to her as I can (doing her no wrong) rather than Christ her Son and Savior shall lack any parcel of His glory; and I am sure that Our Lady will not be displeased with me for so doing; for Our Lady sought His glory here upon earth; she would not now defraud Him in Heaven." Our Lady was good and gracious. The Lord was with her favorably and poured graces upon her plenteously. The Son of God, when he chose to become man, bestowed upon her the unique honor of becoming His Mother. By Him she did the will of the Father. The handmaiden did magnify the Lord. The handmaiden would have all people magnify the Lord.

In his treatment of the status of the Virgin, Latimer took occasion to stress the importance of the use of the *Pater Noster*. This marks the beginning of his efforts, continued for the rest of his life, to encourage his people in the use of what he regarded as the one whole and perfect prayer. No doubt he took the thought from Luther, but no Englishman ever did more than Latimer to establish the place of the Lord's Prayer in Protestant worship and devotion. In the Bristol sermons, of course, his point was that the cult of the Virgin had led to the use of the *Ave Maria* at the expense of the *Pater Noster*. The *Ave Maria,* he insisted, was not a prayer, but a greeting. As a greeting it might still be used, but we were not commanded to use it, and need not always say it in conjunction with the *Pater Noster*. The people, he argued, had been deluded into thinking that their sins might be absolved by the saying of innumerable *Ave Marias,* a practice displeasing to Christ and therefore to Our Lady. The theology in all this was orthodox enough, although it involved distinctions which many of Latimer's lay hearers were probably unable to evaluate precisely and which led to much controversy afterwards.

His third topic was purgatory and the abuses connected with masses for the dead, indulgences, and the like. Perhaps he was incited to treat of it by the recent publication of John Frith's *A Disputation of Purgatory,*[5] in which Frith once again took up the cudgels on behalf of the Lutheran side of the controversy. Here again, although he had undoubtedly preached on the topic before, we have Latimer's first recorded utterances on the subject. There is, he said, a place of purgation for those souls who depart this world with the burden of venial sins still upon them. But the souls in purgatory are happy (here, at least, he varied from Luther, who thought that the souls in purgatory sin ceaselessly by desiring rest and shrinking from their sufferings) because they have certain charity. They are members of the mystical body of Christ; they cannot die; they are sure of final salvation. Moreover, they are concerned for the souls still in this life and pray for them constantly. So far Latimer's ideas were Catholic enough; although mutual intercession was, and still is, a matter of debate, it is an idea held by many Catholic theologians.

What followed, however, was more in Luther's vein. We who are still on earth, he said, have far greater need of the prayers of the souls in purgatory than the latter have of ours. We lack charity. We have envy, rancor, and malice towards one another. We are the inheritors of hell, the adversaries of Christ, the hated of God. We are bound by Scripture, under pain of damnation, to help those in extreme necessity; it is the perishing souls of this world who need our help, not the souls in purgatory, who are already assured of salvation. He urged his hearers to give their money for the relief of the poor and the sick rather than spend it for indulgences and masses for the souls of the dead.

I have tried to report Latimer's own summary of his Bristol sermons in terms which are as unprovocative as possible. There can be no doubt that Latimer's own presentation was quite otherwise. His pulpit manner was excitable, and he was frequently betrayed by his own fervor into saying more than he intended. Afterwards, he could believe—or at least he could say—that his words had been calm and dispassionate, and that his opponents had misunderstood him. In the absence of manuscripts of the sermons (it is likely that he seldom preached from manuscript), it is impossible to say with assurance what his actual words were on this occasion. But subsequent events indicate that he was strident and provocative enough. In his commentary on the sermons, in the midst of his judicious analysis of theological matters, are passages which are certainly echoes of his words from the pulpit. Here are two illustrations.

On pilgrimage:

And as for pilgrimage, you would wonder what juggling there is to get money withal. I dwell within half a mile of the Fossway, and you would wonder to see how they come by flocks out of the west country to many images, but chiefly to the blood of Hales. And they believe verily that it is the very blood that was in Christ's body, shed upon the mount of Calvary for our salvation, and that the sight of it with their bodily eye doth certify them and putteth them out of doubt that they be in clean life, and in a state of salvation without spot of sin, which doth bolden them to many things . . . for as for forgiving their enemies and reconciling their Christian brethren, they cannot away withal; for the sight of that blood doth requite them for the time.[6]

On purgatory:

Consider . . . whether provision for purgatory hath not brought thousands to hell. Debts have not been paid; restitution of evil-gotten lands and goods hath not been made; Christian people (whose necessities we see, to whom whatsoever we do Christ reputeth done to himself, to whom we are bound under pain of damnation to do for as we would be done for ourself) are neglected and suffered to perish; last wills unfulfilled and broken; God's ordinance set aside; and also for purgatory, foundations [of chantries] have been taken for sufficient satisfaction; so we have trifled away the ordinance of God and restitutions. Thus we have gone to hell with masses, diriges, and ringing of many a bell. And who can pill pilgrimages from idolatry, and purge purgatory from robbery, but he shall be in peril to come in suspicion of heresy with them, so that they may pill with pilgrimage and spoil with purgatory? And verily the abuse of them cannot be taken away, but great lucre and vantage shall fall away from them which had liefer have profit with abuse than lack the same with use; and that is the wasp that doth sting them, and maketh them to swell.[7]

Latimer's three sermons gave immediate offense to the vested interests, and also to the learned clergy who might have been sympathetic to his general position but who detected the clear note of heresy in the latter part of his remarks about purgatory. Worse still, the attacks upon practices ratified by centuries of usage outraged many of the faithful and provoked them into unruly demonstrations against the preacher. On the other hand, the considerable Lollard faction in Bristol was delighted. Among the latter was Clement Bays, mayor of the city for that year, whose enthusiasm inspired him (on what authority it is impossible to say) to invite Latimer to preach again on the Wednesday in Easter week. Latimer returned to his parish at West Kington, but the quarrels between the two factions continued and frequently broke out in open riot.

On March 18, a week after the sermons, a priest named Richard Browne, one of the conservative party, wrote a letter[8] of complaint to Dr. Thomas Bagard, chancellor to the bishop of Worcester, in whose diocese the city of Bristol lay. The bishop of Worcester was Ghinucci, an Italian and of course an absentee, so that Bagard was actually the ordinary of the diocese. Browne's letter to Bagard complained that Latimer had said that Our Lady was a sinner, and that neither she or any other saint ought to be worshipped. The town was sorely infected by Latimer's preaching, and Browne recommended that Bagard order the dean of Bristol to forbid him to preach. He added, inaccurately, that Latimer had been inhibited from preaching in his own diocese.[9] Apparently Bagard received at the same time a letter of similar purport from Dr. John Hilsey,[10] prior of the house of the Dominicans at Bristol in whose church one of Latimer's sermons was preached. Hilsey was a person of consequence. No doubt his word carried considerable weight with the chancellor.

When Bagard received these letters he was in London attending a session of Convocation. He therefore had the opportunity to consult upon the matter with Thomas Cromwell, who agreed that Latimer should not be allowed to preach again at Bristol. He was also able to inform Convocation of Latimer's preaching and to procure a copy of the submission of the preceding year.[11] Thus armed, Bagard acted with despatch. He did not follow Browne's recommendation that he work through the dean of Bristol. Instead, he inhibited anyone from preaching within the diocese of Worcester without his specific license. Latimer knew perfectly well that the inhibition was directed against him. He wrote to Morice that "privily they procured an inhibition for all them that had not the bishop's license, which they knew well enough I had not, and so craftily defeated master mayor's appointment, pretending that they were sorry for it." [12] Nevertheless, he obeyed the inhibition, and did not preach again in Bristol until May 18, by which time the wind was favorable once more.

Meanwhile, Latimer's opponents thought it wise to arrange a series of sermons designed to combat his teaching. Three local men—the aforesaid Dr. Hilsey and the prior of St. James and Dr. Roger Edgworth, a canon of Bristol as well as of Salisbury and Wells—undertook to preach against Latimer, apparently with no effect except to stir up further controversy.[13] Whereupon it was decided to import two preachers whose pulpit style was comparable to Latimer's own, and whose reputation as defenders of the old learning was well-established. These were Dr. Edward Powell and Master William Hubberdin.

Dr. Powell [14] was a well-known and influential personage. A graduate of Oriel College, Oxford, he was the author of an effective tract against Luther and had been a frequent preacher at court. He was also a conspicuous pluralist. In addition to prebendaries at Salisbury and Lincoln, he at one time held half a dozen other benefices. He seems to have resided chiefly at Salisbury.

Hubberdin,[15] a graduate of Exeter College, Oxford, was in great demand as a popular preacher. What we know of his character is unfortunately based upon the unfriendly testimony of Latimer and Foxe. To the former he was a man of "no great learning, nor yet of stable wit," who would preach whatever the bishops commanded.[16] To Foxe he was "a right painted pharisee, and a great strayer abroad in all quarters of the realm to deface and impeach the springing of God's holy gospel . . . whose doings and pageants . . . were as good as any interlude." Also according to Foxe, he rode about the country, clad in a long gown which fell to his horse's heels, availing himself of every opportunity to denounce the reformers. The eccentricity of his preaching was the death of him, if a story of Foxe's has any validity. At a time not specified (but evidently some years after the Bristol affair), he was preaching in defense of the sacrament of the altar, and wished to demonstrate that on this subject

Christ, the apostles, and the doctors of the church "danced" together in perfect harmony. "And thus old Hubberdin, as he was dancing with his doctors lustily in the pulpit against the heretics, how he stamped and took on I cannot tell, but 'crash' quoth the pulpit, down cometh the dancer, and there lay Hubberdin, not dancing, but sprawling in the midst of his audience; where altogether he brake not his neck, yet he so brake his leg the same time, and bruised his old bones, that he never came in pulpit more, and died not long after the same." [17] So Foxe, to whose lively anecdotes of the opponents of the reformation we must allow a large rate of discount. In this case, perhaps, our conclusion may be limited to the belief that Hubberdin was a vigorous and effective preacher whose pulpit deportment was not always controlled by the canons of good taste.

Hubberdin's preaching against Latimer began at Easter time, 1533. He preached at St. Thomas' Church on Easter Even and Easter Day, and probably in other churches of Bristol during the week following. Our knowledge of his utterances comes from hostile witnesses—Latimer and his supporters among the townsfolk.[18] He is alleged to have said that the people ought to say at least twenty *Ave Marias* for one *Pater Noster;* he himself said a hundred. The *Pater Noster,* he said, ought to be addressed to the saints. It was presumptuous for a sinner to pray directly to God; moreover, the blood of Christ, without the blood of the martyrs, was insufficient. Rome could not err; all that she decreed was Scripture; it was therefore not necessary that Scripture be written. Indeed, the gospels in English had brought men to heresy; there were twenty or thirty such heretics in Bristol.

All this and more Hubberdin was reported to have said. There is less testimony concerning the utterances of Dr. Powell, but Latimer speaks of him as a stronger antagonist than Hubberdin. Latimer implies that Powell taught that the saints in heaven said the *Ave Maria* constantly,[19] and that pilgrims to the shrines of John Shorn, Saint Anne in the Wood, and Our Lady of Walsingham obeyed the injunction of Christ (Matthew 19: 29) to leave brethren, sisters, father, mother, wife, children, and lands, and would inherit everlasting life.[20]

Whatever the accuracy of these reports may be, it is clear that the preaching of Hubberdin and Powell (and of Dr. Nicholas Wilson, one of the king's chaplains, who came down to Bristol about this time) was as coals to burning coals to kindle strife. Disorder in Bristol was redoubled. Verse libels attacking Latimer were posted on the church doors. One stanza of one of them was an acrostic:

> L for Lollard stands in this place.
> A for error [*sic*] of great iniquity.
> T for traitor to God, lacking grace.
> I for ignorance of the true Trinity.
> M for maintainer of those that nought be.
> E for 'eretic, as learned men saith.
> R for rebeller against Christ's faith.

Latimer's supporters matched this in both zeal and poetic felicity:

> He was a lamb, and thou a wolf shalt prove.
> The blessed Virgin he did not abuse,
> But stocks and stones he preached to remove,
> And pilgrimages, which did men abuse.

Idolatry he would all should refuse,
And cleave unto God's word, it to uphold,
Which thou wouldst hide with face of brass full bold.[21]

At a lower literary level, Dr. Powell prepared charges of heresy to be used against Latimer, and the mayor of Bristol began to take testimony to be used against Powell and Hubberdin.

While these unedifying events were going forward at Bristol, the King's great matter had been hurried to its conclusion. On March 30, the long delayed bulls having arrived from Rome, Thomas Cranmer was consecrated archbishop of Canterbury. On April 17, Convocation formally declared the illegality of Henry's marriage to Catherine. On April 23 at Dunstable, Cranmer, in his capacity as primate and legate, annulled the marriage. On June 1, amidst pageantry of unprecedented splendor, Anne Boleyn was crowned queen in Westminster Abbey.

It was these events which led to the ultimate triumph of Latimer and his supporters at Bristol. In the sermons of Easter Week, Powell and Hubberdin had limited their remarks to matters of theological controversy. National events now led them into indiscretion. Both were stubborn opponents of the divorce; with the courage born of conviction, they both spoke out. Witnesses testified that in a sermon preached on St. Mark's Day, just two days after the annulment of Henry's marriage, Dr. Powell declared that a man who puts away his wife to marry another corrupts the people; if the man is a prince, the corruption is greater by far.[22] It was also reported that a month later, on Ascension Day, Hubberdin said from the pulpit of Temple Church that the pope is the prince of all the world whom all the kings of the world could not destroy. He added, with obvious reference to Cranmer, some indiscreet remarks about bishops who were chosen by kings rather than by the Holy Ghost.[23]

Clement Bays, the mayor, Latimer's ardent supporter, was quick to take advantage of this new development. He found witnesses to testify to the remarks of Powell and Hubberdin, and addressed a memorandum on the matter to Dr. Bagard, chancellor of Worcester. A supplementary memorandum alleged that Dr. Floke, the dean of Bristol (who apparently was among Latimer's opponents), had instructed the clergy at Bristol not to include prayers for the King and Queen in the *memento* of the mass; according to Floke, instructions to that effect had come from Bagard himself. These matters, Bays hinted broadly, were of such gravity that the King's council should be informed of them.[24]

At this time also Bagard received a letter from Dr. Hilsey, the prior of the Dominicans, who had earlier recommended that Latimer be inhibited. Hilsey had changed his front. He now wrote [25] that he had been craftily used by Latimer's opponents, who had persuaded him that Latimer had been guilty of preaching heresy. Since that time he had heard Latimer preach (presumably at West Kington) and had talked with him; he was now convinced that Latimer was merely denouncing abuses. All the preaching against him had only served to promote dissension, and Hilsey urged that Latimer be licensed to preach again at Bristol so that he might amplify his thought and thus satisfy the townspeople who cried out against him.

The direction of the wind was now entirely perceptible to Bagard. He issued the license, and Latimer preached again at Bristol during Rogation Week (May 18-25). But Hilsey, who had gone over lock, stock and barrel to the faction of Latimer and the mayor, was not satisfied. He joined with several others, priests and laymen, in sending a memorandum of the utterances of Powell and Hubberdin to Cromwell and the rest of the King's council. The memorandum, with its testimony to specific charges, is not extant, but the covering letter is. It refers to the "sinistral" preaching of Powell and Hubberdin; Hilsey's is the first of the thirteen signatures to the letter.[26]

Dr. Bagard seems to have felt the weight of Cromwell's displeasure at once, and he naturally took alarm. He had silenced Latimer, who was evidently back in favor; he had licensed (or at least had not inhibited) Powell and Hubberdin, who had denounced the divorce and whose remarks had been reported to the council; it was alleged that he had forbidden his clergy to pray for the King and Queen. To clear himself of the suspicion that he was of the Powell-Hubberdin party he sent off an abject letter to Cromwell. Arguing that the circumstances warranted his original inhibition of Latimer, he reminds Cromwell that it was issued with his approval. He confesses that Latimer's preaching in Rogation Week has been unobjectionable. He promises to inhibit Dr. Wilson from further preaching. He concludes:

This day, before this letter of mine was made ready to seal, Hubberdin came to me desiring me to have a license to preach, but, sir, I warrant you he get no license of me as long as it shall please God, the king's grace, and your mastership that I be in this office, notwithstanding his much instance he makes. Therefore I shall shake him off well enough.[27]

The abject tone of this letter needs no commentary. Cromwell allowed Bagard to squirm for a while. A year later, Bagard was still protesting to Cromwell that he was no supporter of Hubberdin "and other such brabbling preachers," that Hubberdin had preached at Bristol during Bagard's absence in London without his knowledge and without his license, and that Hubberdin and Powell would never be permitted to preach in his diocese again.[28] In the end, Bagard was allowed to retain the chancellorship of Worcester, in which capacity he continued to serve during Latimer's episcopacy and during the Catholic reaction which followed, until his death in 1544.

Late in June or early in July, Cromwell intervened directly in the Bristol affair. He authorized John Bartholomew, collector of customs at Bristol, to appoint a commission to look into the words and behavior of both Latimer and Hubberdin (Powell was not mentioned) and especially the words of Hubberdin concerning the king's majesty. Bartholomew chose as his fellow commissioners William Burton, the abbot of St. Augustine's; John Cable, Thomas Broke, and Richard Tenell, former mayors of Bristol; and Thomas à Bowen, gentleman. This commission sat to take testimony from July 5th until July 11th.[29]

The two principals did not testify. Latimer was presumably in his parish at West Kington. Hubberdin was in prison. He had been examined earlier by the mayor and council of Bristol, and sent up to London, where on July 4 he was committed to the Tower. But there was no lack of witnesses. The testimony against Latimer was not very well organized. Some witnesses were found to testify that he had preached schismatic and erroneous opinions, but others seem to have been frightened off. The warden of the Grey Friars (an opponent of Latimer) alleged that on the first day of the hearing one Gilbert Cogan had come to the house of the Grey Friars to warn him that he should beware how he testified, for "there should come 400 that should testify the contrary." [30]

Latimer's partisans were more efficient. Under the leadership of one John Drews, they had prepared two "books" or bills [31] alleging three articles against Hubberdin—that he had said there were twenty or thirty heretics in Bristol, that he had said that anyone who spoke against the pope or his acts and ordinances was a heretic, and that he had criticized the appointment of bishops by the crown. To each article were affixed numerous signatures. At the foot of one of the bills is the statement that 126 persons had signed, but someone (I suspect it was a suspicious member of the commission) added the note, "44 little more or less, for some be written three or four times." Actually, forty-three separate names appear.

The suspicions of the commissioners were aroused when they began to examine the persons whose names appeared on the bills. One Thomas Butler testified that he had heard Hubberdin say there were twenty or thirty heretics in Bristol, but had not heard him make the other statements attributed to him. And yet, said the commissioners, Butler's name was subscribed to the other two articles as well. Here we must exonerate Butler. The signature affixed to the other two bills is that of *Henry* Butler, not Thomas. But the commission was convinced that the testimony of the witnesses would not agree with the statements in the bills. Rather than protract the hearings, the commissioners voted not to take further testimony and agreed to the suggestion of John Drews that each witness be allowed to make a separate written statement. They recorded their suspicion, however, that Drews would take the opportunity to repair any flaws in the evidence.[32]

The tone of the report of the commissioners to Cromwell was by no means sympathetic to Latimer. It is clear that they believed that the evidence against Hubberdin had been fabricated. It is equally clear, however, that the commission knew the kind of evidence Cromwell wanted. They sent the bills and other evidence against Hubberdin to the council. As far as extant records show, they forwarded no formal statements by witnesses against Latimer. In the covering letter, to be sure, they specified the schismatic opinions with which witnesses had charged him; but no witnesses were named, and the chairman of the commission was careful to add, "for myself, I never heard him preach in Bristol, for I was then sick." [33]

Evidently Latimer's faction knew the commissioners' feelings and intentions, and felt that they should be forestalled. Accordingly, the mayor,

Bays, despatched a letter[34] to Cromwell by the hand of John Drews. After expressions of thanks to Cromwell for appointing a commission to look into Hubberdin's doings, Bays goes on to suggest that the commission has misused its authority, as Drews will report orally in greater detail. This letter is dated July 10, the day before the commission completed its hearings. Assuming the utmost dispatch all around, we may conclude that it reached Cromwell at least twenty-four hours before the arrival of the report of the commissioners.

In reporting these events, I have been careful to speak of the maneuverings of Bays and his friends as the work of "Latimer's faction" rather than of Latimer himself. There is no evidence to connect Latimer directly with the plot (if it was a plot) against Hubberdin; indeed there is no evidence that he was in Bristol after May 25. In all fairness, however, it must be pointed out that West Kington is only a few miles from Bristol; it is entirely possible that he was deeply involved. But such behavior would scarcely have been in character, and the devious activities of the mayor seem to have been designed to "get" Hubberdin rather than to save Latimer, who was never in any particular danger.

Poor Hubberdin had been thrown into the Tower on July 4, 1533. He was still there on July 6, 1535. During that period he wrote at least one plaintive letter to Cromwell, beseeching him to ponder the intentions of the "makers" who had testified against him and begging that he might have a copy of the charges so that he might prove that he "never preached such words nor sentences as hath been laid to my charge, as best knoweth God." [35] For a period during his imprisonment, Hubberdin's miseries were aggravated by the taunts of a Bristol man, a friend of the mayor, who was (for reasons not revealed) thrown into ward with Hubberdin and insisted upon debating with him upon matters of the faith.[36] I cannot find any evidence that Hubberdin was ever brought to trial. His name is not found in the records after July 6, 1535.[37] Except for Foxe's account, I should be inclined to guess that he died in the Tower.

Dr. Powell, Latimer's other principal opponent, managed to stay out of prison for a few months. In July, 1533, letters were sent from the King to the chancellor of Salisbury ordering him to send Powell to London. Powell was sick, but he promised to be with the King by August 18.[38] His alleged words at Bristol had been more offensive than Hubberdin's, and he had committed the additional indiscretion of writing a book against the divorce. Like More and Fisher, he refused to subscribe to the oath to the act of succession and was attainted of treason. He was cast in the Tower not later than June, 1534,[39] and there he remained until his execution in 1541.

Of all those who opposed Latimer at Bristol in 1533, only Dr. John Hilsey emerged with advantage to himself. He was called before the council and presumably was exculpated, although for a while Cranmer was hesitant about granting him a license to preach in the province of Canterbury.[40] But his new protestant views soon brought him into high favor with Cranmer and Cromwell; in 1534 he was one of Cromwell's commissioners to visit the friaries, and in 1535 he succeeded John Fisher as bishop of Rochester.

CHAPTER FOURTEEN

THE TIDE TURNS

The recorded facts of Latimer's career are probably as abundant as can reasonably be expected for a man of his station after a lapse of more than four centuries. Yet there are many hiatuses—silent years, unrecorded crises—which tease the biographer out of thought. One such crisis is adumbrated in a letter written to Latimer by George Joye just at the time the Bristol affair was at its height. Joye, a Cambridge contemporary of Latimer, was one of the most ardent of the first generation of English reformers. Late in 1527, rather than face a process for heresy, he had fled to the Continent. His collaboration and his later quarrels with William Tyndale are well-known, but the details have been imperfectly worked out. He was one of the strangest and most cantankerous of all the pioneers of the English reformation.[1]

Joye's letter [2] to Latimer, dated April 29, 1533, is primarily concerned with a question about which there was much contention among the reformers. When Luther denied the validity of prayers to the saints, he buttressed his argument by denying that the souls of the saints departed were in heaven; instead, he contended, they slept until the day of final judgment. Among the English reformers, John Frith followed Luther in this matter. Tyndale was on the fence. George Joye opposed. "The souls departed sleep not nor lie idle till Doomsday . . . I think that our souls departed live, and doubt not that the Scriptures so sound." Joye had written to this effect to an unknown correspondent in England. The letter (or its contents) came to the knowledge of John Frith, in prison awaiting his own last ordeal, who had written to Tyndale that Joye's views were likely to cause dissensions among the brethren. Tyndale, in turn, had undertaken the thankless task of trying to curb the intractable Joye.[3] Now Joye wrote to Latimer, asking for his views and indicating those passages of Scripture where the truth might be found. We do not have Latimer's answer, but if his Bristol sermons are an accurate guide to his thought at this time, the likelihood is that he sided with Joye.

But for Latimer's biographer the debate over the present status of the souls departed is not the center of interest. It is the latter part of the letter, with its casual allusion to things familiar to both writer and recipient, which suggests some significance now lost:

I would write unto you more, but this bearer goeth hastily hence and may not tarry me. God preserve you and pray for me. I forget you not, neither your good mind toward me. I was full sorry when I heard of that fire that ye suffered whereof Paul speaketh, I Cor. 3, to see your work burned before your face. But be of good cheer, Master Latimer. Paul suffered as great a burning as that when he saw his dull Galatians bewitched and borne back. God is mighty enough to bring them again, and to give you great glory and joy upon your children born and travailed so for again. Such is the chance and fortune of them that must play the pastors and leaders of Christ's unruly flocks. What suffered Moses of his own flock? And yet God brought all to a good end, and was glorified in him and his flock too. Write to my lord of Canterbury and animate him to his office. He is in a perilous place, but yet in a glorious place to plant the gospel. God preserve you.

I confess myself quite unable to find a satisfactory meaning in this intriguing passage. It should be said quickly that Joye evidently is not alluding to any physical "burning"—of books, of manuscripts, or of persons. The "fire" alluded to in I Corinthians 3 is the spiritual fire whereby the preaching of the apostle was tested—"If any man's work shall be burned, he shall suffer loss, but he himself shall be saved; yet so as by fire." The "dull Galatians bewitched and borne back" refers to St. Paul's concern for those Galatian Christians who seemed about to substitute a doctrine of justification by the works of the Jewish ceremonial law for the doctrine of justification by faith alone. Joye might seem therefore to be alluding to some person or persons converted by Latimer to the new religion who had lapsed back into their old beliefs. But this is unlikely. It is much more probable that the letter alludes, in terms veiled to us but perfectly clear to Joye and Latimer, to Latimer's troubles of 1532 and his abjuration before Convocation. The fact that a year had passed between the date of the abjuration and the date of Joye's letter need not present a difficulty, for communication was slow and Joye himself moved frequently from place to place.

Joye's letter, apart from the problems it poses, is of interest as suggesting the closeness of Latimer's relationship with the English reformers on the Continent, and of the importance which was generally attributed to his work. After the Bristol affair, his preaching was matter for discussion among all classes, both in England and abroad. One Robert Panmore was heard in an alehouse to call him a Lollard.[4] John Staunton, a monk, admitted in the confessional that his own orthodoxy had been shaken by Latimer's teaching.[5] Richard Morison, one of Henry's foreign agents, declared that in Latimer and Cranmer lay the only hope for pure religion in England.[6] Carlo Capello, in England on business, wrote to the Signory of Venice that although Latimer had recently stood his trial for heresy, he was now preaching freely against the Pope and the papal authority.[7] Chapuys, the representative of Charles V, wrote his master that there was one preacher—the reference can be only to Latimer—who disseminated more errors than Luther, and that all the bishops save Canterbury wished to have him punished. But, said Chapuys, he had the support of the King, who would long since have declared himself a Lutheran but for fear of a rising against him.[8]

The plain fact was that now more than ever before Henry VIII needed, or believed that he needed, the aid of the leaders of the reforming party. On July 12, after years of delay, the Pope had declared the validity of the King's marriage to Catherine. Henry was firmly determined to appeal the case to a general council of the Church. Meanwhile, the dangerous possibility of a coalition of the papacy, France, and the Empire against England nagged constantly at Henry's mind. As early as the autumn of 1533 he was putting out feelers to discover what support he might count on from the protestant rulers of the German states. He soon learned that in that quarter he was still the Defender of the Faith rather than the friend of the Reformation, and that the German princes had no zeal whatever for the task of pulling Henry's political chestnuts out of the fire. It was immediately desirable, therefore, that Henry should give some practical demonstration of his sympathy with the cause. Accordingly, Latimer and some others of his persuasion were allowed considerable latitude, from the summer of 1533 onward, in preaching without official interference. As a consequence, common gossip, both in official circles and on the streets of London, reported that Henry was on the verge of becoming a Lutheran. The rumor was an exaggeration. Latimer was safe only so long as he confined himself to the reform of abuses. No more than the Pope would Henry have tolerated radical innovations in matters of doctrine. At the very juncture when Latimer was enjoying great freedom, John Frith went to the fire at Smithfield for denying the sacrament of the altar.[9]

No doubt Archbishop Cranmer was largely responsible for the freedom allowed to Latimer during this period. It must have been in the summer of 1533 that he issued to Latimer a license permitting him to preach anywhere within the province of Canterbury. For several months Latimer was much out of his parish; however, his only recorded sermon for the latter half of 1533 was preached in the diocese of his old enemy, Stokesley of London. Earlier in the year, when the controversies at Bristol were at their height, Stokesley had issued an inhibition against Latimer and also a general inhibition against all unlicensed preaching in his diocese;[10] it is clear that Stokesley intended to permit no repetition of the kind of preaching that had occurred in St. Mary Abchurch in 1531. These inhibitions, however, were no deterrent to Latimer, now that he had Cranmer's license for the whole province of Canterbury. On October 3 he preached at the church of the Austin Friars within the city, with the knowledge and consent of George Brown, the prior. The next day Stokesley issued an inhibition against Latimer, whose "pernicious errors" were calculated "to corrupt and infect the people, and to seduce them from approved and received doctrine of the church." All parsons, curates, and vicars of the diocese, and all heads of religious houses, whether exempt or not, were enjoined not to open their pulpits to Latimer until such time as he had purged himself of heresy.[11] The requirement of purgation was a harmless display of pyrotechnics, since Stokesley was not Latimer's ordinary, and Convocation was not likely, at the moment, to back up Stokesley's accusations.

The nullity of Stokesley's action is amply demonstrated by the fact that almost immediately thereafter Latimer was officially employed in the investigation into the affairs of Elizabeth Barton, the Nun of Kent.[12] This ignorant, and perhaps half-mad, servant girl had prophesied, as early as 1526, that if Henry married Anne Boleyn he would lose his kingdom and die within six months. The government had ignored her, and when Henry's continued survival disproved her prophecy the whole episode might have been forgotten. In the meantime, however, her activities had been encouraged by some misguided priests of Canterbury, and she had entered the convent of St. Sepulchre, Canterbury, where she continued to experience ecstasies and visions of one kind or another. She had been interviewed and even encouragd by Archbishop Warham, Bishop Fisher, and Thomas More. In 1533 she announced that her prophecy concerning the king had not failed; Henry, like Saul, had been rejected of God, and was no true king. This was treason. When it was discovered that she was being used as a spearhead of disaffection by prominent personages hostile to Anne and sympathetic to Catherine and Princess Mary (both of whom had been in communication with her), the government determined to proceed against her.

Latimer probably figured only in the early stages of the investigation. Cranmer, Cromwell, and Latimer seem to have served as a commission to conduct the preliminary examination of the Nun and the four priests—Bocking, Rysby, Dering, and Gold—who had stage-managed her pronouncements. From this commission the investigation passed to Star Chamber, with consequences which are well known. In November the accused were required to confess their guilt at Paul's Cross. They were attainted of treason in March, 1534, and on April 20 were executed at Tyburn, the first of the Catholic martyrs of the reign of Henry VIII.

The activities of the Nun of Kent, and the delicate questions relative to the nature of her visions and the uses to which they were put by persons disaffected toward the government, are among the most fascinating problems of Tudor history. But they lie outside the scope of this study. The episode is significant to Latimer's career only in so far as his slight connection with it indicates that he was once more approaching the center of things.

During the height of the controversy at Bristol, Latimer had written to his friend Ralph Morice that he would welcome another opportunity to preach at court, in order that the King might hear for himself the soundness of his doctrine.[13] It was now more than three years since he had preached at Windsor. In the interval he had been called before Convocation and had been required to abjure; he had subsequently been involved in a nasty bit of controversy which had resulted in violence. In spite of all this, there were indications that for the present his preaching would be tolerated. But toleration was one thing, the King's active favor another. It was highly desirable that he should demonstrate to the King that he was safe as well as useful.

It is not clear whether the suggestion that Latimer preach at court during Lent, 1534, originated with Latimer himself or with Cranmer. Cranmer had been criticized severely (no doubt by Stokesley) for having issued to Latimer a preaching license for the whole province of Canterbury, and he was as anxious as his friend that the latter should have an opportunity to vindicate himself. At any rate, we first hear of the proposal in a letter addressed by Cranmer to Richard Sampson, the dean of the Chapel Royal.[14] In it Latimer is described as a man of virtuous life and a sincere preacher of God's word who has lately suffered great obloquy for his preaching, as has the Archbishop for having licensed him. Wherefore, at Cranmer's request, the King has agreed to have Latimer preach at court all the Wednesdays during Lent. Sampson was to make the necessary arrangements, even if another preacher had already been appointed. Latimer had already been instructed to prepare a course of sermons.

Sampson, a man of the old learning, received the order grumpily. He had served on the committee of Convocation which had examined Latimer two years earlier, and he regarded him as dangerous. He felt it necessary to warn Cranmer of the risks. In his reply [15] to the Archbishop's letter, he professed great admiration for Latimer's learning, but he feared his lack of moderation. Wherever Latimer preached there was great dissension. As for the Archbishop's license, Sampson hoped it had been issued only after due consideration of Latimer's recent history.

Although Sampson's professed admiration for Latimer's learning may have been a piece of hypocrisy, his criticism of Latimer's manner of preaching was well founded, as Cranmer very well knew. The Archbishop took the warning in good part. He sent off a long admonitory letter to Latimer.[16] First, in his sermons Latimer was to expound the Gospel, the Epistle, or some other passage of Scripture according to its true sense and meaning. Second, he was not to mention the troubles and quarrels in which he had been involved. He was to be judicious in his manner of speech, so that he should not seem to slander his adversaries. Finally, he was to limit his sermons to an hour, or an hour and a half at the most, lest the King and Queen wax weary at the beginning and have small delight at the end. It would be wise, the letter concludes, if Latimer would come up to London somewhat before Ash Wednesday, "here to prepare all things in a readiness"—which means, I presume, that Cranmer wanted the opportunity to go over the sermons in advance.

As on former occasions, the Lenten preaching was a mixed bag. Nicholas Shaxton, one of the Cambridge reformers and now the King's almoner, was also appointed to preach,[17] as was Dr. Rowland Philips, the vicar of Croydon, representing the old learning.[18] The sermons attracted much attention. Many of the most prominent divines of Oxford and Cambridge came up to hear Latimer and the others preach, and fear was expressed in some quarters that controversy might develop between Latimer and Philips.[19]

The situation was one to delight the theological facet of the King's mind. Had controversy arisen, he would have been happy to resolve it. But all went smoothly. The vicar of Croydon was already in difficulties over the Act of Succession,[20] and it may be presumed that he had no wish to plunge into deeper waters. Latimer for once restrained himself. It was reported that his sermons were very well liked.[21] Probably he followed Cranmer's advice to limit himself to the exposition of Scripture, a function which he could perform effectively when he chose to do so. At any rate, Henry was pleased with his sermons. Latimer justified Cranmer's confidence in him. His availability for high office in the new Anglican hierarchy had been demonstrated, and he was marked out for speedy promotion.

During this Lent of 1534 occurred an episode which it is difficult to assess. While in London, Latimer was lodged with his friend the Archbishop at Lambeth Palace. He was apparently among the group of priests at Lambeth who on April 13 subscribed without demur to the oath of the Act of Succession, the last step in Henry VIII's defiance to the authority of Rome. Rowland Philips subscribed on that day, as did the doctors and chaplains attached to Archbishop Cranmer's staff. The only layman to whom the oath was put on this occasion was Sir Thomas More, who had come by barge from Chelsea at the summons of the King's commissioners. More declined to subscribe. His refusal posed a problem, and the commissioners needed time for discussion. Accordingly, wrote More to his daughter Margaret Roper, "I was . . . commanded to go down into the garden, and thereupon I tarried in the old burned chamber that looketh into the garden and would not go down because of the heat. In that time I saw Master Doctor Latimer come into the garden, and there walked he with divers other doctors and chaplains of my lord of Canterbury, and very merry I saw him, for he laughed, and took one or twain about the neck so handsomely, that if they had been women, I would have weened he had been waxen wanton." [22]

What are we to make of More's description of this scene in the gardens of Lambeth? Does it represent a genuine suspicion on More's part of an abnormality in Latimer's constitution? Or is it merely the ironic musing of one who knew that his own refusal, a few minutes earlier, to subscribe the oath to the Act of Succession would ultimately cost him his life, and who therefore had little patience with the frolickings of a man who, in More's opinion, had just compromised with his conscience? In one way or another More and Latimer had probably seen a good deal of each other. We know that Latimer had little love for More.[23] More's account of the episode at Lambeth, whatever its final implications may be, indicates that the feeling was reciprocal.

In June of 1534 Latimer preached at Exeter under circumstances which bordered on the dramatic. The story is preserved for us in the papers of John Hooker, the Exeter antiquary.[24] According to Hooker, Latimer was sent by the King to preach at Exeter. He preached first in the churchyard of the Grey Friars. Although rain began to fall while he was preaching, the audience stayed on, some because they were fascinated with either the eloquence or the doctrine, others because they hoped to detect heresy. When the preacher became so vehement that his nose began to bleed, his opponents saw in this a sign of God's vengeance. In the end, the friars banned him from further preaching, but not before their warden had been converted to the new doctrines. This warden was no less a person than the celebrated John Cardmaker, who was himself to be martyred in the reign of Queen Mary.[25]

Latimer next preached, according to Hooker, in the parish church of St. Mary Major. The clergy of the church objected, since it was a holy day with high mass and a procession around the parish, but Latimer insisted that the King's commission be obeyed. The church was packed for the sermon, and those who were unable to get in broke the church windows in order to hear the preacher. "The auditory was marvelous great and attentive," says Hooker, except for a disturbance by one Thomas Carew, Esquire. About the middle of the sermon, Carew "approached and drew near the pulpit and there breathed out his intemperate speeches against the preacher, calling him heretic knave, and bade him come down or else he would (as he deeply swore) pull him by the ears, and do to him I cannot tell what. Nevertheless the good man proceeded and made an end to his sermon."

About this time, Latimer was appointed one of the King's chaplains.[26] All signs indicate that he was now in a position of considerable influence. Upon his recommendations, Cranmer issued preaching licenses to a number of men of the reforming party. When it became necessary to issue an injunction to the clergy against public denunciations of the King's matrimony, Latimer was charged by Cranmer with the task of administering the injunction to those for whose licenses he had been responsible.[27] Over in the west country, he took an active interest in the problem of administering the oath to the Act of Succession to those disaffected conservatives to whom Anne was the King's whore rather than the queen of England. He was especially anxious that all gentlemen of lands and arms should stand up and be counted. His earliest extant letter to Cromwell, written in the spring or summer of 1534, is a recommendation that the names of those who had taken the oath should be registered (as had been done with the members of both houses of Parliament) so that it might be surely known who had sworn and who had not.[28]

A none too reliable authority records also Latimer's labors on behalf of the Act of Supremacy, and brings him for the first time into close association with Stephen Gardiner, Foxe's "Wily Winchester." Gardiner, in 1531, had voted without protest in support of Convocation's acknowledgment of the King as supreme head of the English church "as far as the law of Christ allows." He had also been among the first to subscribe to the oath to the Act of Succession. But Gardiner boggled when the Act of Supremacy, which made the former action of Convocation the law of the land and legally completed the separation of the English church from Rome, was introduced into Parliament in the autumn of 1534. Bishop Thirlby later said that Gardiner opposed the measure until the very moment of its passage, and it was probably on this account that for a period of several months Gardiner suffered the loss of royal favor. In the end, however, Gardiner saw his way clear; he was the first of the bishops, after the two archbishops, to sign the formal renunciation of the jurisdiction of the papal see.[29]

Although the nature and extent of Gardiner's opposition to the Act of Supremacy is clouded, there does survive a document which makes certain interesting assertions about it. This is a long series of verses (of no poetic merit whatever) written about 1547 by one William Palmer. The only known copy is a manuscript preserved in the library of Trinity College, Cambridge.[30] Palmer, the author, was as bitterly hostile to Gardiner as was John Foxe, and his assertions must be accepted only with great caution. With respect to the Act of Supremacy, he asserts that Gardiner labored "plainly" against the act, and that at length the King sent Latimer to reason with him. In the course of a long discussion, Gardiner, a canonist, found himself no match for Latimer's theology. But Gardiner still proved stubborn, and in the end the council required him to make a public profession of allegiance and acknowledge the King's supremacy at Paul's Cross. Thus, to his great humiliation, he was proved "Doctor Ignorance" in the hearing of all.

It is difficult to believe that any such profession by Gardiner at Paul's Cross would have gone unrecorded by the chroniclers or by John Foxe, to whom it would have given special delight. On the other hand, Gardiner's determined opposition to the supremacy is confirmed by the testimony of Thirlby. What of the story of Latimer's action on the King's behalf? There is nothing improbable about it. In any case, the significance of the story does not lie in the specific fact, but in its clear implication that in the matter of the supremacy, as in the divorce and the succession, Latimer followed the King's line and perhaps the King's bidding.

By the middle of January, 1535, rumors were abroad that Latimer was slated for a bishopric.[31] Meanwhile rumors of another kind were being circulated by those who hoped to block his promotion. Latimer, it was reported, had "turned the leaf"; on the Wednesday of Ember Week, in a sermon at court before the King, he had declared that the Pope was the highest authority on earth; if the Pope had erred in the matter of the divorce, he should be corrected by a general council, not by the King. Further, Latimer was reported to have said that prayers to Our Lady and the saints were most necessary and that pilgrimages were most acceptable to Almighty God. Interestingly enough, it is possible to trace some of the history of this rumor. It began with Walter Wadland, of Needham Market, a justice of the peace for Suffolk and a stubborn opponent of the new learning.[32] Wadland's intention, evidently, was that this preposterous story might discredit Latimer with his followers in that region. With the speed of all such rumors, it came to one Richard Clotton, servant to Lord Sandys the lord chamberlain. Clotton passed it on to Thomas Fowler, one of the King's gentleman ushers,[33] whence it passed to Sir John Wallop, the King's ambassador in France, whence it passed to Lord Lisle at Calais.[34] This is the direct line of progress; we can only surmise how the rumor fanned out laterally as it advanced. Fortunately the story died of its own absurdity. Latimer suffered no harm from it, but the King was annoyed with Lord Sandys for the latter's share in its dissemination.[35]

While this bit of comedy was running its course, the tyranny which followed so closely upon the Act of Supremacy had begun. In April, John Houghton, the prior of the Charterhouse, and the other Carthusians refused to acknowledge the supremacy. On May 4 they were executed at Tyburn, in their priest's habits, with no previous degradation. Shortly thereafter, as proof that heresy was still as offensive as rebellion, a group of Dutch Anabaptists suffered the same fate. On May 20 Bishop Fisher was elevated to the purple by Pope Paul III; on June 22 he went to the block on Tower Hill. He was followed a month later by Sir Thomas

More, the greatest and most tragic of the Catholic martyrs.

Henry, mindful of his fences, began in the summer of 1535 his formal negotiations for a league with the protestant states of Germany. That the negotiations failed was unquestionably due in large measure to the justifiable suspicion on the part of the Germans that Henry lacked any genuine sympathy with their position. To allay this suspicion Henry promoted four prominent reformers to the episcopal bench. Nicholas Shaxton went to Salisbury, William Barlow to St. Asaph's, John Hilsey to Rochester in succession to Fisher. Hugh Latimer got the see of Worcester.

Latimer's preferment to a bishopric was the reward for services rendered and to be rendered. For six years he had followed the line laid down by the King. The question naturally arises whether or not, during this stage of his career, he was a timeserver, with a quick eye for the main chance. Certainly he shared the average man's reasonable ambition for advancement, and he was quite aware that advancement could come only by the King's favor. On the other hand, he was a distinguished advocate of reform, but not of doctrinal change, long before the question of the divorce arose. Like most of the reformers, he probably believed that the separation of England from the papal jurisdiction would result in the fruition of much that he hoped for. It is not quite fair, as some recent writers have done, to contrast Latimer's compliancy with the fine intransigency of More and Fisher. They died for a cause in which Latimer did not believe. It is much more to the point to compare his conduct, with respect to motive, with that of men like Tunstall and Stokesley and Gardiner, who believed with More but voted with the King. The ancient figure of the oak and the ivy is not without validity. But it is important to realize that there are intermediate degrees of pliancy.

CHAPTER FIFTEEN

BISHOP OF WORCESTER

Since 1497 the diocese of Worcester had had a succession of Italian bishops—Giovanni de Gigli, Silvestro de Gigli, Julio de Medici, and Jerome Ghinucci—who represented the interests of Henry VII and Henry VIII at Rome and whose reward was the revenue of the diocese. The revenues of Salisbury were put to a similar use. When the Act of Supremacy was passed in 1534, Ghinucci had been bishop of Worcester for twelve years; Lorenzo Campeggio, the papal legate who was sent to England to take testimony in the King's "great matter," had been bishop of Salisbury for ten. The dioceses thus ruled *in absentia* by their Italian bishops were probably managed neither better nor worse than those presided over by Englishmen.[1] Except for occasional visitations, most of the bishops were kept from their ecclesiastical domains over long periods by reason of their membership in Parliament and Convocation, and by their varied services to the government at home or abroad. During the absence of the bishop the spiritual functions of the diocese—ordinations, confirmations, and the like—were performed by the suffragan or suffragans; legal affairs were under the control of the bishop's vicar-general; the management of the temporalities was entrusted to lay supervisors who collected the rents and other income and passed them along to the bishop's agent in London. The efficiency or inefficiency of the system depended upon those to whom authority was delegated. The system unquestionably minimized the spiritual functions of the episcopate, but the fault lay chiefly with the Crown, which used the bishoprics as the means of supporting its principal statesmen and diplomatists.

One of the immediate consequences of the separation of England from the Roman obedience was that Ghinucci and Campeggio, no longer of any use at Rome, were deprived of the sees of Worcester and Salisbury. As is the case when a bishop dies, the temporalities were seized by the Crown—that is, the revenues were paid into the royal treasury until the new bishop formally acceded. Rumors that Nicholas Shaxton, the King's almoner and one of the most advanced reformers, would get Salisbury and that Latimer would get Worcester were afloat as early as January, 1535.[2] But Henry moved slowly. Shaxton became bishop of Salisbury in April, but Latimer had to wait until October before all the legalities attendant upon his promotion were completed.

Tradition has portrayed Latimer as a man who, had he been free to follow his own inclination, would gladly have said *"Noló episcopari."* It is true that his four years' tenure of Worcester left him disenchanted with the attractions of a Henrician bishopric; when he was free of the office he is said to have skipped for joy. Some writers believe that in 1549 he declined restoration to the see of Worcester.[3] But in 1535 he was as gratified as any other ambitious churchman by the prospect of his elevation to the bench of bishops, and he was extremely impatient under the delays which postponed his consecration and withheld his revenues.

Latimer's appointment to Worcester followed the form which had been prescribed by law after the Act of Supremacy. Early in August, 1535, the King sent his name to the prior and convent of the cathedral church at Worcester (Worcester did not acquire a dean and chapter until 1540), along with the *congé d'élire* which conferred upon them the right—in practice, the obligation—to elect the King's nominee. On August 20 the election took place in due order, and the royal assent was prepared for Henry's signature and transmission to the archbishop,[4] who could not consecrate until the assent had been received. But Henry withheld his formal assent until Latimer could make satisfactory arrangements for his first-fruits—that is, the payment in advance of the first year's income from the bishopric, which had formerly gone to Rome but now went by law to the Crown. Latimer was at first unable to raise the money. The King, on his part, showed no inclination to be lenient. On September 2 John Gostwyck, one of the commissioners for rating ecclesiastical preferments, wrote to Cromwell that Latimer had become a "hot suitor" in the matter;[5] and two days later Harry Polsted, another commissioner, wrote that Latimer intended to try to persuade the King to allow him to be his own surety for the first-fruits.[6] On the same day Latimer himself wrote to Cromwell that he had been dissuaded from this intention by Queen Anne, who reminded him that a similar proposal by Shaxton had been coldly rejected by the King.[7]

In the end, it was Anne who paid. Whatever her true character may have been, Anne Boleyn was a firm friend of the reformation in various ways, and not least in the practical means by which she assisted some of the reformers to their bishoprics. In April, 1535, she had advanced £200 of her private funds to Nicholas Shaxton to enable him to pay his first-fruits. Now in September she advanced a like amount to Latimer for the same purpose. The inescapable conclusion is that she had more interest and confidence in these appointments than had her royal husband. Her generous loans to Shaxton and Latimer were not repaid during her lifetime; two months after her execution the loans were still listed among the assets of her estate.[8] Henry's known character is sufficient warrant for believing that the debts were ultimately satisfied.

Once his first-fruits were paid, Latimer's affairs proceeded smoothly. On Monday, September 26, 1535, Edward Fox, elect of Hereford; Hugh Latimer, elect of Worcester; and John Hilsey, elect of Rochester, were consecrated in that order at Winchester.[9] Archbishop Cranmer presided; Gardiner of Winchester and Shaxton of Salisbury were the coconsecrators. On October 4, the King at Westminster signed the deed recording that Hugh Latimer, his 'beloved and faithful chaplain," had been duly elected, confirmed, and consecrated. The escheator in the county of Worcester was ordered to deliver the temporalities of the diocese to the bishop-elect.[10] Thus, after weeks of delay, Latimer entered into his reward.

Latimer was well acquainted with the diocese over which he was called to preside; his old parish of West Kington lay just outside its southern border. The diocese was then much larger than it is today; it included the important towns of Worcester, Gloucester, and Bristol, as well as smaller but equally well-known places like Tewkesbury, Warwick, and Stratford-on-Avon. The bishop held title to several "palaces" or residences in addition to the manors and farms from which he derived the greater part of his income. His principal residence was Hartlebury, on the banks of the Severn near Kidderminster, which a little after Latimer's time was described as "a fair manor place" with a moat and a fish pond. He had another residence at Worcester (now the deanery), and others at Alvechurch and at Kempsey on the Severn towards Tewkesbury. Of these, Latimer seems to have made use principally of Hartlebury, although he is said to have restored the house at Alvechurch. The Bishop's London residence was Stroud Place, which was later demolished to make way for Somerset House.[11]

The revenues of Worcester were small in comparison with those of such wealthy sees as London or Winchester. Still, the Bishop's income was considerable. In 1533, two years before Latimer's accession, the income from the spiritualities was £1,049.19s., from the temporalities £979.18s.[12] and this is easily equivalent to £100,000 in the money of our own day. But Latimer never received the full income, and he had difficulty in making ends meet. A letter written to Cromwell on Christmas Eve, 1538, when he had been bishop a little more than three years, tells the story:

> All manner of my receipts, since I was bishop, amounts to four thousand pounds and upward. My first-fruits, reparations, and solutions of my debts, amounts to seventeen hundred pounds. There remaineth in ready money now at my last audit, ending upon Christmas even's even, nine score pounds; of the which, five score pound and five is payable forth withal, for my tenths of this year, other twenty goeth to my new year's gift, and so I have left to myself, to keep my Christmas withal, and to come up [to London] withal, three score pounds. All the rest is spent; if well, that is my duty; if otherwise, that is my folly . . . . It is spent, I say, saving that I have provision for household, in wheat, malt, beeves, and muttons, as much as would sustain my house this half year and more, if I should not go forth of my diocese: and in this standeth much the stay of my house; for I am more inclined to feed many grossly and necessarily, than a few deliciously and voluptuously . . . . as you have always been my good lord, so I desire you to continue, and to take this rude signification of my condition for a new year's gift, and a poor token of my good will toward you, for this time. Another year, and I live, it shall be better; for, I thank my Lord God, I am within forty pounds out of debt, which doth lighten my heart not a little. And shortly cometh on my half-year's rent; and then I shall be afloat again, and come clean out of debt.[13]

This statement is no doubt substantially accurate; Cromwell would have easily detected any gross error. At the beginning of his episcopacy Latimer's position must have been much worse than in 1538, and it is easy to believe Foxe's story that his new year's gift to the King in 1536 was limited to a napkin, although we are at liberty to doubt Foxe's assertion that the napkin was embroidered with a posy reading *"Fornicatores et adulteros judicabit Dominus."*[14]

What manner of bishop was Latimer? The traditional view has turned him into a Victorian prelate of evangelical cast, the shepherd of his flock, concerned chiefly with his diocese, preaching, confirming, admonishing, correcting. But we must remember the probable terms of his commission. Although he was not intended to be a political bishop in the old sense, still he was appointed to serve the national rather than the purely diocesan interest. He was to act as one of the party whips in Parliament and Convocation. As the foremost preacher and popularizer of his day, he was also to proclaim from the pulpits of the land so much of the reformed religion as suited King Henry's purposes at the moment. Such time as remained after the performance of these functions might be devoted to the administration of his diocese.

As far as the extant records indicate, Latimer did not go into his diocese until October, 1536, a year after his consecration. The records are admittedly scant, and he may have made one or more flying visits, but unquestionably he was in London for meetings of Parliament or Convocation during most of this first year. He can be placed in London again during large parts of 1537, 1538, and 1539. As far as it is possible to reconstruct a log of his activities during the forty-five months of his bishopric, it appears he spent about fifteen of those months in his diocese, the remaining thirty in London or elsewhere.

There is no way of knowing how efficiently the diocese was administered during those forty-five months. Only a fragment of a register survives,[15] but the mere absence of records has little significance. Probably the administration continued to function much as it had under Bishop Ghinucci. The same lay supervisors would continue to manage the business affairs. Andrew Whitmay, bishop of Chrysopolis *in partibus infidelium,* continued to act as suffragan, as he had done since 1526 and as he continued to do for two years after Latimer's resignation.[16] In 1538, an additional suffragan was appointed. Dr. Thomas Bagarde, who had been appointed vicar-general of the diocese in 1532, continued to act as chancellor of the diocesan courts; apparently he was an efficient administrator, for, in spite of his preference for the old learning, Latimer gave him the rectory of Ripple in Worcestershire when that living fell vacant in 1536.[17] One or two other diocesan offices continued to be occupied by holdovers from the days of Latimer's predecessors.[18]

In spite of his long periods of absence, Latimer was at great pains to foster the spirit of the new doctrines in his diocese. The earliest instance of this occurs within three months of his institution, in connection with the appointment of a new prior of St. Mary's, Worcester, which since the tenth century had been the cathedral church. For years there had been protests from within against the administration of the old prior William Moore, who had presided over Latimer's election as bishop; in January, 1536, he had been removed or forced to resign. As a pension he was granted the income from one of the priory's manors. In addition, he received an outright gift of 1,000 marks, and a monk had been assigned to serve him and say mass. Obviously he had been well taken care of. But pressure was put upon the King to reinstate him, and Henry, moved by pity, was disposed to do so. Moore was of the old learning, and Latimer firmly opposed his reinstatement. He wrote to Cromwell that, in the pension and the gift, pity for Moore had gone far enough. The Prior's administrative crimes were great. He had been inadequate for his duties; now that he was old and feeble it would be folly to restore him.[19] Fortunately for Latimer, the appointment went to Henry Holbeach, formerly a monk of Crowland and a Cambridge D.D., who subsequently proved a strong right arm to Latimer in putting down "superstition" in the diocese.[20]

A further instance of Latimer's concern for the promotion of the new religion is to be seen in his selection of chaplains. He chose men of known reforming zeal and assigned them to preach frequently in the diocese. Four of these chaplains are named as such in Latimer's letters or elsewhere. One of them, surnamed Bennett, seems to have no recorded history, but his religious coloration is indicated by the charge that on one occasion at Gloucester he preached that if "purgatory priests" were to pray until their tongues were worn to stumps it would not release a single soul from purgatory.[21] Another, called in the records simply Master Garrett or Garrard, was probably the famous Thomas Garrett who in 1528 had been an active disseminator of heretical books in London and Oxford.[22] The identity of the other two chaplains is certain. Dr. Rowland Taylor, a Cambridge D.D., was subsequently domestic chaplain to Archbishop Cranmer, later still a devoted parish priest, and suffered martyrdom under Mary. Rodolf Bradford we have already heard of as being implicated in Latimer's troubles of 1528. Latimer seems to have appointed him to a chaplaincy immediately upon his own elevation.[23]

In Bradford and Holbeach, the prior of Worcester, Latimer seems to have had particular confidence. He promoted Bradford to a benefice in 1536,[24] and in 1537 exerted his influence to secure Holbeach's appointment to preach at court during the following Lent.[25] When he felt the need of an additional suffragan he sent the names of both Bradford and Holbeach to the King for consideration.[26] The choice fell upon Holbeach, who was consecrated with title of Bristol at Lambeth on March 24, 1538. He proved a man of genuine ability. When the priory of St. Mary's Worcester was suppressed in 1540 he became dean of the newly established cathedral chapter. In 1544 he was instituted as bishop of Rochester, and in 1547 he was translated to Lincoln, where he remained until his death in 1551.[27] Bradford, the unsuccessful nominee, seems to have died at Worcester before the end of Latimer's episcopate.

It has often been asserted that Worcester was one of the most backward dioceses in the kingdom. This opinion is based partly upon the old view, now generally discredited, that the diocese must have been badly administered during the reigns of its Italian bishops, and partly upon assertions by Bishops Latimer and Hooper concerning the ignorance of the clergy. Latimer's statement that the curates were intolerably negligent, ignorant, and superstitious was the opening gambit in his effort to impose the new learning upon his diocese, and must not be taken too literally.[28] Hooper's charge was more specific. In 1551, as bishop of Gloucester (a diocese which was carved out of Worcester in 1541), he alleged that of 311 clerks examined during his visitation, ten (3.1%) could not say the Lord's Prayer, thirty (9.6%) could not name its author, 170 (54.6%) could not repeat the commandments, and over two hundred (67%) could not cite Scripture in support of the articles of the Creed.[29] This proportion of ignorance would be shocking if discovered among the clergy of today. It is less so for the sixteenth century. In any case, similar statistics might have been compiled for any other diocese in the realm; there is no reason to believe that the clergy of Worcester were either more or less ignorant than those elsewhere.

What is unquestionably true, however, is that in Worcester, as in most other dioceses, a very considerable portion of both clergy and laity—probably a clear majority—were devoted to the old religion. Since Latimer was conspicuously of the new, there was plenty of hostility to him in his diocese. Some of the more overt expressions of this hostility provoked disciplinary action and thus were written into the public records. Unfortunately the details of these factional quarrels tell us little about Latimer, but they are revealing of the tactics used in local engagements in the long warfare between the old doctrines and the new. As we review the evidence, we must make due allowance for heated tempers, and remember that all the testimony, on both sides, has undergone a considerable amount of partisan refraction.

Opposition to the Bishop, much of it expressed in terms of unseemly abuse, came from both laity and clergy. Thus at Northfield, near Birmingham, one Harry Norton, a layman, denounced Latimer as a "Lollard whoreson" and declared he would gladly carry a fagot seven miles to burn him. He added—so witnesses testified—that he had it from no less an authority than the King's falconer that Latimer's preaching was contrary to the King's wishes, and that the said falconer wondered why the people of Worcester did not pull the Bishop out of his palace. For these exuberant utterances Norton was confined for seven weeks in the Bishop's prison. He later contended that his accusers had a grudge against him over a matter of property, and that Latimer, upon learning the truth, had let him go and had made him and his opponents drink together. Six months after his first offense, however, he was in jail again, on the same charge, except that this time he was said to have offered to carry the fagot sixteen miles instead of seven.[30] Another episode occurred at Kidderminster, where a tailor named Miles Denison—a notorious drunkard, according to witnesses—broke out in furious denunciations of Latimer and his chaplains. The trouble arose when one of the chaplains preached a long "sermon of the New Learning" at high mass; Denison's friends refused to drink with him until mass and sermon were concluded, and his thirst ran away with his discretion.[31]

More disgraceful, if correctly reported, was the conduct of Richard Cornewall, a priest whom Latimer had rebuked for living openly with a concubine. Cornewall denied Latimer's authority to admonish him, saying that the rightful bishop of Worcester (that is, the deposed Ghinucci) was at Rome. He added that he had "set his wench by the bishop's nose," that "if he would marry with her the bishop would be contented that he tilted up her tail in every bush," and that "there ought no man to sit in judgment after he is once suspected in heresy till such time they have made their purgation." [32] Cornewall's objectionable words were spoken just after Christmas, 1537. Just at that time Latimer wrote to Cromwell about an "unpriestly priest, whose damsel was brought to bed alate, not without offense of many; and of another priest also, as lewd as he, of the same town, which hath defiled a young girl alate, of thirteen years of age, and burnt her almost to death." The next sentence in the letter indicates that by this time Latimer was firmly convinced that priests should be permitted to marry—"O unholy and also unchaste chastity, which is preferred in a Christian realm to chaste and holy matrimony." [33] It is highly probable that Richard Cornewall was one of the unnamed priests alluded to in this letter, for in a letter of June, 1538, Latimer specifically mentioned "Master Cornwell and his pretty doing." [34]

One of the principal centers of opposition to Latimer was at Bristol, where from time to time quarrels continued to erupt between the Lollard faction which had supported Latimer in 1533 and the conservatives who had imported Drs. Powell and Hubberdin to oppose him.[35] The commission of laymen which had been appointed to hear the testimony in that controversy continued to function, and their reports to the King and council supply us with the details of attacks upon the Bishop in 1536 and 1537. We learn from those reports that "bills" slandering Latimer and the government were posted in public places at Bristol. It was even charged that some of these were set up by an agent of Reginald Pole, who had recently been created a cardinal by the Pope and who in the popular mind was a symbol of the opposition to the government and its policies. We learn of slanderous attacks upon Latimer in sermons preached by John Kene at Christ Church, Bristol, and by John Rawlins at St. Awence, Bristol. Laymen echoed the words of the preachers. One Henry Jones, a tailor, called the Bishop a false heretic. William Glaskedian, a pewterer, said, "A vengeance on him! I would he had never been born. I trust to see him burned ere I die." Kene, Rawlins, Jones, and Glaskedian were all imprisoned briefly for their indiscretions. The commission's reports are taken up almost entirely with the sayings of Latimer's opponents. But their summary of a sermon by one of his supporters indicates that neither faction had a monopoly on scurrility. In Lent of 1537, Prior William Oliver of the Friars Preachers, an adherent of the new doctrines, declared that a shipload of friars' girdles or a dung cart full of monks' cowls would not avail for justification, and he went on to defend the Bishop against his detractors.[36]

The town of Gloucester was another center of hostility toward Latimer. The mayor said publicly, at the High Cross, "Well, my lord [i.e., Latimer] may be an honest man, but it is much unlike, for he keeps none but heretic knaves about him." In his own house, when the abbot of St. Peter's Gloucester was his guest, the mayor called Latimer a heretic; as a result, he was often invited to dine with the delighted abbot and the monks.[37] But the leader of the opposition to Latimer was not the mayor, but the sheriff, Thomas Bell. Bell was a consequential person, not only in Gloucester, but also in London, where he maintained a house and enjoyed the friendship of such personages as John Stokesley, the bishop of London, and William Kingston, the constable of the Tower. Through them he was able to make his weight felt with members of the parliament and with no less a person than the duke of Norfolk, Thomas Howard, the powerful antagonist of Cromwell.

We first hear of Bell's animus towards Latimer from a letter which he wrote to Stokesley on June 9, 1536.[38] This was the very day of Latimer's famous Convocation sermon,[39] and the letter must have reached Stokesley at a moment when he was prepared to give it the most sympathetic attention. The burden of Bell's discontent was with the radicals whom Latimer had licensed to preach in the diocese. He had licensed not only his chaplains, Masters Garrett and Bennett, who were bad enough, said Bell, but also certain ill-living priests whose conduct was notorious in the diocese.[40] On the other hand, said Bell, the Bishop had refused to license many learned D.D.'s and B.D.'s of the diocese because their doctrine was contrary to his own. Bell's letter concluded with the suggestion that Stokesley, with the support of the duke of Norfolk, might be able to correct the situation in the diocese of Worcester. A few months later Bell was able to boast that he had "trimmed the bishop and his chaplains and had preferred his bill to my lord of Norfolk and to the parliament house, and that he had so handled them that none of his chaplains durst in manner come to Gloucester." [41]

For months Bell was loud and insistent in his denunciations of Latimer. At his house in London, in the presence of divers men of worship in the city, he openly called Latimer by such terms as "heretic," "whoreson heretic," and the like. So confident was he of the strong support of the bishop of London and the duke of Norfolk that he discarded all caution, and spoke these or similar words in the presence of many whose sympathies were with Latimer.[42]

Bell's opposition to Latimer seems to have reached a climax early in 1537, when he and his faction managed to secure the removal of Hugh Rawlins as curate of the church of the Holy Trinity in Gloucester. In this maneuver they seem to have been aided and abetted by John Bell, the archdeacon of Gloucester. Rawlins was evidently of Latimer's party, but the charges against him refer not to his doctrine but to alleged misdemeanors and negligences in the performance of his parochial duties. Rawlins' friends rallied to his defense, and in the end he was restored to his place at Holy Trinity. During the quarrel, Thomas Bell, the sheriff, seems to have defied both Cromwell and Latimer, with the result that he was summoned to London to account for his behavior before Cromwell. We do not know how Cromwell finally disposed of the case, but in the records we hear no more of Bell's opposition to the Bishop.[43]

No doubt it would be a mistake to attach too much significance to these manifestations of opposition to Latimer. Certainly he had many warm friends and admirers, as well as enemies, in his diocese. But the undercurrents of opposition to the reformation were strong and deep. In the diocese of Worcester, where the Bishop was an outspoken leader of the cause of reform, it was inevitable that quarrels should erupt more violently and more frequently than in most other parts of England.

CHAPTER SIXTEEN

THE BISHOP OF WORCESTER AND THE PROGRESS OF DOCTRINE

During his short reign over the diocese of Worcester, Latimer was pretty much in the thick of national affairs. In the Lords and in the upper house of Convocation he was an important member of the government party, the party which was dominated by Cromwell and the King. He participated, somewhat uneasily, in theological deliberations which were significant in the history of the Church of England, if not in the religious life of the English people. At Paul's Cross and elsewhere, he was one of the government's foremost pulpit propagandists. As a result of his close involvement in weighty affairs, this period is the most fully documented of his career.

For almost a year after his consecration, Latimer was in London. Occasionally we catch glimpses of him engaged in the routine details of the work in which his new office involved him. Thus in February, 1536, he acted for Archbishop Cranmer in the matter of censoring and licensing books.[1] In the following month he served with Cranmer and Shaxton in the examination of one Dr. Creukehorne, a priest who claimed to have had visions of the Blessed Virgin and the Holy Trinity.[2] A few days later the same three prelates examined John Lambert, an old Cambridge friend of all of them. Lambert, whose advanced views had got him into trouble with Archbishop Warham in 1532, was now charged by the duke of Norfolk and other conservatives with having preached that prayer to the saints was sinful. According to the curate of St. Margaret Lothbury, who was merely retailing gossip, the bishops instructed Lambert that prayer to the saints was unnecessary but not sinful, and Latimer handled him with particularly severity.[3]

One other brief notice of Latimer must belong to the first weeks or months of his bishopric. It is more personal than these others, and places him close to the center of things. This is the story, in the recently discovered account of Anne Boleyn, written by the younger William Latimer, that Hugh Latimer and Nicholas Shaxton, his brother of Salisbury, often dined at the Queen's table, and that from time to time King Henry joined them to debate points of doctrine.[4] For the moment, the bishops must have felt at ease in Zion. Of the four at dinner, only Henry could have suspected that within a few weeks Anne would go to the block on Tower Hill.

Latimer sat in the Lords for the first time when the Parliament reconvened on February 4, 1536. This was to be the last session of the Reformation Parliament, and the Lords' Journal indicates that the Bishop of Worcester was in regular attendance at its debates. The most important legislation of this session was the act for the suppression of the smaller

111

religious houses; indeed, as we can now see, it was the most revolutionary legislation enacted by any English parliament prior to the twentieth century. Latimer was an important member of the narrow majority which carried the measure through the Lords; the long story of his share in it, and of his subsequent attitude towards the dissolution, will be considered in the next chapter.

One matter that came before Parliament in the last days of this session was unquestionably close to Latimer's heart. This had to do with the universities. In the preceding year, Dr. Richard Layton and Dr. Thomas Legh, acting in their capacities as principal visitors of the monasteries, had visited Oxford and Cambridge and issued injunctions for their reform. In part these injunctions represented the intention of the King to secure control of the revenues of the universities, but they were also, and more importantly, directed toward a drastic revision in the basic program of study.[5] The old textbooks, especially the *Sentences* of Peter Lombard, were forbidden, and the study of the Old and New Testaments was made obligatory. Thus the *coup de grâce* was administered to medieval scholasticism; Duns, as Dr. Layton said, was set in Bocardo. Lectureships in Latin, Greek, and Hebrew were established, and it was provided that exegesis upon the Scriptures should conform to the new learning rather than the old. Into the discard also went the study of the canon law. In all these reforms in the program of studies Latimer must have rejoiced, as he rejoiced also in Cambridge's prudent choice of Thomas Cromwell to be chancellor in succession to the martyred John Fisher. But the new program imposed additional financial burdens upon the universities, and in April, 1536, a bill designed to lighten the load was introduced into Parliament. By this measure, the universities were relieved from the obligation of paying first-fruits and tenths of the income from their spiritualities. In return, the colleges collectively in each university were required to appoint and pay a King Henry VIII lecturer in whatever language or other subject the King might direct. To this measure Latimer could give his whole-hearted support, since the preamble to the statute called attention to "the fervent zeal his majesty hath conceived and beareth . . . principally to the advancement of the sincere and pure doctrine of God's Word and Holy Testament," and added that the King would not "by any means hinder the advancement and setting forth the lively Word of God wherewith his people must be fed, nourished and instructed." [6]

These measures for the reform of the universities were the fruition of much that Latimer had hoped and worked for since that day in 1524 when he himself "began to smell the word of God, and forsook the school-doctors and such fooleries." But the royal injunctions did not work an instantaneous miracle. The conservatives, who were still in the majority at most of the colleges, bowed reluctantly to the King's will, and meantime sought to salvage as much as possible of the old learning. Upon the intransigents at his beloved Cambridge Bishop Latimer kept a watchful eye, and during the next two years he more than once addressed himself to Cromwell with a view to consolidating the gains which had already been made.

To that end, on July 15, 1537, he recommended the appointment of

George Day as master of St. John's—a recommendation which was followed and later backfired, for in the next reign Day proved but a feeble reed for the support of the new doctrine. In the same letter Latimer begged Cromwell to "remember poor Clare Hall, that the master [Dr. John Crayford] neither transgress the statute himself, nor yet bring into his room Mr. [Rowland] Swynbourne of the same house, a man, as they say, of perverse judgment, and too factious for such a cure." [7] Dr. Crayford, who in 1530 had succeeded Dr. Natares as master of Clare and was vice-chancellor for the years 1534-36, needed no prodding to keep him in the way of the reforms. But Swynbourne, who succeeded Crayford in 1539, proved so reactionary that he was removed from office during the reign of Edward VI.[8] Three weeks after writing this letter Latimer again admonished Cromwell with respect to St. John's and Clare, and added, "I can say no more but that all factions and affections be not yet exiled out of Cambridge: and yet my good lord, extend your goodness thereunto, forasmuch as you be their chancellor, that in your time they [the colleges themselves] be not trodden under foot." [9] Again, in May 1538, he prodded Cromwell with respect to both universities: "It were good you would sometimes send for masters of colleges in Cambridge and Oxford, with their statutes; and if the statutes be not good and to the furtherance of good letters, change them. If the masters be not good, but honourers of drawlatches, change them." [10] Clearly, as long as he occupied a position of influence Latimer kept vigil over Cambridge to see that there should be no retrogression.[11]

The act for promoting the new learning at Oxford and Cambridge was the final legislation of the Reformation Parliament, which adjourned *sine die* on April 14, 1536. The last act in the tragedy of Anne Boleyn began a few days later. Jane Seymour was already the acknowledged royal favorite when, on April 24, a commission was secretly formed to hear evidence against Anne. On May 17 she stood her trial for alleged adultery and conspiracy against the King's life; on the same day, the badgered and unhappy Archbishop Cranmer pronounced her marriage to Henry null and void. Two days later, beseeching Jesus "to save my sovereign and master, the king, the most godly, noble, and gentle prince that is," she knelt before the executioner in the Tower. In all this wretched conspiracy Latimer had no part. Nor has he left us any word of his feelings at Anne's death. She had been to him a most gracious sovereign lady. She has sponsored his promotion to a bishopric and had lent him money to pay his first-fruits and tenths. Apparently he was her favorite among the court preachers; he had often dined at her table. He had been her confessor, and probably gave her absolution on the eve of her death.[12] With her passing he lost his most influential friend at court. Never thereafter, as events were to prove, did he enjoy the royal confidence to the same degree. His influence waned rapidly; within a year of his elevation he had passed the peak of his episcopal career. But Latimer could not foresee this. Although he must have grieved for the loss of so good a friend, he probably felt that with the King's marriage to Jane Seymour on May 30 a helpmeet equally sympathetic to the cause of the reformed religion had taken Anne's place. When the long-hoped-for prince was born on October 12, 1537,

Latimer's rejoicings were as loud as any. From Hartlebury he wrote to Cromwell that in Worcestershire there was as much rejoicing as there had been in Judaea at the birth of St. John Baptist. He added, with a quaint mixture of piety and patriotism, "God give us grace to yield due thanks to our Lord God, God of England! for verily he hath showed himself God of England, or rather an English God, if we consider and ponder well all his proceedings with us from time to time." [13] But joy was turned to mourning when Queen Jane died on October 24.

The Reformation Parliament was dissolved on April 14, 1536, and a new parliament assembled on June 8. Convocation, as was the custom, met concurrently. Its business had been predetermined; it was called to consider and approve articles of faith for the Church of England. In the King's opinion the need was great. As a consequence of the separation from Rome, heterodox opinions were being preached more freely than ever before. At the same time, the conservatives were insistent that the breach with Rome implied no alteration in matters of doctrine. The question what the Church of England officially believed and taught was thus posed for the first time. Since February, Cranmer and the bishops (Latimer among them) had been meeting informally at Lambeth, at the King's request, to explore the problem and to formulate articles for presentation to Convocation. As far as can be known they had made little progress when Convocation met for its first session on June 9.

On that day, the five hundred divines who composed the two houses of Convocation repaired first to St. Paul's, where they heard a Mass of the Holy Ghost sung by Bishop Stokesley.[14] They then removed to St. Mary's Chapel to hear the customary Latin sermon. The preacher, by order of Archbishop Cranmer, was Bishop Latimer. The sermon was designed to be the keynote speech of the session; it was recognized as such by all who heard it.

Latimer's Convocation Sermon [15] is far from his best, but because it is summarized in all histories of the English reformation it is undoubtedly his best known. It was also, as far as can be determined, the first of his sermons to be printed. In 1537 the Latin version was printed at Southwark by James Nicolson to be sold by John Gough; [16] in November of the same year an English translation was published by Thomas Berthelet.[17] It must be remembered, however, that the printed texts are far shorter than the spoken sermon, and that it is difficult therefore to evaluate it accurately or to assess its full influence upon its first audience. In that audience the conservatives were in the majority, and unquestionably they were outraged. But they could scarcely have been surprised; the mere presence of Latimer in the pulpit would have warned them what to expect. To many of them, of course, the situation itself was outrageous enough, since the preacher of the day had stood his trial for heresy before a committee of Convocation only four years earlier, and some of those present, like Stokesley, had helped to pass sentence upon him. Now, as they perfectly well knew, he represented the official, the royal will.

The sermon, on Luke 16:8—"the children of this world are in their generation wiser than the children of light"—was in two parts, the first part preached in the morning, the second in the afternoon. Except that it omits the conventional "flowers of rhetoric," the sermon conforms pretty much to the standard pattern of the medieval sermon *ad clerum.* The morning sermon, elaborating the parable of the unjust steward, is the ante-theme; it concludes with the usual bidding-prayer for the King, for his lawful wife Queen Jane, and for all his faithful subjects, "not forgetting those that being departed out of this transitory life, now sleep in the sleep of peace, and rest from their labors in quietness . . . . For all these, and for grace necessary, ye shall say unto God God's prayer, *Pater noster."* The body of the morning sermon was devoted to denunciation, in Latimer's characteristic terminology, of the familiar catalogue of abuses—purgatory, saint-worship, will-works, non-preaching prelates. Theologically, its Lutheran implications are clearest in a short passage in which the Word and the Sacraments are conjoined as the means of salvation. To the clergy of the old learning the comments on purgatory were perhaps the most significant parts of the morning sermon. The clergy had preached, he said, that the souls in purgatory have more need of our help than the suffering souls of this world, and that souls in purgatory can have no help save through us in this world. Of these two preachments, said Latimer, the former was doubtful and the latter manifestly false.[18]

In the sermon of the afternoon, however, Latimer attacked his audience more precisely. With loving attention to detail he embroidered the central motif that many of the clergy, although they were by their profession dedicated to the things of Light, were in fact grandchildren of the Devil and children of the World by his "lemans," Lady Pride, Mistress Avarice, and Dame Hypocrisy.[19] Their actions in convocation during the past seven years had betrayed their ancestry. Every good reform, said the preacher, had come from the King and had been stubbornly resisted by the clergy. They had done their utmost to keep the English Bible and other profitable literature out of the hands of the laity. They had exhumed and burned the body of William Tracy, two years after his death, because in his last will and testament he had forbidden the saying of masses for his soul.[20] They had tried to burn Latimer (he does not name himself, but the allusion is plain) because he would not subscribe to articles which detracted from the supremacy of the King.[21] It was a record, said Latimer, of incredible meanness. How explain it, he asked, save on the assumption that Convocation was controlled by the children of the world?

After further attacks upon "purgatory pick-purse," Latimer offered to Convocation a specific program of reform.[22] It was a sensible program, directed against evils which were generally acknowledged. The bishops, said Latimer, could effect certain reforms at once, if they were men of good will. They could reform procedures in the Court of Arches (the chief consistory court of the archbishop of Canterbury) and in their own consistory courts, where delay, bribery, and money-redemptions were notorious abuses. They could reduce the number of holy days, which were, so it was alleged, the occasions of idleness, dancing, dicing, gluttony, and drunkenness. They could correct the abuses associated with pilgrimages, shrines, and with the veneration of images and relics. It was merely necessary to enforce a constitution which had been in existence for at least three centuries and which provided that people should make pilgrimage only after consultation with their spiritual advisers. The bishops could also see to it that baptism was administered in English, so that the people might know what was said and done. Finally, they could forbid the sale of masses for the dead. Here again, said Latimer, the means of reform was at hand, for Archbishop Simon Islip's mandate of 1350, providing for the suspension of any priest who sold masses, had frequently been reënacted and could be enforced if the bishops willed to do so.

The peroration of the sermon is in one of Latimer's best veins:

If there be neither abroad nor at home any thing to be amended and redressed, my lords, be ye of good cheer, be merry; and at the least, because we have nothing else to do, let us reason the matter how we may be richer. Let us fall to some pleasant communication; after, let us go home even as good as we came hither, that is, right-begotten children of the world, and utterly worldlings. And while we live here, let us all make bone-cheer . . . . But God will come, God will come, he will not tarry long away. He will come upon such a day as we nothing look for him, and at such hour as we know not. He will come and cut us in pieces. He will reward us as he doth the hypocrites. He will set us where wailing shall be, my brethren; where gnashing of teeth shall be, my brethren. And let here be the end of our tragedy, if you will . . . . Come, go to; leave the love of your profit . . . . Love the light, walk in the light, and so be ye the children of light while ye are in this world, that ye may shine in the world that is to come bright as the sun, with the Father, the Son, and the Holy Ghost.[23]

There can be no doubt that a majority of Latimer's audience listened to this sermon with grim dismay. With full allowance for Latimer's well-known extremities of style, they still were aware that his utterances, particularly those touching upon purgatory, foreshadowed decisions which they would shortly be compelled to make. There is no record, however, of any immediate expression of overt hostility to the sermon or the preacher. But it did not go unanswered. Some months later Cromwell was informed by a correspondent that Bishop Gardiner had made an answer to Latimer's sermon, and that the answer "shows that he loveth him never a deal." [24] Unfortunately Gardiner's reply has not been preserved.

Although the conservatives realized that they must give ground, they did not propose to do so without a fight. On the principle that attack is the best defense, the conservative majority in the lower house had prepared a list of sixty-seven *mala dogmata* which needed to be stamped out. In the form of a bill of complaints [25] their proposals were sent to the upper house when it met for its second session on June 16. One of their complaints, a minor one, was that some of the reformers were saying that "Our Lady was no better than any other woman, and like a bag of pepper or saffron when the spice is out." This seems to have been directed in part at Latimer, for he later denied ever having said any such thing.[26] Many of the points touched upon in the bill of complaints referred to extremes of Lutheranism which were not then being advocated by even the most extreme reformers in Convocation. Other points, however, related to matters which the government proposed to reform, and blanket approval for the bill of complaints was therefore out of the question. But the bill provided the means of a delaying action. Debate upon it consumed a great deal of time, with the result that after three weeks Convocation had made no progress whatever with the articles of religion which it had met to formulate.[27]

So Henry, as he had intended from the beginning, was finally "constrained to put his own pen to the book, and to conceive certain articles to be put forth, read and taught for avoiding of all contention."[28] In his labors he is said to have been helped by Archbishop Cranmer. It is probable that Latimer, Shaxton, and Edward Fox also collaborated. On July 11 the articles were brought in by Fox and read to the upper house. Apparently they were adopted without debate by a Convocation which had been taught to obey the King's will. The "Ten Articles," as they are commonly called, thus became the first formulary of the English Church. The handsome manuscript copy on vellum preserved in the British Museum[29] is probably the official copy; it bears the signatures of Thomas Cromwell and fifty-seven bishops, abbots, and priors of the upper house (Latimer's signature is ninth on the list), and of fifty-one deans, archdeacons, and others of the lower house. The names of the signatories are omitted in the printed book, a small quarto, which bears the formal title *Articles Devised by the King's Highness Majesty to Stablish Christian Quietness and Unity Among Us, and to Avoid Contentious Opinions, which Articles be Also Approved by the Consent and Determination of the Whole Clergy of This Realm.*[30]

Five of the articles in the formulary are devoted to faith, five to ceremonies. The first article asserts the absolute and exclusive authority of the Bible and the three creeds in matters of doctrine. The second, third, and fourth treat respectively of the sacraments of baptism, penance, and the Eucharist. The other four sacraments are not mentioned. The articles on baptism and penance are perfectly orthodox; the latter emphasizes works of mercy and charity, in addition to prayer, fasting and almsdeeds, as the fruits of genuine repentance. The article on the Eucharist seems to affirm the Catholic doctrine of transubstantiation, although some Anglican historians see in it merely an affirmation of the Real Presence. The fifth article, dealing with justification, asserts that the merit of Christ is sufficient to salvation, but that good works and charity must concur— a statement that may be regarded as modified Catholicism or modified Lutheranism, according to the point of view.

The second group of articles deals with the "laudable ceremonies used in the church." Images are to be allowed in the churches, but if they are censed or knelt to it must be with the reminder that it is done not to the images but to the honor of God. The saints are to be honored, "but not with that confidence and honor which are due only to God." They may be prayed to, for their intercessions, "so that it be done without any vain superstition, as to think any saint is more merciful than Christ." Such rites and ceremonies as the use of holy water, of ashes on Ash Wednesday, of palms on Palm Sunday, and creeping to the cross on Good Friday may be kept, but the people must be instructed that these ceremonies have no power to remit sin. Finally—and perhaps most significant—the ancient doctrine of purgatory is renounced. That there is a place of purgation after death is not denied, but its location and nature are known only to God. It is permissible and desirable, says the article, to pray for the souls of the dead, and to cause others to pray for them at masses and exequies; but Romish pardons and the *purchase* of masses which purport to "deliver them from their pain and send them straight to heaven" are explicitly condemned.

There can be little doubt that Latimer, like his friend Cranmer, was reasonably well satisfied with the compromise represented by these articles. Those having to do with faith correspond closely to all that he is known to have taught up to this time, as does the article on purgatory. Part of the article on penance must have given him particular satisfaction, for it is virtually a summary of his preaching from the Sermons on the Card onward. The relevant passage reads, "yet all men truly penitent, contrite, and confessed, must needs also bring forth the fruits of penance, that is to say, prayer, fasting, almsdeeds, and must make restitution or satisfaction in will and deed to their neighbors, in such things as they have done them wrong and injury in . . . ." [31]

The Ten Articles survived as the official formulary of the English Church for less than a year. When they were promulgated, the King, through Cromwell, issued also an order prohibiting all preaching except by the bishops or those especially authorized by them. All ordinary preaching licenses were suspended. The purpose of the order was to stamp out debate upon the matters which had been in controversy. There may have been some abatement of public discussion, but the dissatisfactions of the conservatives were in no wise diminished. It may be, too, that there were complaints about the ambiguity of meaning in some of the articles—an ambiguity which was chiefly the result of brevity. Such objections, however, would not have led to a reconsideration of the articles if the King had been satisfied with them. But evidently Henry was not satisfied, although he was the purported author of the articles and they had been issued in his name and by his authority. He was no doubt concerned by the omission of all reference to four of the seven sacraments,[32] and it is certain that he was troubled by the absence of a statement as to the King's position as supreme head of the church. Accordingly he shortly ordered Archbishop Cranmer to assemble a commission of bishops and other divines to reconsider the formulary, with especial attention to the number of the sacraments.

Cranmer's commission of twenty-five began to meet, probably at Lambeth, early in 1537.[33] At their first meeting Cromwell reminded them that the King desired uniformity above all things, and that the debate was to be conducted without acrimony. All questions were to be determined from Scripture, without reference to "unwritten verities." [34] But the issues were too hot, the divines too partisan, for anything resembling harmony. The forces of the old religion were led by Stokesley, Lee of York, Longland of Lincoln, Clerk of Bath, Sampson of Chichester, and Repps of Norwich. The leaders for the new doctrines were Cranmer, Latimer, Shaxton, and Edward Fox. In erudition and vigor the opponents were well matched. As acrimony increased, Cranmer was constrained to remind the disputants that "it beseemeth not men of learning and gravity to make such a babbling and brawling about bare words." [35] The strain was increased when Cromwell brought in Alexander Alesius, a Scottish reformer of the extreme type, to instruct Stokesley on the nature of a sacrament.[36] In all the debate the wisest words seem to have been spoken by Edward Fox, the most moderate of the men of the new learning, who reminded the group that the laity were now in possession of the Bible and therefore in a position to make competent judgment upon the decisions of the commission. "Truth," Fox concluded, "is the daughter of time, and time is the mother of truth; and whatsoever is besieged of truth cannot long continue; and upon whose side truth doth stand, that ought not to be thought . . . that it will ever fail." [37]

Cranmer, Latimer, and the others of the innovators would no doubt have been content to retain the gains which had been made in the Ten Articles. They were opposed to the admission of precise statements concerning the four remaining sacraments; even more, they were opposed to any relaxation of the ban on purgatory. On the latter matter, Latimer prepared a minute for the King which has been preserved.[38] Against purgatory he cited Scripture, Augustine, Jerome, Hilary, Cyprian, Chrysostom. To most of his points the King made annotations of sharp disagreement. Henry's comment on one was, "Herein you do show your carnal wit, which in preaching you dispraise so much." [39] Latimer's last point was from very recent history. If you believe in masses for the dead, he asked the King, why do you suppress monasteries whose founders stipulated the perpetual saying of masses for their souls? Henry's laconic comment was, "Why then do you?"

As the debates continued for weeks and months, Latimer grew increasingly restive. His convictions were strong, and he was as learned as most of his colleagues, but the intense practicality of his mind did not take comfortably to theological hair-splitting. When, in July, some sort of compromise was reached, and a book embodying the revised formulary was being prepared for the King's approval, he wrote to Cromwell in terms of his discontent:

> As for myself, I can nothing else but pray God that when it is done it be well and sufficiently done, so that we shall not need to have any more such doings. For verily, for my part, I had liefer be poor parson of poor Kington again, than to continue thus bishop of Worcester; not for anything I have had to do therein, or can do, but yet forsooth it is a troublous thing to agree upon a doctrine in things of such controversy, with judgments of such diversity, every man (I trust) meaning well, and yet not all meaning one way. But I doubt not but now in the end we shall agree both one with another, and all with the truth, though some will then marvel. And yet, if there be anything uncertain or unpure, I have good hope that the king's highness will *expurgare quicquid est veteris fermenti;* at leastway give it some note, that it may appear he perceiveth it, though he do tolerate it for a time, so giving place for a season to the frailty and gross capacity of his subjects.[40]

It has been debated whether the compromise finally reached represented a victory, however partial, for the old learning. The last sentence quoted above can leave no doubt that Latimer, while assenting to the compromise, felt that enough of the "old ferment" had crept in to be a setback for the reformers. But the new formulary, while distinctly more Catholic in tone and content than the Ten Articles, failed to please the King. Six months after the completion of the work he had still not given it his formal approval. Finally the bishops published it of their own accord; whence it came to be commonly called "The Bishops' Book." Its formal title, however, is *The Institution of a Christian Man, Containing the Exposition or Interpretation of the Common Creed, of the Seven Sacraments, of the Ten Commandments, and of the Pater Noster and the Ave Maria, Justification and Purgatory.*[41]

The formidable title is a sufficient index to the content of this rather bulky quarto. It is, in large part, an elaboration of the Ten Articles. The article on purgatory is virtually the same as in the Articles, and this was a victory for the reformers. On the other hand, the addition of articles on the sacraments of confirmation, holy order, matrimony, and extreme unction was a concession to conservatism, as was the article on the proper use of the Ave Maria. In two other respects the Bishops' Book elaborated upon the Articles. In the discussion of the term "catholic church" as used in the ninth article of the creed, the authority of the Bishop of Rome was expressly denied; and in the article on holy orders the supremacy of the King was explicitly affirmed.

Latimer's disappointment with what he regarded as the retrogressive elements in the Bishops' Book was considerably alleviated by a victory for the reforming party on another front. In the summer of 1537 King Henry finally set the seal of his approval upon an English Bible—not alone upon the principle that it was desirable to have the Scriptures in English, but upon an English version which was actually in being. A large share of the credit for this major victory belongs to Archbishop Cranmer.

It will be remembered that back in 1530 the King had vaguely promised that when the time was ripe the Scriptures in English would be allowed. Latimer's famous letter to the King was a reminder of that promise. Years passed, however, and Henry gave no sign of any further action in the matter. Finally, on December 19, 1534, Cranmer adroitly persuaded the upper house of Convocation to petition the King that the English church might have an English Bible.[42] Obviously neither Tyndale's nor any other existing translation could hope for approval; indeed, no complete English Bible had yet been printed. Convocation therefore proposed that a new translation be made by scholars to be appointed by the King. The petition, with Cromwell's support, was approved, and it appears that the task of making the translation was actually parcelled out among a group of the bishops. The work proceeded haltingly. Gardiner of Winchester is said to have finished his share, but the intransigent Stokesley flatly refused to undertake his, and others probably proceeded at intermediate speeds.[43] On June 9, 1536, a year and a half after the first petition, Convocation again petitioned the King for an English Bible. A few weeks later, just after the promulgation of the Ten Articles,

Cromwell issued to the clergy a set of injunctions—the Royal Injunctions of 1536 [44]—which stipulated, among other things, that before the feast of St. Peter ad Vincula (August 1) 1537, a book of the whole Bible, in both English and Latin, should be provided in every church of the land. Evidently there was still some hope that the bishops, within the year, might complete their translation and publish it along with the Latin.

As Cromwell's deadline approached, however, the work was still unfinished, perhaps not even well begun. Meanwhile Miles Coverdale's *Biblia,* a complete Bible translated from the Latin and the German, had been published, probably at Cologne, in 1535, and had gained a certain amount of popularity.[45] In the summer of 1537 James Nicolson, a Southwark printer, issued two reprints, a folio and a quarto, of Coverdale's Bible. The fact that he could openly do so indicates how greatly the official attitude towards the English Bible had changed. The quarto edition bears upon the title the assertion that it is "set forth by the king's most gracious license." From this some writers have speculated that the King and Cromwell intended that Coverdale's Bible should be placed in the churches to satisfy the injunction of 1536.[46] But this can scarcely have been the case, for on August 4 Cranmer wrote to Cromwell to say that it appeared that the proposed translation by the bishops would not be ready before doomsday, and that he was sending to Cromwell, with recommendation for approval, a Bible "both of a new translation and a new print . . . which in my opinion is very well done." [47] This was the compilation which is commonly called the Matthew Bible.

"Thomas Matthew," it is now generally agreed, was the pseudonym of John Rogers, one of the Cambridge reformers, who was to become in 1553 the protomartyr of the Marian persecutions. The Bible of which he was the editor was a composite made of Tyndale's translation of the Pentateuch; a hitherto unpublished translation of the books from Joshua through 2 Chronicles, believed by most authorities to be also the work of Tyndale and to have been left by him in manuscript; Coverdale's translations of the rest of the Old Testament and the Old Testament Apocrypha; and Tyndale's translation of the New Testament. The work had been printed, probably at Antwerp, at the cost of Edward Whitchurch, a prominent English printer, and Richard Grafton, a member of the Grocers' Company. Apparently it was the printed sheets of this as yet unpublished book which Cranmer sent to Cromwell on August 4, and which through Cromwell's good offices received the approval of the King. In the summer of 1537 the book was published—"set forth with the King's most gracious license."

A puzzling point in connection with this book must be mentioned. The translations of Tyndale had been repeatedly banned; yet two-thirds of the Matthew Bible was Tyndale's work. Grafton, who seems to have urged the work upon Cranmer, was certainly aware of its content. But what of Cranmer, who described the book as a new translation? Had he sampled only those parts which were previously unpublished? Is it just conceivable that he was unfamiliar with the text of Tyndale's Pentateuch and New Testament? Or was he guilty of an audacious piece of deception? And what of Cromwell and the King? No answers to these questions are available. We are left with the ironic spectacle of the King approving, wittingly or unwittingly, a Bible much of which he had previously condemned.

There is abundant evidence that Latimer shared Cranmer's enthusiasm for the Matthew Bible. When the Archbishop learned that the King had approved it, he wrote again to Cromwell to say that his satisfaction was greater than if he had been given a thousand pounds, and added, "you may reckon me your bondman for the same, and I dare be bold to say so may ye do my lord of Worcester." [48] Clearly Latimer had backed the book and had urged Cranmer to recommend it to Cromwell. The same conclusion must be drawn from two letters written to Cromwell by Richard Grafton in an attempt to secure exclusive rights to the book and to prevent it from being pirated. In one letter Grafton assured Cromwell that Cranmer, Latimer, and Shaxton would be grateful for any additional favors to the book.[49] In the other he says that the same three bishops stand ready to require that copies be placed in the churches of their dioceses.[50] Probably he already had Latimer's assurance that he intended to do so. Shortly after Grafton's letter was written, Latimer issued to the clergy of his diocese a set of injunctions which called attention to the fact that the King had granted that the Scriptures might be read in English. The injunction required that every priest with a cure of soul should "provide to have of your own a whole bible, if ye can conveniently, or at least a new Testament, both in Latin and English, before the feast of the nativity of our Lord next ensuing." [51]

CHAPTER SEVENTEEN

THE BISHOP OF WORCESTER AND THE DISSOLUTION OF THE MONASTERIES

Plans looking towards the suppression of the monasteries had been set in train just at the time of Latimer's nomination to the see of Worcester. The work was virtually finished when he resigned his bishopric in 1539. Although he did not directly participate in the dissolution, he commented freely, in letters and sermons, upon the progress of the work. An analysis of his attitude towards the suppression is important to an understanding of his opinions at this time.

In July, 1535, the king had issued to Cromwell, now vice-gerent in matters ecclesiastical, a commission to make a general visitation of all churches, abbeys, monasteries, and collegiate bodies in the kingdom. Until further notice, the bishops were prohibited from making visitations in their own dioceses. It was obvious that the church was to be reconstructed along national lines. Men like Latimer were heartened by the prospect, but churchmen of the old order were shocked and dismayed. Cromwell's visitation began in July. The visitors, of whom Drs. Layton, Legh, and London are the best known, fanned out over the country, armed with twenty-five injunctions for the better ordering of the houses of religion, and with eighty-six articles of inquiry by means of which they might discern the facts as to the conduct of the monks, friars, and nuns, and their management of the properties entrusted to them.[1] The visitations were carried out with almost indecent haste, lest the religious houses should sell their treasures in order to forestall confiscation.

The reports of the visitors ("comperts," they were called) painted a black picture of corruption and abuse. About these reports there has been much debate.[2] Protestant historians formerly accepted enthusiastically the record of financial mismanagement, the mulcting of the superstitious laity at the shrines, the cohabitation of monks and nuns, and the graver crime of sodomy. On the other hand, Catholic writers have contended with spirit that these abuses were exceptional rather than usual, and that on the whole the monks, friars, and nuns were considerably more virtuous and efficient than their brothers and sisters in the world. Impartial modern historians, conscious of Cromwell's intention to destroy the system and aware of the generally unsavory character of his principal visitors, have inclined to favor the Catholic interpretation. Indeed, it is impossible to read the visitors' reports as they are summarized in the *Letters and Papers . . . of Henry VIII* without the strong conviction that their monotonous pattern displays little of that concern for truth which recognizes infinite gradations of merit and depravity in human conduct.

The reports of the visitors were all in by the end of January, 1536, and shortly afterwards some kind of summary of them was presented to Parliament when it reassembled on February 4. There has been much controversy also as to the nature of this report to Parliament. Was there, or was there not, on the table in the Chapter House, a mysterious "black book" containing the comperts? If there was such a book, did it also contain the sworn confessions of monks and nuns to crimes of the blackest sort? Black book or not, Latimer himself is a sufficient authority for believing that a report of some kind was made. "When their enormities were first read in the parliament-house," he said in a sermon preached at court in 1549, "they were so great and abominable that there was nothing but 'down with them.' "[3] The accuracy of his recollection has been called into question, on the ground that he was speaking thirteen years after the event.[4] But this was the first parliament in which he sat, and the lapse of thirteen years is not likely to have blurred his vivid memory. Besides, he was talking to a courtly audience, many of whom had first-hand knowledge of the facts. It may be taken as true that a report was made to Parliament, and that some of the members, if only a vocal minority, were shocked, or professed to be shocked, at what they heard.

Before formal legislation was introduced to deal with the alleged abuses, it was desirable that the public mind should be prepared for it.

In London, propaganda looking to that end was systematically disseminated from press and pulpit. Of the sermons preached at Paul's Cross, that by Cranmer was the most nearly official: the Archbishop repeated the now customary repudiation of papal authority; he denounced purgatory, images, and the worship of the saints; and he assured his hearers that the secularization of the monasteries would result in a reduction in taxes.[5] Latimer, a more effective preacher than Cranmer, took his turn at the Cross on March 12. One of his audience reported him as saying that "bishops, abbots, priors, parsons, canons resident, priests and all were strong thieves, yea dukes, lords, and all; the king . . . made a marvelous good act of Parliament that certain men should sow every of them two acres of hemp, but it were all too little, were it so much more, to hang the thieves in England. Bishops, abbots, with such other, should not have so many servants, nor so many dishes, but to go to the first foundation, and keep hospitality to feed the needy people, not jolly fellows with golden chains and velvet gowns . . . ."[6] No doubt the sermon has been crudely and inaccurately reported. It seems unlikely that Latimer would have included the whole of the episcopacy and the nobility with the abbots and the priors in one general condemnation. But one thing is clear. It was the reform, not the abolition, of the religious houses that Latimer was advocating.

Although the conservatives had to move warily in their counterpropaganda, they were not without means of personal retaliation. Against Latimer they now used a device which they had tried a year before. This consisted in spreading rumors that he had "turned the leaf" and had repudiated his most cherished opinions. One William Bragges, a priest, went about saying that Latimer, on his knees at Paul's Cross, had retracted all that he had ever said against auricular confession and prayers to the saints. But one of Latimer's supporters, knowing that the Bishop had never preached against auricular confessions, confronted the rumormonger. When pressed, Bragges admitted that on the occasion when Latimer was supposed to have made this astonishing retraction, he, Bragges, had stood so far from the Cross that he had been unable to hear the preacher's words. But he had been assured that Latimer had recanted by no less a person than Latimer's old antagonist John Stokesley, the bishop of London. The whole thing, wrote Latimer's friend, was a plot on the part of the "great papistical murderers both of soul and body." Evidently the rumor was widely disseminated and widely accepted, for in the end Latimer was impelled to deny it publicly at the Cross.[7]

On March 11, 1536, the government presented to the parliament the bill which was to work a revolution. Characteristically, it was less drastic than had been expected, or at least it seemed so on the surface. For the time being, the larger religious houses could breathe more easily. Only those with incomes of less than £200 were to be suppressed, and the bill made provision for the dispossessed religious, for pensioners, and for the continuation, in part at least, of the provisions of the founders. Despite its apparent moderation, the bill seems to have met with plenty of opposition. In the upper house, Stokesley, for example, is said to have foreseen that the great abbeys would not long survive.[8] Even in the lower house the opposition was sufficiently strong to require the King to resort to threats of falling heads.[9] In the end, with the support of those who were intimidated or suborned, and of the children of this world who foresaw the profit to themselves, and of those who sincerely hoped for reform of the orders, the bill was passed into law. The immediate consequence was the suppression of 376 small houses, and the diversion to the Crown of an annual income said to have totaled £32,000.

There can be no doubt that Latimer played a leading part in steering the bill for the suppression of the smaller monasteries through the Lords. Afterwards, for a time at least, he continued to be an important spokesman for the government's policy, as can be seen from his activities during the Pilgrimage of Grace. The causes of the Lincolnshire and Yorkshire revolts which go by this name were manifold, but they found their focus in a protest against the suppression of the religious houses.[10] In October, 1536, when the risings began, Latimer had gone into his diocese, perhaps for the first time. As the intensity of the rebellion grew, he returned to London to take his part, as the most effective preacher in the governmental party, in the work of counter-propaganda. Sermons at Paul's Cross were an important channel for the official party line, and during several weeks in London Latimer probably went frequently to the Cross to denounce the rebels. Only one of these sermons survives—that of November 5, 1536. In its extant form [11] it is such a bald summary of the preacher's words that it has little interest either as a sermon or as a commentary upon events. The short passage which bears directly upon the revolt does touch, however, upon one of the most interesting features of the Pilgrimage of Grace—the claim of the rebels that they were the King's loyal subjects bent only upon driving out his disloyal advisers. Thus, says Latimer, they are deluded into doing the devil's work.[12] There was more to the sermon than this, of course, and there were other sermons.

It is not surprising that Latimer was one of those singled out for special attack in the North. All the "bishops of the new learning"—Cranmer, Latimer, Hilsey, Shaxton, Barlow—were accused by the rebels of having subverted the laws of the realm and the true faith of Christ.[13] In presenting their grievances to the King, the leaders demanded that the church be granted its old accustomed privileges, that the suppressed houses of religion be restored, and that the bishops of the new learning, along with Cromwell and others, be delivered up to the rebels or else banished from the realm. Ballads attacking Cromwell and the bishops were circulated.[14] Against Latimer the rebels revived the old charge that he had abjured and borne a fagot for his preaching.[15] It is illustrative of Henry's deviousness that in replying to the rebels' articles he ignored their attacks upon the reforming bishops and chose to speak of Edward Fox and Stephen Gardiner as his chief spiritual counselors.[16]

The Pilgrimage of Grace was over by Christmas, 1536. In spite of the King's promises of amnesty, the leaders were imprisoned and executed. We hear of Latimer in connection with two of them. In March 1537, he and Cromwell, acting presumably as *agents provocateurs,* interviewed the Lord Darcy in the Tower.[17] On this occasion Darcy repeated his protest that throughout the rebellion his loyalty to the King had never wavered. To this Latimer replied, "Marry, but in the mean season ye played not the part of a faithful subject, in holding with the people in a commotion and a disturbance."[18] Another reference places Latimer in a kindlier light. In the Public Record Office there survives a letter written to him by a Katherine Bigod, perhaps the widow of Sir Francis Bigod who was hanged for heading the insurrection at Beverley. The distressed lady thanks the Bishop for having interceded on her behalf with the King, and begs him to continue to be her good lord, "for I have no other of my friends that dare speak of the same."[19]

From the first, Latimer hoped that the government's program was one of genuine reform. No doubt he approved the suppression of the small houses. But he looked forward to the survival of the larger houses as centers of the new learning. In this he was encouraged by Cromwell's injunctions of 1535, which provided, inter alia, for the maintenance of promising young monks and friars at the universities, for the daily reading and exposition of the English Scriptures in each religious house, and for offerings to the poor in place of offerings to relics and images.[20] No doubt Latimer was naïve in accepting the injunctions at their face value, but as late as March, 1537, we find him writing to Cromwell in terms of such reforms. He is speaking of Furness Abbey in Lancashire, shortly before the surrender of that great Cistercian house. The comperts, he says, have indeed disclosed great "fedities" at Furness, and the monks are foolish praters. It is not their extinction that he urges, however, but rather that men of learning and judgment may be put over them, lest they perish in their ignorance.[21]

It appears also that at first Latimer had some hope that the income from the suppressed small houses would be devoted to the uses of religion and education. In this hope he was encouraged by Queen Anne. One of the most interesting details in the recently discovered biography of her by William Latimer bears upon this very point. When she discovered that the houses with incomes under £200 were to be suppressed, she told Hugh Latimer that in his next sermon before the king he should attempt "to dissuade the utter subversion of the said houses and to induce [the King] to convert them to some better use." Accordingly he preached on Luke 20:16—"He shall come and destroy these husbandmen, and shall give the vineyard to others"—from which he argued that since the vineyard was not destroyed but let out to others, so the King should "revert the abbeys and priories to places of study and good letters and to the continual relief of the poor."[22]

The vineyard was indeed let out to others, but not in ways which Latimer had expected or for purposes in which he could rejoice. There is no need to repeat here the familiar story of the sale of monastic lands to the acquisitive "new men" or of the questionable methods by which, within four years, all the religious houses, small and great, friaries and nunneries as well as monasteries, were dissolved and the religious orders banished from the land. It will be sufficient for us to examine the record of Latimer's dissatisfaction with the results, and his efforts to salvage something from the wreckage.

It must have been after the great abbeys began to fall that he dared to utter his famous protest against the base uses to which some of the abbey churches were being put. He tells us about it in a sermon preached at court in 1549. He had got on the subject of horses:

> Horses for a king be good and necessary, if they be well used; but horses are not to be preferred above poor men. I was once offended with the king's [i.e., Henry VIII's] horses, and therefore took occasion to speak in the presence of the king's majesty that dead is, when abbeys stood. Abbeys were ordained for the comfort of the poor: wherefore I said, it was not decent that the king's horses should be kept in them, as many were at that time; the living of poor men thereby minished and taken away. But afterward a certain nobleman said to me, "What hast thou to do with the king's horses?" I answered and said, "I spake my conscience, as God's word directed me." He said, "Horses be the maintenances and part of a king's honor, and also of his realm; wherefore in speaking against them, ye are against the king's honor." I answered, "God teacheth what honor is decent for the king, and for all other men according unto their vocations. God appointeth every king a sufficient living for his state and degree, both by lands and other customs; and it is lawful for every king to enjoy the same goods and possessions. But to extort and take away the right of the poor is against the honor of the king. If you do move the king to do after that matter, then you speak against the honor of the king; for I full certify you, extortioners, violent oppressors, ingrossers of tenements and lands, through whose covetousness villages decay and fall down, the king's liege people for lack of sustenance are famished and decayed—they be those which speak against the honor of the king."[23]

These were bold words, spoken as they must have been about the year 1538. They are the words of a man who disapproved of the national policy. They also supply something of an answer to those who question the extent to which the monasteries before the dissolution contributed to the relief of the poor. Latimer, who knew the system intimately and who disapproved of whatever elements of superstition and chicanery he found in it, seems to have had no doubt that the monasteries had not entirely neglected their responsibilities towards God's poor. He was quite sure, moreover, that the new owners of the monastic properties were bad landlords, and that upon their shoulders, and indirectly upon the shoulders of the King, must rest the blame for the economic distress which followed the dissolution.

As he watched the extirpation of the monasteries and friaries in his own diocese,[24] Latimer sought valiantly (and, one must suppose, at the risk of losing royal favor) to have some of the revenues of the dissolved houses diverted to the public interest. Thus in letters [25] to Cromwell he refers to efforts that he has made on behalf of Tewkesbury and Bristol, both of which places would be greatly benefited, he says, if the income from the suppressed houses there could be applied to the welfare of the community. He has left a fuller record of his efforts to salvage the revenues of the houses in and about Gloucester. In a letter written in the summer of 1538 he appeals to Cromwell on behalf of the free grammar school of St. Mary de Crypt in that city. The school had been recently founded by the bequest of John Coke, late alderman of Gloucester. Now Coke's widow sought to purchase lands formerly belonging to the abbeys of

Gloucester and Llanthony, the income of which she proposed to devote to the maintenance of the school. Latimer supported the project enthusiastically, and his efforts were partly successful.[26] He made a similar plea on behalf of his episcopal city of Worcester. When the Franciscan and Dominican friaries in that town were confiscated, he wrote to Cromwell that the bridge and the city walls were in grievous need of repair, and that there was no provision for the school formerly maintained by the Guild of the Holy Trinity. He himself had been supporting the schoolmaster out of his own income. Now if His Majesty would bestow the properties of the Greyfriars and the Blackfriars upon the corporation, the school could be maintained, the walls and bridge repaired, and the "lip-laboring of a few lewd friars should be turned into right praying of the whole city and town for the king's majesty and all his grace's posterity."[27] Here again Latimer's appeal met with success, for in 1539 the two friaries were granted to the citizens of Worcester.[28]

In one other respect Latimer was opposed to the policy of the Crown. He had no objection to the pensions granted to the displaced religious by the newly established Court of Augmentations, but he strongly disapproved of the government's attempts to evade the pensions by providing some of the mitered abbots to bishoprics, and converting some of the monks into secular priests with cures of souls.[29] In this attitude he was motivated by his zeal for the reform of religion and by his insistence upon the importance of the preaching office. His opposition was not to the religious as such; indeed he wrote to Cromwell urging that the prior and friars of the Dominican house at Worcester be allowed to retain their faculties as preachers.[30] Presumably they were well disposed towards the new doctrines. His opposition was to those who had no capacity for preaching. It were better that such be pensioned off than that they should be sent as unpreaching prelates into a world which hungered and thirsted for the Word.

It would be unsafe to generalize too positively from an admittedly fragmentary record of Latimer's opinions with respect to the dissolution of the monasteries. But the record as we have it is remarkably consistent. As the antagonist of all the elements of superstition in the old religion, Latimer participated with characteristic vigor, as we shall see, in pulling down the shrines. Similarly, he had supported and promoted the government's measures for the suppression of the small monasteries, not only because he was a good party man, but also because he thought their revenues would be diverted to the cause of education and pure religion. Had he had the disposition of the affairs of the larger houses, he would have had them continue and multiply their charitable services to the community, and he would have made them the centers for the study and dissemination of the pure word of God. When at last he realized that, in the government's policy of total extirpation, avarice and rapacity were wearing the mask of reform, he still continued to advocate the moderate program of reform in which he believed.

His latest letter on the subject sets forth his considered opinion. It was written to Cromwell in December, 1538, just a few months before he resigned his bishopric. It concerns the approaching surrender of the priory of Great Malvern, and the relevant paragraphs may well be set down in his own words:

But now, sir, another thing that, by your favour, I might be a motioner unto you, at the request of an honest man, the prior [Richard Whitborne] of Great Malvern, in my diocese, though not of my diocese;[31] referring the success of the whole matter to your only approved wisdom and benign goodness, in any case: for I know that I do play the fool, but yet with my foolishness I somewhat quiet an unquiet man, and mitigate his heaviness: which I am bold to do with you, for that I know, by experience, your goodness, that you will bear with fools in their frailness. This man both heareth and feareth (as he saith) the suppression of his house, which, though he will be conformable in all points to the king's highness' pleasure, and yours once known . . . yet nevertheless . . . he would be an humble suitor . . . for the upstanding of his foresaid house, and continuance of the same to many good purposes: not in monkery, he meaneth not so, God forbid, but any other ways as should be thought and seem good to the king's majesty: as *to maintain teaching, preaching, study, with praying, and* (to which he is much given) *good housekeeping;* for to the virtue of hospitality he hath been greatly inclined from his beginning, and is very much commended in these parts for the same. So, if five hundred marks to the king's highness, with two hundred marks to yourself, for your good will, might occasion the promotion of his intent, at least way for the time of his life, he doubteth not to make his friends for the same, if so little could bring so much to pass. The man is old, a good housekeeper, feedeth many, and that daily, for the country is poor and full of penury. *And alas, my good lord, shall we not see two or three in every shire changed to such a remedy?*[32]

Two sentences in this paragraph have been intentionally put in italics in order to emphasize what seems to have been Latimer's final effort to effect a possible compromise between rapacity and reform. The effort failed, and Latimer's allusion to his own folly proved to be amply warranted. For it cannot be doubted that his pertinacity in trying to salvage something from the wreckage of English monasticism contributed in large measure to the punishment which was shortly to be visited upon him.

CHAPTER EIGHTEEN

THE BISHOP OF WORCESTER AND THE DESTRUCTION OF THE SHRINES

Early in 1538, when the surrender of the larger monasteries was beginning, the church and the government began the systematic "exposure" and destruction of some of the shrines, relics, and images which to the faithful were objects of special devotion. The inspiration for this seems to have been the zeal of the reforming bishops, especially Cranmer, Latimer, and John Hilsey of Rochester, for the putting down of superstition. The program won the warm support of Cromwell and the King,[1] who were not unaware of the immense wealth amassed at some of the shrines, and who were also determined to stamp out all those elements of the old religion which in any way symbolized the power or influence of the church as against the state. The program reached its climax in October, 1538, with the destruction of the shrine of St. Thomas à Becket. The vast treasure at Canterbury was impounded. The bones and other relics of the martyr were destroyed. Because he had once defied a king of England, Becket was posthumously declared a rebel. All statues and pictures of him were removed from the churches, and his name was deleted from the calendar of the saints.

The fact that Bishop Latimer was a prime mover in the destruction of the shrines is not inconsistent with his moderate attitude towards the monasteries. In their systematic and generous relief of the poor, and in their potential as places of study and teaching, the monasteries stood for those works of mercy and piety to which he attached great importance. On the other hand, the shrines and relics, most of which were in the custody of the monks, were the symbols of those voluntary works which he at first deprecated and finally condemned. To him, the holy land of Walsingham was not holy at all. His answer to those who argued that the abuse was small, and that common people would resent the change, was simply that shrines and pilgrimages were impediments to righteousness.[2]

Latimer began the work of destroying the shrines and wonder-working images in his own diocese even before the national program was formulated. In the priory of St. Mary, Worcester, Latimer's cathedral church, the image of Our Lady of Worcester was an object of great local devotion. In August, 1537, upon order of Latimer and Prior Holbeach, who was a friend of the new doctrines, the statue was stripped of its handsome garments and proved to be but the effigy of an unidentified bishop of the Middle Ages. The revelation caused trouble. On the feast of the Assumption one Thomas Emans entered the Lady chapel, kissed the feet of the image and said an Ave and a Pater Noster before it. Then he addressed the people. "Though Our Lady's coat and jewels be taken away from her, the similitude of this is no worse to pray unto . . . than it was before." This much by his own confession. Witnesses testified that he also said, "Ye that be disposed to offer, the figure is no worse than it was before, and the lucre and profit of this town is decayed through this . . . . I trust to see the day that they shall be stripped as naked that stripped her." It is small wonder that Emans found himself in trouble with the bishop and the prior and that he was committed to ward.[3]

The stripping of Our Lady of Worcester was a local foreshadowing of what was about to occur on a larger scale. Early in February, 1538, at the command of the bishops, a collection of relics and images was carted up to London.[4] The first object of public condemnation was the famous Rood of Boxley, "the Rood of Grace in Kent." On February 24, Bishop Hilsey, preaching at Paul's Cross before an audience which was largely hostile, exhibited the mechanism by which the image was made to roll its eyes, open and close its mouth, and nod or shake its head in response to questions asked of it. Then the image was smashed to pieces, the people gathering up the fragments, some to burn them in disapproval, others to preserve them as relics.[5]

Latimer was no doubt present and helpful at the destruction of the Rood of Boxley. Later the same day he officiated at the degradation of the Rood of Ramsbury. According to tradition, the combined strength of sixteen oxen and seven horses would be insufficient to move this image. Now Latimer picked it up unassisted and hurled it out the west door of Paul's. Then the two bishops proceeded to the destruction of other images which had been brought up for the purpose.[6]

To us the spectacle is scarcely edifying, but Latimer seems to have enjoyed himself immensely. He was eager for another round-up in midsummer. On June 13 he wrote to Cromwell: "I trust your lordship will bestow our great Sibyll [the statue of Our Lady of Worcester] to some good purpose, *ut pereat memoria cum sonitu.* She hath been the devil's instrument to bring many (I fear) to eternal fire: now she herself, with her old sister of Walsingham, her young sister of Ipswich, with their other two sisters of Doncaster and Penrice, would make a jolly muster in Smithfield; they would not be all day in burning." [7] His recommendations were followed, but the burning seems to have occurred at Chelsea, not Smithfield, with Cromwell presiding.[8]

Among the images brought to London that summer was one called Darvell Gathern, which was an object of particular devotion in Wales. Local legend affirmed that Darvell Gathern, if and when it were burned, would destroy a forest. The legend suggested to some one the monstrous jest of using the image as fuel at the burning of Friar Forest, who was executed at Smithfield on May 22, 1538. In this melancholy affair Latimer had a prominent part.

John Forest was of the Observant Friars of Greenwich.[9] In April, 1538, it was alleged that he had used the confessional to encourage penitents to deny the royal supremacy. He was charged with treason and heresy (the latter because he had uttered opinions which were without scriptural foundation) and committed to Newgate, where he was examined by Cranmer and Latimer. After a few days in Newgate, he was brought before Cranmer and other bishops at Lambeth; he abjured his heresy, and was sentenced to do penance at Paul's Cross on Sunday, May 12, when Latimer was scheduled to preach. Before that date, however, the Whitefriars and the Friars Observant who were imprisoned with him counseled him that he would still be made to suffer for treason, and at the Cross he withdrew his abjuration and refused to bear his fagot, despite Latimer's request to the audience "to pray heartily unto God to convert the said friar from his said obstinacy and proud mind." Accordingly Forest was found guilty of both treason and heresy. He was condemned to be hanged in chains for the one and burned for the other.

Latimer was appointed to preach the sermon at Forest's execution. On May 18th he wrote to Cromwell about the arrangements.

Salutem in Christo pluriman. And, sir, if it be your pleasure, as it is, that I shall play the fool after my customable manner when Forest shall suffer, I would wish that my stage stood near unto Forest; for I would endeavor myself so to content the people that therewith I might also convert Forest, God so helping, or rather altogether working: wherefore I would that he should hear what I shall say, *si forte, etc.* Forest, as I hear, is not duly accompanied in Newgate for his amendment, with the White Friars of Doncaster, and monks of the Charterhouse, in a fit chamber, more like to indurate than to mollify: whether through the fault of the sheriff or of the jailer, or both, no man could sooner discern than your lordship. Some think he is rather comforted in his way than discouraged; some think he is allowed both to hear mass and also to receive the sacrament; which if it be so, it is enough to confirm him in his obstinacy, as though he were to suffer for a just cause . . . . It is to be feared that some instilled into him, that though he had persevered in his abjuration, yet he should have suffered afterward for treason: and so by that he might have been induced to refuse his abjuration. If he would yet with heart return to his abjuration, I would wish his pardon; such is my foolishness.[10]

Forest was executed before an audience said to have numbered ten thousand. Latimer preached as scheduled, from a platform built especially for the occasion. Close by were two other platforms—one for Forest to stand upon, the other for the dignitaries who were present. It was widely advertised that Latimer's sermon would begin at 8 A.M. and would last for three hours.[11] The event was a spectacle of such magnitude that it was recorded by several of the chroniclers. The variations in their narratives are instructive.

The account which has been most generally followed by historians is that of Edward Hall. Hall asserts that Forest would have been pardoned at the last moment had he agreed to recant, but that in spite of Latimer's arguments and exhortations he refused to recant and to the end maintained a stubborn silence. When the fire began to rage beneath him, he "caught hold upon the ladder, which he would not let go, but so unpatiently took his death that no man that ever put his trust in God never so unquietly nor so ungodly ended his life: if men might judge him by his outward man he appeared to have little knowledge of God and his sincere truth, and less trust in him at his ending." [12]

At the opposite pole from this grimly protestant narrative is the version given by Antonio de Gueras, a Spaniard residing in London. De Gueras asserts that after an hour Forest interrupted the sermon to charge that Latimer was the tool of the King, who had rewarded him with a bishopric. After an extended debate, Latimer once more urged the friar to submit, promising that the King would reward him with a good living.

At this point, says the Spanish chronicler, Forest made an attempt to appeal to the Duke of Norfolk, who was sitting with the King's council on the adjacent platform. But Cromwell intervened, Forest was hung up, and the flames were kindled beneath him. When the fire touched his feet, he first pulled them up, then lowered them calmly into the flames. As the fire consumed him, he said many prayers in Latin, his last words being "Domine miserere mei." When the image of Darvell Gathern was thrown into the flames, a miracle occurred. A dove, white as snow, appeared out of the heavens, and for a long time hovered over the body of the dead friar.[13]

It is a relief to turn from the harshness of Hall and the fancies[14] of the Spaniard to the relative objectivity of Charles Wriothesley. Wriothesley also records that Forest interrupted to accuse Latimer of timeserving and to declare that he would not renounce his allegiance to the Pope even if an angel from heaven should enjoin him to do so. So Forest was burned for his treason and with him Darvell Gathern, "which idol was of wood like a man at arms in his harness, having a little spear in his hand and a casket of iron about his neck with a riband, the which people of North Wales honored as a saint."[15]

Wriothesley's account of the tragedy is strongly protestant in tone, but it has the merit of not charging Forest with either knavery or cowardice. Most readers will agree that Wriothesley seems a better witness than either Hall or De Gueras. Even so, we can feel sure of little more than that Latimer preached, that Forest challenged his integrity, and that in the end Forest died bravely.

Probably no episode in Latimer's career has provoked more unfavorable comment than the fact that he preached at the execution of Friar Forest. Catholic writers have denounced him for it, and even his protestant biographers have felt constrained to apologize for him.[16] Both attitudes are based upon humanitarian considerations with which the sixteenth century was unfamiliar. Latimer's only extant comment upon the episode is the letter quoted above. There is no reason to believe that he suffered any squeamishness of conscience over Forest's death. His comments upon the execution of the Anabaptists in October, 1538 (Latimer was in his diocese at this time and was probably not directly involved), and upon the execution of the Lord Admiral Seymour in 1549, indicate that he shared with the governing classes of the age the view that death was the necessary way with heretics and traitors.[17]

The final notice of Latimer in connection with the suppression of the shrines comes in the autumn of 1538. Evidently he had no part in the desecration of the shrine of St. Thomas à Becket in October, for at that very time he was busy in his own diocese examining the Blood of Hayles. The Cistercian abbey of Hayles in Gloucestershire had been founded in the thirteenth century by Richard, earl of Cornwall, whose son Edmund, after the death of his father, presented the abbey with its famous relic, a vial said to have contained a portion of the Most Precious Blood.[18] The relic was for centuries a famous object of pilgrimage. As rector of West Kington, Latimer himself had commented disparagingly upon the hordes of pilgrims traveling along the Fossway to the shrine.[19]

When Abbot Whalley, in 1537, opposed the surrender of the house to the Crown, he was replaced by Stephen Segar, the last abbot, who surrendered the abbey peacefully in 1538 and was duly given a pension. Shortly before the surrender Abbot Stephen himself wrote to Cromwell expressing doubt as to the authenticity of the relic, but denying the allegation, which had been made at Paul's Cross by Bishop Hilsey, that the vial contained duck's blood which was renewed weekly by the custodians. Segar was unwilling on his own authority to suppress or destroy the relic, and he requested that Cromwell appoint a commission to investigate it.[20] Cromwell complied; the commission consisted of Latimer as bishop, Abbot Stephen, Holbeach the prior of Worcester, and Richard Tracy, Esquire.[21]

Latimer wrote to Cromwell on October 28, 1538:

Sir, we have been bolting and sifting the blood of Hayles all this forenoon. It was wondrously closely and craftily enclosed and stopped up, for taking of care.

And it cleaveth fast to the bottom of the little glass that it is in. And verily it seemeth to be an unctuous gum and compound of many things. It hath a certain unctuous moistness, and though it seem somewhat like blood when it is in the glass, yet when any parcel of the same is taken out, it turneth to a yellowness, and is cleaving like glue. But we have not yet examined all the monks; and therefore this my brother abbot shall tell your lordship what he hath seen and heard in this matter. And in the end your lordship shall know altogether. But we perceive not, from your commission, whether we shall send it up or leave it here, or certify thereof as we know.[22]

The formal report of the commission enlarges upon the statements in Latimer's letter, but does not differ from them in any respect. Both the letter and the report are temperate accounts of what was really discovered. A good many Protestant historians, however, have preferred to repeat Bishop Hilsey's earlier allegation that the Blood of Hayles was the blood of a duck, regularly renewed, and have amplified it by saying that the vial in which it was contained had a transparent side which was held up to the view of generous pilgrims and an opaque side which was for those whose gifts were not in proportion to their means.[23] Nothing in the letter or in the report indicts the monks of Hayles of any such chicanery, or indicates that they had been guilty of anything beyond the credulity common to their epoch. The Blood of Hayles, on order of Cromwell, was sent up to London, where Bishop Hilsey "exposed" it at Paul's Cross on November 24, declaring it "to be no blood, but honey clarified and colored with saffron, as it had been evidently proved before the king and his council."[24]

CHAPTER NINETEEN

THE BISHOP IN HIS DIOCESE

Bishop Latimer can be placed in his diocese with certainty at only three periods during his régime—from October until Christmas in 1536, from late July until Christmas in 1537, and from mid-June of 1538 until mid-January, 1539. Probably he was there for shorter periods at other times. But it was a three-days' journey over bad roads between London and his favorite manor of Hartlebury, just outside Worcester, and there cannot have been much casual shuttling back and forth.

Nothing is known of his visit in 1536 except the few details set forth in three letters which he wrote to Cromwell from Hartlebury. In the earliest of these he tells of having examined a Bristol youth named John Scurfield. Scurfield, only nineteen years old, had been zealous in informing against certain "sacramentaries" of Bristol who were denying the sacrament of the altar; apparently he had also spoken slightingly of Cromwell and the Bishop. For his indiscretion Scurfield was imprisoned for a time at Bristol. Then, at Cromwell's insistence, he was brought to Hartlebury to be examined by Latimer, who dealt with him leniently because of his youth and simplicity.[1] In another letter Latimer enclosed a Latin prophecy, not very meaningful, which was evidently regarded as seditious.[2] In the third, he spoke chiefly of the benefices which he had given to Drs. Bagard and Bradford.[3]

It may have been during his return journey to London at the close of 1536 that Latimer stopped off at Oxford to hear a lecture by Dr. Richard Smith of Merton College, the Regius professor of divinity. Smith was an ardent supporter of the old religion; many years afterwards he was appointed to dispute with Cranmer, Latimer, and Ridley at Oxford. Out of the episode of Latimer's visit to Smith's lecture room developed a tale which is almost certainly apocryphal. According to this story, which Strype attributed to Peter Martyr, Smith was warned of Latimer's visit, and hastily substituted for his ordinary lecture an earnest exposition of the doctrine of justification. The Bishop thanked him for his lecture, admitted that he had been misinformed about Smith's doctrine, and promised to recommend him favorably to the King. But some of Smith's colleagues rebuked him, and the next day he publicly acknowledged that he had deliberately taught what he did not believe because he was afraid of Latimer. He hoped that his audience would attribute his weakness to his youth. Whereupon he plucked off his cap, and at the sight of his gray hairs the audience was reduced to laughter.[4] It is a good yarn, but it does less than justice to an able man.

During the first half of the year 1537 Latimer was in London. As the debates over the Bishop's Book dragged on he was eager to return to Worcester, partly because several members of his household in the Strand had come down with the plague,[5] partly because he was keen to begin a formal visitation of his diocese and put into effect the King's injunctions of August, 1536, with respect to the reform of religion. In a letter to Cromwell dated July 15, 1537, he wrote somewhat plaintively, "I pray God preserve you, and send you hither shortly again, that we might end and go home into our diocese, and do some good there."[6]

Late in July he was back at Hartlebury to begin his visitation.[7] In October he issued his famous injunctions.[8] As far as can be discovered, these represent the first formal effort by a bishop to implement the royal injunction of 1536 that every religious house and every church should provide itself with the Bible in English, and to take advantage of the fact that the King, in granting royal license for the Matthew Bible, had provided the means by which the injunction might be obeyed. The injunctions survive in two forms. One set is addressed to the prior and convent of St. Mary's Worcester. The other set is addressed to all parsons, vicars, and other curates of the diocese.

In both sets the preamble speaks of the ignorance of the clergy of the diocese and points to the remedy in the study of the Scriptures, now available in English by the King's gracious license. The injunctions for St. Mary's enjoin the prior to provide a whole Bible in English, to be chained in some accessible place in either the church or the cloister. By the following Christmas, each member of the community is to have his own copy of the New Testament in English. There is to be a Scripture lecture every day, with compulsory attendance, and a chapter is to be read each day at dinner and supper. The customary services in the choir are to be curtailed, and preaching is to be emphasized. Other articles provide for the employment of a schoolmaster and the distribution of alms.

The injunctions to the parsons, vicars, and curates likewise emphasize the study of the Scriptures in English. Each parish church is to be provided with a whole Bible, or at least the New Testament, in both Latin and English. Each clerk with a cure of souls is to study a chapter a day, comparing the English and the Latin. The young are to be carefully instructed, and no young person is to receive the sacrament until he or she is able to recite the *Pater noster* in English. The parsons and curates themselves are to say the *Pater noster*, the Creed, and the Commandments frequently, and each one is to provide himself with a copy of the Bishops' Book and study it diligently. Preaching is to be regular and frequent, and the old ceremonies are to be discouraged. The people are to be carefully instructed in matters of the faith.

Latimer's injunctions bear the unmistakable stamp of his own views. He omitted many of the points which were emphasized in the Royal Injunctions of 1536—for example those touching upon the royal supremacy, the abrogation of superfluous holidays, the superstitious veneration of images and relics, the morals of the clergy, the maintenance of students at the universities, and the repair of chancels. On all of these matters he had strong convictions, but evidently he felt that they were sufficiently taken care of in the Royal Injunctions, a copy of which every clergyman of the diocese was required to have. Instead, Latimer chose to place the emphasis upon the regular and systematic study of the Scriptures by the clergy. He insisted upon the importance of teaching children to read English, and of encouraging the laity to read both the Bible and other fruitful books. He magnified the preaching office of the church.

It is possible that in preparing his injunctions Latimer had the advice and assistance of Archbishop Cranmer, for a year later Cranmer issued to the diocese of Hereford (whose bishop, the moderate Edward Fox, had recently died) a set of injunctions which in emphasis and at times in phrasing are remarkably like Latimer's.[9] In view of the known influence of Cranmer upon Latimer, it is reasonable to suppose that Latimer's injunctions, despite their priority, owe something to Cranmer's thought. But it is certain that Latimer himself was responsible for the final form in which his injunctions were issued. They have his characteristic vigor and directness. The short injunction to the clergy to "excite and stir up your parishioners to the necessary works of God, works of mercy and charity" is an instance. The corresponding injunction in Cranmer's set is three times as long, much more theological, much less emphatic.

No detailed record of Latimer's episcopal visitation of 1537 survives, but a number of letters written to Cromwell from remote parts of the diocese as well as from Hartlebury throw a little light upon the problems which confronted him. In October he was in Warwick, "that blind end of my diocese." From there on October 14 he wrote a letter to Cromwell which is of considerable interest because it relates to the collegiate church of the Holy Trinity at Stratford-on-Avon, the church in which Shakespeare was baptized and in the chancel of which he is buried. Latimer had visited the church a few days earlier and had found it badly run down. The warden, Dr. John Bell,[10] was a nonresident. He was, however, a person of consequence in the diocese. He was archdeacon of Gloucester, and under the last three Italian bishops he had been chancellor of the diocese. He had been superseded in the latter office before Latimer became bishop, but he continued as archdeacon throughout Latimer's régime, and in 1539 was appointed bishop in succession to Latimer. Also, he was of the old religion, and it is evident that Latimer had a poor opinion of him. Now, in October, 1537, additional preferment having come to him, he had offered to resign the wardenship of the Stratford church upon condition that he be paid a pension of £22 [11] a year out of his successor's income. Cromwell had recommended the appointment of Anthony Barker as Bell's successor, and Latimer wrote to Cromwell that he would give the post to Barker, since the latter seemed a man of "honest conversation, and also not without good letters." Latimer stipulated, however, that Bell's pension should be chargeable to Barker alone, not to his successors or to the college. The bishop added his fervent hope that Cromwell himself

would persuade Master Barker to tarry upon it, keep house in it, preach at it and about it, to the reformation of that blind end of my diocese. For else what are we the better for either his great literature and good conversation, if my diocese shall not taste and have experience thereof? And the houses (I trow) be toward ruin and decay, and the whole town far out of frame for lack of residence. When the head is far off, the body is the worse.[12]

The tone of this letter suggests that Latimer felt something less than enthusiasm for Cromwell's nominee. His suspicions were justified, for Barker failed to maintain discipline. In January 1539, Latimer was forced to report upon him unfavorably to Cromwell:

Sir, I like not these honey-mouthed men, when I do see no acts nor deeds according to their words. Master Anthony Barker had never had the wardenship of Stratford at my hands, saving at contemplation of your lordship's letter. I am sure your lordship can bolt out what should be meant by such instructions as master Anthony Barker gave to his parish priest, whose voluntary confession without any provocation of me, I do send unto your lordship, written with his own hand, his name subscribed; Mr. Lucy with all my house being at the publishing of the same.[13]

The Master Lucy referred to in this letter was none other than William Lucy of Charlcote, the father of the Sir Thomas Lucy on whose preserves the youthful Shakespeare is supposed to have poached. William Lucy was a stanch friend of the reformation, and one of Latimer's strongest supporters in the diocese. So were John Combes, John Greville, and a number of others whose names are familiar to all lovers of Shakespeare's Stratford. But at Stratford there was also an influential faction which was bitterly opposed to Latimer and his doctrines. The leader of this group was William Clopton, the owner of New Place, whose heirs sold that handsome property to Shakespeare in 1597. In the spring and summer of

1537 these opposing forces engaged in a row which kept the neighborhood in an uproar for several months, and which caused Bishop Latimer a good deal of trouble and anxiety.[14]

The center of the controversy was Edward Large, to whom Latimer had given the rectorship of Bishop's Hampton (now Hampton Lucy), a parish a few miles from Stratford. Large's advocacy of advanced doctrines had enraged the conservatives of the neighborhood. Large himself thought that he had been imperfectly understood. He therefore undertook to clarify his position in a sermon preached at Hampton on Easter Monday, 1537. It is to be feared that he timed his *apologia* badly, for the day was a festive one, being the occasion of the annual church-ale and also of the wedding of a Hampton girl to a man of substance from Stratford. The folk of both parishes (including John Combes, and William Lucy's wife and two brothers, although Lucy himself was not present) were out in force, and the conservatives were prepared for battle. Large preached for two hours. He was reported to have said, among much else which has not been recorded, that anyone who repeated Our Lady's Psalter would be damned, and that Ember Days were called after a woman named Ember who had been the mistress of one of the popes. Whether he said these things or not, it is certain that his sermon infuriated his opponents. Before he had finished Large was interrupted by an artisan named William Coton. A disgraceful row ensued, as a result of which both Large and Coton were jailed for disturbing the peace. Coton remained in Warwick jail for some weeks. Large was brought before a local jury and bound over to appear before a grand jury at Warwick on May 29. On that day he was indicted (for heresy, it would appear) and held for trial at the next assizes.

While the priest was awaiting trial, Cromwell, probably at Latimer's suggestion, appointed Masters Lucy, Combes, and Greville to serve as a commission to investigate the charges against Large. Coton, the first witness examined by them, freely confessed his error in publicly denouncing the priest, and the commission agreed to recommend that he be let off if he would make public profession of his guilt. The commission next examined Thomas Bayer (Badger), the foreman of the local jury which had examined Large, who admitted that the jury had called no witnesses, but had acted upon common gossip and a "bill" (that is, an unsworn statement) signed by numerous Stratford men. The commission's attempt to round up the signatories to this bill proved ineffective. But the two who were brought in declared that they were hazy about Large's sermon, and refused to swear to the statements in the bill.

At this juncture William Clopton, the leader of the party opposed to Large, offered to bring in a cloud of witnesses to swear to the priest's heretical utterances. When Lucy expressed doubt that those of Hampton would so swear, Clopton replied that if they would not it would be because they were intimidated by Lucy, their landlord. A day or so later the commission learned that Clopton had prepared a new bill against Large to be sent up to London, and he had succeeded in getting a great many signatures. In this new bill charges of treason were added to those of heresy.

All this occurred early in July, while Bishop Latimer was in London, deep in the closing debates over the Bishops' Book. When Lucy rode up to London to report on the state of the case, Cromwell and the Bishop approved the penalty suggested for Richard Coton. Accordingly on Sunday, July 14, Coton was carried from the Warwick jail to Bishop's Hampton, where in the church, after mass, he publicly acknowledged that he had defamed the character of the priest. Then in the afternoon Masters Greville and Combes examined the members of Hampton parish. Lucy disqualified himself because of Clopton's charge that the people were intimidated by him. Faced with the requirement of testifying under oath, Large's parishioners were unable to remember having heard him make any of the extreme statements which had been attributed to him.

When, late in July, Large appeared before the judges at Warwick, Lucy and his fellow commissioners confidently expected that the case would be dismissed for lack of evidence. But they reckoned without the pertinacity of William Clopton. On the morning of the trial, Lucy rode over to Warwick to get the ear of the judges, but Clopton was there before him and had secured the sympathetic attention of Judge Fitzherbert, a friend of the old religion and no friend of Thomas Cromwell. When Lucy attempted to report the insufficiency of the evidence against Large, Fitzherbert snubbed him publicly (to the delight of the Clopton faction) and threatened to hold him as an accessory. Then at the session at Warwick Hall it was learned that the original charges against Large had been dropped. Clopton's bill, charging heresy and treason, was made the subject of a fresh indictment, and Large was bound over to stand trial at the next session.

It was at this juncture that Lucy wrote letters to Latimer and Cromwell, setting forth his version of the controversy and urging that Cromwell intervene on Large's behalf. The letter to Latimer was plaintive, and suggested, without saying so directly, that Latimer had not dealt with the case as vigorously or as efficiently as he might have done. He urged Latimer to send his chaplain, Dr. Rowland Taylor, to investigate the facts, or better still, to come himself. He continued:

I have gotten me for meddling in this matter displeasure not only of most part of Stratford and of the most part of all this country but also of the most part of the gentlemen in this shire . . . my lord, I do most fervently, instantly, and earnestly desire you, require you, and pray you, as you favor God's word and the truth of Christ's gospel and as you have been a setter forward of it hitherto, to open this matter unto my lord privy seal [Cromwell] that it may be heard before him, and then I doubt not but truth shall have place. And of this matter dependeth and hangeth much more than this matter only. Your lordship must pardon me though herein I be somewhat plain.[15]

There can be no doubt that Latimer's sympathies were with Large, and that his failure to deal energetically with the case was due to his preoccupation with grave matters in London. By the time he received Lucy's letter (which is dated July 21) he was at Hartlebury, and he immediately wrote to Cromwell:

Now, my good lord privy seal, show your charitable goodness in this matter of Mr. Lucy. I have sent unto your lordship his letters. If that Mr. William Clopton may be suffered thus to rage, it will be but folly for any true preachers to come into that part of my diocese. I heartily require herein both the use of your authority and also of your counsel; and that you would send for the priest and also that Mr. Clopton, and to reduce him into some order; and, according to justice, to end the matter, which is now at length made treason, and so not appertaining to my court. And in what case are they in, that hath veiled treason so long! But I refer all things to your approved wisdom, and singular favour towards the truth of God's word and execution of justice, that good master Lucy be not discouraged in his hearty goodness.

Yours, this St. James' day [July 25], even now going to horse, when master Lucy's servant came to me, which, if your lordship be at leisure, can tell the whole process.[16]

Apparently Cromwell was slow to take action, for on September 6 Latimer wrote to him again to say that there are few such gentlemen in the realm as Master Lucy, who is on his way to Cromwell to report further on the case of the priest of Hampton.[17] On October 6, from Pershore where he was visiting the house of the Benedictines, Latimer wrote yet again to urge "that your good lordship will extend your goodness to that poor priest, sir Large, in my conscience injured and wronged by means of one Mr. Clopton, which neither did hear him, nor, if he had, could judge his doctrine; but zealously, for lack of right judgment, stirred the people against him." [18]

Cromwell seems to have taken action in October. Apparently he ordered the case against Large to be dismissed; there was no trial at the Warwick assizes, and the priest was restored to his parochial duties. Latimer's last word to Cromwell on the matter, written while he was visiting the collegiate churches at Stratford and Warwick, seems to suggest that Large was let off with an admonition to be more cautious in his future utterances:

As for Sir Large, your commandment shall be done, whose cause, in my mind, your lordship doth judge rightly: malice to be in one part, and simplicity in the other. But God shall reward you, that will not suffer malice to prevail. *Postridie Edwardi* at Warwick, visiting and busily always.[19]

Queen Jane Seymour died on October 24, 1537, twelve days after the birth of Prince Edward. A few days later Latimer was summoned to court to participate in the solemnities of her funeral. Accordingly he broke off his diocesan visitation and returned to London. The difficult journey was hard on him, and once in London he took to his bed at his house in the Strand. There he was nursed by a Mistress Elizabeth Statham, a pious friend of many of the reformers. When he took a turn for the worse she had him moved to her husband's house in Milk Street, in the parish of St. Mary Magdalen,[20] whence he wrote to Cromwell, on November 8, that he was "in a faint weariness over all my body, but chiefly in the small of my back: but I have a good nurse, good Mistress Statham, which . . . doth pymper me with all diligence: for I fear a consumption. But it maketh little matter for me." [21] He was still able to be diligent in business, however; in the same letter he urged the appointment of either Richard Gorton or John Clarke, both monks of Westminster, as successor to the deceased prior of Coventry.[22]

He recovered sufficiently to take part in the final stages of the prolonged obsequies for Queen Jane. The Queen lay in state at Hampton Court until November 12, when the coffin, surmounted by a magnificent effigy of the dead queen, was conveyed to Windsor. On the funeral journey the body was accompanied by a great throng of black-clad lords and ladies, gentlemen and gentlewomen, and by Princess Mary as chief mourner. At

Windsor the body was placed in St. George's Chapel, where on the following day, with a great company of bishops and mitered abbots in the stalls, Archbishop Cranmer sang the solemn mass of requiem and Bishop Latimer preached the sermon. Afterwards there was a great feast in Windsor Castle for all who had been present at the burial.[23]

This account of the state funeral for Jane Seymour may serve as a reminder that, whatever changes in doctrine may have been sanctioned by the Ten Articles and the Bishops' Book, there had been no change in the ancient forms of catholic worship and ceremonial. Oddly in contrast to the pageantry of the Queen's funeral are the spirit and intention of the will of Humphrey Monmouth, draper and alderman of London, who died just ten days after the Queen was buried. Monmouth had been for years a valiant supporter of the reformed religion; it was he who had financed William Tyndale back in 1523, when the latter was seeking the leisure to translate the New Testament, and he appears to have enjoyed the friendship of most of the leading English reformers. Now he had died, and his will stipulated that he should be buried in the forenoon, with neither bells ringing nor priests singing, but only a sermon by Dr. Crome. The will further provided that, instead of the usual "trental" of thirty masses for the soul of the deceased, thirty sermons were to be preached by Bishop Latimer, Dr. Barnes, Dr. Crome, and Mr. Taylor the parson of St. Peter's Cornhill. "And after every sermon *Te Deum* to be sung, to give laud and praise to God for the king that hath extinguished and put down the power of the bishop of Rome, and hath caused the word of God to be preached sincerely and truly, and that he may so proceed that we may have the very true knowledge of Scripture as Christ taught and left to his apostles." [24] The will provided that the preachers have 13s. 6d. for each sermon, and that Cromwell and Audley, the lord chancellor, each be given a silver cup of the value of £10, so that they would not interfere with the provisions of the will.[25] It has not been recorded whether Latimer had the opportunity to preach any of Monmouth's memorial sermons before his return to Worcester, but in any case he would certainly have done so when he was back in London the following year.

Latimer must have returned to Hartlebury shortly after the funeral of Jane Seymour. There is no further record of his diocesan visitation, however. The last that we hear of him in his diocese in 1537 is in two letters written to Cromwell at the Christmas season. In one of them he takes the opportunity to sing the praises of his old Cambridge friend, Dr. Robert Barnes, who at the moment was high in favor with Cromwell and the King. Barnes had been visiting Latimer at Hartlebury. Latimer writes of him: "Mr. doctor Barnes hath preached here with me at Hartlebury, and at my request at Worcester, and also at Evesham. Surely he is alone in handling a piece of Scripture, and in setting forth of Christ he hath no fellow. I wish that the king's grace might once hear him." He adds that two monks of Evesham, a great Benedictine monastery in Worcestershire, have been preaching in quite the opposite vein, and recommends that Cromwell investigate them.[26]

During the first half of 1538 Latimer was back in London. Neither Parliament nor Convocation was in session during this period, but other matters were going forward in which he was vitally interested. The destruction of the shrines has already been mentioned. Throughout the spring, Coverdale and his publisher Grafton were busy with plans for the revision of the Matthew Bible—the revision which came to be known as the Great Bible after its publication the following year. During the same period German theologians were in London conferring with a committee of English divines in an attempt to find some sort of doctrinal compromise which would make possible a political alliance between Henry VIII and the protestant states of Germany. There is no record that Latimer was directly involved in these conferences, or in the work of Coverdale, but his concern for them would have been sufficient to keep him in the capital.

In the middle of June, however, he returned to Hartlebury for his longest and, as it turned out, his last period of residence. Although he was not very well, and complained a good deal of sleeplessness,[27] he was able to keep up an animated correspondence with Cromwell upon various matters of business. Some of these matters, having to do with the monasteries and the shrines, we have already heard about. The others may be considered briefly.

A good many letters of this period reflect his trouble and anxiety over the collegiate church of St. Mary at Warwick. The previous year he had visited the church (which had a dean, five canons, ten priest vicars, and six choristers) and had found it run down despite its income of more than £334. Now the lecturer on Scripture required by Latimer's injunctions was unpaid, as were the vicars and the choristers. Latimer was minded to pay the lecturer out of his own funds, but he expressed the hope that the King might augment the church's income by granting it "some piece of some broken abbey." Part of the difficulty at Warwick seems to have been due to maladministration by Master Watwood, one of the canons, who acted as treasurer. So at least it was reported to Latimer by John Knightley the dean and two of the canons.[28] The Bishop duly sent their report to Cromwell and added that Watwood was a lecher and a fighter.[29] Watwood retaliated with charges against the Bishop. The altercation dragged on for weeks, but in the end Cromwell seems to have reduced Watwood to order. Latimer's amazement at the transformation is palpable as he writes to Cromwell, "you be indeed *scius artifex* and hath a good hand to renew old bottles, and to polish them and make them apt to receive new wine . . . . What a work you have wrought upon this man Master Watwood." [30]

A recurrent topic in Latimer's letters of this period is the disposition of confiscated monastic properties. Although he was not entirely in sympathy with the government's policy, he was concerned that his friends and supporters in Worcestershire should receive their share of the manors which were being sold off. In one instance at least he did so against his own interest. Since his income as bishop had never been sufficient for his needs, he determined, in the summer of 1538, to request for himself some of the lands of the Cistercian abbey of Bordesley, which was about to be suppressed. But Thomas Evaunce, a man of substance in Worcester, was even more forehanded. In yielding his own claim, Latimer wrote one of his most attractive letters to Cromwell:

And, sir, I was minded to have been a suitor to your lordship, seeing I cannot attain to the use of my park at Allchurch, for my preferment to some good part of the demesne of Berslay, for my money, which is even at hand, to relief of my great need to such things. For I trow no man, having the name of so many things, hath the use of so few as I, handled indeed like a ward. But now, hearing that this bearer, Mr. Evance, hath begun and entered into the same suit beforehand with your lordship, and is put in comfort of the same to be furthered therein, as I perceive by a letter come to him alate, I leave my purpose to begin for myself, and wish good success to his beginning; very loth to hinder or let any man's suit begun . . . . And you have been so good, and hath showed your goodness so largely unto me, that many men doth think that my poor remembrance with a word or two unto your lordship should further their causes with you. But yet methink you smile at one thing, that I, a man of so little policy, so little experience and activity, so little wit and wisdom, would take upon me to judge another man politic and expert, active, witty and wise. Well, sir, if I have done but only that made you to smile, to the refreshing of your mind in the midst of your matters, I have not done nothing . . . . [31]

At the close of this letter, and in several other letters of the period, Latimer begs Cromwell to act favorably upon the suit of Mistress Statham, the good woman who had nursed him in his illness the preceding year.[32] At his request, Archbishop Cranmer also put in a word for her.[33] It is likely that she and her husband had applied to Cromwell for some suppressed monastic properties in or around London. He was similarly active on behalf of a Mr. Butler of Droitwich,[34] of Henry Tracy of Todington in Gloucestershire,[35] and of the brothers Thomas and Robert Acton of Sutton Park, Tenbury.[36] The mother of the Actons was a niece of Humphrey Monmouth. Latimer wrote of Thomas Acton as his "godsib and friend," and he supported Robert when the latter coveted the estate of Anthony Throgmorton, whose loyalty to the government was suspect.

One of Bishop Latimer's suits on behalf of his friends was not without its comic overtones. A Master Nevell, who is identified only as a servant of the Bishop, was a suitor for lands belonging to the suppressed house of the Austin Friars at Droitwich. He was also a suitor for the hand of an unnamed widow. On June 13, 1538, Latimer wrote to Cromwell that Nevell, "making himself sure of his suit, hath got the widow, trusting surely in your lordship's goodness for the performance of the same, not without pledging of my poor honesty in the same behalf." [37] But there were several other applicants for Droitwich.[38] In spite of repeated hints from Latimer, Cromwell finally granted the lands belonging to the friary to Mr. John Pye of Chippenham, Wiltshire. On June 25, Latimer wrote to Cromwell in terms of humorous exasperation:

Ah, my good lord privy seal, what should I say? . . . with an honest gentlewoman my poor honesty I pledged, which is now distained, and my poor credence, the greatest treasure that I have, not a little minished: for that in Durtwich and here about the same we be fallen into the dirt, and be all-to dirtied, even up to the ears; we be jeered, mocked and laughed to scorn . . . . A wily Pye hath wilily gone between us and home, when we thought nothing less, but, as good simple souls, made all cocksure. In good faith I would wish to Mr. Pye as good a thing as it, and better too; but not so, and after that matter, to the defeating of a suit begun and near hand obtained; which if I had suspected, I could perchance have prevented, saving that I would not show myself to mistrust your pretense nor to have either in doubt or fear your enterprise. But it is now too late to call yesterday again, and to go about to undo that that is done. For Master Pye doth say that the king hath given it to him. I pray God much good might it do him; for I will no longer anguish myself with a matter that I cannot remedy. But I commit altogether to God and to your high discretion, which I am sure meant rightly, and with the loss of the same (*ut in humanis fit rebus*) sought opportunity.[39]

Latimer's letters to Cromwell in the latter half of 1538 are taken up with such matters as these, as well as with the destruction of the shrines and with the repeated expressions of hope that some of the monasteries might be reserved to the uses of education and a reformed religion. As one reads through the letters of this year in chronological sequence, one detects a note of increasing uneasiness, and then of querulousness, instead of the friendliness and self-confidence which marked the letters from Hartlebury in the two preceding years. The sparkle of humor is still there; but, as in the letter just quoted, there is an overlayer of complaint and even of anger. It is as if Latimer realized that he no longer had the full confidence of the vicar-general, and that, within the government, factions adverse to himself were gathering force. Such suspicions, if he had them, were quite correct. The correspondence ends with a letter of April 2, 1539, written from Sutton Tenbury, the home of his friends the Actons. It is the letter, already quoted, commenting on the amazing reform of Master Watwood. Almost immediately after writing it, Latimer returned to London, to take part in the debates which led to the Act of the Six Articles and to the loss of his bishopric.

CHAPTER TWENTY

THE SIX ARTICLES

There is every reason to believe that during the first few months of his bishopric Latimer was of the inner circle at court, or at least of that part of it over which Queen Anne Boleyn presided. Anne had helped to raise him to the episcopal bench; unquestionably she continued to give him her full support until her fall. Probably he continued to enjoy a share of royal favor during the brief tenure of Anne's successor, since the Seymours were of the reforming party. Thereafter, however, he seems to have preached less frequently at court, and from the correspondence with Thomas Cromwell it appears that his direct association with the King virtually ceased. True enough, in the autumn of 1538 he was presented with a stag which had been shot in one of the royal forests, but his expressions of gratitude for the gift were sent through Cromwell,[1] as were all his requests for favors of any sort during this period.

It is possible that the withdrawal of royal favor was due in part to the bluntness of Latimer's preaching. Not so long after Henry's death George Joye asserted that "M. Latimer in the king's day that dead is did openly before him and his nobles vehemently and continually inveigh against adultery, and . . . exhorted him and his council to punish it according to God's law or by the sword." [2] If this statement is to be relied upon, it may well be that Henry, whose standards in these matters were more relaxed than Latimer's, found the topic wearisome. Even if Latimer's themes were less personal, we may be sure that his court sermons frequently dealt with matters which touched the King closely. He himself tells of an occasion when someone about the court accused him of preaching "seditious doctrine"—a curious phrase—before the King. To his critic he replied, "Sir, what form of preaching would you appoint me to preach before a king? Would you have me for to preach nothing as concerning a king in the king's sermon?" Then, on his knees, he addressed himself to King Henry:

> I never thought myself worthy, nor I never sued to be a preacher before your Grace, but I was called to it, and would be willing, if you mislike me, to give place to my betters . . . . But if your Grace allow me for a preacher, I would desire your Grace to give me leave to discharge my conscience; give me leave to frame my doctrine according to mine audience: I had been a very dolt to have preached so at the borders of your realm, as I preach before your Grace.[3]

Certain of his friends expected that he would go to the Tower on this occasion, but the "Lord directed the king's heart." As time passed, however, the King found such preaching little to his taste. He must have been less than charmed with Latimer's criticism of the disposition of monastic lands, and of the base uses to which some of the abbeys were being put. Nor did he share to the full Latimer's enthusiasm for the destruction of the shrines. Latimer himself reports the King's reluctance to permit the public denunciation of the Blood of Hayles.[4]

It is probable, however, that the principal reason for Henry's coolness was Latimer's increasing advocacy of some of the views of the German reformers.[5] In this, of course, Latimer was merely following Cranmer. Both men, and their followers, were misled by Henry's apparent readiness, in the years between 1535 and 1538, to effect some sort of doctrinal compromise with the Germans. They must have known full well that Henry's primary concern was for a political alliance upon which he could fall back in the event of a possible combination of Francis I, Charles V, and the papacy against him. But they were encouraged to believe that he was also ready to accept some of the doctrinal and practical reforms upon which the Germans insisted. In this belief, Cranmer was prepared, by 1538, to abandon the Catholic doctrine of transubstantiation, although he still held to a belief in the Real Presence.[6] Probably Latimer was more than ready to adopt the same position. Unquestionably both men would have been willing to have both the bread and the wine administered to the laity, a point upon which the Germans insisted. With respect to the marriage of the clergy, another vital matter, there can be no doubt as to the views of Cranmer and Latimer. In letters to Cromwell, Latimer had openly advocated that priests should be allowed to marry.[7] Cranmer had gone farther; he had married a wife. If it be asked why, in the sequel, Latimer was punished for such opinions and Cranmer was not, the answer must be that Cranmer was still useful to the King and Latimer was not, and that Henry had a genuine fondness for Cranmer but not for Latimer.

In the autumn of 1538, the reformers had clear warning that the

King's views had not changed. Henry presided in person at the trial of John Lambert, their old Cambridge friend, who was charged with denying the Real Presence in the sacrament of the altar. Lambert was condemned as a heretic and burned at Smithfield.[8] At the same time a royal proclamation[9] imposed severe restrictions upon the publication and sale of English books, including Bibles; forbade disputation about the sacrament of the altar except by learned divines; ordered that married priests be deprived of their livings; and specifically allowed such ancient ceremonies as the use of holy water, creeping to the cross on Good Friday, the use of candles at Candlemas, and the like.

The religious reaction implicit in this proclamation was in part attributable to the fact that a relaxation of international tensions had relieved Henry of any sense of urgency in the matter of alliance with the Germans. But it represents also the growing influence upon the King of Stephen Gardiner, bishop of Winchester, and the beginning of the decline of Thomas Cromwell.

Cromwell had served his King well. In his management of the suppression of the religious orders, he had fulfilled his promise to make Henry the wealthiest prince in Europe. To achieve this end he had used the services and influence of the reformers, just as the King had done in the matter of the divorce. But Cromwell had gone far beyond the King in supporting the doctrinal principles of the new learning; in spite of some debate on the subject by modern writers, it seems clear that he was the genuine, if not a wise or scrupulous, friend of the English reformation.[10] By the close of the year 1538 the work of the suppression was so far accomplished as to make its completion automatic, and Henry needed to rely less upon the services of a minister whose practical usefulness was over and whose doctrine was distasteful.

In this resolution Henry had the support and encouragement of Stephen Gardiner, one of the ablest men in the kingdom.[11] It is probable that Gardiner, who had been created bishop of Winchester in 1531, expected promotion to the see of Canterbury upon the death of Archbishop Warham in 1533, and was bitterly disappointed when the primacy was given to Cranmer instead. But he smothered his disappointment and continued to serve the King ably, both as a diplomatist and as the author of distinguished and influential books defending Henry's assumption of the supremacy. On the other hand, his doctrinal conservatism made him completely unsympathetic with the views of the reformers and their supporter Cromwell. By virtue of his position and abilities, he became the leader of the party of the opposition to Cromwell. In this opposition, Gardiner was warmly supported by Thomas Howard, duke of Norfolk, one of the most influential of the King's council; by John Stokesley, bishop of London; and by a clear majority of both the lay and clerical members of the House of Lords. He could rely also upon the sympathy of a majority of the nation at large. It was this party which gradually gathered strength and power as Henry's dependence upon Cromwell waned. It was this party, under Gardiner's leadership, which in 1539 encouraged Henry to say to the reformers, "Thus far and no farther," and sustained Henry during the remainder of his reign in what is usually known as the Catholic reaction.

A new parliament met on April 28, 1539. The speech from the throne, read by the Lord Chancellor, announced that the principal business of the session would be the adoption of legislation to establish uniformity of religious opinion. It was obvious to everyone who could discern the signs of the times that the act, when passed, would be reactionary. But with a fine gesture of impartiality the Lords appointed a committee of prelates representing both the conservative and the radical positions to formulate a measure for the consideration of the whole house. The new learning was represented by Cranmer, Latimer of Worcester, and Goodrich of Ely; the old, by Lee of York, Tunstall of Durham, Clerk of Bath, Capon (*alias* Salcot) of Bangor, and Aldrich of Carlisle.[12] The committee was presided over by Cromwell, a layman, who by reason of his position as the King's vicar-general for ecclesiastical affairs took precedence over both archbishops.

As was no doubt intended and expected from the first, the committee's deliberations were fruitless. The conservatives had a numerical majority, but this was neutralized by the rank and influence of the Vicar-General and the Archbishop of Canterbury. The committee wrangled for ten days, while Parliament waited and transacted other business. Many years later, Latimer alluded to the discussions of this period. He speaks of a bishop "which ever cried 'unity, unity,' but he would have a popish unity." Unless the unity be according to God's word, Latimer adds, it is better to have war than peace.[13] Again, he says, "it was objected and said unto me, that I was singular; that no man thought as I thought; that I loved singularity in all that I did; and that I took a way contrary to the king and the whole parliament: and that I was travailed with them that had better wits than I, that I was contrary to them all." [14] If this passage tells us nothing of the points on which Latimer manifested such singularity, it nevertheless suggests that in committee he could be as vehement as in the pulpit.

Finally, on May 16, the Duke of Norfolk announced to the Lords that there was no likelihood that the committee could agree. He therefore ventured to suggest that the peers should consider six articles which might be incorporated into the proposed law: that in the sacrament of the altar the natural body and blood of Christ is really present under the form of bread and wine, and that after the consecration no substance of bread or wine remains; that communion in both kinds is not necessary, according to God's law; that priests may not marry; that vows of chastity or widowhood must be kept; that private masses must be continued; that auricular confession is expedient and necessary.

Unquestionably the King had much to do with the formulation of these articles, as he had had with the formulation of the Ten Articles of 1536. But it is significant of the times that whereas the Ten Articles were proposed to Convocation by a bishop, the Six Articles were now proposed by a lay peer to a legislative body made up partly of laymen. There is no indication, however, that the lay peers participated in the debates upon the articles. They knew that the King expected their affirmative votes, and were prepared to give them when the division was called for. Meanwhile, they were content to leave debate to the bishops.

No formal record of the debates has survived. A conservative peer who sat through them reported that Cranmer, Latimer, Shaxton, and two or three others argued stubbornly against the articles for three days, while Archbishop Lee, Gardiner, Tunstall, and Stokesley led in support of the proposals. On the fourth day, however, the King himself came into the house, spoke with all the weight of his royal learning in support of the articles, and "confounded" the opposition. Whereupon "My lord of Canterbury and all these bishops have given their opinions, and come into us, save Salisbury [Shaxton], who yet continueth a lewd [ignorant] fool." The same commentator reports that Cromwell raised no objection to the articles, and that the lay peers approved them unanimously.[15]

During the preliminaries to the final passage of the act, the rights of Convocation were not completely ignored. On June 2 the articles were sent to both houses of Convocation by Cromwell with the request that they submit opinions to the Lords. In the lower house, which was overwhelmingly conservative, there seems to have been little or no debate; all except two members agreed to accept the opinions of the King and the bishops. In the upper house, however, the debate followed the pattern of that which had taken place in the Lords, and a brief record [16] of these deliberations furnishes some hints as to the points on which the reformers held out most stubbornly. Apparently they gave in readily enough in the matters of transubstantiation, private masses, and vows of chastity. But Cranmer, Latimer, Shaxton, and a few others persisted in the opinion that priests might be allowed to marry. The same group had the support of a few of the conservatives in the opinion that auricular confession, while "very requisite and expedient," is not expressly enjoined in the Scriptures. Cranmer and Barlow of St. David's were alone in insisting that both the bread and the wine should be administered at the communion.

"An Act Abolishing Diversity of Opinions," [17] commonly called the "Act of the Six Articles," was written into the statute books on June 28, 1539. As finally passed, it embodied not only the six articles but also, at the insistence of the King, penal clauses of exceptional severity. Anyone who denied transubstantiation was to be declared a heretic and burnt, and his lands and goods forfeited. First offenders against the other five articles were to be punished with imprisonment and forfeiture of property; second offenders, by death. Priests who had married were required to put away their wives. Any person who refused to go to confession or receive the sacrament at the accustomed times would be fined and imprisoned for the first offense, treated as a felon for the second. Fortunately these fierce penalties were never put into effect. Although several hundred persons were indicted in the first few weeks after the law was enacted, they were shortly freed under the King's general pardon.

Although the Six Articles were not so reactionary as has been sometimes asserted, there can be no doubt that they represented a setback to principles to which Cranmer, Latimer, and the other reformers were dedicated. Nevertheless it is clear that all of these, save possibly Shaxton, voted for the bill at its final reading. It is possible, of course, to interpret their acquiescence as mere timeserving. On the other hand, it must be remembered that they were dealing with a king whose shifting policies made it necessary for them to walk warily in their efforts to secure their ends. Latimer himself said that their method with Henry was to wear him down gradually, as the slow dropping of water wears down a stone.[18] More than once before, reaction had been followed by re-reaction. Successful political behavior, like successful living, is a compromise between what is desirable and what is possible, and in the summer of 1539 the reformers no doubt felt that they could afford to bide their time. They could not know that the influence of Cromwell was about to end, and that the Tudor reaction, under the aegis of Gardiner and his party, and with the support of the nation at large, would continue until the death of King Henry in 1547.

Three days after the Act of the Six Articles became law, Latimer and Shaxton were tricked into resigning their bishoprics. The engineer of the deception was Thomas Cromwell who, according to Latimer's own statement in 1546, came to him with the story that "it was His Majesty's pleasure that he should resign it, which His Majesty after denied, and pitied his condition." [19] Probably Shaxton's resignation was procured in the same way.

If, as Latimer was led to believe, the King was unaware of Cromwell's maneuver, it is not difficult to guess at the latter's motive. He had helped in the promotion of the men of the new doctrines to the episcopate. Now that his influence was waning, he may have sought to improve his own situation by securing the resignations of two of the more radical bishops. Moreover, Cromwell had reason for private animosity toward Shaxton, who had frequently complained of Cromwell's interference; on one occasion Cromwell had said that Shaxton had "a stomach more meet for an emperor than for a bishop." [20] Cromwell may have had similar but less acute feelings about Latimer, whose letters to him were sometimes couched in language of apostolic exhortation.

On the other hand, Latimer's statement of the circumstances of his resignation may have been innocently unfair to Cromwell. It is equally possible that the Vicar-General was indeed merely acting as the King's agent, and that Henry's later protestation of ignorance and regret was a characteristic piece of hypocrisy. In any case, it is certain that the King was glad to be rid of the bishops of Worcester and Salisbury, whose usefulness to him was at an end. Once he learned of Cromwell's deception (as he must shortly have done) he could have declined to accept the resignations or, if they had already been accepted, he could have restored the two men to office. The fact that he did neither would seem to indicate that he approved of Cromwell's action, either before or after the event.

Nevertheless, the story was allowed to circulate that Latimer and Shaxton had resigned in protest against the Act of the Six Articles. A correspondent of Lady Lisle, wife of the governor of Calais, writing to inform her that Latimer and Shaxton had resigned their sees, added, "They be not of the wisest sort methinks, for few nowadays will leave and give over such promotions for keeping of opinion." [21] This represents the public interpretation of what had occurred. The government's failure to deny it tended to promote the protestant tradition that Latimer's resignation was an act of heroic protest and self-sacrifice. Thus it is not surprising that John

Foxe, writing in 1563, asserted that "being distressed through the strait-ness of the time, so that either he must lose the quiet of a good conscience, or else forsake his bishopric, he [Latimer] did of his own free accord re-sign his pastorship." [22] Twelve years later, Lord North, writing to Richard Cox, bishop of Ely, to admonish him to be more amenable to the will of Queen Elizabeth in matters of religion, added, "Here meseems you will say unto me that you are determined to leave your bishopric in her majesty's hands to dispose thereof at her good pleasure, and I know that you have so reported amongst your friends. Your wife hath also counseled you to be a Latimer in these days, glorying as it were to stand against your natural prince." [23] So the tradition grew, and persisted until the discovery and publication of the document which contains Latimer's own statement that he was the victim of Cromwell's sharp practice.

The probability is that Latimer felt no inclination whatever to resign his bishopric. He was unquestionably distressed, as were all the reformers, by the reactionary nature of the Six Articles. But the new law did not require actual subscription to the articles; it merely required that no one should openly defy them. At this stage of his thought, acquiescence to the articles need have done no violence to Latimer's conscience. He had not preached against transubstantiation. He had not taken a wife. The articles did not forbid or restrict the English Scriptures, nor did they encourage the improper veneration of saints and relics; and these were the matters about which Latimer's convictions were strongest. The article permitting private masses did indeed give some aid and comfort to his old enemy "purgatory pickpurse," but not enough to provoke him to extreme action.

John Foxe is responsible also for the tradition that Latimer gave over his office with unmixed pleasure. Says Foxe, "At what time he first put off his rochet in his chamber among his friends, suddenly he gave a skip on the floor for joy, feeling his shoulder so light, and being discharged (as he said) of such a heavy burden." [24] Some relief he may well have felt. Tem-peramentally he was not suited to the work of administering a diocese. More-over, as his letters clearly show, he had little freedom of independent action; every major decision, almost every appointment to a benefice, had to be submitted to Cromwell for approval. Nor were the financial rewards of the office at all commensurate with those of his predecessors. Nevertheless, it is certain that Latimer's feelings were not entirely those of joy at being relieved of the burdens of office. There is chagrin in the passage quoted above in which he tells how he was tricked into resigning, and there is more than a hint of bitterness in those passages in his later sermons in which he alludes to himself as a "quondam." In the presence of his friends he may have skipped for joy, but in the privacy of his thoughts he unquestion-ably regretted the loss of rochet and miter.

For a few days Latimer may have thought that his resignation would be pleasing to the King. He may even have expected some sort of *quid pro quo*—perhaps a parish from whose pulpit he could continue in the preaching office which he valued so highly. But to the public (and perhaps to the King) his resignation had been made to appear an act of protest against the government's policies. According to modern democratic theory, such a protest seems natural enough. But in Tudor political theory the holder of public office who resigned in protest against the policies of his prince came dangerously close to treason. It was the will of God that the prince should rule and that the subject should obey. It was the subject's duty to submit obediently to the royal will, committing to God the ultimate issues of right against wrong, truth against falsehood.[25] It was on this principle that Cranmer submitted to the Six Articles, put away his wife, and retained his archbishopric.[26] It was made to appear that Latimer had deliberately flouted this principle by his resignation of the see of Worcester. Such apparent disobedience to the will of the prince could not go unpunished. Accordingly Latimer was imprisoned for several months, and then he was put to silence. The order forbidding him to preach was not rescinded until after the death of Henry VIII.

CHAPTER TWENTY-ONE

THE SILENT YEARS

For a few days the resignations of Latimer and Shaxton were kept quiet. But the news soon leaked out. Shaxton wrote to Cromwell, evidently before July 7, that he had been asked by those who received his resignation to keep it secret, but it was now known throughout the city. Meanwhile Shaxton was puzzled. Should he put away his servants, and should he dress like a priest or like a bishop?[1] The answer was that not only had Latimer and Shaxton resigned their sees; they were also to be deprived of all outward signs of their episcopal orders. A few days after his resignation, Latimer was seen at Lambeth wearing a priest's gown and a sarcenet tippet, and with no attendants.[2] Those who saw him correctly interpreted the significance of his costume.

By that time, however, there was no need for further attempts at secrecy, for on July 7, less than a week after the resignations, the King sent to the prior and convent of St. Mary's, Worcester, the *congé d' élire* for the election of John Bell as bishop in succession to Hugh Latimer, "clerk,"[3] and at the same time he set in motion the machinery for the translation of Capon *alias* Salcot from Bangor to Salisbury. Both Salcot and Bell were of the old learning. Bell, it will be recalled, was archdeacon of Worcester, and one of those who had made matters difficult for Latimer in and about Gloucester. On August 4, the deed restoring to him the temporalities of the diocese was signed[4], and he was consecrated by Cranmer on August 17.[5] The whole proceeding was conducted with a dispatch in marked contrast to the delays which had held up Latimer's consecration for many weeks in 1535.

It appears also that the government acted quickly in cutting off Latimer's revenues from his diocese. Before his resignation he had sent his commissary to collect the annual payment known as the "Pentecostal" because it was due on Whitsunday. This was a small sum to be paid by each household of the diocese; in return, at Pentecost, they received the bishop's absolution. For Worcester, according to Latimer, the total was £55. Since in 1539 Whitsunday fell on May 25, the money was legally owing to Latimer. But the fees were denied him, on the pretext that to collect them would be to "incite sedition." The fees had already been collected, however, and there can be little doubt that the money was diverted into the royal treasury.[6]

Meanwhile it was generally felt that Latimer was in grave danger. Rumors that he had attempted to flee the country circulated freely. One report had him apprehended at Gravesend—"what his intent was, God knows."[7] According to another, he had been taken at Rochester and brought back to be lodged in the Tower.[8] Since both of these reports were written at about the same time that he was seen with Archbishop Cranmer at Lambeth, they probably represent reckless rumor-mongering. If he had actually made an unsuccessful attempt to flee, Latimer would certainly have been dealt with more severely than was the case.

While these rumors flew about, the King had already decided upon the temporary disposition of the two bishops. Latimer was placed in ward in the London house of Richard Sampson, bishop of Chichester; Shaxton was placed in the custody of John Clerk, bishop of Bath and Wells. Both were to remain in confinement during the King's pleasure.

Latimer's imprisonment at Chichester's London establishment, in Chancery Lane overlooking Lincoln's Inn Fields, was not rigorous. Sampson was an old antagonist, but he was evidently neither disposed nor empowered to treat his prisoner with severity. Nevertheless Latimer was more than a little alarmed at the danger in his situation. Ten years later, in one of his court sermons, he spoke of his imprisonment and his apprehensions:

> When I was with the bishop of Chichester in ward, (I was not so with him but my friends might come to me, and talk with me,) I was desirous to hear of execution done, as there was every week some, in one place of the city or other; for there was three weeks' sessions at Newgate, and fortnight sessions at the Marshalsea, and so forth: I was desirous, I say, to hear of execution, because I looked that my part should have been therein. I looked every day to be called to it myself.[9]

The passage of ten years had probably distilled out of these words the immediacy of the terror which Latimer must have felt, during the long days of the summer of 1539, as he lived in hourly expectation of word that sentence had been passed upon himself. Perhaps there was some alleviation of his fears when, after a few weeks, he was removed from London to Sampson's episcopal palace at Chichester, where he would be less likely to receive a daily budget of news concerning executions in the city. Here he was attended by John Tyndale and William Farley, two friends whose further identity is not known; thus it would appear that some vestige of his former dignity was allowed him.[10]

Meanwhile the feeling that Latimer and Shaxton were in jeopardy seems to have been general. An interesting letter from Marillac, the French ambassador, to Francis I repeats the current gossip that the two bishops could save their lives only by revoking what they had preached.[11] This feeling was at once the fear of their friends and the hope of their enemies. In ale-houses, barber shops, and even—it was said—at bishops' tables, they were denounced as "false knaves and whoresons" who richly deserved the fires at Smithfield.[12] Their friends, on the other hand, had to be more discreet. One of Latimer's admirers, whose identity has not been preserved, is said to have written to the King, "Consider, sire, what a singular man he is, and cast not that away in one hour which nature and art hath been so many years in breeding and perfecting." [13] As far as the record shows, however, only Dr. Crome dared to speak publicly in their defense. They were, he said openly at Aldermary Church, as honest and good after their resignation as they were before. Their merit did not leave them when they put aside their offices, any more than a lord mayor or a sheriff lost his honesty when his year in office expired.[14] From this, it would appear that the attacks upon Latimer and Shaxton at this time were directed not against their doctrines, but against their supposed temerity in resigning in opposition to the Six Articles. For his rashness, Dr. Crome was temporarily put to silence, and was for a time in danger of severer punishment.

In spite of fears and rumors, Latimer's life was probably not in danger at this time. Both Latimer and Shaxton had served the King well, and now that they could no longer trouble him from the bench of bishops he had no need to use extreme measures against them. The token punishment of mild imprisonment was sufficient for what the world believed to be their opposition to the royal infallibility. Indeed, Henry may have felt some qualms of conscience at the way in which Latimer especially had been treated, for he almost immediately granted him a considerable pension of a hundred marks (£66. 13s. 4d.) a year, to be paid by the Court of Augmentations. Although the amount was small in comparison with the revenues of his bishopric, it was still a substantial sum, being roughly the equivalent of £3,000 in the money of our own day. Since it was net, and Latimer no longer had an establishment to maintain, he was probably as well off financially as he had been as a bishop, and much better off than he had been as parson of West Kington. At Michaelmas (September 29) 1539, although only three months had elapsed since his resignation, Latimer received a payment for the half-year *ending* on that date.[15] Thereafter, the records show, his pension was paid him in semi-annual installments during the rest of Henry VIII's reign and on into the reign of Edward VI.[16] Thus it was that in 1550, preaching at Stamford, he was able to say, "I have enough, I thank God, and I need not to beg. I would every preacher were as well provided as myself."

The news of the pension, however, did not entirely dispel the belief that Latimer would be made to suffer the extreme penalty. A communication of George Constantyne, one of the less prominent Cambridge reformers, reflects the current uncertainties. Constantyne, on his way from Bristol to Slebeck in South Wales, had stopped off to sup with John Barlow, the dean of the collegiate church at Westbury. In the course of the conversation he reported the news of Latimer's pension. The Dean's first comment was that he was glad, for now he might get the £30 which Latimer owed him. But, said he, "I am sure that he shall never receive a penny of his pension, for he shall be hanged, I warrant him, ere Christmas." Said Constantyne, "Nay, God forbid! for I think he will neither write nor preach contrary to the act of Parliament, he is too wise." "But he shall be examined," said the Dean, "and I warrant he will never subscribe." When Constantyne pointed out that subscription to the act was not required, the Dean insisted, "Well, ye shall see that a way will be found for him." All this Constantyne faithfully reported to Cromwell, and added, "I pray you, was not one of the best preachers in Christendom bishop of Worcester? And now there is one made [i.e., Bell] that never preached that I heard, unless it were the pope's law . . . ." [17]

For a time after the passage of the Act of the Six Articles, particularly at the end of the year 1539 while the work of suppressing the last of the monasteries was going forward, Cromwell seemed to have recovered much of his former influence. For the time being, Gardiner was cast into shadow. As Cromwell concluded the negotiations for the marriage of Henry to Anne of Cleves, some of the reformers were led to hope that the pendulum of royal favor was about to swing to their side once more. The treaty for the marriage was concluded on October 4. Shortly thereafter John Burchardus wrote to Philip Melanchthon that all good men had the highest hope that the Six Articles would be abrogated and the "true doctrines" of religion would be once again received. The King, said Burchardus, seemed already displeased with the promulgation of the Act, had stayed all executions under it, and was ill disposed towards Gardiner and the others who had promoted it.[18] Shortly thereafter, Melanchthon addressed a long epistle to the King in which he eloquently besought Henry to bring about the repeal of the statute and to spare the lives of Latimer, Shaxton, and Crome, whom he describes as the "lanterns of light" of the English church.[19]

The expectation that the position of the reformers would be improved by the marriage to Anne proved ill founded. Henry's reaction to the lady whom he ungallantly called the "Flanders mare" is well known. It is interesting but fruitless to speculate upon the course the English reformation might have taken if Anne had fulfilled the promise of Holbein's dainty miniature and had bewitched Henry as Anne Boleyn had done years before and as Catharine Howard was to do a few months later. Henry, as it turned out, was not bewitched; the marriage was speedily annulled; and Cromwell, who had urged and negotiated the marriage, fell into deep disfavor from which he never managed to extricate himself. Although he was created Earl of Essex in April, 1540, his attainder followed in less than two months, and on July 28 he went to the scaffold on Tower Hill.

Meanwhile Latimer remained in ward. In the autumn he would have heard of the executions of the abbots of Glastonbury, Reading, and Colchester for resisting the seizure of the last of the great abbeys. By March he would have learned that Gardiner was back in power. He would have listened with mixed feelings to accounts of the spirited but fruitless theological controversies in which his old friends Robert Barnes, Thomas Garrett, and Jerome Barlow the vicar of Stepney had engaged the Bishop of Winchester, as a result of which, after unsatisfactory recantations, all three men were imprisoned.[20] When he received the news that Edmund Bonner and Nicholas Heath, both staunchly conservative, had been consecrated as bishops of London and Rochester respectively, he would have realized that there was little likelihood that the King was about to veer again in the direction of the new doctrines. But as the months of his imprisonment were extended to almost a year, he would also have grown more hopeful that his own life might be spared.

In May, 1540, however, his uncertainty was quickened once more when his nominal jailer, Richard Sampson, was himself imprisoned in the Tower under suspicion of having given aid and comfort to some who had denied the King's supremacy. As it turned out, Sampson was shortly able to clear himself of the charges. Meanwhile, however, Ralph Sadler, one of the King's principal secretaries, inquired what disposition was to be made of Latimer, and was informed that he was to remain a prisoner in Sampson's house until the King could devise what to do with him.[21]

Latimer was finally released in July, 1540, when Henry issued a general pardon to all those who had been imprisoned under the Act of the Six Articles. Frivolous gossip reported that Latimer might be restored to the bishopric.[22] The fact was quite otherwise. By order of the King he was prohibited from preaching, and was forbidden to come within ten miles of London, of the universities, or of his former diocese.[23] For one to whom preaching was the very breath of life, the sentence was as severe as might be, short of actual incarceration.

Just as Latimer was released, the last act in the tragedy of Barnes, Garrett, and Barlow was completed. All three had been specifically excepted from the general pardon which had effected Latimer's release. They were attainted of heresy by act of parliament, and on July 30, 1540, they perished in the flames at Smithfield. With their deaths, Latimer lost two, perhaps three, of his closest friends. He had been in intimate association with Barnes since the meetings at the White Horse at Cambridge back in the 1520's. He had made Garrett his chaplain. With Barlow, his associations were perhaps less close, although the two men must have known each other well. Certainly, as Latimer went into indeterminate exile, his heart was the heavier for their deaths.

A letter written about this time by Richard Hilles indicates the emotions of the reformers as so many of their leaders seemed to be passing from the scene. It was addressed to Henry Bullinger, the disciple of Zwingli. We have sinned, says Hilles, by attributing the success of our cause, not to God, but to ourselves and the learning of our leaders. But now God "has taken them all away. And here I mean Queen Anne, who was beheaded, together with her brother; also the Lord Cromwell, with Latimer and other bishops. Oh, the great wrath and indignation of God! yea, rather the far greater mass of our sins, by reason of which the tender severity of God could not but inflict upon us this punishment."[24]

There are few authenticated details of Latimer's life for the period between July, 1540, and May, 1546, when he was once again in trouble for his religious views. These are almost literally the silent years. Since he was forbidden to stay in London or to return to his beloved Cambridge, he unquestionably spent those years with friends here and there in the country. One historian [25] places him for a time in the household of Catherine Parr during the brief period between the death of her second husband, John Neville Baron Latimer, in January, 1543, and her marriage to King Henry in July of the same year; but there is apparently no evidence for this beyond the fact that Catherine Parr was known to be sympathetic to the new doctrines. It would seem probable also that some part of these years were spent in or near his old home at Thurcaston in Leicestershire.

It is almost certain that during this period Latimer was a frequent guest of his friends and relatives the Glovers of Baxterley in Warwickshire, which is about twenty miles as the crow flies from Thurcaston. Since Baxterley was in the diocese of Coventry, Latimer could reside there without violating the prohibition against his coming into his old diocese of Worcester. It will be remembered that one of his nieces had married Robert Glover, who was to be martyred at Coventry in 1555.[26] Robert was the younger brother of John Glover, a man of some substance who had properties at Baxterley and at Mancetter four miles away. It is probable that at this time the John Glovers were living at Mancetter, the Robert Glovers at Baxterley; in the home of his niece and her husband and their child Hugh, the exiled preacher would have found a ready welcome. Indeed, it is a tradition that it was through his teaching that the Glovers, John and Robert, became such devoted adherents of the reformed religion.

At Baxterley (or if not there, then some other place in Warwickshire) Latimer was visited, about 1545, by Thomas Becon, the younger reformer who remembered so vividly Latimer's sermons at Cambridge in 1528 and 1529. Becon reported that when he was with Latimer and his friends he felt that he was "clean delivered from Egypt and quietly placed in the new glorious Jerusalem." [27] It was also during this time in Warwickshire that Latimer "converted" John Olde, who later was one of the translators of Erasmus' paraphrase of the New Testament, and for whom, in 1549, Latimer was instrumental in procuring the vicarage of Cubbington in Warwick.[28] Olde's statement of his debt to Latimer is very precise: "I acknowledge and from the bottom of my heart unfeignedly confess that the reverend father of blessed memory, Hugh Latimer, was to the very death a right worthy instrument and minister of God, by whose most wholesome doctrine, sincere example of godly life, and constant friendship toward me, it hath pleased the almighty Lord to open unto me (among many other the most unworthy) the true Christian faith." [29] Olde wrote these words in 1556; in the same book he speaks of his "first entry into the gospel ten or eleven years ago," [30] and thus the date of his conversion is fixed as 1545 or 1546. Since Thomas Becon includes Olde among those with whom he talked in Warwickshire, it appears that Latimer, even though forbidden to preach, was the center of a group among whom he vigorously promoted his cause. It was probably this group which Latimer invited the young John Foxe to join for a period of two or three months in 1545. The future martyrologist had just resigned his fellowship at Magdalen College, Oxford, to avoid expulsion for his refusal to take priest's orders (his refusal was grounded in his objection to the requirement of celibacy). But Foxe, in need of employment, was in search of a schoolmaster's post, and was unable to accept Latimer's invitation. Although Foxe did not find a school, he did get a job as tutor to the sons of William Lucy of Charlcote.[31]. We have seen how close was the association between Lucy and Latimer while the latter was bishop of Worcester. It is pleasant to suppose that it was partly through Latimer's good offices that John Foxe became the tutor to the thirteen-year-old Thomas Lucy who in his later years, according to popular tradition, provided Shakespeare with the model for Justice Shallow.[32].

Although the years during which Latimer was silenced were in most respects a period of Catholic reaction in England, it might be more proper to think of them as the time during which the contending forces were held pretty much in equilibrium. Partly this was the result of the King's matrimonial adventures. The hopes of the reformers were raised by the marriage to Anne of Cleves, only to be cast down when that marriage was annulled and the King, within a short time, married Catherine Howard, the niece of the duke of Norfolk. But this triumph of the Catholic faction was short-lived. Catherine's pre-nuptial unchastity and her adulteries after she became queen were exposed, and on February 13, 1542, she went the way of Anne Boleyn on Tower Hill. So great was Henry's rage and grief that he remained a widower for a year and a half. His marriage to Catherine Parr in July, 1543, brought him under the influence, as far as he could be influenced, of a wife whose sympathies were with the new religion. She is said to have promoted the cause gently, but so insistently that at times she came dangerously close to the limits of the King's patience. It is recorded that once after a bout of theological debate with his last queen Henry petulantly exclaimed, "A good hearing it is when women become such clerks; and a thing much to my comfort to come in mine old days to be taught by my wife." [33]

It was Archbishop Cranmer, however, rather than Catherine Parr who was most successful in keeping the forces of reaction in reasonable control. In 1542, when the conservative bishops in Convocation attempted to supplant the Great Bible (the revision of the Matthew Bible which in 1539 became the first "authorized" English version) with a new and more Catholic translation, it was Cranmer who killed the proposal by persuading the King to order that the matter be referred to the universities. Cranmer was less successful in exercising a restraining influence upon the King when the third formulary of the English church was in preparation in the spring of 1543. This document, commonly known as the "King's Book" to distinguish it from the "Bishops' Book" of 1537, was published in May with the title *A Necessary Doctrine and Erudition for Any Christian Man*.[34] It affirmed transubstantiation more precisely than the Ten Articles and the Bishops' Book had done, and in other respects also was more Catholic than the earlier formularies. But a copy of the book with annotations by the King and replies to the annotations by Cranmer [35] indicates that the Archbishop had the courage to oppose the King on a number of disputed points. At the same time, Cranmer was engaged in preparing an English version of the litany (substantially the same as that still used in the Anglican communion) and in preparing a book of homilies expounding fundamental Christian doctrine. The latter was submitted to convocation in 1543, but it was not approved and published until the reign of Edward VI. It is clear from all these activities that Cranmer had not despaired of victory for the new doctrines. One can only admire his patient, quiet persistence in promoting his cause during a period when the general political situation was so adverse to it. By the beginning of 1546 he had made such progress that he believed the King was once more prepared to be sympathetic to reform. While Gardiner was on embassy to Charles V, the Archbishop attempted to persuade the King to abolish such practices as the covering of images in Lent and creeping to the cross on Good Friday. But in this effort he was outmaneuvered by Gardiner, who persuaded Henry that such a gesture towards reform would disturb the equilibrium of his own negotiations with Charles V and Francis I.

It must have been just about the time of this small setback to Cranmer's plans that Latimer returned to London. If the King's order forbidding him the city was still in effect (and there is no record that it had been rescinded) this was a step involving considerable risk. John Foxe provides us with the means of guessing at Latimer's reason for taking it. Foxe reports that "a little after he had renounced his bishopric, first he was almost slain, but sore bruised, with the fall of a tree. Then, coming up to London for remedy, he was molested and troubled of the bishops, whereby he was again in no little danger; and at length was cast into the Tower, where he continually remained a prisoner, till the time that blessed king Edward entered his crown, by means whereof the golden mouth of this preacher, long shut up before, was now opened again." [36] Here, as is so often the case, Foxe's chronology is disappointingly vague, so that we cannot be sure of the date of Latimer's injury. But since we know from other sources that Latimer was "troubled of the bishops" in the spring of 1546, it is a safe guess that he came up to London "for remedy"—that is, to consult physicians—shortly before that time.

Latimer's presence in London might have gone unnoticed or have been winked at had he not got himself involved in the affairs of Dr. Edward Crome. In April of 1546 Crome's effervescence had bubbled over once again. An act of Parliament of the preceding year had abolished some of the chantries (endowments for the saying of masses for the dead) and their revenues had come to the Crown. The background of the act was thus financial rather than doctrinal, but Crome, preaching at the Mercer's Chapel, contended that the very passage of the act argued for the non-existence of purgatory. He was called before the Council and required to recant. His first public recantation was unsatisfactory, and he was required to make a second appearance at the Cross. In the meantime some of his friends had been implicated. Among these was Latimer.

The examination of Crome began in May, 1546. On the thirteenth, Latimer, John Taylor *alias* Cardmaker (the vicar of St. Bride's, who was "converted" by Latimer at Exeter in 1535), and two others were brought before the Council for having "comforted Crome in his folly." [37] Specifically, Latimer was charged with having encouraged Crome to make his first evasive recantation "wherein he [Crome] satisfied not his promise to the king's majesty, but craftily said and promised one thing in appearance, and meant in deed another . . . ." [38]

All that is known of Latimer's appearance before the Council is contained in the Council's report to Sir William Petre, the secretary of state. This document is signed by the lord chancellor (Wriothesley), the duke of Norfolk, the earl of Essex, the bishops of Durham (Tunstall) and Winchester (Gardiner), the comptroller (Sir John Gage), Anthony Browne, and Anthony Wingfield. All these men were opponents of the new doctrines, a fact which must be borne in mind in evaluating both Latimer's conduct and their report of it.

According to this report, Latimer admitted having talked sundry times with Crome about his recantation. But he refused to reveal the nature of his advice to Crome, with the result that the Council put him under oath and required his written answers to a set of questions which they had prepared. He was put in a quiet place to write his answers while the Council proceeded with the examination of the vicar of St. Bride's and the others.

In a short time, after he had answered only two or three of the questions, Latimer balked and asked to speak to the Council. They sent Tunstall and Sir John Gage to him, but he demanded that he be allowed to speak to the whole Council. When they finally heard him, he said that the questions were devised to trick him, and he refused to proceed with his answers without more time for study. The whole procedure against him was extreme, he said, since Crome's views, not his own, were under suspicion; the Turks would treat a man more fairly. Besides, he doubted that it was the King's pleasure that he should be so examined; he had been deceived the same way seven years before, when Cromwell pretended that the King wished him to resign his bishopric. He demanded that he be allowed to present his case directly to the King. Finally, he charged that the proceeding against him was inspired by the malice of some of the Council. He specifically named Gardiner, with whom he had once had words in the King's presence, and who, Latimer felt, had never forgiven his Convocation sermon of 1536.

Such charges, by an obviously angry man, could not fail to annoy the Council. Gardiner replied with asperity, "proving by remembrance of things passed between us, that he did me much wrong; for I declared plainly, how much I had loved, favored, and done for his person, and that he had no cause to be offended with me, though I were not content with his doctrine, when the same was not of the sort that appertained." Further, Gardiner rebuked his unfavorable comparison of England with Turkey, and pointed out that the King could not be troubled to speak with every particular person who was called up before the Council. Finally, said Gardiner, the questions were not designed to trap Latimer; they pertained only to matters of fact, not of doctrine.

In the end, Latimer was forced to give his answers to the interrogatories. But he did so, reported the Council, "in such sort, as we be, for the purpose, as wise almost as we were before; saving that by the same he doth so open himself, as it should appear that he is as Crome was; which we shall this night know thoroughly, for this afternoon my lord of Worcester [Nicholas Heath, who had succeeded John Bell] and the rest of the doctors talk frankly with him, in the matter of the articles, to fish out the bottom of his stomach, whereby his majesty, at his coming, shall see further in him; and thus shall we leave to cumber his highness any further with him, till his grace's coming hither."

From the passage just quoted, it appears either that the questions put to Latimer were not so free of doctrinal import as Gardiner said they were, or that Latimer's impetuosity led him to plunge into the whirlpool of doctrine instead of confining his answers to the nature of the advice he had given Crome. We can make a fairly accurate guess as to the topics in which Latimer became embroiled after he had been turned over to the "doctors" for examination upon the "matter of the articles"—that is, the Six Articles. Crome's assertion in the trouble-making sermon that the abolition of chantries argued the nonexistence of purgatory was but an extension of the reasoning which Latimer had used ten years before in his paper-debate with the King. At that time he had said, "The founding of monasteries argued purgatory to be; so the putting of them down argueth it not to be." [39] Now he could scarcely have failed to come to Crome's support on this point.

But it appears that he became involved also in a much more dangerous matter than the debate over purgatory—namely, the nature of the mass. According to the first of the Six Articles, any unorthodoxy on this point meant death without the privilege of recantation. Up until this time, whatever his private views may have been, he had not dealt openly with this explosive topic, and as we shall see he did not formally reject the doctrine of transubstantiation until 1548. But during the silent years of his exile he had read and studied much, and he had certainly begun to have doubts about the doctrine of the mass as a propitiatory sacrifice. That he was now questioned concerning his views on this topic seems certain from the following passage from his last sermon before Edward VI. As far as can be ascertained from the available evidence, it can refer to no occasion other than his examination in 1546:

> When I was in examination, I was asked many questions, and it was said to me, What did Christ that we should do: a bishop gathered that upon these words, *Hoc facite in mei recordationem,* " Do this in remembrance of me." Then said he to me, "How know ye that they ate it, before he said, *Hoc est corpus meum,* 'This is my body'?" I answered again and said, "How know ye that they did not it?" &c. So I brought unto him the place of Paul abovesaid; and that in thanksgiving is none oblation; and when he gave thanks it was not his body, for he gave thanks in the beginning of the supper, before they eat any manner of thing at all; as his accustomed manner was to do.[40]

This passage is obviously garbled and therefore obscure as to details. Also there can be little doubt that while it refers to Latimer's examination in 1546, it is strongly colored by the opinions which he had come to hold in 1550. But it seems clear that in 1546 Latimer argued, from the ordering of the clauses in St. Paul's account of the Last Supper, that the critical words *Hoc est corpus meum* could not properly be adduced in support of the mass as a propitiatory sacrifice. From evidence to be presented in the next chapter it is certain that he had not yet accepted any alternative theory. But it was hazardous enough to question the orthodox opinion. It may be, as is sometimes asserted, that Latimer was brought before the King to answer for his opinions. There is no reason whatever to doubt Foxe's clear statement that he was imprisoned in the Tower [41] and remained there for more than a year and a half. A government agent was sent to search his things "in the country" [42] (probably at Baxterley) in the expectation that heretical literature would be found among them. There can be no doubt that he was in serious danger—far more so than when he resigned his bishopric in 1539. This time there was no mild confinement in the London house of a bishop; the grim walls of the Tower symbolize the gravity of his situation.

The seriousness of Latimer's situation may be estimated from the parallel case of Anne Askew.[43] This woman, of good Yorkshire family, was one of the more extreme gospelers. In March, 1546, she had been examined for denying the sacrament of the altar, but at that time she had been released. In June she was examined again and imprisoned in Newgate. She was put to the rack in the hope that she would incriminate others who held similar views, but in spite of the torture she kept her own counsel. Shortly before her condemnation she asked that Latimer be allowed to visit her, but this request was of course denied. She died in the fires at Smithfield in July, 1546. At her execution the preacher was Nicholas Shaxton, the former bishop of Salisbury, whose heroism over the Six Articles had now been reduced to abject submission to the old order. His complete change of face is one of the major ironies, perhaps one of the major tragedies, of the English reformation.

Latimer's offense was the same in kind, if not in degree, as Anne Askew's. Why then was he not punished in the same way? We can only suppose that time operated in his favor. Even as Anne Askew died, the ever delicate equilibrium of international affairs had been disturbed. The Emperor Charles V was making war against the Schmalkaldic League of German protestants, and Henry, to restore the balance, was sympathetic to a proposal for a league with the Germans against the Emperor and the Pope. This would have involved further doctrinal changes. In September, according to Cranmer,[44] Henry was prepared to substitute a communion service for the mass. Meanwhile both Gardiner and the Duke of Norfolk had fallen into disfavor. Power in the Privy Council passed to Edward Seymour, earl of Hertford, the brother of Jane Seymour and uncle of young Prince Edward. Both Seymour and his wife were sympathetic to the reformers. No doubt it was Hertford, supported by Cranmer, who saved Latimer from suffering the same fate as Anne Askew. But apparently he remained in the Tower until after the death of Henry VIII.

CHAPTER TWENTY-TWO

RETURN TO THE PULPIT

Henry VIII died on January 20, 1547. The nine-year-old heir to the throne was forthwith proclaimed King Edward VI. The late king's will named sixteen executors who were presumably to serve as a council of regency until the new king should attain his majority at the age of eighteen. The men whom Henry had appointed represented a nice balance between the old religion and the new. But by a brilliant if unscrupulous *coup d' état* which resulted in the scrapping of Henry's will, Edward Seymour procured his own election as Lord Protector.[1] Assuming the title of duke of Somerset, he thus became the virtual ruler of England.

Somerset, like all the Seymours, was a friend of the new religious doctrines. During the three years of his regime the heresy laws were relaxed and then repealed (the Act of the Six Articles was formally abolished by the Act of Repeal on December 2, 1547). Restrictions upon the Bible were removed, and the first English prayer book was introduced. But Somerset was not a radical. He was not in sympathy with the fiercely protestant reforms which are often associated with his name but actually occurred during the rule of his successor, John Dudley, earl of Warwick. Nor did he attempt any wholesale suppression of those who favored the old religion. Gardiner, to be sure, was excluded from the Council and subsequently imprisoned, but that was a matter of political expediency. On the whole, with due allowance for his partisanship, Somerset's religious policy was one of wise moderation. The late Professor Pollard, Somerset's best biographer, has summed up the religious temper of his regime by reference to a passage—perhaps in Somerset's own words—from the preamble to the Act of Repeal. "But as in a tempest or winter, one course and garment is convenient, in calm or warm weather a more liberal case or lighter garment, both may and ought to be followed and used." [2]

With the wind favorable once more, Latimer was released from the Tower, presumably by the terms of the general pardon issued in the name of Edward VI on February 20, 1547, the day of his coronation. We do not hear of Latimer, however, until the close of the year 1547, when his name was included, along with those of John Knox, Matthew Parker, Edmund Grindal and others, in a list of persons who since July had been licensed to preach under the ecclesiastical seal.[3] The chronicler John Stow reported that on January 1, 1548, Latimer preached for the first time in almost eight years.[4] Thereafter his services as preacher and propagandizer seem to have been much in demand.

Latimer resumed his preaching at a time when there was much embittered hostility to the famous Royal Injunctions of 1547 [5] for the reform of religion, and there is reason to believe that his first sermons were preached to counter that opposition. The Injunctions, which had been issued on

July 31, were in most respects moderate. One article[6] reiterated the requirement that each parish should purchase a copy of the "whole Bible of the largest volume in English"—that is, the Great Bible. The same article required each parish to buy a copy of the newly published English translation of Erasmus' paraphrase of the Gospels and the Acts. At high mass, the Gospel and the Epistle were to be read in English.[7] When there was no other sermon, the priest was to read from one of the *Homilies*,[8] the doctrinal essays which had been prepared chiefly by Cranmer in 1543 and were now, by the authority of the Council, published for the first time.[9] The articles also made provision for education. Every holder of a benefice worth £100 was to maintain a student at one of the universities, and to support an additional student for each additional £100 of income.[10] Chantry priests were to be diligent in their auxiliary functions as schoolmasters.[11]

Such were some of the moderate and reasonable provisions of the Injunctions. The conservative clergy opposed the articles concerning Erasmus' *Paraphrase* and Cranmer's *Homilies;* Gardiner and Edmund Bonner, the bishop of London, were both imprisoned briefly for their refusal to accept them. But the articles which provoked popular hostility were those which called for the removal of "abused" images from the churches and for the suppression of certain customary ceremonies.[12] In parish after parish, as the votive candles were extinguished and the beloved images were pulled down by reforming priests and church-wardens, bitter quarrels and often physical violence broke out between the contending factions. Some of the priests were handled so roughly that in December, 1547, the protector issued a proclamation imposing severe penalties for violent words or acts against the clergy.[13] The situation promised to get out of hand, and Latimer appears to have been one of those called upon to defend the Injunctions at Paul's Cross.

According to Stow, Latimer preached at the Cross on four Sundays in January 1548—January 1, 8, 15, and 29.[14] Our only knowledge of the content of these sermons is Stow's statement that on the eighth "he affirmed that whatsoever the clergy commanded ought to be obeyed; but he also declared that the clergy are such as sit in Moses' chair and break not their Master's commandment, adding nothing thereto nor taking anything therefrom; and such a clergy must be obeyed of all men, both high and low."[15] Brief as it is, this statement suggests that the purpose of this sermon was to support the Injunctions and the proclamation against disrespect to the clergy, and to answer the attacks of the conservatives upon those priests who were overzealous in casting out images and otherwise enforcing the Injunctions.

During this same month of January, Latimer preached at Paul's Cross a series of four sermons which are commonly called the Sermons on the Plough. Some of these may be identical with the Sunday sermons just mentioned. But the one which is extant, and should properly be called the "Sermon on the Ploughers," was preached on Wednesday, January 18;[16] it was the last of the series, and the likelihood is that all four of the Sermons on the Plough were preached on Wednesdays. If so, Latimer must have preached at least eight sermons at Paul's Cross during January, 1548, a remarkable testimonial to the value which the government attached to his preaching.

It has not generally been noted that the Sermon on the Ploughers was preached in the interests of the Injunctions of 1547. That it was will be clear to anyone who will first read the Injunctions and then read the sermon. It touches upon the *Homilies* (especially that "Of a True and Lively Faith," which·dealt with justification).[17] It pleads for the appointment and adequate compensation of teachers and schoolmasters, and for the maintenance of divinity students at the universities.[18] It attacks images (all of them, not just those which are abused) and the use of candles, palms, ashes, and holy water.[19] It pleads for the use of English in the services of the church.[20] It touches also upon a matter not treated in the Injunctions—the nature of the mass and, more basically, the nature of the atoning work of Christ. The inclusion of this topic points to the fact that the Act of the Six Articles had been repealed a month before, and that Cranmer and his associates, including Latimer, were well advanced in their plans to substitute a communion service for the mass.[21]

In the three earlier sermons, we are told in the fourth sermon, Latimer had compared the people to God's field, God's plough-land, and the Word of God to the seed to be sown in the field. But in this fourth sermon his topic was the ploughers, the preachers of the Word, and the need for preaching prelates (by "prelates" he meant all clergy with a cure of souls). This was one of his favorite themes, and in the Sermon on the Ploughers all other matters are subordinated to it. The function of the preacher, he emphasized, was to bring the people to a living faith, and the function of a living faith was to bring the individual to salvation. This in turn would induce in men collectively that righteousness of life which alone can create a true commonwealth.[22] Accordingly he attacked those unpreaching prelates who were lorders and loiterers, hawkers and hunters, and those who were so busy with their temporal offices under the Crown that they had no time for preaching.[23] He condemned both the clerical loiterers and the clerical politicians as spiritual enclosers who hindered church ploughing, just as the enclosers for pasturage had cut off the ploughlands from "bodily" ploughing. Both the spiritual enclosers and the physical enclosers had more concern for their private "commodity" than for the establishment of a flourishing Christian commonwealth.[24] "A Christian Commonwealth"—it is a concept of which we shall hear more in Latimer's court sermons of the following year.

Against the nonpreaching prelates Latimer loosed all his gifts of irony. They were, he said, engaged in the work of the devil and of "that Italian bishop yonder, his chaplain." [25] He continues:

And now I would ask a strange question: who is the most diligentest bishop and prelate in all England, that passeth all the rest in doing his office? I can tell, for I know him who it is; I know him well . . . I will tell you: it is the devil. He is the most diligent preacher of all other; he is never out of his diocese; he is never from his cure . . . . he is ever at his plough: no lording or loitering can hinder him; he is ever applying his business, ye shall never find him idle, I warrant you. And his office is to hinder religion, to maintain superstition, to set up idolatry, to teach all kind of popery.[26]

The Sermon on the Ploughers was printed, shortly after its delivery, by John Day in a small octavo volume with title-page as follows: *A Notable Sermon of The Reverend Father Master Hugh Latimer, which he preached in the Shrouds at Paul's Church in London, on the XVIII day of January.*

The year of Our Lord MDXLVIII. The reference to the "shrouds" tells us that the sermon was preached on a rainy day and therefore not at Paul's Cross itself but in the enclosed place used for the Paul's Cross Sermons in inclement weather. Nothing in the volume indicates the source of the printer's copy for the sermon. It may have been based on Latimer's own manuscript, or it may have been made from notes taken by a member of the audience, as was the copy for the sermons which were printed in the following year.

The Sermon on the Ploughers is generally, and quite properly, regarded as one of the finest of Latimer's extant sermons. No outline or extended quotation can do justice to its qualities. Its excellence for the reader is due in part to the fact that it was more fully and accurately recorded than most of the others, so that it is possible to admire the design and construction of the whole. Partly its appeal arises from the skill with which the preacher is able to sustain the extended metaphor of the ploughers throughout the sermon. Its greatest merit, however, is the lively concreteness which, even in those parts which are most theological, remains picturesque and colorful after the lapse of four centuries.

In Lent of 1548 Latimer preached a series of sermons before the court at Westminster. By this time his fame was so great that the Chapel Royal could not accommodate the throng which wanted to hear him. A special pulpit was built for him in the private gardens of Westminster Palace, so that, says Stow, "he might be heard of more than four times as many people as could have stood in the king's chapel." [27] The Lenten sermons of this year have not been preserved, but from the preacher's references to them in a sermon of 1550 we know that one of the principal topics was an appeal to venal officials to make restitution of any monies of which they had defrauded the government. "I have now preached three Lents," said Latimer in 1550. "The first time I preached restitution." Then he repeated some of his old thunder. "If thou wilt not make restitution, thou shalt go to the devil for it. Now choose thee either restitution, or endless damnation." [28]

In one case, Latimer's words of 1548 achieved dramatic results. John Bradford,[29] later to be a martyr under Mary, and Sir John Harington,[30] treasurer of the King's camps and buildings, made secret restitution of more than £500 of which they (or at least Harington) had defrauded the King. Latimer himself told part of the story [31] without revealing names —he referred to Bradford only as a "good man" and made no allusion whatever to Harington—but it is possible to amplify Latimer's story from Bradford's letters [32] and from the records of the Privy Council. The peculations had occurred while Bradford was serving as Harington's secretary. Shortly thereafter Bradford had come to London to study law at the Inner Temple. Latimer's sermon on restitution so moved him that he immediately wrote Harington begging him to make restitution. Harington demurred, saying that he had not the money. Bradford then took counsel of Latimer, who advised that he confess and throw himself on the mercy of the Protector if Harington had not come around within fourteen days. Finally Harington agreed to pay on installments, over a period of years, if the money might be given secretly to Latimer to be turned over to the Council. Bradford's troublesome conscience urged him to hold out for full restitution at once, but Latimer persuaded him to accept Harington's proposal. The result was, according to Latimer, that Harington returned £20 in Lent 1548, £320 in Lent 1549, and £180.10s. in Lent 1550 [33]—a total of £520.10s. The records of the Privy Council record that Latimer turned over to the Council £373 in March, 1549, and £104 in March, 1550 [34]—a total of £477. The discrepancy between the two sets of figures is probably to be explained by the fact that for his share in the negotiations the Council gave Latimer a reward of £50, a handsome sum and a welcome addition to the honorarium of £20 which he received for the Lenten sermons of 1548. Another consequence of the transaction was that Bradford forsook the law for the study of divinity. He shortly became one of the most ardent of the reformers, and in 1555 he went to the fires of Smithfield with an eagerness which bordered on the psychotic.

The Paul's Cross sermons and the Lenten sermons are the only records which survive of Latimer's preaching in 1548. Because of his great reputation, he must have preached, in London and elsewhere, many sermons of which we now can have no knowledge. He was certainly one of the many preachers who throughout the year 1548 preached at the Cross in support of the government's policy against the mass and in favor of the new communion service. He must have been frequently employed also on other matters. Of such employment, however, there is only one surviving record. In April, 1548, he served with Cranmer and others on the King's commission which examined certain avowed Anabaptists,[35] whose doctrines —especially the denial of the Incarnation and of the authority of secular princes—he abhorred. But on this occasion the offenders recanted, and it was unnecessary to take extreme measures against them.

In the light of subsequent events, the most significant fact of Latimer's career in the year 1548 was his formal renunciation of the doctrine of transubstantiation. When he was in London during this period, Latimer made his home with Archbishop Cranmer at Lambeth Palace, where he took part in the discussions then going forward with both English and Continental theologians on the nature of the communion. It was Cranmer's great hope that out of their deliberations would emerge a truly catholic formula which would be acceptable to all the diverse elements among the reformers. Many of the problems which had vexed such discussions in the past were now pretty much resolved. Cranmer was assured that the government would back him in a formula which rejected the view that the mass was a sacrifice and provided for a communion in which both the bread and the wine would be administered to the laity.

The present debate on the mysteries of the communion was concerned with the question as to what theory should replace the Roman doctrine of transubstantiation, which held that after the prayer of consecration at the mass no substance of the bread and wine remained in the elements.

Some of the English reformers held to the Lutheran theory of consubstantiation—a theory never precisely stated by Luther but generally defined as the substantial presence and combination of the body of Christ *with* the bread and wine. The more extreme reformers held with the Swiss theologian Zwingli an opinion which has been wittily called the "real absence." This party insisted that the bread and wine were but bread and wine, and that the communion was merely a memorial and not of a sacramental nature at all. There were many other shades of opinion.

In the discussions at Lambeth, Archbishop Cranmer proved too conservative and deliberate to satisfy the radicals. He had long been doubtful about the validity of the transubstantialist theory, but he was slow to arrive at an alternative. Even Latimer, more prone to hasty judgment than Cranmer, was cautious. The discontent of the radicals is summed up in a letter written in August, 1548, by Bartholomew Traheron, an extreme Zwinglian, to Heinrich Bullinger, Zwingli's Swiss disciple. After asserting, inaccurately, that the leading English reformers were of Zwingli's opinion, Traheron continues:

> I except the archbishop of Canterbury and Latimer, and a very few learned men besides; for from among the nobility I know not one whose opinions are otherwise than what they ought to be. As to Canterbury, he conducts himself in such a way, I know not how, as that the people do not think much of him, and the nobility regard him as lukewarm. In other respects he is a kind and good-natured man. As to Latimer, though he does not clearly understand the true doctrine of the eucharist, he is nevertheless more favorable than Luther or even Bucer. I am quite sure that he will never be a hindrance to this cause. For, being a man of admirable talents, he sees more clearly into the subject than the others, and is desirous to come into our sentiments, but is slow to decide, and cannot without much difficulty and even timidity renounce an opinion which he has once imbibed. But there is good hope that he will some time or other come over to our side altogether. For he is so far from avoiding any of our friends, that he rather seeks their company, and most anxiously listens to them while discoursing upon this subject, as one who is beyond measure desirous that the whole truth may be laid open to him, and even that he may be thoroughly convinced.[36]

By the end of September, the views of Latimer and Cranmer had developed to the point where even Traheron was contented. He wrote again to Bullinger, "But that you may add yet more to the praises of God, you must know that Latimer has come over to our opinion respecting the true doctrine of the eucharist, together with the archbishop of Canterbury and the other bishops who heretofore seemed to be Lutherans." [37]

Traheron's statement as to the date of Latimer's final rejection of the doctrine of transubstantiation is approximately correct. Although he had been wavering since 1546, when he was sent to the Tower for irregular opinions on the subject,[38] he had evidently been reluctant to make a complete break. That he had done so by 1548 is attested in his own statement in 1554 that he had abandoned belief in transubstantiation about seven years earlier.[39] But Traheron was wrong in his assertion that Latimer and Cranmer had "come over to our opinion," if by that he meant that they had taken the Zwinglian position. They had abandoned belief in the Corporal Presence in the Roman sense, and it is doubtful that they had ever accepted the Lutheran view. But they held firmly to a belief in the Real Spiritual Presence, an opinion which they seem to have derived from the great German theologian Martin Bucer. They rejected the Zwinglian view of the communion as a mere memorial.

In the debate over transubstantiation Cranmer was the leader,[40] Latimer the follower. The whole topic might have been passed over in a few words except for two important considerations. The first of these is that many writers have attributed to Latimer certain extreme views which he never maintained. It has therefore seemed desirable to emphasize the fact that on this topic he shared the opinions of the moderate Anglicans. The second consideration is more important. While it is not true, as some historians have maintained, that the reformation was primarily or even chiefly a quarrel over transubstantiation, it is certainly true that in this matter the conservatives would tolerate no heterodox opinions. On the field of transubstantiation many of the major battles of the reformation were fought. When Cranmer, Latimer and other leaders of reform in England broke with transubstantiation, they burned their bridges. In the next reign, they might have retreated to previously prepared positions in the quarrels over such matters as justification or even the supremacy. Over transubstantiation there could be no retreat. Those who had denied it could surrender—or die.

CHAPTER TWENTY-THREE

APOSTLE TO THE ENGLISH

The awesome but affectionate title "Apostle to the English" which such men as John Foxe and Bishop Ridley applied to Latimer unquestionably reflects the interpretation which they placed upon the whole of his life's work. To some modern students it has seemed more nearly applicable to the closing years of his career, when he became, as Canon Dixon puts it, the Jeremiah of the English reformation, no longer primarily concerned with the "Italian bishop yonder," but hurling thunderbolts at abuses in the Anglican church and at the economic, political, social, and moral ills which infected his beloved England. Such restriction of attention to the last phase of Latimer's life is mistaken, as I hope this study has shown, but it is nevertheless understandable in light of the fact that only five of his extant sermons belong to the period between 1525 and 1540, whereas the remaining thirty-eight all belong to the period between 1548 and 1552. As we turn to a consideration of these later sermons, it will be well to bear in mind that his contemporary reputation was less dependent upon them than upon hundreds of earlier sermons, all but five of them now lost, which represent his long warfare with what he regarded as the enemy.

It will be convenient, before we examine the first group of these later sermons, to set down the few discoverable facts of Latimer's life for the period from the end of 1548 to the end of 1549. During much of this period he certainly lived at Lambeth with Archbishop Cranmer. It has been suggested that he had some share in the intensive work which preceded the final formulation of the first English prayer book, which was formally authorized on January 21, 1549, by the first Act of Uniformity. If so, his participation was purely advisory, for there is no trace of his style in that most beautiful of liturgies. At Lambeth at this time he would have met Peter Martyr, Martin Bucer, Paul Fagius, and other Continental theologians who came to England to escape the *Interim,* that uneasy truce between German Catholics and Protestants which proved intolerable to the latter. There is evidence, too, of his occasional preaching, some of which must have been turbulent; for it is recorded that at some time in the year 1549 the church wardens of St. Margaret's, Westminster, were forced to pay out 1*s.* 6*d.* for "mending of divers pews that were broken when Dr. Latimer did preach." [1] In April, 1549, he served on Cranmer's commission which examined and imprisoned Jane Boucher, a woman whose anabaptist convictions led her to deny the Incarnation; but neither he nor Cranmer had anything to do with her sentence and execution the following year.[2] The most interesting personal record of this period is the fact that on January 8, 1549, the House of Commons petitioned the Lord Protector that Latimer be restored as bishop of his old diocese of Worcester.[3] This was unquestionably a gesture of respect to Latimer; it was also an attack upon the conservative views of the incumbent, Nicholas Heath, who had succeeded John Bell in 1543. Nothing came of the petition. At the moment it did not suit the Protector's book to remove Heath summarily. There is no reliable evidence as to Latimer's reaction to the suggestion of his reappointment to the episcopal bench, but his satiric references to himself as a "quondam," in the sermons of this year, suggest that he would have been glad for the refusal of the appointment.

During Lent of 1549 Latimer preached before the court at Westminster the series of seven Friday sermons for which, with the Sermon on the Ploughers, he is now chiefly remembered. They were preserved through the piety of one Thomas Some, of whom nothing more is known than that he was of the reformed religion, that he was an ardent admirer of Latimer, and that he was adept at some kind of shorthand writing. Some's admiration of "good father Latimer" was boundless. But his shorthand, as he ruefully confessed, was inadequate to keep pace with the torrent of Latimer's eloquence. "And let no man be grieved," Some wrote, "though it be not so exactly done as he did speak it; for in very deed I am not able so to do, to write word for word as he did speak: that passeth my capacity, though I had twenty men's wits, and no fewer hands to write withal." [4]

In spite of many omissions and many palpable distortions, Some rushed his transcripts of the sermons to the press. With a dedication by Some to the duchess of Suffolk, they were published by John Day and William

Seres in 1549, the year of their delivery.[5] There is no evidence that Latimer himself saw the copy before it went to press. If he had seen it, he might have corrected or amplified some of the passages which Some had botched. On the other hand, it would be unfair to attribute all the imperfections in the extant sermons to Thomas Some's deficiencies as a stenographer. The incoherence was no doubt partly due to Latimer's digressive style. As one reads, one suspects that Some took down the digressions at the expense of the central themes. The result is that we must admire the sermons for their effective and picturesque details rather than for their power of sustained thought.[6]

In spite of their incoherence, it is not difficult to perceive the central topics of the separate sermons. The first deals with the office and function of a king. The second, with many digressions, is an attack on those who deplored the fact that a boy was sitting on the throne of England. The third and fourth are pleas for upright magistrates, with incidental replies to the critics of the preceding sermons. The fifth reiterates the themes of the first three. The sixth, the most incoherent of them all, is primarily a defense of the royal supremacy. The seventh is structurally the best and the most exclusively religious in content; it was preached on Good Friday, and is an eloquent meditation upon Christ's agony in Gethsemane. It would not be very helpful, however, to consider the sermons separately. They overlap in content; the same topics recur again and again. It will be more illuminating to consider leading ideas and specific problems as they are treated in the sermons collectively. To do so understandingly, we must first examine their background.

Young Edward VI inherited from his father not only a kingdom but also a whole complex of social and economic ills. Some of these were directly the result of Henry VIII's shortsightedness and rapacity. Others were labor-pains brought on by the impending birth of modern economic man, but they were no less painful for being inevitable. The religious troubles have already been mentioned. On the economic side, the most serious difficulties were those arising from the agrarian problem,[7] the resultant displacements of labor, and an inflated currency. The dissolution of the monasteries, originally represented as a device to stamp out corruption in the religious orders, had been followed by the sale of the monastic lands to enterprising and often unscrupulous "new men"—rising courtiers, land-hungry merchants, and the like—who had none of the old feudal ideal of the landowner's responsibility towards his tenants and workers. To the "new men" land was purely an investment to be used in whatever way would bring in the greatest profit. Many of the new landlords were rack-renters, and virtually all of them were enclosers—that is, wherever possible they converted arable land and commons formerly used for the grazing of cattle into pasturage for sheep, since the production and export of wool was now England's most profitable business. Enclosures were nothing new. The sale of the monastic lands merely expanded and accelerated a process which was an unavoidable aspect of the decline of the feudal system and the rise of modern "business."

By the time of Edward's accession in 1547 the social and economic dislocations resulting from rack-renting and enclosures were critical. The yeoman, the backbone of the old agrarian economy, was in many cases forced off the land by rising rents; where he managed to hold on, his standard of living was sharply reduced. Farm laborers were thrown out of work; as Latimer put it, "For whereas we have been a great many of house-holders and inhabitants, there is now but a shepherd and his dog." Many of them had no recourse except to vagabondage, against which the severest measures were ineffective. The surplus of labor kept wages down, in spite of the fact that the period was otherwise one of inflation brought on by repeated debasement of the coinage to meet the rising cost of government.

Such, in brief summary, were the critical problems confronting Edward VI or, more exactly, confronting the Protector Somerset. In 1547 and 1548 small but significant risings of the common folk occurred in various parts of England, and petitions for the redress of grievances had been addressed to the King.[8] Somerset was alarmed. He was also genuinely concerned for the public welfare. In June, 1548, he issued a proclamation describing the evils resulting from enclosure, and calling attention to the existing statutes restricting the practice. In Parliament various measures of control were proposed, but most of them were allowed to die, since the Commons actually represented the landowners rather than the people at large. Nor did Somerset's policy have the full support of the Privy Council, where the Earl of Warwick was the principal spokesman of the opposition.

To reforming preachers like Latimer, and to laymen who shared their views, the economic and social distress of the mid-century was far more than an economic problem.[9] Although they were probably more aware of inexorable economic forces than modern writers give them credit for, their approach to a solution of the problem was primarily moral and religious. For in their view, the reformation of religion, with the open Bible as its symbol and its textbook, should have driven out the old corruption and ushered in a new era of righteousness. Its failure to do so was distressing, and they looked for a solution in the faith that was in them. The long story of their gropings has often been told, most effectively by Tawney in his *Religion and the Rise of Capitalism*. The later compromises of Puritanism with the "realities" of business furnish abundant material for cynical reflection. But there can be no doubt of the earnestness and sincerity of the conviction of Latimer and others like him that a religious solution to the problem must be found. They had no doubt that if it could not be found the just wrath of heaven would shortly be visited upon England for her sins.

Beginning, as nearly as we can tell, with the Sermon on the Ploughers in January, 1548, Latimer had been one of the most vocal of critics of the existing order. Another such critic was Thomas Lever,[10] a fellow of St. John's College, Cambridge, who at the age of twenty-seven was just coming into prominence as a preacher. Still another was the layman John Hales,[11] of whom we shall hear more in a moment. In the preaching and writing of these men the word "commonwealth" occurred with such frequency that by some of their opponents they were called "Commonwealths" or "Commonwealth men." Modern historians often speak of them as the "Commonwealth Party." They were not a party in the sense that they had an organization. But they were a party in the sense that they had a common program or theory, which may be summed up in the words of Hales: "It may not be lawful for every man to use his own as him listeth, but every man must use that he hath to the most benefit of his country." [12] As the late Professor Pollard put it, they held "that man was born not to himself, but primarily for the services of God and then for that of the state." [13]

It cannot now be determined to what extent the teaching of the "Commonwealths" influenced the policy of Somerset or, conversely, to what extent their views must be regarded as a reflection of that policy and perhaps propagandizing for it. It may have been partly as a result of their agitation that Somerset, in June, 1548, appointed commissions to investigate enclosures in several of the shires. [14] The only one of these which seems actively to have functioned was that headed by the aforementioned John Hales, in many ways the most articulate of the "Commonwealths." In the latter part of 1548 Hales' commission heard the testimony of witnesses in some of the midland counties. Somerset's opponents took the view that the commission's activities merely served to stir up unrest. It is in connection with such local disturbances that we encounter the name of Latimer among the "Commonwealth Men." In October, 1548, Sir Anthony Auchar wrote to Cecil as follows:

Sir, as a poor man may require you, be plain with my lord's grace [Somerset] that under the pretense of simplicity and poverty there may rest much mischief. So do I fear there doth in these men called Commonwealths and their adherents. To declare unto you the state of the gentlemen (I mean as well the greatest as the lowest) I assure you they are in such doubt that almost they dare touch none of them [the disturbers of the peace], not for that they are afraid of them, but for that some of them have been sent up and come away without punishment, and that Commonwealth called Latimer hath gotten the pardon of others (and so they speak manifestly) that I may well gather some of them to be in jealousy of my lord's friendship, yea and to be plain, think my lord's grace rather to will the decay of the gentlemen than otherwise . . . . Assuring you that if words may do harm or may be treason or any ill come of them, there was never none that ever spake so vilely as these called Commonwealths do. [15]

Although Somerset's commission on enclosures accomplished little of practical significance, it bore speculative fruit in the celebrated tract called *A Discourse of the Common Weal of this Realm of England.* First printed in 1581 as the work of "W.S." (at one time absurdly identified with William Shakespeare), the tract was obviously written about 1549; scholars are now pretty generally agreed that its author was John Hales. It takes the form of a dialogue in which the problem of enclosures is discussed with philosophic calm against the background of the work of the enclosures commission. The principal speakers are the "knight," who acts as interlocutor and describes existing conditions, and the "doctor," who points to the cause of the troubles and suggests the remedies which will produce a Christian commonwealth. Other speakers are the husbandman and the capper. The "knight" is easily identifiable as Hales. Miss Lamond, the modern editor of the *Discourse,* tentatively identified the "doctor" as Latimer. [16] The language used by the "doctor" is unlike Latimer's, but his ideas bear a remarkable resemblance to some of those advanced in the sermons.

For our purposes, however, the identity of the "doctor" is of minor importance. What is important is the fact that Latimer's court sermons of 1549 were part of the current thought concerning the Christian commonwealth as reflected in the *Discourse* and elsewhere. They were preached on behalf of the policies of Somerset and the ideals of the "commonwealth men" to a courtly audience, many of whom were themselves enclosers and rack-renters who were little likely to listen sympathetically to the preacher's views.

From beginning to end, Latimer's Friday Sermons propound the Tudor theory of monarchy. The theory itself was a commonplace; what is interesting in Latimer's treatment of it is the intensely ethical and religious undergirding which he provides for it. In a protestant commonwealth released from obedience to the universal church, all authority, temporal and spiritual, rests with the monarch. The king has his authority from God. It is therefore his duty to be godly in his life, to walk according to God's holy Word.[17] His first concern must be the study of the Scriptures.[18] Save for recreation when he is weary of state affairs, he must not dance and banquet, hawk and hunt. He must carry the Bible with him constantly and study it all the days of his life. Thus, and thus only, will he truly flourish. He will have the dread of God ever before his eyes. When his counselors, his "claw-backs," advise him badly, he will have a pair of spectacles, one lens of which is faith and the other charity, through which to perceive their motives.

As for worldly wealth, says Latimer, the king must have sufficient for his honor.[19] He may lawfully tax his subjects for all just purposes. But he must not have so much that his subjects are impoverished.[20] Nor may he permit any of his subjects to have too much at the expense of those who are poorer than themselves.[21] It rests with the king to determine equitably how much is "sufficient" either for himself or for any of his subjects; here again, he may not trust his counselors in the government, who are guided by self-interest.[22] To redress cases of inequity, he must always be ready to hear the complaints of his subjects, the little, unimportant people as well as the great.[23] He must see to it that his judges and magistrates do the same, else he will be as guilty of injustice as they.[24]

All this imposes a heavy responsibility upon the king. But for his support he has the Holy Scriptures. He will also seek wisdom through prayer, as did Solomon.[25] Moreover—this is a characteristic touch—the king can look for guidance from his godly preachers. For God, says Latimer, has two swords.[26] The king, wielding the temporal sword, may correct transgressors, even the clergy. But the clergy, wielding the spiritual sword, may correct the king, as Moses corrected Pharoah and as Micaiah corrected Ahab. Thus Latimer appropriated to the Tudor preacher something of the function of the prophet of Israel—and not a little of that of the bishop of Rome.

Since the Friday Sermons of 1549 were addressed to the King and his court, it is not surprising that Latimer speaks far more of the duty of kings and magistrates than he does of the duty of the subject. But the subject's responsibilities are clear by implication, and in later sermons are explicitly affirmed.[27] The subject too must be guided by the Word, which will be clarified for him by the study of the Bible, by prayer, and by the admonitions of godly preachers. The subject's duty, of course, is to deal justly with his fellow man and to serve the king as he would serve God. As in all Tudor theorizing upon government, rebellion against the king is unthinkable. If the king is unjust, the subject must endure injustice patiently. The subject may seek redress by all legal means. If these fail, he must be passively obedient in all temporal matters. Heaven will punish the king for his injustice, as it will reward the subject for his patience. In the meantime, the subject will seek consolation in prayer.

This was the theory which should have produced the Christian commonwealth. But the actual fell far short of the ideal. In criticizing and describing the actual, Latimer is at his picturesque best. Everywhere he finds evidence of greed and avarice—of "private commodity." The brewer waters his ale; the clothier stretches his cloth to get an extra yard to a piece, then conceals his deception by thickening the cloth with flock-powder.[28] The physician, the lawyer, the merchant, the landlord—all are infected:

> As for example, the physician: if the poor man be diseased, he can have no help without too much. And of the lawyer, the poor man can get no counsel, expedition, nor help in his matter, except he give him too much. At merchants' hands no kind of ware can be had, except we give for it too much. You landlords, you rent-raisers, I may say you step-lords, you unnatural lords, you have for your possessions yearly too much. For that [which] here before went [for] twenty or forty pound by year . . . now is let for fifty or an hundred pound by year. Of this too much cometh this monstrous and portentous dearth made by man, notwithstanding God doth send us plentifully the fruits of the earth, mercifully, contrary unto our deserts . . . .[29]

He is particularly severe, of course, against enclosers and against the "carnal gospelers" who have embraced the reformed religion only that they might get abbey and chantry lands to exploit. The law, he says, is unable to cope with the evil: "We have good statutes made for the commonwealth, as touching commoners, enclosers; many meetings and sessions; but in the end of the matter there cometh nothing forth. Well, well . . . from whence it cometh I know, even from the devil." [30]

He speaks plainly to his courtly audience:

> I will tell you, my lords and masters, this is not for the king's honor . . . . it is the king's honor that the commonwealth be advanced; that the dearth of these foresaid things be provided for, and the commodities of this realm so employed, as it may be to the setting his subjects on work, and keeping them from idleness. And herein resteth the king's honor and his office.[31]

Such an admonition could only have aroused the antagonism of an audience in which many were rack-renters and enclosers. It is not surprising that one of them, when asked how he liked Latimer, replied, "Marry, even as I liked him always: a seditious fellow."[32] Many of his hearers must have been pinched also by his attacks upon corruption in the government and the courts. Throughout the sermons he lashes out against bribe-takers, many of whom recoiled when money was offered to them directly, but accepted it through their wives or their servants.[33] He tells of one murderer who got off by paying a crown to each of twelve jurors; and of another, a woman guilty of infanticide, who got off by bribing a judge who hanged another woman, unable to meet his price, for stealing a few rags off a hedge.[34] So common is the evil among government officers that bribes are referred to lightly as "gentle rewards." But changing the name does not palliate the crime. Officials who take bribes are thieves—"princely thieves." They may not hold up wayfarers on Shooters Hill or Standgate Hole, but they are thieves just the same.[35]

The principal reason for this corruption, says Latimer, is that officials must pay, and pay excessively, for their posts. The price of an office ranges from £200 to £2,000, and the purchaser must get his money back. The evil will be remedied when the King gives the offices to able, qualified men—wise men, men of activity, in whom is the truth—and pays them well for their services.[36] Closely related to the corruption in the sale of government offices is that in the sale of ecclesiastical benefices. The fault is with the patrons. Latimer tells of a suitor for a benefice who sent the patron a dish of apples. At first the patron was indignant; "This is no apple matter." But when he found ten gold pieces in each apple he was ready enough to give the benefice to the applicant. "Get you a graft of that tree," Latimer concludes, "and I warrant you it will stand in better stead than all St. Paul's learning." [37]

The consequence of this wholesale giving and taking of bribes is that poor men cannot get their suits heard in the courts or by the proper authorities. Latimer himself was known to be sympathetic to such suitors; he confesses that he was thought a nuisance for his intervention on their behalf. He cannot, he says, go into the Archbishop's garden at Lambeth to read his book but what he is besieged by poor men seeking his aid in getting their suits heard. He even rebukes the Protector himself for his negligence in this regard (effectively, it would seem, since Somerset set up a Court of Requests in his own house for the hearing of complaints),[38] and urges the King to emulate Solomon's readiness to hear complaints himself.[39]

In the Friday Sermons, however, Latimer did not limit his jeremiads to corruption in government. There are repeated denunciations against the decline in national morality, especially sexual morality. "I hear say," he laments, "that there is such a whoredom in England as never was seen the like." [40] He points out that measures taken in 1546 to suppress the "stews" of the Bankside have not been notably efficacious.[41] The brothels still flourished, many of them having removed to the "immune" precinct of St. Martin-le-grand.[42]

Within Latimer's generalized attack upon sexual irregularity there is more specific criticism of laxity in the laws of marriage and divorce. He speaks especially of the practice of the noble and wealthy of arranging the marriage of infant children—even the kidnapping and forced marriage of wards [43]—"for joining lands to lands, possessions to possessions, neither the virtuous education or living being regarded; but in the infancy such marriages be made, to the displeasure of God, and breach of espousals." [44] The result of infant marriages is subsequent adultery and divorce. In this particular point there may have been a reference to a contemporary *cause célèbre:* the marquis of Southampton had just put away his wife for adultery and, contrary to canon law, had married Elizabeth Cobham, to the outrage of Somerset who, through the Privy Council, declared the second marriage illegal.[45]

As we read these repeated and sustained attacks upon personal immorality and public corruption, we are inevitably led to wonder what rate of discount must be allowed to the reforming zeal of the preacher. The late Professor Pollard, whose expert knowledge of the period is unsurpassed, was inclined to think that the evils of enforced marriage and divorce were no greater then than in earlier and later periods,[46] and the experience of the ages, from the Hebrew prophets to the present, indicates a fairly constant percentage of sexual irregularity. On the other hand, there can be little doubt of the accuracy of Latimer's picture of economic distress and of the corruption in government. The former is attested by the statutes as well as by the evidence of Latimer's contemporaries.[47] The latter is likewise attested by the record, and by Francis Bacon's famous comparison of his own corrupt judicial record with that of his predecessors.

Latimer was at one with his contemporaries and his predecessors back through the Middle Ages in seeing the mortal sin of covetousness as the basis of all economic and social ills. He had little hope for the amelioration of either the sin or its consequences by statute. Nor does it appear that he believed, like John Hales, that reform might come through an appeal to self-interest. Certainly he did not anticipate the idea of the social contract. His hope of remedy, as far as he had any, lay in cutting at the root of covetousness by means of "Godly preaching." To the twentieth century the notion may appear naïve, but it must be remembered that Latimer and his fellows had good reason to know the power of the pulpit as a medium of propaganda, and they did not entirely despair of its power to inculcate virtue as well as to sway opinion.

Latimer is quite precise in his convictions of the importance of preaching. His starting point is St. Paul's famous words in Romans 10:13-15— "For whosoever shall call upon the name of the Lord shall be saved. How then shall they call on him in whom they have not believed? And how shall they believe in him of whom they have not heard? And how shall they hear without a preacher? And how shall they preach except they be sent?" This was the *Scala Coeli*—"the true ladder that bringeth a man to heaven"— of which Latimer speaks repeatedly in his Friday Sermons.[48] But there was another rung in the ladder which might lead to the betterment of this world. By preaching, men may be brought through faith to salvation. But by salvation they may also be brought to righteousness, and by righteousness the commonwealth may be saved.

It was because he believed so strongly that without preaching there could be neither personal salvation nor a Christian commonwealth that Latimer reiterated, in his Friday Sermons, the attack on "nonpreaching prelates" which had been the central theme of the Sermon on the Ploughers. It is the duty of patrons to see to it that benefices go to "godly preachers." It is the duty of incumbents to preach and read the Homilies regularly.[49] The "strawberry preachers" who come but once a year must be made to preach or give up their livings. Displaced chantry-priests, who have no skill as preachers, must be given pensions as provided by law; they must not, to evade the pension, be entrusted with parishes.[50]

Perhaps his sharpest attacks are directed against bishops who are themselves unpreaching prelates and permit nonpreaching prelates in their dioceses. He alludes to a bishop (Tunstall) who is busier as president of a council than in his episcopal duties.[51] He speaks darkly of another who commits all his work to a suffragan;[52] he rebukes Veysey of Exeter for inactivity and calls Coverdale, then preaching in Devonshire, Veysey's "suffragan."[53]

He tells of a bishop on visitation to a certain parish who was offended when the great bell could not be rung for him because the clapper was broken. One of the parish said, "Why, my lord, doth your lordship make so great a matter of the bell that lacketh a clapper? Here is a bell" —pointing to the pulpit—"that hath lacked a clapper this twenty years. We have a parson that fetcheth out of this benefice fifty pound every year, but we never see him." "I warrant you," Latimer concludes his story, "the bishop was an unpreaching prelate. He could find fault with the bell that wanted a clapper to ring him into the town, but he could not find any fault with the parson that preached not at his benefice." [54] Against non-functioning bishops Latimer suggests a drastic remedy: "Make them quondams. Out with them; cast them out of their office: what should they do with cures that will not look them it."[55] At one point he makes the radical suggestion that if there are not sufficient godly preachers to fill the bishoprics, there are enough learned laymen to supply the need. Let them be ordained and consecrated, all in good order. Lest the suggestion seem too extreme, Latimer reminds his hearers that many laymen are already enjoying the income from ecclesiastical endowments, and cites the case of Sir Thomas Smith, the secretary of state, who was provost of Eton and dean of Carlisle.[56]

Latimer had too much sense of humor, however, to believe that the laity unanimously shared his own enthusiasm for preaching. He tells of a London woman whose sovereign remedy for insomnia was to go to the sermon at St. Thomas of Acres, where she never failed of a good nap. But, he says, it is better that she go, whatever her purpose, than that she stay at home. "For with what mind soever ye come, though ye come for an ill purpose, yet peradventure ye may chance to be caught ere ye go; the preacher may chance to catch you on his hook." [57] Where the people love not to hear preaching, the fault lies still with unpreaching prelates. He illustrates the point with an anecdote from his own experience:

I came once myself to a place, riding on a journey homeward from London, and I sent word over night into the town that I would preach there in the morning, because it was holiday; and methought it was a holiday's work. The church stood in my way, and I took my horse and my company and went thither. I thought I should have found a great company in the church, and when I came there, the church door was fast locked. I tarried there half an hour and more: at last the key was found, and one of the parish comes to me and says, "Sir, this is a busy day with us, we cannot hear you; it is Robin Hood's day [May 1, when it was the custom to collect money for the May games]. The parish are gone abroad to gather for Robin Hood: I pray you let them not." I was fain there to give place to Robin Hood: I thought my rochet should have been regarded, though I were not; but it would not serve, it was fain to give place to Robin Hood's men.

At this the audience laughed, and Latimer drove home his point:

It is no laughing matter, my friends, it is a weeping matter, a heavy matter; a heavy matter, under the pretense of gathering for Robin Hood, a traitor and a thief, to put out a preacher, to have his office less esteemed; to prefer Robin Hood before the ministration of God's word: and all this hath come of unpreaching prelates.[58]

In preaching, then, lay England's hope. It was necessary to provide godly preachers, and that concern underlies the anxiety over education which runs through the Friday Sermons. To Latimer all education was education for godliness. Any impediment to education was an impediment to godliness. For this reason he was seriously disturbed by the consequences of the statute of 1547 by which the chantries were finally abolished.[59] The chantry-priests had been the local schoolmasters, and one clause of the statute provided that purchasers of chantry-lands should continue to devote part of the income to the "education of youth in virtue and godliness." By the new owners, this provision was pretty generally honored in the breach rather than the observance. Somerset himself, although he was responsible for the educational provision of the statute, caused the income of some of the chantry-endowments which were retained by the Crown to be diverted to military and other expenditures.[60] It was in protest against this abuse that Latimer had said, in the Sermon on the Ploughers, "for the love of God appoint teachers and schoolmasters, you that have charge of youth; and give the teachers stipends worthy of their pains, that they may bring them up in grammar, in logic, in rhetoric, in philosophy, in the civil law, and in that which I cannot leave unspoken of, the word of God." [61] The theme is repeated again and again in the Friday Sermons of 1549.

In the field of education, however, Latimer's primary concern was with the universities, especially his beloved Cambridge. In the mid-century the universities were unquestionably in the doldrums,[62] partly because of a dearth of distinguished teachers. There was another problem. From their foundation the universities had been primarily concerned with the education of the higher clergy, whose ranks had been recruited very largely from the yeoman class. Now many of the yeomen were in straitened circumstances and unable to maintain their sons at the university. Nor were the young men otherwise maintained, in spite of frequent injunctions to holders of well-paying benefices to provide exhibitions for one or more students. The result was a sharp decline in the number of divinity students, their places being taken by the sons of courtiers and wealthy merchants whose interest, when it was not solely in education for gentility, was in humane rather than theological study.

To Latimer, mindful of Paul's "And how shall they preach except they be sent?" this change in student personnel could have only one consequence—a decline in the number of "godly preachers." It is therefore to this matter that he addresses himself in the Friday sermons. One of his attacks on the "gold-coast" students has been quoted in an earlier chapter.[63] One more passage must serve as a summary of his thought on the subject:

It would pity a man's heart to hear that that I hear of the state of Cambridge; what it is in Oxford I cannot tell. There be few do study divinity, but so many as of necessity must furnish the colleges [*i.e.,* who hold fellowships]; for their livings be so small, and victuals so dear, that they tarry not there, but go other where to seek livings; and so they go about. Now there be a few gentlemen, and they study a little divinity. Alas, what is that? It will come to pass that we shall have nothing but a little English divinity, that will bring the realm into a very barbarousness and utter decay of learning. It is not that, I wis, that will keep out the supremacy of the bishop of Rome.

Here will I make a supplication, that ye bestow so much to the finding [i.e., the support] of scholars of good wits, of poor men's sons, to exercise the office of salvation, in relieving of scholars, as ye were wont to bestow in pilgrimage-matters, in trentals, in masses, in pardons, in purgatory-matters. Ye bestowed that liberally, bountifully; but this was not well spent . . . . You may be sure, if you bestow your goods on this wise, ye shall bestow it well, to support and uphold God's word, wherein ye shall please God.[64]

This emphasis on education and godly preaching may serve us as a needed reminder that Latimer's Friday Sermons, while primarily social and economic in their implications, were still full of vigorous preaching on behalf of the reformed religion. In the sermons as originally preached, there was probably a great deal more than Thomas Some was able to take down. In the sermons as we have them are echoes of the old pleas for the Bible in English in Latimer's attacks upon the "Dr. Dubbers" who say that the people do not need the Scriptures.[65] There are even surprised comments upon his discovery, made while he was browsing in the Archbishop's library at Lambeth, that some of the scholastic writers were acquainted with the Bible![66] A number of fine passages, echoing the Homily, expound the doctrine that faith only justifies.[67] Other passages are obviously defenses of recent legislation pertaining to the church. The attacks on prayers to the saints reflects the fact that quarrels over the removal of images still raged.[68]. The denunciation of the "popish mass"[69] and the praise of the communion service are obvious defenses of the new Prayer Book, which had just been issued, although it did not come into general use until the following June.

It is obvious that at many points in the Friday Sermons Latimer was acting as a spokesman for the government. This will be the more apparent from a consideration of two topics not yet mentioned. The first is Latimer's discussion of the problem of the King's minority and the succession. The theory had been advanced by some opponents of the government's policies, particularly on religious matters, that laws enacted during the King's minority were invalid, or at best only temporary. Somerset and his party were thus attacked through the King. In some cases these attacks took the extreme form of expressions of fear for the country's safety with a boy-king on the throne. Thus on January 21, 1549, in a speech before the Commons,[70] Dr. John Story, the first Regius professor of civil law at Oxford, dared to quote from Ecclesiastes 10:16 the words, "Woe unto thee, O land, when thy king is a child." For his temerity Story was imprisoned briefly, then went to Louvain where he remained until 1555. But Story was only one member of a faction which included such formidable personages as Bishops Gardiner and Bonner. A strong counter-propaganda was needed. Accordingly, Latimer's first two Friday Sermons were largely directed against this faction.

To Ecclesiastes 10:16 he opposed Ecclesiastes 10:17 as it reads in the Vulgate—"Blessed is the land whose king is noble." He continues:

What people are they that say "The king is but a child"? Have we not a noble king? Was there ever a king so noble; so godly; brought up with so noble counsellors; so excellent and well learned schoolmasters? I will tell you this, and I speak it even as I think: his majesty hath more godly wit and understanding, more learning and knowledge at this age, than twenty of his progenitors, that I could name, had at any time of their life.[71]

The preacher is able to cite scriptural precedents for boy-kings—including David in his second childhood![72] Edward is the natural king, given by God.[73] He is wise. His council takes pains day and night for the profit of the commonwealth. Yet some wicked people will say, "Tush, this gear will not tarry: it is but my lord Protector's or my lord of Canterbury's doing: the king is a child, and he knoweth not of it." "Jesu mercy!" Latimer continues. "How like are we Englishmen to the Jews, ever stubborn, stiff-necked, and walking in by-ways!" [74]

For the sake of the succession, the King must make a godly marriage —and with an English wife.[75] The marriage ought not to be merely political; if it is based on affection and esteem, the King will not be tempted to adultery and divorce. From such a union, in the fullness of time, will come a true English heir to the English throne.[76] In the meantime, Mary and Elizabeth are the King's true heirs. They must marry Englishmen. If either marries a foreigner, let her never come to the throne. A foreign king is the worst fate that Latimer can imagine for England, for it will bring back the "strange religion." If that fate should befall, it will be punishment for England's vices.[77] "Therefore, to avoid this plague, let us amend our lives," lest God "plague us with a strange king, for our unrepentant heart." [78]

Thus in the matter of the King's minority Latimer promoted and defended the authority of the protectorate. He did so also in his remarks upon the affair of Thomas Seymour, the Protector's brother.[79] Thomas Seymour was an ambitious man. At the accession of Edward he was created Baron Seymour of Sudeley, became a member of the Privy Council, and shortly succeeded Warwick as Lord High Admiral. In many ways, during the next three years, he was a thorn in the Protector's side. His marriage to Catherine Parr within a few months of the death of Henry VIII gave offense, as did his attempted familiarities with the fifteen-year-old Princess Elizabeth, who lived in their household under the protection of Catherine. After Catherine's death in September, 1548, he hoped to marry Elizabeth, a scheme which Somerset opposed with threats of imprisonment in the Tower. He was guilty of various kinds of official corruption; he organized a faction within the Council in opposition against his brother; and it is certain that he hoped to become co-protector, if he did not plot to usurp Somerset's position altogether. One of his minor offenses was that he attempted to win the support of the young King by supplying him with money—a point noted here only because in 1548 some of the money went to Latimer for his court sermons.[80] At last the Council prepared a set of charges against him and on March 4, 1549, he was attainted of treason by act of Parliament. He was beheaded on Tower Hill on March 22. Historians ever since have been debating the degree of his guilt, the legality of the procedure by which he was convicted, and above all the responsibility of his brother the Protector for his death.

Whatever the true answers to these questions may have been, immediately after the Lord Admiral's death certain of his faction loudly asserted that his execution was judicial murder instigated by Somerset. Latimer, in the last five of his Friday Sermons, undertook, or was assigned, to answer these charges. In the sermon of March 24, two days after the execution, he reproved those who challenged the decrees of Council and Parliament, and exhorted his audience to accept the decisions of constituted authority.[81] The following week he spoke precisely in answer to those who saw proof of innocence in the courage with which the Admiral went to his death. He alleged that Sudeley, in the Tower awaiting execution, had addressed letters to the Princesses Mary and Elizabeth, urging them to conspire against the Protector. On the block he had said to the servant of the lieutenant of the Tower, "Bid my servant speed the thing that he wots of." The words were overheard, and the letters were found in the servant's shoe. Latimer further charged, with grudging admiration, that Sudeley had been able to manufacture both the pen and the ink with which the letters were written.[82] In the same sermon Latimer asserted that he had met, years before, a prostitute condemned for robbery who, before she was hanged at Tyburn, confessed that her first fall from virtue had been wrought by the Lord Admiral.[83] The following week Latimer defended the attainder, arguing that the Admiral received as much justice as if he had been tried by the Lords.[84] Two weeks later, in his Good Friday sermon, Latimer added yet another item to his bill of particulars: the Lord Admiral had been a contemner of religion. When Catherine Parr instituted family prayer, "the admiral gets him out of the way, like a mole digging in the earth." [85]

It is not surprising that Latimer's allegations of treason, fornication, and irreligion provoked the Lord Admiral's faction to indignant protest. Latimer complained that they made "such a huzzing and buzzing in the preacher's ear, that it maketh him oftentimes to forget his matter." [86] Specifically the Admiral's friends branded Latimer's statements as lies and charged that he had been suborned by the Lord Protector and the Council.[87] Some alleged, however, that he had been suborned by the duchess of Somerset, the Protector's wife,[88] who was popularly believed to be piqued because protocol required her to yield precedence to the Admiral's wife, Catherine Parr, as former queen.[89] In either case, his enemies likened Latimer to Dr. Ralph Shaw, the prebendary of St. Paul's, whose services Richard Crookback suborned to proclaim the illegitimacy of the sons of Edward IV.[90]

By any modern standard, Latimer's attacks upon the dead Lord Admiral were in shocking taste. They have offended even his most sympathetic biographers. All that can be said in extenuation is that in such matters, as in so many others, Tudor standards were not ours. Even here, however, we are on uncertain ground, for the passages referring to the Lord Admiral were deleted from all except the first edition of the sermons. If we turn from the question of taste to questions of fact, it must be recorded first that Latimer indignantly and publicly denied that he was suborned or that he had lied. He had, he said, never discussed the Lord Admiral with the duchess of Somerset.[91] As for Council and Parliament—"The council needs not my lie for the defense of that that they do . . . . Although the men of the parliament-house can defend themselves yet have I spoken this of good zeal, and a good ground of the admiral's writing; I have not feigned or lied one jot." [92] Unfortunately, all the specific charges laid by Latimer to the Lord Admiral rest upon Latimer's unsupported statements. In the end, they must be judged in terms of the known character of the Lord Admiral on the one hand, and the known character of Latimer on the other. The advantage seems to rest with Latimer.[93]

Here, then, as in so much else in the Friday Sermons, Latimer was speaking semi-officially on behalf of the Protector's government and policies. The point has been emphasized, because most writers, in their admiration for the picturesque effectiveness of the sermons, have lost sight of the propaganda in them. The fact that the sermons contain propaganda need in no way weaken our belief in the preacher's sincerity. All of Latimer's convictions led him to support the Protector's policies; when called upon to preach at Westminster, he could defend them with all the force of his eloquence.

CHAPTER TWENTY-FOUR

THE LAST SERMONS

Latimer was about fifty-seven years old when he preached the Friday Sermons of 1549. In terms of the average life expectancy of the sixteenth century he was an old man. He so regarded himself, and he was so regarded by his admirers. Thomas Some, who collected the 1549 sermons, spoke of him as "father Latimer," [1] and expressed the hope that he might "live long among us in a flourishing old age." [2] No doubt the impression that he had reached the age when the grasshopper is a burden was enhanced by the frailty of his body and the frequent bouts of illness of which he complained from the age of forty onward. In the year following the Friday Sermons he suffered a sickness which led him to believe that he was at the point of death. In view of this fact, there was probably no foundation for the rumor which circulated in February 1550, that the government was once more about to give him a bishopric.[3]

He was not so old or so ill, however, that he was unable to keep a watchful eye upon the rebellions and uprisings which erupted in several parts of England in the summer of 1549. The first of these, the rising in Cornwall and Devonshire, was touched off by the new Prayer Book, which the law required to be used in all churches beginning June 9, 1549. The Cornishmen, with some justice, protested that the English service was to them just as foreign as the old Latin, and they clamored for the restoration of the mass, the revival of the Act of the Six Articles, and a general return to the ways of the old religion. The Cornish revolt was not put down until the middle of August; in the meantime rebellion had reared its head elsewhere. In Oxfordshire, where many a stubborn priest was hanged from his own church steeple, the revolt was primarily against religious innovation. In Yorkshire, Northampton, Norfolk, and Suffolk, however, the risings, while not unrelated to religion, were provoked chiefly by social and economic grievances. The most formidable of these was the rising in Norfolk, commonly called Kett's Rebellion.[4] Under the leadership of Robert Kett, the Norfolk rebels confiscated some of the common lands which had been enclosed, and instituted a kind of local communism which was finally crushed by an army of foreign mercenaries under the command of the earl of Warwick.

The revolts of 1549 constituted a grave embarrassment for the Protector Somerset. In a sense his religious policies had provoked the risings in Cornwall and Oxfordshire. On the other hand, the rebellions in Norfolk and elsewhere were protests against the evils which Somerset himself had sought to remedy; while he could have no sympathy with rebellion, he did have a sympathetic understanding of its causes. His handling of the situation, once the revolts had broken out, was far from vigorous; it was Warwick, rather than Somerset, who emerged from the crisis as the strong man in the government. The result was that in October, 1549, Somerset was deposed by the Council and sent to the Tower for a time. He again became a member of the Privy Council in February, 1550, and for the better part of two years he strove to maneuver himself back into his former position of power. In the end, charges of treason and felony were trumped up against him, and he was executed on January 22, 1552.

With the fall of Somerset the control of the government passed to Warwick, who shortly assumed the title of Duke of Northumberland. The new government abandoned Somerset's policies with respect to enclosures. On the other hand, from expediency rather than conviction, Northumberland became the supporter of the extremists among the reformers of relegion. During his regime Gardiner was deprived of his bishopric and placed under closer confinement. Heath, Bonner, and Tunstall were removed from the sees of Worcester, London, and Durham. John Hooper, the "father of nonconformity," was appointed to the see of Gloucester, and touched off the first of the controversies over the use of vestments. Nicholas Ridley was translated from Rochester to London, with the result that St. Paul's and the city churches were stripped of their altars. It is small wonder that Northumberland was regarded as the patron of protestantism. But he was a "new man," and behind his religious policies was the practical necessity of winning the support of the other "new men" and keeping the old Catholic families out of power. Northumberland's cynicism in matters of religion is sufficiently indicated by the fact that in his hour of extremity under Mary he professed to be a Catholic.

It was therefore after a period of rebellion and a turnover in the government that Latimer, during Lent, 1550, preached at court for the last time. This year the principal Lenten preachers were John Hooper and Thomas Lever; as far as the record shows, Latimer preached but a single sermon. The minor role assigned to him may have been due to his recent illness. "When I was appointed to preach here," he said to his audience, "I was new come out of a sickness, whereof I looked to have died, and weak as I was, yet nevertheless, when I was appointed unto it, I took it upon me." [5] And again, "I think I shall no more come here; for I think I have not long to live; so that I judge I take my leave now of the court forever, and shall no more come in this place." [6] But it is also possible that he was made to play third fiddle to Hooper and Lever because he was known to have been strongly sympathetic to the fallen Somerset and his policies. "The Last Sermon Preached before King Edward the Sixth," as it is commonly called,[7] is the longest of Latimer's extant sermons. At the outset he announced his intention of preaching for three or four hours ("I know it will be so long, in case I be not commanded to the contrary" [8]), and it is likely that he did so. From its length we may conclude that the printed sermon more nearly approximates the spoken sermon than any of the others.[9]

It is not necessary to summarize the sermon in great detail. Its text was Luke 12:15—"Take heed and beware of covetousness"—and it repeated the old attack upon covetousness, the evil root from which spring enclosures, corruption in government and in private morals, and so on. It should be emphasized, however, that this was a courageous sermon, preached as it was before a court at which Northumberland, not Somerset, was now the principal figure. Northumberland's sympathy lay entirely with the enclosures, not with the recent rebels; yet Latimer spoke as follows of the rebellions of 1549:

> Covetousness was the cause of rebellion this last summer; and both parties had covetousness, as well the gentlemen as the commons. Both parties had covetousness, for both parties had an inordinate desire to have that they had not: and that is covetousness, an inordinate desire to have that one hath not.
>
> The commons would have had from the gentlemen such things as they desired: the gentlemen would none of it; and so was there covetousness on both sides. The commons thought they had a right to the things that they inordinately sought to have. But what then? They must not come to it that way. Now on the other side, the gentlemen had a desire to keep that they had, and so they rebelled too against the king's commandment, and against such good order as he and his council would have set in the realm. And thus both parties had covetousness, and both parties did rebel.[10]

Then, lest there be any doubt as to whose interests lay closest to the preacher's heart:

> They [the commons] are equal with you. Peers of the realm must needs be. The poorest ploughman is in Christ equal with the greatest prince that is. Let them, therefore, have sufficient to maintain them, and to find them their necessaries. A plough-land must have sheep; yea, they must have sheep to dung their ground for bearing of corn; for if they have no sheep to help fat the ground, they shall have but bare corn and thin. They must have swine for their food, to make their veneries or bacon of . . . . They must have other cattle: as horses to draw their plow, and for carriage of things to the markets; and kine for their milk and cheese, which they must live upon and pay their rents. These cattle must have pasture, which pasture if they lack, the rest must needs fail them: and pasture they cannot have, if the land be taken in, and enclosed from them.[11]

There was much more in the same vein. Latimer was heavily ironic with those who said that his preaching against covetousness the preceding year had been an incitement to rebellion. They argued, he said, post hoc, propter hoc, and reminded him of the famous story, told by Sir Thomas More,[12] of the old man who attributed the formation of the Goodwin Sands at the mouth of Sandwich Haven to the building of the steeple of Tenterton church.[13] He warned the Council, now headed by Northumberland, to live righteously and govern justly during the minority of the King.[14] Towards the end, he even demanded that the young King, in the interest of justice, begin to exercise his own office.[15]

It is small wonder that Latimer was not invited to preach at court again. Northumberland, for all his support of the reformed religion, was not the man to encourage such direct criticism of his government. Latimer himself believed that this would be his last appearance at Westminster, and referred to the sermon as his *ultimum vale*.[16] He was thinking principally of the state of his health. Perhaps he spoke the more freely on that account. His health improved, however, to the extent that he was able to preach pretty regularly for the next three years. But it appears that never again did he preach at court. In later sermons he spoke more than once of honest preachers whose mouths were stopped because they had reproved the wicked.[17] It is impossible to avoid the inference that he was referring to his own exclusion from the pulpit which had been erected especially for him in the gardens of Westminster Palace.

For a year or so after his last court sermon, Latimer may have continued to live at Lambeth with Archbishop Cranmer, as he had done during the three preceding years.[18] In January, 1551, he was appointed to a commission of thirty-one persons, headed by Cranmer, which was charged with the duty of correcting and punishing Anabaptists and others who refused to administer the sacraments according to the prescriptions of the Book of Common Prayer.[19] Presumably he was in London ready to serve. The activities of the commission have not been recorded beyond the fact that in April, presumably after examination by this group, a Fleming named George van Paris was burned at Smithfield for irregular views on the nature of Christ.[20] In October, 1551, Latimer was named a member of a commission of thirty-two persons to reform and codify the canon law,[21] a project which was especially dear to Cranmer and the bishops. But this group never functioned; two weeks later, it was replaced by a more manageable commission of eight members.[22] Apart from these brief notices, there is nothing to connect Latimer with London between early in 1550 and the autumn of 1553. Presumably he had no share in the formulation of the second Edwardine Prayer Book, which was approved by the Second Act of Uniformity in January, 1552, or with the Forty-three Articles, the forerunners of the famous Thirty-nine.

Latimer certainly spent much of this period with friends and relatives in the provinces. We find him preaching at Stamford, not far from his old home at Thurcaston; at Leicester itself, where he received a gift of pears and wine for his sermon—in addition, it is to be hoped, to a more substantial fee;[23] at Melton Mowbray, where the honorarium was 2s. 8d. and the great bell was rung to call the people to the sermon.[24] These are but the scattered extant records of what must have been a great deal of itinerant preaching. Much of the time he was with the Glovers at Baxterley. He was probably there at Christmas, 1551, and certainly in the early summer of the same year. No doubt it was there that he was visited by John Bradford and enjoyed a cheese which had been sent to Bradford by Master Traves, the minister of Blakly.[25] He can be placed most frequently, however, in the household of the dowager duchess of Suffolk at

Grimsthorpe in Lincolnshire, where many of the extant sermons were preached.

Katherine Brandon, duchess of Suffolk,[26] was at this time a widow in her early thirties. She had been the fourth wife of Charles Brandon, duke of Suffolk, his third wife having been Mary Tudor, sister of Henry VIII. Suffolk died in 1545, leaving two sons by his fourth marriage. Both boys died of the sweating sickness in 1551. The Duchess had long been sympathetic to the innovations in religion, and after the death of her husband and her sons she devoted herself zealously to the cause of reform both in London and in Lincolnshire, where her principal estates lay. A woman of considerable abilities, she was described by Fuller as "a lady of sharp wit and sure hand to thrust it home." On more than one occasion she exercised her wit at the expense of Stephen Gardiner, a self-indulgence for which she was made to pay dearly when Gardiner became chancellor under Queen Mary. Her principal residence outside of London was Grimsthorpe, which had been virtually rebuilt by the late Duke in expectation of Henry VIII's visit there when he went on progress in 1541. It was in the chapel at Grimsthorpe and perhaps in some of the neighboring parish churches that Latimer frequently preached in 1552.

We cannot now determine when the friendship between Latimer and the Duchess began. Her admiration for him probably antedated the court sermons of 1549, for the first printed version of those sermons was dedicated to her and bore her coat-of-arms on the reverse of the title-page. She became his friend and patroness, and he became her adviser in matters of religion. Apparently he admonished her freely. One wonders if there are direct hits at her in some of the criticisms of women in the Lincolnshire sermons—for example, in the reference to "Mistress Pilate, which took a nap in the morning, as such fine damsels are wont to do," [27] or in the passage explicating the words "Mary pondered all these things in her heart" —"She did not as our well-spoken dames do; she took not in hand to preach: she knew that silence in a woman is a great virtue." [28] Whether these and other passages refer to the Duchess or not, it is certain that privately Latimer gave her blunt counsel. In 1559, four years after his death, she wrote to Cecil, ". . . my father Latimer was wont to say to me, 'I will be bold to write you another time as I hear, and what I think; and if not I shall hold my peace, and pray God to amend it'." [29] For her part, she was a generous friend to him, as is evidenced in the following passage from a letter written in June, 1552, to Cecil inviting him to hunt in her park. Evidently a buck which she had promised him accompanied the letter:

By the late coming of this buck to you, you shall perceive that wild things be not ready at command, for truly I have caused my keeper, yea and went forth with him myself on Saturday at night after I came home (which was a novelty for me) but so desirous was I to have had one for Mr. Latimer to have sent after him to his niece's churching [probably Mary Glover at Baxterley]. But there is no remedy but she must be churched without it . . . . [30]

Probably Latimer was still at Grimsthorpe when the Duchess remarried early in 1553.[31] Her new husband was Richard Bertie, a man of distinctly inferior rank. It has been suggested that Latimer officiated at the wedding.[32] In spite of the difference in rank, the Duchess's second marriage was a happy one. During the severities of Mary's reign, she and Bertie were forced to take refuge on the Continent. After the accession of Elizabeth they returned to England. The Duchess lived on until 1580. Her continuing devotion to Latimer's memory is reflected in the fact that all the early editions of his collected sermons were dedicated to her by their editor.

That editor was Augustine Bernher, a Swiss (he described himself as a "Helvetian") residing in England. It is probable that he came to England in the late 1540's; the precise date is not discoverable. An ardent reformer, he became the intimate of the Glovers of Baxterley and Mancetter, of John Bradford, of John Careless, and of others whose names are enrolled in the catalogue of the Marian martyrs. He himself escaped serious trouble in Mary's reign, during part of which he served as one of the ministers of the "Christian congregation" in London, a group which met secretly for protestant worship all through the period of persecution.[33] At some time or other he must have received Anglican orders, for in the reign of Elizabeth he became rector of Southam (or Sutton), where, in Strype's phrase, "he died in peace." [34]

Bernher's friendship with Latimer may have come through their common association with the Glovers. He became a devoted disciple of the great preacher. He referred to Latimer as his "master," and to himself as Latimer's "servant." The relationship was certainly as much that of friends between whom there was a great difference in age as that of master and servant. Bernher looked up to Latimer as the "apostle to the English," and out of that devotion collected the later sermons and saw them through the press. For this, if for no other reason, he deserves the gratitude of later generations.

In the dedication of the 1562 collection to the duchess of Suffolk, Bernher gives us, in addition to some biographical details which will appear in their proper place, the following account of Latimer's work during the reign of Edward VI:

Now when he was thus delivered [from the Tower, in 1547], did he give himself up to the pleasures of the world, to delicateness or idleness? No, assuredly; but even then most of all he began to set forth his plough, and to till the ground of the Lord, and to sow the corn of God's word, behaving himself as a faithful messenger of God, being afraid of no man; telling all degrees their duties faithfully and truly, without respect of persons, or any kind of flattery. In the which his painful travails he continued all King Edward's time, preaching for the most part every Sunday two sermons, to the great shame, confusion, and damnation of a great number of our fat-bellied unpreaching prelates. For he, being a sore bruised man, and above three-score and seven years of age,[35] took notwithstanding all these pains in preaching, and besides this, every morning ordinarily, winter and summer, about two of the clock in the morning, he was at his book most diligently. And besides this, how careful he was for the preservation of the church of God, and for the good success of the gospel, they can bear record, which at that time were in authority; whom continually by his letters he admonished of their duties, and assisted with his godly counsel. But when the time approached, the which God had appointed for the punishment of the carnal gospelers and hypocrites which most wickedly abused the same, how faithfully he did admonish, both privately and openly, all kinds of men, they that were then about him can bear record. But one thing amongst others is principally to be noted, that God not only gave unto him His Spirit most plenteously and comfortably to preach His word unto His church, but also by the same Spirit he did most evidently prophesy of all those kinds of plagues, which in very deed afterwards ensued; so plainly, I say, as though he had seen them before his eyes: so that, if England ever had a prophet, he was one: and amongst other things he ever affirmed that the preaching of the gospel would cost him his life, to the which thing he did most cheerfully arm and prepare himself, being persuaded that Winchester was kept in the Tower for the same purpose.[36]

Latimer's gift of prophecy (or his ability to discern the signs of the times) was sound enough with respect to his own martyrdom, but it led him astray, as we shall see,[37] in his belief that "wily Winchester" was his chief enemy.

The first collection of Latimer's sermons edited by Bernher was published by John Day in 1562. Its title-page reads in part: 27 *Sermons Preached by the Right Reverend Father in God and Constant Martyr of Jesus Christ, Master Hugh Latimer, as well such as in times past have been printed, as certain other coming to our hands of late, which were yet never set forth in print.*[38] The volume is in two parts. Part one contains Thomas Some's dedication to the Duchess of Suffolk and all the sermons which had previously appeared in print (that is, the Convocation Sermon of 1536, the Sermon on the Ploughers, the sermons before King Edward VI, and the sermon at Stamford, the last-named having been separately printed by Day in 1550). Part two has a separate title-page which reads as follows: *Certain Other Sermons Preached by the Right Reverend Father in God, Master Hugh Latimer, in Lincolnshire, the Year of Our Lord 1553. Collected and gathered by Augustine Bernher an Helvetian: and albeit not so fully and perfectly gathered as they were uttered; yet nevertheless truly, to the singular commodity and profit of the simple ignorant, who with fervent zeal and diligent reading, desire to be better taught and instructed.* In this context "Lincolnshire" probably means Grimsthorpe, since Bernher indicates in the dedication that all the sermons in the volume were preached there. The date "1553" is palpably incorrect, as will appear in a moment. This part of the collection, with the dedication by Bernher to the Duchess of Suffolk, consists of seven sermons on the Lord's Prayer and nine sermons on texts from the Gospels or Epistles for the following days: the 20th, 21st, 23rd, and 24th Sundays after Trinity; All Saints Day; St. Andrew's Day (November 30th); and the 1st, 2nd, and 3rd Sundays in Advent. At the end of the sermons on the Lord's Prayer is the specific statement that they were preached at Grimsthorpe in 1552. The other nine sermons are described merely as having been preached in Lincolnshire, and they are not dated. It is obvious that these sermons could not have been preached in 1553, for all of these Sundays fell later than September 13, by which time in the year 1553 Latimer was imprisoned in the Tower. On the other hand, if the sermons were all preached on the days to which the texts are applicable, they could not all have been preached in 1552, for, as Demaus pointed out, there were only twenty-three Sundays after Trinity Sunday in that year.[39] They could all have been preached in 1550, when there were twenty-five Sundays after Trinity, or in 1551, when there were twenty-seven. But although there is a certain continuity in the sermons (for example, back-references to the preceding sermon) it is by no means certain that they were all preached in the same year. All that can be said with certainty is that Bernher, like Latimer's later editors, arranged the sermons according to the calendar of the Christian year.

The first eleven sermons in this 1562 collection were evidently based upon earlier printed copies, with some editorial revision by Bernher—for example, the excision of the direct attacks upon the Lord Admiral. All that we know of the provenance of the remaining sixteen—the Grimsthorpe and "Lincolnshire" sermons—is to be found in the words "not so fully and perfectly gathered as they were uttered" from the title-page of Part II, and the additional statement *"exceptae per me Augustinum Bernerum Heluetium"* at the conclusion of the sermons on the Lord's Prayer. Bernher was unquestionably the "gatherer."

In 1571-72 the printer John Day put out an enlarged collection of Latimer's sermons, again with Bernher as editor. This volume bears the title *Fruitful Sermons Preached by the Right Reverend Father and Constant Martyr of Jesus Christ M. Hugh Latimer, newly imprinted: with others, not heretofore set forth in print.*[40] This book is in three parts. Part I contains the Convocation Sermon, the Sermon on the Ploughers, the eight sermons preached before Edward VI, and the Stamford Sermons. Part II contains the Lord's Prayer and Lincolnshire Sermons first published in the 1562 volumes. Part III, however, contains twelve sermons not previously published. These are on texts from the Gospels or Epistles for the following days: St. Simon and St. Jude's Day (October 28), Christmas, St. Stephen's Day (December 26), St. John Evangelist's Day (December 27), Epiphany (January 6), the first five Sundays after Epiphany, Septuagesima Sunday, and Sexagesima Sunday. The first four of these sermons are dated 1552. The fifth, that for Epiphany, is dated 1553. For the remaining seven no year is given, but the day of the month is stated in each case, and reference to the church calendar indicates that they must have been preached in 1552—that is, that they are earlier by almost a year than the first five.[41] Once again, however, the editor chose to arrange them according to the days of the Christian year rather than in the order of their delivery. All the sermons are described in the text as having been preached at Grimsthorpe except that for Christmas Day, which is assigned to Baxterley. In this there is some error, for Baxterley and Grimsthorpe are too far apart for Latimer to have preached at one on December 25 and at the other on December 26 (St. Stephen's Day). As Demaus suggests, the editor may have written "Baxterley" by mistake, or Latimer may have repeated on Christmas 1552 a sermon preached at Baxterley the preceding Christmas.

Fruitful Sermons was frequently reprinted.[42] In 1578 the sermon which Latimer had preached against the Pilgrimage of Grace in 1536 was added to the collection.[43] With this edition, the corpus of Bishop Latimer's printed sermons is complete.

Latimer's biographers, and historians generally, have dealt rather summarily with the later sermons; literary historians ignore them entirely. This neglect is understandable. In those passages which attack enclosers, bribe-takers, nonpreaching prelates and the like, Latimer seems merely to be repeating himself. On the other hand, since the sermons were addressed to small congregations in the country, there are many passages which are very like the parish priest admonishing and instructing his little flock in elementary matters of morality and religion; and these passages are likely to be dismissed as uncharacteristic of Latimer at his best. Moreover, the extremes of language so characteristic of the court sermons are noticeably moderated in the later sermons, perhaps because Latimer was accommodating his style to a different audience, or perhaps because the language was toned down by Augustine Bernher.

In regard to political theorizing, the later sermons must be regarded as a necessary sequel to the Edward VI sermons. The court sermons stressed the duties of kings and magistrates; the later sermons, addressed mostly to servants and retainers of the Duchess of Suffolk, stressed the duties of the subject. Although there are passages outlining the duties of the prince,[44] the emphasis of the later sermons is upon the subject's duty of obedience. The topic is developed most fully in the Stamford sermons,[45] the text of which was "Yield to Caesar that belongeth to Caesar, and to God that belongeth to God." But it recurs in most of the others. In the St. Stephen's day sermon at Grimsthorpe, for instance, Latimer said:

> I think of this matter we cannot speak too much; for it is a thing most necessary to be known. For if the parents of our Savior were content to be obedient unto a heathen king, how much more should we show ourselves obedient unto our natural king, which feedeth us with the holy word of God, and seeketh not alone our bodily health and wealth, but also the health of the soul.[46]

In other sermons this thought is developed and illustrated in various ways, including a long passage, rather obtrusively out of keeping with the rest of the sermon, on the necessity of paying taxes cheerfully.[47]

There is, however, an important exception to the general rule of obedience. If the prince and the parliament make laws against God, the subject may refuse to obey, but always quietly, passively, without commotion or active rebellion:

> When laws are made against God and his word, then I ought more to obey God than man. Then I may refuse to obey with a good conscience: yet for all that I may not rise up against the magistrates, nor make any uproar; for if I do so, I sin damnably. I must be content to suffer whatsoever God shall lay upon me, yet I may not obey their wicked laws to do them. Only in such a case men may refuse to obey; else in all the other matters we ought to obey. What laws soever they make as concerning outward things we ought to obey, and in no wise to rebel, although they be never so hard, noisome and hurtful. Our duty is to obey, and commit all matters unto God; not doubting but that God will punish them, when they do contrary to their office and calling.[48]

It is difficult to tell, from the sermons, how far Latimer believed the individual might go in following this typically protestant notion of passive resistance, involving as it does the dangerous principle of private judgment. It is clear that he believed that there should be no resistance whatever to laws involving secular affairs. He specifically urges obedience to the laws pertaining to apparel, abstinence from meat, vagabondage, and usury.[49] His later history indicates that he probably meant only that the individual should refuse to obey any laws which might subsequently be passed for the restoration of the old religion and obedience to Rome.

Closely related to the passages on obedience to the prince are the numerous references in the later sermons to the duty of the servant towards his master. Since the servants at Grimsthorpe were compelled to attend the sermons, it is not surprising that the preacher frequently addresses them directly, not primarily on matters of doctrine ("Such obscure questions pertain not to you that are ignorant and unlearned" [50]) but upon their simple duties of doing a full day's work, keeping sober, and obeying their masters.[51] All this is developed in terms of the traditional views that class distinctions are part of the divine plan and that all work, be it that of the prince or that of the servant, is a form of service to God,[52] the latter opinion being one which was given particular prominence in the teaching of Luther. Above all, the principle of order, the proper relationship of class to class, rank to rank, must be maintained.[53] If maintenance of the principle results in misery for the individual (as when a subject suffers from the tyranny of his prince or a servant from the cruelty of his master) he must have faith in God's justice. Either he is being punished for his sins or he is being tried in the fire of tribulation. At the last, all will be well.[54]

In the later sermons, however, the economic and social teaching is subordinated to the religious. From this point of view, the seven sermons on the Lord's Prayer are the most interesting. Strictly speaking, they were not sermons at all, but lectures to the servants and the household of the Duchess of Suffolk.[55] Latimer's long devotion to the Lord's Prayer has already been noted. Like Luther, he spoke of it as the perfect prayer, taught us by the perfect Schoolmaster. He had used it for years as the bidding prayer of his more formal sermons; it was so used in each of the sermons at the court of Edward VI. At the end of his Stamford sermon of November 9, 1550, he said,

Marvel not that I use at the sermon's end to make prayer, for I do it not of singularity: but when I am at home, and in the country where I go, sometime when the poor people come and ask at me, I appose [question] them myself, or cause my servant to appose them, of the Lord's prayer; and they answer some, 'I can say my Latin *Pater-noster*,' some, 'I can say the old *Pater-noster,* but not the new.' Therefore that all that cannot say it may learn, I use before the sermon and after to say it. Wherefore now I beseech you, let us say it together: 'Our Father, which art' etc.[56]

The Grimsthorpe lectures are therefore the fruit of this long devotion; no doubt Latimer used the same lectures, or others like them, many times over. There is nothing very original about the lectures; each explicates one of the seven petitions in terms both of ancient and medieval commentary and of Lutheran or even Calvinistic interpretation.[57] There is also much conventional moralizing. They are remarkable, however, for their intense sincerity, seldom marred by the pyrotechnics characteristic of the sermons which Latimer preached to larger and more distinguished audiences, and for their clarity and coherence, qualities for which Latimer's sermons are not always notable and which in this case may be the result of skillful editorial pruning by Augustine Bernher.

In passing, it may be said that the Lord's Prayer sermons and the others of this later period are, for Latimer, remarkably free from attacks on the religion of Rome. Latimer would not have been Latimer without occasional thrusts at "the Italian bishop yonder" and his old enemies, pilgrimages and relics.[58] But the attacks upon the Anabaptists, who at the moment seemed the more dangerous adversaries, are quite as numerous and even more fervent than those upon the old religion.[59] He attacks them for their theology, their communism, their opposition to war. The sermons, however, are critical of Anabaptists or papists only in passing. Their theme is righteousness, and more than once the preacher confesses that it flourishes no better under the new learning than it did under the old.

Although Latimer's preaching was never primarily doctrinal, there is a good deal of doctrine in the later sermons. Since none of it represents original thinking by Latimer, we need speak of it only briefly. Several passages assert far more clearly and explicitly than it is stated anywhere in the earlier sermons the doctrine that "faith only justifies." The following will serve as illustration:

> For when we well consider the works of the law, which the law requireth, and again, how we do them, we shall find that we may not be justified by our doings: for the flesh reigneth in us; it beareth rule and letteth the Spirit, and so we never fulfil the law. Certain it is that they that believe in Christ have the Holy Ghost, which ruleth and governeth them: yet for all that there be a great many lacks in them; so that if they would go about to be saved by their works, they should come too short; for their works are not able to answer the requests of the law. And so Christ should be but a judge, which should give every one according to his merits, and should not deserve for us. If we had no other help but that, then we should go all to the devil. But God, the everlasting, be praised, we have a remedy and a sure helper! Christ, the Son of the living God, hath fulfilled the law for us, to deliver us from sin. Such is the office of Christ, to deliver us from the law and the wrath of it. The law required a perfect righteousness and holiness: now all they that believe in Christ, they are holy and righteous, for he hath fulfilled the law for us which believe in him: we be reputed just through faith in Christ. What required the law of us? Marry, righteousness and holiness. This we have, we are righteous; but how? Not by our works, for our works are not able to make us just, and deliver us from our sins; but we are just by this, that our sins are pardoned unto us through faith which we have in Christ our Savior: for he, through his fulfilling of the law, took away the curse of the law from our heads.[60]

This is clear—and elementary, as was fitting for an audience composed of the Duchess of Suffolk's servants. Less clear (but no more opaque than Article **XVII** of the Forty-three Articles) are the occasional passages which touch upon election and predestination. Anticipating the usual objections to these doctrines, he contents himself with a catalogue of the "notes" or signs of election—a sense of sin, a true and lively faith, a desire of amendment, and so on.[61] But he makes no attempt to grapple with the basic problem. "Think that God hath chosen those that believe in Christ," he says, "and that Christ is the book of life. . . . So we need not go about to trouble ourselves with curious questions of the predestination of God." [62] In defense of this apparent evasiveness, it may be pointed out that when Latimer spoke these words Calvin's *De Praedestinatione* had not yet been published, and that such able theologians as Cranmer and Ridley were still mindful of Melanchthon's advice to "think well concerning any such formula of doctrine." [63]

We must glance also, in this brief summary of the doctrinal content of the last sermons, at Latimer's expressed opinions of the Eucharist. The matter is important because of the centrality of the Eucharistic controversy in the disputations and the heresy proceedings at Oxford in 1554 and 1555. On this topic, as on justification by faith, there are clearer statements in the later sermons than in the earlier. The following, from the sermon for St. John Evangelist's Day (December 27), 1552, is Latimer's last known statement concerning the mystery of the communion prior to the Oxford disputations:

> . . . when the bread is consecrated, when the words are spoken over it, then it is such an office that it beareth the name of the body and blood of Christ. Like as the magistrates because of their office are called *Dii*, "Gods"; so the bread representeth His body, so that we go unto it worthily, and receive it with a good faith. Then we be assured that we feed upon Him spiritually. And like as the bread nourisheth the body, so the soul feedeth upon the very body and blood of Christ by faith, by believing Him to be a Savior which delivered man from his sin.[64]

As is usually the case in the utterances of the more responsible Anglican divines of the mid-sixteenth century on the subject of the communion, it is impossible to be sure of the exact theological coloration of this statement. Probably the word *representeth* (which was changed by an editor to *presenteth* in the editions of 1584 and 1596, to bring it into closer conformity to Elizabethan Anglicanism) is to be regarded as a Zwinglian tint. Apart from this, however, the emphasis upon the Real Spiritual Presence seems to conform pretty much to Latimer's earlier opinions, to the view implied in the first Prayer Book (but not the second), and to the position maintained by Latimer in the disputations at Oxford two years later. It was the position from which he felt there could be no retreat.

It may not be amiss to conclude this brief survey of Latimer's last sermons by bringing together what he himself had to say about his own preaching. First, as to the length of his sermons. It was a general principle in medieval preaching that a sermon should be no shorter than a low mass, no longer than a high mass. Latimer evidently discarded that principle along with the mass. In the last sermon before Edward VI he announced his intention of preaching for three or four hours.[65] It is not unlikely that his more formal sermons, modeled upon the traditional sermon *ad clerum,* generally ran to some such length. The later sermons, designed for a smaller and less critical group, were shorter. Even so, the originals were longer than the extant printed sermons as they were "gathered imperfectly" by Augustine Bernher. Thus, in the fifth sermon on the Lord's Prayer the preacher confessed that he had been "long" in his previous sermons and would be short in this one. As printed, however, the fifth sermon is the longest of the seven. The present writer has experimented with the shortest of the Lord's Prayer sermons, the third. Reading aloud at what is for him breath-taking speed, he cannot get through the sermon in less than a half-hour. He requires about fifty minutes to read it at what he regards as a good pace for effective delivery. If we make due allowance for passages which dropped out in transcription, it is a fair guess that Latimer took about an hour to deliver the sermon. One reason for the length of the court sermons was Latimer's gift for extemporizing. Whether or not this is to be regarded as merit or a defect in a preacher depends upon the use which is made of it. Latimer's extemporizing usually took the form of apposite digressions. There can be no doubt that in most cases the digressions were effective and that they represent the effort of a shrewd tactician to keep or regain the attention of a difficult audience. The comparative freedom of the later sermons from such digressions may perhaps be explained by the fact that they were delivered to small audiences in a private chapel or in a small parish church, a speaking situation in which aggressive inattention was less likely to occur than in the "preaching place" at Westminster.

Even a casual reader of the sermons will be struck with the fact that there is a good deal of repetition in them, particularly in those which belong to a series. This repetitiousness was intentional, and grew out of his realization that in preaching, as in pedagogy and pugilism, it is profitable to strike repeated blows at the same spot. "I have a manner of teaching," he says in one place, "which is very tedious to them that be learned. I am wont ever to repeat those things which I have said before, which repetitions are nothing pleasant to the learned: but it is no matter, I care not for them; I seek more the profit of those which be ignorant, than to please learned men." [66] In another sermon he tells the story of a friar whose servant complained that he always preached on the Ten Commandments. The friar, saying that the servant must therefore be well grounded, demanded that the man repeat the commandments, whereupon the unfortunate servant rattled off the list of the seven deadly sins. "Therefore," Latimer concludes, "be not offended with me, when I tell you one thing two or three times." [67]

From all this, it is apparent that Latimer's preaching was not calculated merely to provoke his audience to admiration of the performance. He was unquestionably aware of his own virtuosity in the pulpit, and sometimes, one suspects, was guilty of using it for its own sake. But not often. His own best summary of the seriousness of his purpose and the use to which he put his talent is to be found in his reply to an unnamed bishop who had labeled his preaching "unfruitful":

. . . whether it be unfruitful or no, I cannot tell; it lieth not in me to make it fruitful: and [if] God work not in your hearts, my preaching can do you but little good. I am God's instrument but for a time; it is He that must give the increase: and yet preaching is necessary; for take away preaching, and take away salvation.[68]

CHAPTER TWENTY-FIVE

THE DEBATE ON THE SACRAMENT OF THE ALTAR

King Edward VI, always a sickly child, was stricken with consumption early in 1553 and died on July 6. Within a fortnight Northumberland's bold attempt to establish Lady Jane Grey as Edward's successor collapsed. Mary Tudor was proclaimed sovereign on July 19, amidst demonstrations of popular approval. Northumberland, quickly convicted of treason, was executed on Tower Hill on August 21. Poor Lady Jane and her husband, Northumberland's son Guildford Dudley, were spared for six months more. Their execution in February, 1554, followed the abortive rebellion led by Sir Thomas Wyatt, the son of the poet—a rebellion which was on the surface a protest against Mary's proposed marriage with Philip of Spain, but which was fundamentally an attempt to preserve the reformed religion.

Throughout Edward's reign Mary had managed, in the face of every obstacle, to hear mass daily in her private chapel. In so far as her devout Catholicism meant the old doctrines, the old liturgy, the old ceremonials and customs, her views were shared by a majority of her people. But to Mary, whose habit of mind was more Spanish than English, Catholicism meant England's reconciliation to Rome. So dogged was her determination to consummate the reconciliation that she probably never understood that most of her countrymen, even those who thought of themselves as Catholics, were either indifferent or hostile to the prospect of a return to obedience to Rome. When it came, the reconciliation was accepted by most as the law of the land, but without enthusiasm.

There is no need to repeat here in detail the familiar story of the steps by which the old religion was restored. The funeral of Edward VI was symbolic of what was about to occur. Mary, reluctantly following the cautious advice of her cousin Charles V, permitted the official funeral in Westminster Abbey to be conducted by Archbishop Cranmer according to the forms of the English service. But Mary was not present. Instead she was chief among four hundred mourners at a solemn requiem mass for the dead king in the chapel of the Tower of London. The celebrant was Stephen Gardiner, who upon Mary's accession had been released from the Tower, restored to the see of Winchester, and appointed to the lord chancellorship. Immediately, to the joy of a majority, the mass was informally restored in all the churches of England; it was officially restored by Convocation in October, 1553. A year later, the Pope having at last agreed not to press for the return of confiscated church property, Cardinal Reginald Pole arrived in England as papal legate to absolve the kingdom of its former heresy and schism. On January 4, 1555, Parliament passed the Act of Reconciliation, whereby the ecclesiastical legislation of the last two reigns was repealed and England returned to the Roman obedience.

From the beginning of Mary's reign it was evident that the restoration of the mass was to be the critical point of conflict between the old religion and the new. For months after Mary's accession the government's official preachers proclaimed the validity and efficacy of the mass at Paul's Cross and elsewhere with a frequency and efficiency which outmatched the earlier efforts of Edward's preachers to promote the Book of Common Prayer. Inevitably, in an age when religious toleration was undreamed of, the leaders of the attack upon the mass were faced with a choice between recantation, exile, or death. A few recanted. Many, not all of them lacking in courage, elected to continue their fight from Basle or Frankfort or Geneva. But many also chose to stay, with the almost certain knowledge that unless they recanted they would burn. It is nonsense to say that at the beginning they faced nothing more than imprisonment. To be sure, the wholesale executions which began in 1555 were not originally anticipated. But the fate of the leaders who stood their ground was never in doubt. Persistent denial of the sacrament of the altar had been the one intolerable heresy since the time of Wyclif. No one knew it better than such men as Cranmer, Latimer, and Ridley.

In fairness, however, it must be pointed out that the government preferred that the leaders of the reformed religion go into voluntary exile, and gave them abundant opportunity for escape. To execute them would only further alienate the strong minority who shared their views. Cranmer could easily have fled if he had cared to do so. Hooper, the most radical of the Edwardine bishops, and John Rogers, the first of the Marian martyrs, were given every chance to escape.[1] Latimer was virtually invited to run away. Their refusal to run is an interesting problem for the psychologist. No single explanation will serve for all cases; deep within the unconscious of each one were motives which for lack of evidence must forever escape us. Here and there we find hints. The letters of John Bradford reflect something very like the Freudian death-wish. Hooper seems to have been moved to a fanatical emulation of St. Paul. Cranmer and Latimer present the most interesting problems. Both middle-of-the-roaders, they might well have been expected to join the exiles at Geneva. They could have done so without loss of face. It would not have been a case of deserting their more humble followers, for there was as yet no intimation that over three hundred would be executed for religion. In the case of Latimer, the cynic might say that he was too old and ill for successful flight. But the order for his appearance before the Privy Council reached him in the country, probably at Baxterley, and he voluntarily made the arduous journey to London. He could as easily have proceeded to the nearest seaport, and thence to safety overseas. The explanation in terms of age and illness will not bear examination. Whatever the deepest motive may have been, his determination to stand, like that of Cranmer and the others, must be seen as a magnificently courageous recognition of the fact that where great issues are involved there comes a time when the bravest men cannot give ground. In this connection Latimer's record is of particular interest. Twenty-five years earlier he had submitted to Wolsey. In 1533 he had submitted to Convocation. Had he not been deceived by Cromwell in 1539, he probably would have accepted the Six Articles and retained his bishopric.

It had not been an especially heroic record. But all of these submissions were over relatively minor matters of abused ceremonials and customs. In each case he could feel that real progress had been made in the causes which he cherished, and that further progress was possible in the foreseeable future. In his thinking, as in Cranmer's, the critical change had come in 1548, when he finally rejected the doctrine of the mass as a propitiatory sacrifice. In his view, the restoration of the mass meant the return of all the abuses against which he had fought for so long. Nor did there appear to be much likelihood of another change in the near future. The martyrs could not know, in 1553, that Mary had only five years to live. She was only thirty-seven. Even if she lived to be no older than her father Henry, her reign would last for another twenty years, during which time the cause might be hopelessly lost. Clearly the time was at hand for passive resistance, preached so consistently by all the reformers, to those laws of the land which contravened the laws of God.

Latimer's long ordeal began within two months of Mary's accession. On September 4, 1553, an order was issued for his appearance before the Privy Council.[2] A few days later a pursuivant was sent into the country probably to Baxterley, to serve the summons. According to both Foxe and Bernher, Latimer had six hours' advance warning of his coming, through the good offices of John Careless, a Coventry weaver, who had somehow got wind of the pursuivant's mission. But Latimer, declining to take advantage of the warning, prepared himself for the journey to London; the pursuivant was astonished to find the old preacher waiting quietly for the summons. To the officer's expressions of surprise Latimer is reported to have answered:

My friend, you be a welcome messenger to me. And be it known unto you, and to all the world, that I go as willingly to London at this present, being called by my prince to render a reckoning of my doctrine, as ever I was at any place in the world. I doubt not but that God, as He hath made me worthy to preach His word before two excellent princes, so will He able me to witness the same unto the third, either to her comfort or discomfort eternally.[3]

Whereupon the pursuivant rode off, declaring that he had orders to deliver the summons but not to tarry for Latimer nor conduct him to London—"by whose sudden departure," say both Foxe and Bernher, "it was manifest that they would not have him appear, but rather to have fled out of the realm." [4]

Latimer was in London by September 13. His way into the city took him through Smithfield, haunted with the ghosts of Friar Forest and the Carthusian martyrs, of Frith, Barnes, and Garrett, of the maid of Kent and Joan Boucher; and he is reported to have said—"merrily"— that Smithfield had long groaned for him.[5]

He appeared before the Privy Council on September 13. Among his examiners were Stephen Gardiner, Cuthbert Tunstall (himself but lately released from prison and restored to the see of Durham), and William Paget, to whose youthful lecture on Melanchthon, thirty years before, Latimer's own disputation for the B.D. had been an impassioned reply. Foxe says that he was mocked and taunted by the Council,[6] but this is unlikely, since such examinations were usually conducted with at least the outward appearance of judicial calm. Latimer's own attitude was certainly intransigent. One of the Council, presumably Gardiner, spoke much of the need for unity in the church, but Latimer would only reply, "Yea, sir, but in verity, not in popery. Better is a diversity than an unity in popery." The clerk of the Council laconically recorded that "for his seditious demeanor [Latimer] was committed to the Tower, there to remain a close prisoner, having attended upon him one Austey [Bernher] his servant."

At his coming to the Tower next day, one chronicler records, Latimer said to one of the warders named Rutter, "What, my old friend, how do you? I am now come to be your neighbor again." [8] Forthwith he was lodged in the "Garden House" close by the residence of the lieutenant of the Tower. On the same day, September 14, Archbishop Cranmer, charged with treason in connection with the plot to enthrone Lady Jane Grey, was also brought to the Tower and confined "over the gate against the water-gate," [9] where the Duke of Somerset had awaited execution. Bishop Ridley, who had openly preached on behalf of Lady Jane's cause, had already been in the Tower for several weeks. There can be no doubt that these three—Cranmer, Latimer and Ridley—were regarded by the government as the arch-heretics. On this point we have the testimony of Ridley himself, in a letter to Bradford: "For when the state of religion was once altered, and persecution began to wax whole, no man doubted but Cranmer, Latimer, and Ridley should have been the first to have been called to the stake." [10] As it turned out, they were not the first to be called; Rogers, Hooper, Bradford himself, and many others were called before them. But the government dealt with the cases of Cranmer, Latimer, and Ridley more carefully and more spectacularly than with those of any of the others.

The three distinguished prisoners for religion remained in the Tower for six months. Most of that time they were kept apart, as punishment (said Ridley) for their refusal to attend mass.[11] But they managed to exchange both oral and written communications through the agency of the faithful and courageous Augustine Bernher, who nominally attended upon Latimer but seems to have been admitted freely to the company of the others. Foxe indicates they were subjected to "cruel and unmerciful handling," but he particularizes only about Latimer's suffering from the cold, confined as he was throughout the winter in a room without a fire. The story was known to many, says Foxe, that on one occasion Latimer remarked to an attendant that he was about to deceive the lieutenant of the Tower. That official, fearing that some plan for escape had been hatched, post-hasted to Latimer for an explanation. "Yea, master lieutenant, so I said," said Latimer, "for you look, I think, that I should burn; but except ye let me have some fire, I am like to deceive your expectation, for I am like here to starve for cold." [12]

From the first, the three bishops were aware that their trial, when it came, would center about the nature of the sacrament of the altar. On this topic Ridley held the most advanced views, and he forthwith undertook the task of setting down his opinions in writing. A tract called *A Brief Declaration of the Lord's Supper*[13] which he wrote in the Tower was published, probably at Zurich, shortly after his death, the manuscript having been entrusted to Augustine Bernher. Our more immediate interest, however, is in a little treatise, published at Zurich in 1556, with the title *Certain Godly, Learned and Comfortable Conferences between the Two Reverend Fathers and Holy Martyrs of Christ, D. Nicholas Ridley Late Bishop of London, and Mr. Hugh Latimer, Sometime Bishop of Worcester during the Time of their Imprisonments.*[14] From the content of the book itself, and from Ridley's letters, we learn something of the history of this volume.

As a first step in the evolution of this curious work, Ridley, in the Tower, had written down eleven reasons why he abstained from the mass. This document was carried by Bernher to Latimer, with a request for the latter's opinion of it. Latimer added his own brief comment (always in agreement, and sometimes with additional supporting argument) to each of Ridley's eleven points. He also appended a little essay of his own attacking the doctrine of the mass as a propitiatory sacrifice. The substance of the essay is in the sentence, "I have read over of late the New Testament three or four times deliberately; yet can I not find there neither the popish consecration, nor yet their transubstantiation, nor their oblation, nor their adoration, which be the very sinews and marrow-bones of the mass." [15] It concludes with words of encouragement to Ridley and an acknowledgment of the writer's own weakness.

Lo! sir, here have I blotted your paper and played the fool egregiously. But so I thought better, than not to do your request at this time. Pardon me, and pray for me: pray for me, I say, pray for me, I say. For I am sometime so fearful, that I would creep into a mouse-hole; sometime God doth visit me again with His comfort. So He cometh and goeth, to teach me to feel and to know my infirmity, to the intent to give thanks to Him that is worthy, lest I should not rob Him of His duty, as many do, and almost all the world.[16]

In spite of Latimer's protestations of weakness, Ridley evidently regarded Latimer as a stronger and braver man than himself, for a little later he sent by Bernher another set of opinions, in the preface to which he begged Latimer to give him "one draught more to comfort my stomach" lest in the time of trial he should play the part of a "white-livered knight." Latimer, he added, was an old and expert warrior, whereas he (Ridley) was but young and inexpert.[17]

Ridley wrote his share of the second "conference" in expectation that he would shortly be examined by "Diotrophes and his warriors," by whom he evidently meant Gardiner and the Council. This "conference" took the form of a series of anticipated objections to his former arguments against the mass and his own replies to the objections. Once again Latimer was asked to add his comments,[18] and he did so to nine of Ridley's fourteen points. In most cases these add little or nothing to Ridley's arguments; Latimer repeatedly remarks that Ridley has said all that can be said. At one point he warns Ridley against too much reliance upon anxious study. "You shall prevail more with praying than with studying, though mixture be best; for so one shall alleviate the tediousness of the other. I intend not to contend much with them in words, after a reasonable account of my faith given; for it shall be but in vain." [19] In another place he gently charges that Ridley, under the pretense of seeking counsel, is really priming him with arguments. "Sir, I begin now to smell what you mean: by travailing thus with me, you use me as Bilney once did, when he converted me. Pretending as though he would be taught of me, he sought ways and means to teach me; and so do you." [20]

In this piecemeal fashion the manuscript of *Certain Godly, Learned, and Comfortable Conferences* was compiled. Ridley himself added the initials "N.R." and "H.L." to indicate the parts written by each author. It does not appear that either Ridley or Latimer intended that the tract should be published. But at some time before the two men were removed from the Tower to Oxford it was entrusted, along with the manuscript of Ridley's treatise on the Lord's Supper, to the care of Master George Shipside, Ridley's brother-in-law. By him a copy was sent to Nicholas Grimald,[21] the well-known poet and later one of the principal contributors to the famous *Book of Songs and Sonnets,* commonly called *Tottel's Miscellany.* Grimald, at one time an ardent reformer and the author of a Latin poem in praise of Latimer, had been Ridley's chaplain at the time of the Bishop's arrest. Latterly he had displayed a tendency to bow the knee to Baal, as Ridley expressed it. Shipside, however, had no knowledge of this. When Grimald expressed a desire to see everything that Ridley had written since his imprisonment, Shipside trustingly sent copies along. Immediately thereafter someone—almost certainly Grimald, although Ridley was at first reluctant to think so—revealed the contents of the manuscripts to the authorities. Shipside was arrested on the charge of possessing heretical literature, but he had already hidden the originals or sent them abroad and refused to disclose their whereabouts.[22] Bernher, who (as the text of the *Conferences* clearly stated) had been the amanuensis of part of it, was also in some danger,[23] but he seems to have escaped arrest. In the end, the original manuscript was carried abroad, and the work was printed at Zurich in 1556, after the death of its authors. It seems to have been seen through the press by John Olde, whom Latimer had converted at Baxterley in the later years of King Henry's reign. Two editions were published in that year, and a third was published in London in 1572. A condensed and badly garbled version was included by Foxe in his *Acts and Monuments.*

Thus for a period of weeks or months the prisoners in the Tower managed to communicate in spite of their separate confinement, and to exchange opinions on the topic upon which they were certain to be examined. It must have been during this period that Latimer was given a last chance to change his opinions and thus escape being brought to trial. At least we have it on the evidence of Dr. William Turner, the nonconformist dean of Wells who spent the years of Mary's reign on the Continent, that Chancellor Gardiner "offered in his own name, as it was reported unto me, pardon unto Master Latimer, if he would turn from his religion." [24] The evidence is in the nature of hearsay, but it is probably accurate. If so, it is further testimony to the government's reluctance, at least at the first, to proceed with extreme measures against Latimer. If the offer was indeed made, it certainly met with a firm refusal.

Towards the end of the period of their imprisonment in the Tower, circumstances made it impossible that Cranmer, Latimer, and Ridley be kept any longer in separate confinement. Scores of those who had been involved in Wyatt's rebellion were brought in to the Tower, and in order to make room for the newcomers the three distinguished prisoners for religion were put together in a single room or cell,[25] where they remained until they were removed to Oxford in March, 1554. No doubt their confinement was physically more onerous than it had been when they were lodged separately, particularly after John Bradford was added to their number. But they had their Bibles with them, and according to Latimer they read and reread the New Testament, "with great deliberation and painful study," searching for texts on the nature of the Holy Communion. "I assure you," he adds, "as I will answer at the tribunal throne of God's majesty, we could find in the testament of Christ's body and blood no other presence but a spiritual presence; nor that the mass was any sacrifice for sins . . . ." [26]

Late in February or early in March of 1554, the Privy Council determined to stage at Oxford a disputation on the subject of the mass. The whole affair was planned with elaborate care. The disputants in support of the doctrine were to be the best-learned men of both universities; those assigned to oppose were Cranmer, Latimer, and Ridley. It is not to be supposed, however, that the question was to be decided on its merits. The performance was designed to be a formal affirmation of the doctrine of transubstantiation by the leading scholars of the realm, and a formal condemnation of the most distinguished opponents of the doctrine.

In accordance with this plan, the Council, on March 10, 1554, instructed the lieutenant of the Tower to deliver the "bodies" of Cranmer, Latimer, and Ridley to Sir John Williams, by whom they were to be conveyed to Oxford.[27] A few days later the transfer was made, the prisoners and their attendants traveling by way of Windsor, where the party broke the journey for a time.[28] The precise date of their arrival at Oxford cannot be determined, but Bishop Ridley says that it was a little before Easter,[29] which in 1554 occurred on March 25. During the three or four weeks before the beginning of the formal proceedings on April 14, the three bishops were lodged in Bocardo, the notorious Oxford prison which Miles Coverdale bitterly described as "a stinking and filthy prison for drunkards, whores, and harlots, and the vilest sort of people." [30] With the coming in of Cranmer, Latimer, and Ridley, however, Bocardo became, as Ridley wittily put it, a "very college of quondams." [31]

The three bishops had been permitted to bring only such books and personal belongings as they could carry with them.[32] At first they were allowed to retain their personal servants, who had the liberty of the town, and the bishops themselves were permitted to take exercise upon the walls of their prison and to have visitors. They were disappointed, however, that no members of the university came to see them; their keepers assured them this neglect was due to the unanimous hostility of the university towards them. But then one or two disturbances occurred in Bocardo— once, a coal fell out of the chimney and burned a hole in the floor, another time an alcoholic prisoner became unmanageable. Rumors flew about the town that the bishops had attempted to escape and had been prevented only by the alertness of the warders. As a result, their privileges were taken away from them. They were no longer permitted to exercise upon the prison wall; no visitors were admitted to them; their servants were forbidden to leave the prison; upon order of the mayor, the "Book of the Communion" was taken from them. In spite of these restraints, they retained their health and good spirits—were, in fact, "merry in God." [33]

It must have been during the comparatively brief period of their joint confinement in Bocardo that Latimer wrote the three letters which are all that survive of his correspondence for the period between his going to the Tower in September, 1553, and his death in November, 1555.[34] One of these, preserved by Foxe, is a charming note to Mistress Wilkinson, a widow whose home was in Soper Lane, London, but who at the time was staying in Oxfordshire.[35] The gifts referred to were no doubt food and clothing. The note reads, in its entirety:

> If the gift of a pot of cold water shall not be in oblivion with God, how can God forget your manifold and bountiful gifts, when he shall say unto you, "I was in prison, and you visited me"? God grant us all to do and suffer while we be here as may be his will and pleasure! Amen. Yours in Bocardo,
>
> Hugh Latimer.[36]

The other letters are too long to be quoted in their entirety. Although they add nothing to our factual knowledge of Latimer's circumstances during this period, they are wonderfully indicative of his courage and resolution in this time of tribulation. One, first printed by Strype,[37] is addressed to "one in prison for the profession of the Gospel" whose friends were apparently ready to pay a considerable sum of money for his release. With many citations from Scriptures Latimer warns his correspondent that it is "not lawful for money to redeem yourself out of the cross, unless you would go about to exchange glory for shame, and to sell your inheritance for a mess of pottage . . . ." [38] The other is an "epistle general" of the kind which so many of the Marian martyrs undertook to write. Also first printed by Strype,[39] it is addressed to "all unfeigned lovers of God's truth, out of a prison in Oxford, called Bocardo." It is without doubt one of the most beautiful and affecting of Latimer's extant compositions. The first few sentences read as follows:

> Brethren, the time is come when the Lord's ground will be known: I mean, it will now appear who hath received God's gospel in their hearts in deed, to the taking of good root therein. For such will not shrink for a little heat or sunburning weather; but stoutly stand and grow, even maugre the malice of all burning sun and tempests. For he that hath played the wise builder, and laid his foundation on a rock, will not be afraid that every drizzling rain or mist shall hurt his buildings, but will stand, although a great tempest do come, and drops of rain as big as fir-fagots. But they that have builded upon a sand will be afraid, though they see but a cloud arise a little black, and no rain or wind doth once touch them; no, not so much as to lie one week in prison, to trust God with their lives which gave them.[40]

The remainder of the letter, which runs to something over three thousand words, is a plea to the brethren, in terms of the imagery of the storm and with examples from the "patriarchs, good kings, prophets, apostles, evangelists, martyrs, holy saints, and children of God," to endure the blast until the day break and the shadows flee away.

While Cranmer, Latimer, and Ridley languished in Bocardo, elaborate preparations for the disputation were going forward. Three articles or questions on the mass were formulated by the lower house of Convocation and forwarded to the universities. Each university selected its own delegates to the disputation, which was to be presided over by Dr. Hugh Weston, dean of Westminster, rector of Lincoln College, Oxford, and prolocutor of the lower house of Convocation.[41]

The formalities which preceded the disputations will suggest the importance which was attached to the affair.[42] On Friday, April 13, the Cambridge delegates arrived at Oxford and took up their lodgings at the Cross Inn, where two beadles presented the vice-chancellor of Cambridge with a ceremonial gift of a dish of apples and a gallon of wine from the vice-chancellor of Oxford. Later in the day the delegates of both universities met with Dr. Weston at Lincoln College. At 9 the next morning, Saturday, April 14, they repaired to the church of St. Mary the Virgin, where the Cambridge divines were incorporated as Oxford D.D.'s and the Oxford divines as Cambridge D.D.'s. Then a mass of the Holy Ghost was celebrated, the choral parts being sung by the choirmen of Christchurch. Afterward the Queen's commission was read, the three articles to be debated were subscribed by all those who had not already done so, and the whole company went in solemn procession to Christchurch for psalm and collect. Then most of the company repaired once more to Lincoln College for dinner with the mayor of the town. After dinner, they returned to St. Mary's, and the official disputants, to the number of thirty-three, took their places in the choir before the altar, while the main body of the church was filled with members of the university and townspeople eager to hear the first round of the disputation.

It had already been determined that each of the three bishops should be called separately, and that once the disputation had begun they should be given no further opportunity for communication. In deference to his rank, Archbishop Cranmer was brought in first.[43] Weston, in his scarlet gown, spoke briefly, reviewing Cranmer's history and urging that he now subscribe affirmatively to the three articles which were to be debated, as follows:

First, in the sacrament of the altar is the natural body of Christ, conceived of the Virgin Mary, and also His blood, present really under the forms of bread and wine, by virtue of God's word pronounced by the priest.

Secondly, there remaineth no substance of bread and wine after the consecration, nor any other substance, but the substance of God and man.

Thirdly, the lively sacrifice of the church is in the mass propitiatory as well for the quick as the dead.[44]

After some lively debate as to the meaning of terms, Cranmer declared that the three propositions—that is, the strictly Roman doctrine of the Real Presence, the doctrine of transubstantiation, and the doctrine of the mass as a propitiatory sacrifice—were without foundation in Scripture. Accordingly, he was ordered to write out his opinions and be prepared to debate the following Monday. He was then taken back to Bocardo, and Bishop Ridley was brought in. Ridley's answers were likewise sharply in the negative, and he was ordered to debate on the following Tuesday.

Finally Latimer was led in. Foxe describes him as dressed "with a kerchief, and two or three caps on his head, his spectacles hanging by a string at his breast, and a staff in his hand." [45] The absurdity of Latimer's appearance, as hinted by Foxe, may suggest the onset of the physical or mental breakdown which, as we shall hear, occurred a little later. But as yet there was no sign of weakening of the mental or moral fiber. Because of his age, he was allowed to sit while the articles were read to him. He too denied them, and was appointed to dispute on the Wednesday following. Whereupon he argued that because of age, sickness, and lack of books he was no more prepared to dispute with the learned divines than a "captain of Calais" would be. Nevertheless, he said, in seven readings of the New Testament since his imprisonment he had been able to find "neither the marrow-bones nor sinews" of the mass, and on Wednesday he would deliver his opinion to the doctors, although he would not dispute formally. The commissioners were annoyed by the vigor of his language, and Weston offered to prove from the New Testament that the mass had both marrow-bones and sinews. "That you will never do, master doctor," replied Latimer, and began to explain what he meant by those terms. But he was silenced, and the beadles led him away.

The disputations began on Monday, April 16, in the divinity school. Cranmer's debate [46] with the doctors, lasting from 8 A.M. to 2 P.M., was in general conducted in Latin and according to the formal principles of medieval disputation, as was Ridley's on the following day.[47] For each of the disputations a chief opponent had been formally designated. Cranmer's opponent was Dr. William Chidsey of Christchurch, formerly a prebendary of St. Paul's and now canon of Windsor. Ridley's opponent was Dr. Richard Smith of Merton, Regius professor of divinity at Oxford —the same Richard Smith whose alleged pusillanimity in preaching before Bishop Latimer in 1536 or 1537 was reported so gleefully by Peter Martyr.[48] Both Cranmer and Ridley complained that the debates were interrupted by unseemly interludes in which the representatives of the universities lost both their tempers and their Latin, and substituted vituperation for logic.

Latimer's turn came on Wednesday the eighteenth.[49] When the old preacher was brought in to the divinity school at 8 A.M., he was greeted by the laughter and hissing of the audience. He was faint and ill, and in constant fear of vomiting. He begged that the proceeding be kept short, and that he be allowed to speak in English, since his Latin was rusty. He was not able, he said, to dispute formally, but he handed up to Dr. Weston, the prolocutor, his written opinion on the three articles under debate. He was not permitted to read it aloud, as he wished to do. Fortunately, however, several manuscript copies survive.[50] His views concerning the sacrament were set forth with clarity and simplicity, without the subtleties and the excessive qualifications that characterized the arguments of Cranmer and Ridley. A few paragraphs will serve as illustration:

Concerning the first conclusion [the article referring to the Roman doctrine of the real corporal presence], me thinketh it is set forth with certain new terms, lately found, that be obscure, and do not sound according to the scripture. Nevertheless, however I understand it, thus do I answer, although not without peril of my life. I say that there is none other presence of Christ required than a spiritual presence; and this presence is sufficient for a Christian man, as the presence by the which we both abide in Christ, and Christ in us, to the obtaining of eternal life, if we persevere in his true gospel. And the same presence may be called a real presence, because to the faithful believer there is the real or spiritual body of Christ: which thing I here rehearse, lest some sycophant or scorner should suppose me, with the anabaptist, to make nothing else of the sacrament but a bare and naked sign. As for that which is feigned of many, I, for my part take it for a papistical invention. And therefore I think it utterly to be rejected from among God's children, that seek their Savior in faith; and be taught among the fleshly papists, that will be again under the yoke of antichrist.

Concerning the second conclusion [transubstantiation], I dare be bold to say, that it hath no stay nor ground of God's holy word; but is a thing invented and found out by man, and therefore to be reputed and had as false; and, I had almost said, as the mother and nurse of all other errors. It were good for my masters and lords, the transubstantiators, to take better heed to their doctrine, lest they conspire with the Nestorians. For the Nestorians deny that Christ had a natural body: and I cannot see how the papists can avoid it: for they would contain the natural body which Christ had (sin excepted) against all truth into a wafer cake.

The third conclusion [the mass as a propitiatory sacrifice], as I understand it, seemeth subtly to sow sedition against the offering which Christ himself offered for us in his own person, and for all, and never again to be done; according to the scriptures written in God's book . . . . I will speak nothing of the wonderful presumptions of man, that dare attempt this thing without any manifest calling: specially that which intrudeth to the overthrowing and fruitless-making (if not wholly, yet partly) of the cross of Christ.[51]

The remainder of Latimer's written statement is given over to citation of Scripture in support of his opinions, and to the emphatic exposition of his conviction that the restoration of the mass, particularly of masses paid for by the faithful, would mean the return of all the old abuses. He complains also of his treatment at the preliminary session the preceding Saturday. He, who in his time had preached for two or three hours without interruption before two kings, had not been suffered to speak for a quarter of an hour in defense of his opinions. And why? Because he had said he could not find in the New Testament the marrow-bones and sinews of the mass. If their "bread-god" has flesh and marrow-bones and sinews (this of course implies complete disregard of the scholastic distinction between substance and accidents) and were indeed the corporal Body and Blood of Christ, surely the Scriptures would say so. But they do not. Nor was this the opinion of only "old Hugh Latimer," of whom they might say that he "doted for age" or that his "wits were gone." It was concurred in by Cranmer, Ridley, and Bradford after the four had read the New Testament seven times over in a fruitless search for evidence of the presence of the "marrow-bones."

The latter part of Latimer's written statement is replete with indications that in spite of age and illness he retained much of his old gift for the mordant and provocative phrase. At one point he even expresses doubt that the scholarly attainments of Dr. Weston (whom he accuses of having changed theological coats at Mary's accession) were such as to qualify him to preside over the disputation. Perhaps it was fortunate that Latimer was not permitted to read the statement to the assembled divines.

Dr. Richard Smith, Ridley's chief opponent of the day before, had likewise been assigned the task of leading the disputation with Latimer. In spite of Latimer's refusal, Smith did make some effort to engage him in formal disputation. But the old preacher skilfully evaded Smith's attempts at syllogistic debate. In this evasion he was unintentionally abetted by Dr. Weston and some of the others, especially Dr. William Tresham, a former vice-chancellor of Oxford. Still brooding over Latimer's denial of the marrow-bones of the mass the preceding Saturday, they began to hurl citations from Scripture and the fathers at Latimer as soon as the session began. They continued to do so, in defiance of the rules of order, throughout Dr. Smith's half-hearted attempts at disputation. Sometimes Latimer capped their quotations. At other times, he insisted that they misinterpreted their texts. Whenever his memory or erudition failed him, he fell back upon "my lord of Canterbury's book"—that is, Cranmer's *Defense of the True and Catholic Doctrine of the Sacrament*—alleging that all the answers to his opponents' arguments could be found in that work. In this there was a certain element of unintended humor, for Cranmer in his disputation had several times insisted that he held to Ridley's opinions. It is not surprising that the Bishop of Gloucester later remarked with some exasperation, "Latimer leaneth to Cranmer, Cranmer to Ridley, and Ridley to the singularity of his own wit: so that if you overthrow the singularity of Ridley's wit, then must needs the religion of Cranmer and Latimer fall also." [52]

On the whole, despite the superior weight of learning arrayed against him, Latimer came through the controversy very creditably. Repeatedly and doggedly, he denied the corporal presence in the sacrament and insisted upon the spiritual. At the end, Weston said, "You never agreed with the Tigurines [Zwinglians], or Germans [Lutherans], or with the church, or with yourself. Your stubbornness cometh of a vainglory, which is to no purpose; for it will do you no good when a fagot is in your beard. And we see all by your own confession, how little cause you have to be stubborn, for your learning is in feoffer's hold.[53] The queen's grace is merciful, if ye will turn." Latimer's reply was weary but firm. "You shall have no hope in me to turn. I pray for the queen daily, even from the bottom of my heart, that she may turn from this religion." [54] Thus Latimer's debate with the doctors was concluded, having lasted about three hours.

On the following Friday,[55] the divines of the two universities assembled once again in the church of St. Mary the Virgin, this time for the formal condemnation of the three bishops and their opinions. Cranmer, Latimer, and Ridley, brought together before their quondam opponents, now their judges, were solemnly informed that they had been overcome in disputation. Cranmer ventured to protest once more at the irregular fashion in which the disputations had been conducted, but he was shouted down. Then the three articles on the mass were read once more by Dr. Weston, and the three bishops were given a final opportunity to subscribe them. But they stood by their former opinions, and Dr. Weston proceeded to their condemnation as heretics, whereby they, their followers, and their patrons were declared to be cut off from the church. Each of the condemned men was given an opportunity to comment upon the sentence. Cranmer appealed from their judgment to the judgment of God, trusting to be present with Him in heaven for whose presence in the altar I am thus condemned." Ridley remarked that the sentence would send them sooner to heaven than they would have come in the course of nature. Latimer said, "I thank God most heartily, that he hath prolonged my life to this end, that I may in this case glorify God by that kind of death." Dr. Weston so far forgot his judicial status as to reply, "If you go to heaven by this faith, then will I never come thither, as I am thus persuaded." Whereupon the three bishops were removed to their places of separate confinement—Cranmer to Bocardo, Ridley to the sheriff's house next the prison, and Latimer to the house of a bailiff elsewhere in the town.

The next day, Saturday, April 20, the last ceremonial in the elaborate program was enacted. After a high mass at St. Mary's, the learned divines went in solemn procession through the streets of Oxford. At the end came Dr. Weston bearing the Sacrament, with four doctors holding the canopy over him. As the procession passed Bocardo, Cranmer was required to watch it from the prison window, Ridley from the sheriff's house. But Latimer's place of confinement being off the route, he was brought to Carfax to see the procession and the Sacrament. In some confusion of mind, he thought he was being taken out to be burned, and he urged Augustine Cooper, the bailiff, to make a quick fire. When he saw the Sacrament, says Foxe, "he ran as fast as his old bones would carry him, to one Spenser's shop, and would not look towards it."

In his expectation of speedy execution, Latimer failed to reckon with the government's cautious plan that all should be done according to due process of law. He could not know that he would be required to live through eighteen months more of confinement before the foredoomed end.

CHAPTER TWENTY-SIX

THE MARTYRDOM

A few days after the termination of the spectacle at Oxford, Dr. Weston rendered an official report of the proceedings to Convocation and presumably also to the Privy Council. The latter body was faced with a dilemma. The old statutes for the burning of heretics had been repealed in the preceding reign. Mary's first and second parliaments, in spite of pressure from the Council, had been reluctant to enact a new heresy bill. When the second parliament was dissolved, on May 5, 1554, there was still no statute on the books which provided adequate punishment for the condemned heretics, Cranmer, Latimer, and Ridley. On May 3 the Council, knowing that there was no hope of securing suitable legislation from the parliament which was about to be dissolved, adopted a resolution that "the judges and the queen's highness's learned counsel should be called together and their opinions demanded what they think in law her highness may do touching the cases of the said Cranmer, Ridley and Latimer, being already by both the universities of Oxford and Cambridge judged to be obstinate heretics, which matter is the rather to be consulted upon for that the said Cranmer is already attainted."[1]

If the judges and the learned counsel actually convened, it must have been only to recommend continued pressure upon Parliament for the enactment of a new heresy statute. As it turned out, Mary's next parliament, which began its sessions on November 12, 1554, proved acquiescent. It was this parliament which petitioned for and received Rome's absolution for the nation's former heresy and schism, and in January, 1555, passed the Great Act of Reconciliation. It also reenacted, on December 15, 1554, the old statute *De haeretico comburendo,* a law originally designed for the punishment of Lollardy.

By that time, nine months had passed since the Oxford disputations. The three bishops remained in separate confinement, Cranmer in Bocardo, Latimer and Ridley in the houses of the bailiff and the sheriff respectively. The Privy Council kept a watchful eye upon their affairs and made careful provision for their maintenance. On May 3, 1554, Council ordered that the town authorities be reimbursed for expenses up to that time, and a subsequent order in Council reveals that they were allowed one pound per week for each bishop and his servant,[2] a sufficient sum. The bailiffs kept occasional accounts of their expenditures, and in some instances the record is quite precise. On October 1, 1554, for instance, the dinner provided for the prisoners consisted of bread and butter, oysters, eggs, salt ling, fresh salmon, pears, cheese, wine and beer—a repast which seems sumptuous in contrast to the British austerity diet of today. The total cost of this meal was 2s. 6d., or 10d. per bishop.[3] The regular provision for food and clothing was also supplemented by occasional gifts from admirers. Bishop Ridley speaks of presents from known and unknown friends,[4] and a letter of Robert Glover reveals that on one occasion he sent two shirts to Latimer and two to Augustine Bernher, and at the same time forwarded from an anonymous friend the substantial sum of £6. 13s. 4d. to provide for the greater comfort of Cranmer, Latimer, and Ridley.[5]

In spite of what seems to have been generous provision for their maintenance, the three prisoners suffered greatly from their isolation from each other. "We are now so ordered and straitly watched," wrote Ridley, "that scantly our servants dare do anything for us: so much talk and so many tales (as is said) are told of us abroad. One of us cannot easily nor shortly be of knowledge of another's mind . . . ."[6] Their separation became the more grievous when the authorities decreed that they might no longer have their familiar servants. They missed especially the faithful Augustine Bernher, who was himself reduced to a state of great anxiety at being cut off from access to Latimer and the others. Thereafter Bernher seems to have divided his time between Oxford and London, carrying messages and news to and from the prisoners for religion in both places. The Oxford prisoners were given new servants who at first refused to render anything more than perfunctory service. Gradually, however, the bishops won their confidence, and it became possible once more to exchange messages and to effect an equitable distribution of the gifts of money, food, and clothing.[7]

Even more distressing than the difficulty of communicating with each other was the uncertainty of Cranmer, Latimer, and Ridley concerning their own fate. They had no doubt that they would be burned, but they could not know when. As the weeks and months passed their tension increased. Throughout the spring of 1554, while Parliament was sitting, they must have been in daily expectation of the enactment of a new heresy law which would make it possible for the government to despatch them. When they learned that Parliament had been dissolved, they did not know what to expect. The prisoners for religion in London and elsewhere suffered from the same uncertainty. To relieve their tensions they wrote letters—so many and such long letters that one who reads through them comes to the conclusion that the authors suffered from a monstrous *cacoethes scribendi* induced by long periods of enforced solitude. They wrote to friends and relatives, to each other, and in more apostolic vein to England, to the universities, to the Christian world at large. They were supplied with writing materials by the pertinacious audacity of Augustine Bernher and others like him, with the connivance of warders and bailiffs. By the same means the letters were smuggled out of the prisons and delivered to the addressees. Copies of many of them came ultimately into the hands of John Foxe and Miles Coverdale. The former printed them in his famous *Acts and Monuments,* the latter in a thick quarto volume entitled *Certain Most Godly, Fruitful, and Comfortable Letters of Such True Saints and Holy Martyrs of God, as in the Late Bloody Persecution Here within This Realm, Gave Their Lives for the Defense of Christ's Holy Gospel.* In all this frenetic correspondence Latimer had no part other than to write the three letters described in the preceding chapter, all of which were probably written before the disputations at Oxford. Foxe attributes this lack of epistolary zeal to the feebleness of old age. But Bishop Ridley supplies us with an additional explanation. "Master Latimer," he wrote to Bradford, "was crazed, but I hear now, thanks be to God, that he amendeth again." [8] With misguided partisanship some writers [9] have attempted to explain away the word "crazed" by emphasizing that in the sixteenth century it usually meant physical illness. But it could also mean mentally disordered. Foxe's references to eccentricity of dress and behavior suggest that during the disputations in April, 1554, Latimer displayed some of the symptoms of nervous and mental collapse and that the same symptoms were present at the final trial in October, 1555. If the collapse was more complete at some time during the intervening months, when Bishop Ridley's letter was written, there would be no reason for surprise and certainly no need for concealment or apology. Latimer was old and ill; the mental strain and anxiety had been unrelieved for months. Who can say what uncertainties about the wisdom of his course clouded his mind during the long, silent vigils? Archbishop Cranmer repeatedly recanted before the end, and repeatedly he recanted his recantations. There is no reason to believe that Latimer was less sensitive, less beset by doubts than Cranmer.[10] The same lack of certitude which induced such vacillation in the Archbishop might well have brought on nervous collapse in the case of Latimer. The matter for wonder is not that for a time he may have broken under the strain. It is rather that, if he did so, he made so good a recovery and was able in the end to face his judges and the flames with calmness and courage.

Like many others in time of crisis, he found his release in constant prayer. Foxe and Bernher both say that during his long imprisonment he was accustomed to pray so long and so fervently that often he could not rise from his knees without help. The same authorities declare (upon what evidence it is impossible to say) that in his prayers he made three principal petitions. He prayed that "the gospel" might be restored to England once again, that the Princess Elizabeth might be spared to be a comfort to that comfortless realm, and that he himself might be given "grace to stand to his doctrine until his death, that he might give his heart blood for the same." [11]

On December 15, 1554, Parliament reënacted the old statute for the punishment of heretics. The executions under it began in February, 1555. Within the next three years over three hundred perished in the flames at Smithfield and elsewhere. Many of these were men who can be properly regarded as the fathers of the Church of England. But the great majority were Anabaptists, obscure sectarians and sacramentaries whom the former group would probably have punished with equal severity had the power been vested in them. With all allowance, however, for the barbarities of an age which held human life cheaply, the number and the severity of the executions still strike us with horror. The effort to fix final responsibility has never met with much success. In the older protestant histories of the period, Queen Mary, Cardinal Pole, Bishop Gardiner, and Bishop Bonner are the objects of special attack. More temperate modern research has tended to correct the old picture of the latter three as "great bloody persecutors." [12] There remains the difficult problem of Mary's direct responsibility for the persecutions. As a result of her unhappy marriage and her failure to give birth to an heir to the throne, she was unquestionably in a condition of hysteria during much of this period. In this state of mind she may well have encouraged or at least have permitted executions which a more normal woman holding the same religious opinions might have restrained. Whatever her responsibility, it was shared by her husband Philip, whose training and habit of mind caused him to have every sympathy for the methods of the Spanish inquisition.

The first of the martyrs was John Rogers, editor of the Matthew Bible and latterly a prebendary of St. Paul's, who went to the flames at Smithfield on February 4, 1555. Shortly thereafter John Bradford, expecting that he would be next, wrote to Cranmer, Latimer, and Ridley, "Our brother Rogers hath broken the ice valiantly. . . . And for your part, make you ready; for we are but your gentlemen ushers: 'The marriage of the Lamb is prepared, come unto the marriage'." [13] But Bradford was not executed until June 30. Rogers was followed on February 8 by Laurence Saunders, sometime rector of All Hallows Bread Street, burned at Coventry; and on the next day by Bishop Hooper at Gloucester and Dr. Rowland Taylor at Hadley in Suffolk, where he was rector. Dr. Taylor will be remembered as having been one of Latimer's chaplains when the latter was bishop of Worcester. Both he and Saunders, shortly before their execution, wrote letters addressed jointly to the three bishops imprisoned at Oxford. Although the letters add nothing to the factual record, they eloquently attest the courage with which these two martyrs faced the prospect of a horrible death. They attest also the veneration in which Cranmer, Latimer, and Ridley were held by their younger disciples. To Saunders they were "a town set upon a hill, a candle upon a candle-stick, a spectacle unto the world." [14] To Taylor they were his "dear fathers and brethren." [15]

Throughout the succeeding months the executions continued in ever increasing numbers. As the winter passed, and then spring and summer and early autumn, the three bishops at Oxford were in daily expectation of their own summons and were bewildered that no summons came. The delay in dealing with the three arch-heretics can be explained only by the government's hope that they would recant and thus deal a crippling blow to the opposition. But in the cases of Latimer and Ridley these hopes were never realized, and Cranmer's distressing vacillations did not occur until after his brother-bishops had perished.

At last in September, 1555, the Church determined to despatch the three Oxford prisoners. Cranmer's case was delayed by formalities arising from his status as archbishop; there followed the long and tragic period of alternating weakness and strength which culminated in his martyrdom on March 21, 1556. The last examination [16] of Bishops Latimer and Rid-ley began on September 30 before a commission appointed by the papal legate, Cardinal Pole. The commission consisted of John White, bishop of Lincoln, James Brooks, bishop of Gloucester, and John Holyman, bishop of Bristol, all recent appointees to the episcopal bench. They were charged with full authority to examine Latimer and Ridley, "pretensed bishops of Worcester and London," upon the erroneous opinions which they had long held and which they had publicly maintained the preceding year at Oxford. If the accused would recant and submit to the Church, the com-mission were empowered to reconcile them to the Holy Father the Pope. If they stoutly and stubbornly maintained their erroneous opinions, the commission would proceed against them to the full extent of the law.

The hearings began in the divinity school at Oxford at 8 A.M. on September 30. The commissioners sat in the high seats of the lecturers, which seats were now, as befitted the gravity of the occasion, furnished with velvet cushions and trimmed with cloth of tissue. Ridley was brought in first, Latimer meantime being kept waiting in an ante-chamber. The "pretensed" bishop of London stood bare-headed while the notary read the commission of the examining bishops, but he hastily put on his cap when the Pope and the papal legate were named. There followed an altercation between Ridley and White, the presiding bishop, and a good deal of undignified on-capping and off-capping by Ridley whenever the names of the Pope or the Cardinal recurred. Finally, the beadle took Ridley's cap away and the examination continued in more orderly fashion. White's long charge to Ridley was chiefly declarative of the supremacy of Rome, with Ridley frequently interposing an objection. When the ar-ticles of heresy [17] were finally read, Ridley once more denied the Corporal Presence and the propitiatory nature of the sacrament. With a good deal of technical reasoning, he affirmed the Real Spiritual Presence. Finally, he was ordered to appear the next day at the church of St. Mary the Virgin to make formal renunciation of his opinions.

After the removal of Ridley, Latimer was brought in, "his hat in his hand, having a kerchief on his head, and upon it a night-cap or two, and a great cap (such as townsmen use, with two broad flaps to button under the chin), wearing an old thread-bare Bristol frieze-gown girdled to his body with a penny leather girdle, at the which hanged by a long string of leather his Testament, and his spectacles without case depending upon his neck upon his breast." He complained that he had been kept waiting so long, with only the cold walls of the antechamber to gaze upon, and Bishop White apologized gravely.[18]

Latimer listened quietly as White spoke at length on the importance of unity in the church. White's address, quiet and restrained throughout, concluded with a direct exhortation: "Let not vain-glory have the upper hand, humiliate yourself, captivate your understanding, subdue your reason, submit yourself to the determination of the church, do not force us to do all that we may do, let us rest in that part which we most heartily desire, and I, for my part, again with all my heart exhort you." [19]

Latimer, having been given permission to sit, replied for the most part with matching restraint. He could not find in Scripture, he said, authority for the supremacy of Rome, whose bishops ruled not according to the will of God, but according to their own will. When the old scoffing manner flared up at one point, the audience laughed, and Latimer rebuked them with, "Why, my masters, this is no laughing matter. I answer upon life and death, 'Vae vobis qui ridetis nunc, quoniam flebitis'." [20] A slight interchange of personalities between Latimer and the Bishop of Gloucester led to another small outburst. "Lo," said Latimer, "you look for learning at my hands which have gone so long to the school of oblivion, making the bare walls my library; keeping me so long in prison, without book or pen or ink." [21] But the Bishop of Lincoln, cutting short these asperities, proceeded to a reading of the articles, which were the same as those put to Ridley—that the two bishops had openly denied the real corporal presence in the sacrament of the altar, that they had denied transubstantiation, that they had denied that the mass was a propitiatory sacrifice, that these opinions had been condemned as heretical by the learned of both universities, and that all the premises (that is, the four preceding articles) were universally known to be true.

Protesting that his answers were not to be regarded as an admission of the pope's jurisdiction, Latimer nevertheless made brief answers to all the articles. To the first, he denied the Corporal Presence of the Body of Christ in the sacrament of the altar, but affirmed once more the Real Spiritual Presence. To the second, he asserted that after the consecration there was a change in the elements, but it was a change in dignity, not in substance; the bread was still bread, the wine still wine, but they were no longer common, having been sanctified by God's word. To the third article, he denied that the mass was a propitiatory sacrifice. He seems to have been confused in his mind by the legal phraseology of the fourth and fifth articles, but after a little delay he admitted their truth. The notaries duly recorded his affirmative answers to all five articles—that is, his full confession to the truth of all the charges against him.

Then Bishop White said to him, "Master Latimer, we mean not that these your answers shall be prejudicial to you. Tomorrow you shall appear before us again, and then it shall be lawful for you to alter and change what you will. We give you respite till tomorrow, trusting that, after you have pondered well all things against tomorrow, you will not be ashamed to confess the truth."

Latimer replied pathetically, "Nay, my lords, I beseech you to do with me now as it shall please your lordships: I pray you let not me be troubled tomorrow again." Then, when Lincoln insisted upon his further appearance, "Truly, my lord, as for my part I require no respite, for I am at a point; you shall give me respite in vain: therefore I pray you let me not trouble you tomorrow." [22]

But the court, resolved that all things must be done in order, and hopeful to the last that a heretic might recant, declined to consider the old preacher's request. He was committed to the mayor of Oxford, with the order that he appear at St. Mary's the next morning at eight.

At St. Mary's on October 1 Bishops White, Brooks, and Holyman were enthroned in the choir. Below and some distance in front of them was a table covered with a silken cloth for the prisoners at the bar. Benches for the dignitaries of the university were arranged in such a way as to hold back the press of townsmen and gownsmen who thronged the church in eagerness to be present at what they realized was an historic occasion. Bishop Ridley was brought in first and after a repetition of the off-capping and on-capping of the preceding day was seated at the silk-covered table. After some preliminary wrangling over the authority of Rome, he offered his written opinion on the sacrament of the altar. The court, after glancing over the opinion, refused him permission to read it aloud, on the ground that it was partly irrelevant, since it was largely a denial of the authority of the court, and partly blasphemous. Then the five articles were read once more; in answer to each article Ridley referred the judges to his written opinions. The Bishops of Gloucester and Lincoln urged him to forsake reliance upon private judgment—it was at this point that Gloucester made his celebrated remark that "Latimer leaneth to Cranmer, Cranmer to Ridley, and Ridley to the singularity of his own wit" [23]—and submit himself to the opinion of the church. But Ridley persisted in the assertions that his opinions were grounded in God's word, and the court was left with no recourse but to deliver the sentence of condemnation.

Ridley was led away and preparations were made for dealing with Latimer. The silken cloth was removed from the table, on the ground that Latimer was not a doctor of divinity. As the old preacher seated himself he noted the absence of the cloth and immediately laid an old felt hat on the table and rested his elbows upon it. Before his judges had time to speak, he rebuked them for not managing the crowd better, protesting that his "evil" back, injured years before by a falling tree, had been hurt by the press of the multitude. As on the preceding day, Bishop White apologized, promising that at his departure there would be better order. Latimer bowed deeply, not without irony. [24]

The formal proceeding began with Lincoln's renewed plea that Latimer recant. But the old man interrupted him. "Your lordship often doth inculke the catholic church, as though I should deny the same. No, my lord, I confess there is a catholic church, to the determination of which I will stand; but not the church which you call catholic, which sooner might be termed diabolic. . . . Christ gave knowledge that the disciples should have persecution and trouble. How think you then, my lords, is it most like that the see of Rome, which hath been a continual persecutor, is rather the church, or that small flock which hath continually been persecuted of it, even to death?" [25] He remained deaf to all of the bishop of Lincoln's further argument.

When the five articles were read by the notary, Latimer made affirmative answers substantively identical with those of the day before. Bishop White made the last formal plea for recantation, to which Latimer replied that he neither could nor would deny his Master Christ and His truth. Whereupon the bishop of Lincoln read the condemnation. The prisoner was declared a heretic and excommunicated with the greater excommunication. It was ordered that he be degraded from the degree of bishop, from priesthood, and from all other ecclesiastical order, and that he be delivered to the secular powers to receive due punishment according to the temporal laws.

Latimer received the sentence quietly. He asked for, and was denied, permission to defend further his refusal of the pope's authority. Then he asked whether he might appeal the sentence to the next general council which should be truly called in God's name. Bishop White agreed that he might, but could not refrain from adding that it would be long before such a council as Latimer had in mind would be convened. It is not clear whether this witticism was directed at Latimer or at the Council of Trent, then in its tenth year. In either case, White's last gesture towards Latimer was kindly. "Now he is your prisoner, master mayor," he said, but he ordered that the old man be kept in the church until the crowd had been cleared away, so that he might suffer no further injury.[26]

Fifteen days elapsed between the sentence and the execution. During this period Ridley composed his long letter of farewell addressed to his friends and relatives, to Cambridge and his own college of Pembroke, to Canterbury, Westminster, England and the world. It is a long document, occasionally rhapsodic,[27] but revealing Ridley with all his powers unimpaired. From Latimer, old and broken, came no word of any kind. Cardinal Pole sent Peter de Soto, the Spanish friar who was now teaching in Peter Martyr's place at Oxford, to make a final effort to bring the condemned men to repentance.[28] But the friar's efforts were fruitless, and the execution for Ridley and Latimer was set for October 16.

On October 15 came their formal degradation. We have no account of this painful ceremony as used in Latimer's case, but it was certainly identical in form with the degradation of Ridley, which is described in detail by Foxe.[29] Dr. Brooks, bishop of Gloucester, Dr. Marshall, the vice-chancellor of Oxford, and several heads of colleges repaired to the house of Master Irish, the mayor, where Ridley was imprisoned. There, with Ridley protesting and resisting at every step, they put upon him the surplice and other vestments of a priest, but not those of a bishop, since according to Rome he had never truly been a bishop and was therefore not degraded from episcopal dignity. One by one the garments were removed, with Bishop Brooks reading the solemn Latin sentence of degradation. Part of the ceremony required that the chalice and wafer be put in Ridley's hands, then removed as a sign that he might no longer perform the sacrament. Ridley refused to hold the chalice and wafer, which then had to be held forcibly in his hand. Such were the details of Ridley's degradation. Latimer was subjected to the same indignity, probably on the same day by the same officials. If a spark of the old fire remained, it is unlikely that he played his part more submissively than Ridley.

Meanwhile, preparations for the execution the next day were completed. The furze for kindling and the wood for fagots had been brought in from the country at a cost to the bailiffs of 17s. 4d. The post for the stake was in place, and the chains and staples for securing the victims to the stake had been forged. Four laborers were engaged to do the preparatory work and to build and feed the fire at the appointed time.[30]

The place of execution, says Foxe,[31] was "upon the north side of the town, in the ditch over against Balliol College." There the stake had been set up, and thither the whole town and university repaired on the morning of October 16, 1555. On a platform hard by sat Lord Williams of Thame, who had been commanded to preside at the execution, together with the vice-chancellor of the university and other dignitaries.

Ridley, wearing a furred black gown and a bishop's tippet, was conducted to the place of execution by Master Irish, then mayor of Oxford, and an alderman. As he passed Bocardo, Ridley looked up at the window, hoping to catch a glimpse of Cranmer, but the Archbishop was then in disputation with the Spanish friar and was thus prevented from waving a last farewell to his colleagues. At that moment Latimer, dressed in his shabby gown of Bristol frieze and with his large townsman's cap buttoned about his ears, was brought out of the house where he had been confined. To Ridley's "Oh, be ye there?" Latimer replied, "Yea, have after as fast as I can follow." Then Ridley embraced the older man and said, "Be of good heart, brother, for God will either assuage the fury of the flame, or else strengthen us to abide it."

Arrived at the place of execution, both men spent some time upon their knees in prayer. Then they settled themselves to hear the sermon, which was preached by Dr. Richard Smith, one of the divines with whom they had disputed the previous year. Smith's sermon was mercifully short, lasting but a quarter of an hour. He denounced their heresies, especially their alleged Zwinglianism, and (using the same argument that Latimer had advanced years before against the Lord Admiral and the Anabaptists) declared that their dying for their cause was no sign of holiness, for, he said, "the goodness of the cause, and not the order of death, maketh the holiness of the person." His text, inevitably, was St. Paul's "Though I give my body to be burned and have not charity, it profiteth me nothing." At times during the sermon Latimer and Ridley expressed their disapprobation by glance and gesture. When it was over Ridley invited Latimer to make answer, but Latimer deferred to Ridley. Both men fell to their knees, and Ridley asked permission of Lord Williams to speak. While Lord Williams hesitated, uncertain of the proper procedure, Ridley began to answer Smith's sermon, but the bailiff and Dr. Marshall, the vice-chancellor of the university, stopped his mouth with their hands. "Master Ridley," said Marshall, "if you will revoke your erroneous opinions, and recant the same, you shall not only have liberty so to do, but also the benefit of a subject; that is, have your life."

"Not otherwise?" asked Ridley.

"No," said Marshall. "Therefore, if you will not do so, then there is no remedy but you must suffer for your deserts."

Ridley said, "Well, so long as the breath is in my body, I will never deny my Lord Christ, and His known truth: God's will be done in me. I commit our cause to Almighty God, which shall indifferently judge all." To which Latimer added, "Well! there is nothing hid but it shall be opened."

So they prepared themselves for the flames, with Cranmer watching from the wall of Bocardo. Ridley gave his gown and tippet to his brother-in-law, Master Shipside (from whom Foxe may have got these details). He gave his truss, his watch, and some trifles he had about him to by-standers. Latimer gave nothing, having nothing to give. But when the keeper stripped off his poor outer garments, and he stood only in his shroud, it seemed to his friends among the bystanders that "whereas in his clothes he appeared a withered and crooked silly old man, he now stood bolt upright, as comely a father as one might lightly behold."

They were chained to the stake, and the gorse and fagots of wood were built up about them. Master Shipside had provided himself with two little bags of gunpowder, and he was permitted to tie one about the neck of each of the condemned men, that they might have a quicker death.[32] As the torch was applied, Latimer spoke his famous words. At least Foxe says he spoke them, and I would not take them from him. "Be of good comfort, Master Ridley, and play the man. We shall this day light such a candle, by God's grace, in England, as I trust shall never be put out." As the flames mounted, Ridley cried out in a loud voice, "In manus tuas, Domine, commendo spiritum meum: Domine recipe spiritum meum." And then in English repeatedly, "Lord, Lord, receive my spirit." Latimer seemed to some who were present to embrace the flames and to stroke his face as if to bathe it with fire, the while he too cried loudly, "Oh Father of heaven, receive my soul."

Ridley's death was horrible beyond words. The fire beneath him failed to burn vigorously (his brother-in-law, intent upon hastening the end, made matters worse by adding more fagots which further smothered the flames) and he suffered agonies before the fire reached the gunpowder. Latimer had a kindlier fate. Either the gunpowder was ignited almost at once or he lost consciousness, for he seemed to suffer little pain and he died quickly.

So ended the mortal career of Hugh Latimer. In the months and years which followed, his memory was kept alive by friend and enemy alike. Many a heretic, in the trials which preceded his own execution, courageously grounded his faith on the religion of Cranmer, Latimer, and Ridley, who "did preach the gospel truly." Conversely, against many of them the specific charge was made that they had "commended and approved the doctrine of Thomas Cranmer, Nicholas Ridley, and Hugh Latimer, concerning the sacrament of the altar." When Cardinal Pole made his visitation of Cambridge, after the bodies of Martin Bucer and Paul Fagius had been disinterred from their place of burial in the church of St. Mary the Great and publicly burned, the preacher of the occasion, a Master Peacock, thundered in Latin against heresy and heretics and spoke especially of Bilney, Cranmer, Latimer, and Ridley, all Cambridge men.[33] In 1560, when, upon order of Archbishop Parker, Bucer and Fagius were posthumously restored to their honors, the public orator, Acworth, declared that Cambridge alone had "played the mad bedlam against the dead." Oxford had burned Latimer, Ridley, and Cranmer, but she had burned them alive, not dead.[34]

By that time, Latimer's reputation as the martyred apostle to the English was firmly established. Three years later he was permanently enshrined in the pages of John Foxe, where his story was destined to be read by generations of readers. His sermons were printed again and again in the next two centuries, and his famous words about the candle which would not be put out became the watchword of English protestantism. For almost three hundred years English historians, with the understandable exception of Roman Catholic writers, spoke of him only in terms of veneration and love. James Anthony Froude, writing in the middle years of the nineteenth century, was bold to say that Latimer, at the time of his trial, was "the greatest man then living in the world," an hyperbole which represents the culmination of the tradition.

Froude's words have a peculiar significance. Thirty years before they were written, the leaders of the Oxford Movement, in their growing hostility towards the English reformation, had begun to denigrate the memory of Latimer and the other reformers. No one had spoken against them more injudiciously than Hurrell Froude, James Anthony's brother. As a young man the historian had himself been on the fringes of the Oxford Movement, but his early interest soon turned to antagonism and disgust. It is almost certain that his unrestrained praise of Latimer was a reaction against his brother's unrestrained condemnation. But there was another and more curious consequence of the attacks upon the reformers by John Henry Newman, Hurrell Froude, and their associates. In 1839, when the Oxford Movement was approaching its acrimonious climax, the Reverend C. P. Golightly conceived a plan for requiring the critics of the English reformation to declare themselves. He and his friends would solicit subscriptions for a memorial to the Oxford martyrs. The critics would be placed in awkward position. If they subscribed, they would in a sense be reversing their field; if they refused to subscribe, they would have declared themselves irrevocably the friends of Rome. The plan succeeded. The money was raised; Newman and his chief disciples declined to subscribe. Today the Martyrs' Memorial stands in St. Giles Street, aesthetically depressing to all who see it, and saddening to those who remember its history. But Latimer has another and better memorial than this. It is the collection of his sermons, preserved by the piety of his friends, from which the words still ring out in the tones of the living voice.

NOTES AND BIBLIOGRAPHY

In the notes the titles of the works cited are given in brief. Full titles, with place and date of publication, are given in the bibliography. Throughout the notes the following abbreviations are used:

Foxe John Foxe, *The Acts and Monuments.* [Edited by R. R. Mendham and Josiah Pratt]. 4th edition, revised and corrected by Josiah Pratt. 8 volumes, London, [1875]. (References to the first edition of Foxe are always specified as such.)

LP *Letters and Papers, Foreign and Domestic, of the Reign of Henry VIII.* 21 volumes and addenda. London, 1862-1910.

STC *A Short-Title Catalogue of Books Printed in England, Scotland, and Ireland, and of English Books Printed Abroad, 1475-1640.* Compiled by A. W. Pollard and G. R. Redgrave. London, 1926.

Strype John Strype, *Ecclesiastical Memorials.* Clarendon Press Edition. 3 volumes in six parts. Oxford, 1822.

VCH *Victoria History of the Counties of England.*

Works *The Works of Hugh Latimer,* edited by George E. Corrie. The Parker Society. 2 volumes, Cambridge, 1844, 1845.

In general, the bibliography is limited to works cited in the text and notes. It includes also a few books which are not directly cited but to which any writer on this period must be highly indebted.

NOTES

CHAPTER ONE

Student and Priest

1. First Sermon before Edward VI. *Works*, I. 101.
2. *ibid.*, I. 102.
3. Foxe, VII. 437.
4. Some account of the manor of Thurcaston will be found in Nichols, *The History and Antiquities of the County of Leicester*, Vol. IV, Pt. 2.
5. Foxe, *loc.cit.*
6. Nichols, *op. cit.*, I, 496: and *DNB*. *s.v.* Sampson, Thomas.
7. Stowe MS 958.
8. Dugdale, *Antiquities of Warwickshire*, II. 1054.
9. In the dedication of Latimer's later sermons to the Duchess of Suffolk. Latimer, *Works*, I. 320.
10. Foxe, VII. 463.
11. See below, p.4.
12. Foxe, VII. 437.
13. "I myself have been of that dangerous, perilous and damnable opinion [of the necessity of voluntary works] till I was thirty years of age." Sermon of Twelfth Day. *Works*, II. 137.
14. The opinions of other writers should be noted. Canon Corrie (Latimer, *Works*, I. i-ii) favors the year 1491. Demaus (*Hugh Latimer*, pp.14-15) argues for the year 1485, and is followed by Gairdner (*DNB*, *s.v.* Latimer). The Carlyles (*Hugh Latimer*, p.4) follow Corrie; but they seem unaware of the conflicting testimony.
15. Foxe, VII. 437.
16. *Narratives of the Days of the Reformation*, p.218.
17. Sixth Sermon before Edward VI. *Works*, I. 197.
18. See above, p.1.
19. An excellent brief account of the program in arts and divinity will be found in *Grace Book A*, Introduction, pp.xx-xxvii.
20. "Cauciones domini pynder domini latemer et domini browne et sunt due pecie argentee." *Grace Book B, Part I.* 248.
21. "Item conceditur Hugoni Latymer ut xii termini in quorum quolibet excepto uno ordinario audiuit etsi non secundam formam statuti sufficiant sibi ad respondendum quaes-

22. tioni." *Grace Book Gamma*, p.78.
22. *e.g.* in Venn, *Alumni Cantabrigienses*, Part I, III. 49.
23. It is based upon the assertion in Foxe, VII. 451, that Latimer was once a pupil of Dr. John Watson, who was a fellow of Peterhouse from 1501 to 1516, when he became master of Christ's (see *DNB*, *s.v.* Watson, John). From Watson's association with Christ's some writers have also suggested the possible connection of Latimer with that house. But Latimer must have been a pupil of Watson's long before 1516, if ever.
24. "Etiam circa festum Purificationis proxime sequens eligebantur in socios istius Collegii Dominus Johannes Powel et Dominus Willelmus Pyndar in artibus baccalaurei et Dominus Hugo Latymer quaestionista." Quoted from the registers by Christopher Wordsworth, *Ecclesiastical Biography*, II. 446.
25. *Calendar of State Papers Domestic, 1547-1580*, p.16. The letter, dated May 18, 1549, was apparently first printed by Demaus, p.448.
26. There is a portrait of him in the hall of the college. Forbes, *Clare College 1326-1926*, Chapter III, Plate 28.
27. Forbes, *op. cit.*, I. 33-35.
28. Demaus, p.23, says that the annual stipend for a fellow was £ 1. 3 *s.* 4 *d.* The amount seems probable, but I have been unable to discover the source of the statement.
29. It has been estimated that fewer than half of the matriculates proceeded to the half-degree of B.A. and that fewer than six percent completed the whole course. Coulton, *Medieval Panorama*, p.409.
30. An excellent brief account of Erasmus at Cambridge will be found in Mullinger, *The University of Cambridge from the Earliest Times to the Royal Injunctions of 1535*, pp.491-506.
31. "Item, conceditur Domino Latymer ut lectiones ordinariae novem terminorum audite cum quatuor responsionibus quarum una erat in

die cinerum altera in finali determinatione et due alie in grammatica quarum altera in die commensaciones altera in scolis publicis sufficiant sibi ad incipiendum in artibus sic ut soluat Universitati 13 sol. iiij d." *Grace Book Gamma*, p.116.

32. *Grace Book B, Part II*, p.19. The date is here given specifically—May 8, 1514.

33. Sermon on the Epistle for the Twenty-first Sunday after Trinity. *Works*, I. 499.

34. Venn, *Alumni Cantabrigienses, Part I*, III. 49.

35. In three letters of this period one 'Latimer' is mentioned as the servant of Richard de la Pole, father of the future cardinal. *LP*, II. Nos. 2410, 3690, App. No. 39. But there is no way of identifying this Latimer with Hugh.

36. Harleian MS 422, ff.34-36. For a discussion of this MS, see below, p.26.

37. *Grace Book B, Part II*. p.105.

38. Until the publication in 1906 of H. P. Stokes' monograph, *The Chaplains and the Chapel of the University of Cambridge*. To this work, both for its general account of the chaplaincy and for specific references to Latimer, I am greatly indebted.

39. See, for example, Demaus, p.24.

40. Ridley, *Works*, p.406.

41. The details of this paragraph will be found in Stokes, *Chaplains and the Chapel, passim*.

42. The date of the resignation of his predecessor, John Ostaby, is not recorded, but Latimer's name appears as *capellanus* from 1522 to 1529.

43. Harleian MS 422, f.34.

44. For instance, "Item Magistro Lattymer pro clavibus ac emendatione serarum in scolis publicis . . . xxii d; xxiid; xiii d." *Grace Book B, Part II*. pp.101, 102. This is for the year

1522. Similar entries are scattered through the Grace Books for these years.

45. The entry for 1523 reads as follows: "Audito compoto Magistri lathemer pro tribus annis finitis ad Festum Michaelis anno Domini Mo 523 per Johannem Edmundes vicecancellarium, doctorem grene, W. Sowd, Johannem Smyth in theologia bachalarios, remanet in Bursa communi xxx *li* ix *s* x *d*." *Grace Book B, Part II*, p.111. The entries for 1526 and 1528 are at pp.134 and 137. By 1526 the cash balance had been reduced to 49 *s*. 4 *d*. In 1528 it had dwindled to 28 *s*. The auditors approved the accounts for both years. The expenditures were probably for much needed repairs.

46. *Grace Book B, Part II*. p.102.

47. *ibid.*, pp.107-108.

48. *Valor Ecclesiasticus*, III. 505-506.

49. *Grace Book B, Part II*. pp.124, 135, 142.

50. In 1515, during the tenure of Ostaby, the payments for bearing the cross "pro anno elapso" were lumped at 6 *s*. 4 *d*. Stokes, *Chaplains and the Chapel*, p.45.

51. Stokes, *op. cit.*, pp.44-45.

52. Stokes (p.44) is mistaken in his statement that Heath was Latimer's immediate successor as bishop of Worcester.

53. *Grace Book B, Part II*. p.114.

54. Demaus (p.207) so interprets it emphatically.

55. *Grace Book B, Part II*. p.197. "Item Magistro latomero theologiae baccaulario ad mandatum vicecancellarii in vino . . . vii *d*." He is similarly referred to in 1533-4 in a fragment of the diary of John Meers preserved in *Grace Book A*, p.224. It may be remarked also that Foxe always refers to him as "Master Latimer".

CHAPTER TWO

The Cambridge Reformers

1. *LP*, XVI. No. 101.

2. Mullinger, *The University of Cambridge*, pp.498-500.

3. For Bilney, see Foxe, IV, 619-656; *DNB;* and Rupp, *Studies in the Making of the English Protestant Tradition*, pp.22-31.

4. Letter to Sir Edward Baynton. *Works*, II. 330.

5. Venn, *Alumni Cantabrigienses, Part I*. p.152. He took both the B.A. and the LL.B. in 1520.

6. Foxe, IV. 635. The Latin original

was printed by Foxe in his edition of 1563, p.465.

7. Stafford is not listed in the *DNB*. He receives some attention in Mullinger, *University of Cambridge*, pp.567-568, 608-609.

8. According to earlier writers he died in 1530, but his will was proved in 1529. *Calendar of Wills Proved in Vice-Chancellor's Court at Cambridge, 1501-1765*, p.65.

9. George Joye, *Refutation of the Bishop of Winchester's Dark Declaration*, f. xxxi. The pertinent passage is quoted in the appendix to Foxe, IV. 754.

10. Foxe, IV. 656.

11. A marginal note in Foxe (*loc. cit.*) refers the reader to Nicholas Ridley and Edmund Grindal.

12. Reasonably full lists of the names of the converts are given in Strype, I (1). 568-569, and by Mullinger, pp.572-573.

13. F. Madan, "The Day-Book of John Dorne, Bookseller in Oxford." *Collectanea, First Series* (Oxford His-

torical Society Publications, vol. V). pp.71-177.

14. It is often asserted that heretical books were also burned at Oxford and Cambridge a few days later. But see the present writer's "A Note on the Burning of Lutheran Books in England in 1521." [Univ. of Penn'a] *Library Chronicle*, XVIII (1952). 68-71.

15. The most recent discussions of the White Horse are in H. Maynard Smith, *Henry VIII and the Reformation* and Rupp, *Studies in the Making of the English Protestant Tradition*.

16. Mullinger, *University of Cambridge*, pp.572-573.

17. Maynard Smith, *ob. cit.*, p.225.

18. The best full-length account of Fisher is still Bridgett's *Life*.

19. It was the forty-third article in a list of forty-four. *LP*, IV, Pt. 3. No. 6075.

20. Cotton MS Titus B.I. Quoted by Strype, I (1). 78.

CHAPTER THREE

Convert

1. Owst, *Literature and Pulpit in Medieval England*, pp.99-100.

2. Letter to Sir Edward Baynton. Foxe, VII. 489; and *Works*, II. 332.

3. Harleian MSS 422. f.84. See below, pp.24-26.

4. Foxe, IV. 656. See also Foxe, VII. 437.

5. Foxe, IV. 656.

6. Harleian MS 422, f. 84. See below, p.26.

7. *DNB*, s.v. Paget.

8. The First Sermon on the Lord's Prayer. *Works*, I. 334-335.

9. In 1536 Wm. Stevyns wrote that he had heard Latimer say, in a sermon preached at Cambridge, "If ever I had amendment of my sinful life, the occasion thereof came by

auricular confession." *LP*, X. No. 1201. (SP 1/104/221).

10. *Grace Book B, Part II*. p.114.

11. Third Sermon Preached before Edward VI. *Works* I. 138.

12. See Note 2 to this chapter.

13. Foxe, VII. 452.

14. Mozley, *William Tyndale*, pp.17-21.

15. For Barnes, see Rupp, *Studies in the Making of the English Protestant Tradition*, pp.31-46, and the article by Gairdner in *DNB*.

16. Harleian MS 422, f. 84.

17. Foxe, VII. 438.

18. Foxe (VII. 451) associates Bullock's criticism of Latimer with the Sermon on the Card of 1529. But Bullock died before July 4, 1526. See *DNB*.

CHAPTER FOUR

Latimer, Bishop West, and Cardinal Wolsey

1. Foxe, ed. 1563, p.1297.

2. Foxe, VII. 451-452.

3. The only modern account of West

is that in the *DNB*.

4. *LP*, IV, Pt. 1. Nos. 1258, 1264.

5. *LP*, IV, Pt. 1. No. 1272.

6. Wilkins, *Concilia*, III. 712.
7. The fullest modern accounts are those by Gairdner in the *DNB* and Rupp, *Studies in the Making of the English Protestant Tradition,* pp. 31-46. A different version is given by the present writer in "Robert Barnes and the Burning of the Books," *Huntington Library Quarterly,* XIV (1951). 211-221.
8. In his *A Supplication unto Henry the Eighth* (*STC*, 1470).
9. The text of the MS was first printed in Strype, III (1). 368-372. The dialogue in the following paragraph is taken *verbatim* from the manuscript.
10. This Tyrell seems to have been a self-appointed hammer of the heretics. I can discover nothing of him save that he was a fellow of King's (Foxe, VII, 452) and that he proceeded M.A. along with Latimer and others in 1514 (*Grace Book B, Part II.* p.19.)
11. Strype, III (1). 368.
12. The handwriting is unlike that in other documents known to be in Morice's autograph. On the other hand, as officials of the Public Record Office point out, there is enough similarity to suggest that the present manuscript might have been

written by Morice in extreme haste.
13. C.C.C. Camb. Cod. CXIX. 15. The text, in Latin, is printed in *Works,* II. 467-468. An English translation is given at pp.295-297.
14. See above, p.8.
15. Cooper, *Annals,* I. 311.
16. See above, p.7.
17. "Item conceditur vice cancellario doctoribus Crome Cranmer et Imar magistris Latemer Stafford Mydylton et Aldryge autoritas discernendi an nostre rei publice commodum sit, legibusque nostris ac usui earum consonum integram racionem omnium expensarum tocius anni audituribus reddi huius compoti, et quod prefatorum decretum nunc et futuris annis semper habeatur ratum et firmum." *Grace Book Gamma,* p.226.
18. "Item conceditur magistro vicecancellario [Edmunds] doctori Smyth magistris Latemer et Langford ut habeant autoritatem assignandi et augendi stipendium oratoris ex erario communi pro tempore magistri Daye et concesserunt illi iiij *li* annuatim. Et pro laboribus quos superioribus diebus sustinuit—xxvj *s* viii *d.*" *Grace Book Gamma,* p.237.

CHAPTER FIVE
The Testing of Little Bilney

1. West Register, f. 33. Foxe, VII. 770.
2. The best modern account of Tunstall is Sturge, *Cuthbert Tunstall.*
3. Foxe, VIII. 636n.
4. All of this is documented in Strype, I (1). 113-134.
5. The following account of Bilney's troubles is based on Foxe, IV. 619-656. See also *DNB* and Rupp, *Studies in the Making of the Eng-*

lish Protestant Tradition, pp.22-31.
6. Strype, I (1). 122.
7. Rupp, p.27.
8. Seventh Sermon before King Edward VI. *Works,* I. 222. Latimer again referred to Bilney's depression in the Sermon on the Gospel for the Second Sunday in Advent. *Works,* II. 51-52.
9. The First Sermon on the Lord's Prayer. *Works,* I. 334-336.

CHAPTER SIX
The English Bible

1. See above, p.18.
2. Foxe, VII. 438.
3. *A preservative, or triacle, agaynst the poyson of Pelagius.* (*STC.* 24368). Preface, "To Mr. Hugh Latimer."

4. *The Catechism on Thomas Becon,* pp.424-425.
5. Maitland, *Essays on Subjects Connected with the Reformation in England,* pp.1-41.
6. Wilkins, *Concilia*, III. 713.

7. See above, pp.22-23.
8. *Grace Book B, Part II.* p.145.
9. Foxe, VII. 773 (Appendix V). It should be pointed out that the compiler of the notes to Foxe perceived the connection between Moryson's letter and the episode described in the next paragraph. But he did not push the matter to its obvious conclusion.
10. Strype, I (1). 487.
11. See the letters of Bishop Longland to Wolsey, dated March 3 and March 5, 1528. *LP, IV, Pt. 2.* Nos. 4004 and 4017. For the details of Garrett's career, see *DNB,* and below, pp.107, 110, 155.
12. Strype is in error in giving the vice-chancellor's name as John Redman. The vice-chancellor for 1527-8 was John Edmunds. Strype errs also in speaking of Frith as if he were the translator of the New Testament. Frith had been busy in circulating copies, however.
13. For these men see Cooper, *Athenae Cantabrigienses,* I, and Venn, *Alumni Cantabrigienses, s.v.* Brad-

ford, Nicholson, Richard Smith, Simon Smith.
14. See above, pp.24-26.
15. Demaus, p.67, quite properly points out that Latimer could not have been convicted judicially at any time before he was tried by Convocation in 1532 (see below, pp.76-81) else at that time he would have been treated as a relapsed heretic. But Demaus' further argument that in 1528 Latimer could not have subscribed to articles required by Wolsey will not hold. The case of Bilney is parallel. Sir Thomas More (*Dialogue,* p.213) says that Wolsey (probably in 1526) accepted Bilney's "corporal" oath (that is an oath solemnized by touching the Bible or the sacrament) that he would not preach any further heresy; and this corresponds with Bilney's own statement in 1528 that he had previously been before the cardinal, but "not judicially." Yet in 1528 Bilney was not treated as a relapsed heretic.
16. *Grace Book B, Part II.* p.140.

CHAPTER SEVEN

The Sermons on the Card

1. It will be remembered that the celebrated case of Richard Hunne had its origin in Hunne's resistance to the payment of mortuary fees. For a recent summary of the Hunne case, see Ogle, *The Tragedy of the Lollards' Tower.*
2. Foxe, VII. 438.
3. Becon, *The Jewel of Joy,* In *The Catechism of Thomas Becon,* etc., p.425. See also Bailey, *Thomas Becon and the Reformation of the Church of England,* pp.2-6.
4. Since this account of the Sermons on the Card is necessarily based upon Foxe alone, a single reference will perhaps suffice. The summaries of the sermons are given in Foxe, VII. 439-449. Details of attendant circumstances are at pp.438-439, 449-451.
5. Cooper, *Athenae Cantabrigienses,* I, 40; III, 121.
6. *Literature and Pulpit,* pp.99-100. Owst cities particularly a "Moralization of the Game of Cards" by the Dominican John of Reinfelden (MS Egerton 2419).

7. For Buckenham, see *DNB* and Mozley, *William Tyndale,* pp.304, 333.
8. Foxe, VII. 449.
9. *loc. cit.*
10. Foxe also includes Bullock of King's in the list, but this is a mistake, for Bullock was dead by this time. In his first edition (p.1307) Foxe also lists Nicholas West as having preached against Latimer at this time, but West's name is removed from the later editions.
11. Cooper, *Annals,* I. 310.
12. *Athenae Cantabrigienses,* I. 64; III. 90. See also pp.80-81 of the present work.
13. For Baynes see *DNB.*
14. Lamb, *A Collection of Letters, Statutes, and Other Documents from the MS Library of Corpus Christi College,* pp.14-15.
15. *ibid.,* pp.15-18.
16. The "sum" of Redman's letter and of Latimer's reply are given in Foxe, VII. 453-454. The letters are not otherwise preserved.

CHAPTER EIGHT
The King's Great Matter

1. Fox, one of the most attractive English ecclesiastics of this period, has yet to find a biographer. For Gardiner, see James A. Muller, *Stephen Gardiner and the Tudor Reaction.*
2. For Cranmer, see Pollard, *Thomas Cranmer and the English Reformation.*
3. Cotton MS Vespasian B.V. See Pollard, *op. cit.,* pp.41-42.
4. Lamb, *A Collection of Letters, Statutes and Other Documents,* pp.19-20.
5. Cotton MS Vitellius B.XIII. f.51 ff. Printed in Burnett, *The History of the Reformation,* I (2). 136-140. The next seven paragraphs are based upon this document.
6. Dr. Buckmaster's Latin speech to the delegates upon his presentation

of the report is printed in Lamb. *op. cit.,* pp.20-22.
7. See Buckmaster's letter to Dr. Edmunds, printed in Lamb, *op. cit.,* pp.23-25.
8. *ibid.*
9. For Butts, see *DNB.*
10. Foxe, VII. 454.
11. *LP,* VIII. p.317.
12. *ibid.*
13. For Philips, see *DNB.*
14. Demaus, p.96.
15. Alexander Aless to Queen Elizabeth, Sept. 1, 1559. *Calendar of State Papers, Foreign Series, of the Reign of Elizabeth,* I. 524.
16. *LP, loc. cit.*
17. *LP,* V. p.749.
18. Lamb, *loc. cit.*
19. *LP,* V. p.749.

CHAPTER NINE
Of Heretical Books

1. Buckmaster to Edmunds. In Lamb, *A Collection of Letters, Statutes, and Documents,* pp.23-25.
2. Foxe, VII. 454.
3. For Nix (or Nykke), see *DNB.* He had been an implacable opponent of Tyndale's New Testament, and he was to be, in 1531, the presiding dignitary of the commission which sentenced Bilney.
4. The letter is printed in Lamb, *A Collection of Letters, Statutes, and Documents,* pp.26-27.
5. Hall, *Chronicle,* p.771.
6. Printed in Wilkins, *Concilia,* III. 727-737.
7. On the difficult problem of these primers, see Butterworth, *The English Primers (1529-1545),* pp.11-46.
8. Hall, *Chronicle,* p.771.
9. Hall, *loc. cit.*
10. *STC,* 7775-6. Printed in Pollard, *Records of the English Bible.*
11. The Rev. Josiah Pratt. See the note in Foxe, VII. 777.
12. *LP,* V. No. 751.
13. Butterworth, *The English Primers,* pp.18-46.
14. P.R.O., S.P. 6/7.pp.189 ff. and 301

ff. Demaus (p.112, note 1) speaks of "many manuscript copies." I know of only these two.
15. Foxe, ed 1563, pp.1344-48.
16. Foxe, VII. 506-511. Printed also in *Works,* II. 297-309.
17. One interesting variation is the reading "barbarous glosses" for "Banbury glosses" in Foxe's text. See the notes in Foxe, VII. 777, 796. But Rev. J. B. Mozley writes me that he has discovered support for "Banbury glosses" in a sermon by John Newell (Harleian MS 425, f.119).
18. *History of England,* II. 103-104.
19. *History of the Church of England,* I. 42-45.
20. Gairdner. *Lollardy,* II. 261-263, and the article on Latimer in *DNB;* and H. Maynard Smith, *Henry VIII and the Reformation,* pp.324-325.
21. H. Maynard Smith, *loc. cit.*
22. Foxe, VII. 509. *Works,* II. 305.
23. Foxe, *loc. cit.*
24. Foxe, VII. 508-509. *Works,* II. 303-304.
25. As do most other writers. Cf. Demaus, p.112.

CHAPTER TEN
West Kington

1. Foxe, VII. 454. Foxe's statement is probably substantially correct. The see of Salisbury at that time was held by the Italian Campeggio, an absentee. Presumably the Crown could dictate provision to benefices nominally in the gift of the Italian bishops (Salisbury and Worcester) who represented the Tudor interests at Rome. The parish of West Kington is now in the diocese of Gloucester and Bristol, whose bishops are the patrons.

2. *Valor Ecclesiasticus.* II. 134.

3. "Quarto decimo die mensis Januarii, anno 1530 [1531], Magister Richardus Hilley Vicarius Generalis, in domo residentiae infra clausum Canonicorum Sarum situata Ecclesiam parochialem de West Kington in Archidiaconatu Wiltes. Sarum Dioc., per mortem Domini Will.Dowdyng ultimi Rectoris ejusdem vacantem atque ad collationem Domini Laurencii Sarum episcopi pleno jure spectantem, Magistri Hugoni Latymer, presbytero, Sacrae Theologiae Baccalaurio, auctoritate qua fungebatur contulit, ac ipsum Rectorem dictae Ecclesiae de canonica obedientia &C. juratum instituit canonice in eadem cum suis juribus &c et Scriptum fecit Archidiacono Wiltes.et ejus officiali pro ipsius inductione, &s." Campeggio Register, f.24. Printed in the appendix to Foxe, VII. 773-774.

4. *loc. cit.*

5. Aubrey, *Wiltshire,* pp.87-88.

6. Jackson's note to Aubrey, *loc. cit.* How long the church and the window will survive is a question. As these words are written, a letter from the last incumbent, the Rev. Harold Higgins, informs me that upon his retirement in 1950 at the age of eighty-two no new appointment to the rectory was made. It is proposed to unite West Kington, with a population of only two hundred, to a neighboring parish.

7. Letter to Archbishop Warham. Foxe, VII. 456. *Works,* II. 474.

8. Letter to Sir Edward Baynton. Foxe, VII. 490. Works, II. 334.

9. *ibid.* Foxe, VII. 485. *Works,* II, 323.

10. Second letter to Sir Edward Baynton. Foxe, VII. 491. *Works,* II. 335.

11. See the references given above in Note 5 to Chapter V.

12. For Crome, see *DNB.*

13. Letter to Dr. Sherwood. Foxe, VII. 480. *Works,* II. 469 (English translation, p.310).

14. Sherwood's letter, in Latin, is in Foxe, VII. 478-480. Latimer's reply, likewise in Latin, is at pp.480-483. The original of Latimer's letter is printed in *Works,* II. 468-474. Canon Corrie provides an English translation in *Works,* II. 309-317.

15. Foxe, VII. 483-484.

16. Harleian MS 422, ff.88-89. The text was first printed in Strype, I (2). 175. It is also printed in *Works,* II. 317-321. The date of this letter is uncertain. In it Latimer alludes to a sermon preached by Hubberdin on Ascension Day (May 18), and it is known that Hubberdin preached at Bristol on that day in 1533 (see below, p.90). But a reference to "the honest priest that he last year was martyred by you in Kent"—i.e., Thomas Hitton, executed February 20, 1529/30—suggests that the letter was written in 1531. I am inclined to accept the earlier date.

17. *Works,* II. 318-320.

18. The only modern account of Stokesley is that in the *DNB.*

19. Wilkins, *Concilia,* III. 725. The minute concludes: "Sed ulterior deliberatio eorum in aliud tempus dilata est."

20. On this point, see especially Rupp, *Studies in the Making of the English Protestant Tradition,* pp.29-30.

21. First letter to Sir Edward Baynton. Foxe, VII. 488. *Works,* II. 330-331.

22. Crome's recantation is preserved in Stokesley's Register, f.138ᵛ, and is printed as part of Document XVI in the appendix (unpaged) to Foxe, V.

23. Foxe, IV. 680-688.

24. Foxe, IV. 688-694.

25. Chambers, *Thomas More,* pp.274-282, makes a good general defense of Lord Chancellor More's treatment of heretics. But Foxe's charges that Tewkesbury was mistreated by More remain unrefuted.

CHAPTER ELEVEN

The Sermon at St. Mary Abchurch

1. The factual details concerning this episode are all drawn from the correspondence between Latimer and Sir Edward Baynton. This consisted of Latimer's reply to a letter of Baynton's which has not been preserved, Baynton's reply to Latimer's letter, and a second letter from Latimer to Baynton. The original MS letters are not extant, but they were printed by Foxe (VII. 484-498). Latimer's letters, but not Baynton's, are printed also in *Works,* II. 322-351.
2. Foxe, VII. 485.
3. *ibid.*
4. *ibid.,* p.484.
5. *ibid.,* p.486.
6. *ibid.,* pp. 484-485.
7. *ibid.*
8. The recently discovered life of Anne Boleyn by William Latimer the younger records that Anne visited Baynton at Bromham about this time. Bodleian MS Don. C. 42. To be published in the *Bodleian Quarterly Record.*
9. Foxe, VII. 486-487.
10. *ibid.,* p.487.
11. *ibid.*
12. *ibid.,* p.486.
13. *ibid.,* p.489.
14. *ibid.,* pp.489-490.
15. *ibid.,* pp.490-491.
16. *ibid.,* p.492.
17. *ibid.,* p.494.
18. *ibid.*
19. *ibid.,* pp.494-495.
20. *ibid.,* p.495.
21. *ibid.,* pp.495-497.
22. *ibid.,* p.497.
23. *ibid.,* p.498.

CHAPTER TWELVE

Before Convocation

1. The long citation is printed in Foxe VII. 455.
2. Foxe, VII. 498.
3. Sermon Preached at Stamford. *Works,* I. 294-295.
4. The original articles, in Latin are in the Tunstall Register, f.142. These were printed by Foxe in his first (1563) edition, p.1334. In later editions of the *Acts and Monuments* Foxe gave them in English translation, with some variation in numbering. A different English translation, but with numbering corresponding to Foxe's, is in Harleian MS 425, f.13-14. The original Latin articles are printed in Foxe, VII. Appendix 6.
5. The Crome articles are also in Harleian MS 425, f.13.
6. Wilkins, *Concilia,* III. 747.
7. Foxe, VII. 456-458. *Works,* II. 474-478. An English translation, by Canon Corrie, is in *Works,* II. 351-356.
8. *Works,* II. 353-354.
9. *ibid.,* pp.355-356.
10. "xxj° die mensis Martii Anno domini Millesimo quingentesimo xxxj *mo* [i.e., 1532]. Mr. Hugo Latimer ... confessus est et recognovit fidem suam sic sentiendo prout sequitur." The sixteen articles follow. Tunstall Register, f.142, and Foxe, VII. Appendix VI.
11. Wilkins, *Concilia,* III. 747.
12. See above, note 4.
13. Convocation Sermon. *Works,* I. 46.
14. Wilkins, *Concilia,* III. 747.
15. "Et postea differebat dominus locum tenens [i.e. Stokesley] juramentum ad subscribendum articulis praedictis, et ad praesentandum se coram reverendissimo 10. Aprilis ...." Wilkins, *loc. cit.*
16. See above, pp.46-47.
17. Harleian MS 6989, f.158. *Works,* II. 356-357.
18. Wilkins, III. 748.
19. *ibid.*
20. *ibid.*
21. The unfriendly witness was Dr. Wilson, one of the king's chaplains. *LP,* VI. No. 433, article 6 (SP 6/1/19). The text of this document is partially undecipherable. According to Wilson, when Latimer appealed to the king the latter replied, "Mr. Latimer, I [advertise that ye] have good learning. It were pity but ye [did not conduct yourself] much better than ye have,

for you . . . and to be abjured; and I will not take [upon me to be] a suitor to the bishops for you [but leave you to do such] penance as ye have deserved; [and if ye attempt] such things again ye sha [!!] . . . a faggot to burn you . . . ."

The words in square brackets are Gairdner's conjectural restorations.
22. Wilkins, *loc. cit.*
23. *ibid.*
24. See the account of Bainham in *DNB* and in Foxe, IV. 697-706.
25. Harleian MS 422, ff.90-91.

CHAPTER THIRTEEN
Latimer at Bristol

1. The best study of Cromwell is R. B. Merriman's *Life and Letters of Thomas Cromwell.*
2. In the letter to Ralph Morice. Foxe, VII. 473.
3. The following summary is based upon Latimer's letter to Ralph Morice printed in Foxe VII. 473-477 (and in *Works*, II. 457-466) ; and upon the "Articles untruly, unjustly, falsely, uncharitably imputed to me Hugh Latimer, by Dr. Powell of Salisbury" printed in Foxe VII. 466-473 (and in *Works*, II. 225-239).
4. The figure of images as "lay-folks' books" has been traced back into the early Middle Ages. Owst, *Literature and Pulpit*, pp.137-138.
5. *STC*, 11387.
6. Letter to Morice. Foxe, VII. 476. *Works*, II. 363-364.
7. Foxe, VII. 475-476. *Works*, II. 363. The last sentence, however, is from the "Articles". Foxe, VII. 472. *Works*, II. 238.
8. *LP*, VI. No. 246 (Cotton MS Cleopatra E.V. f.363). The letter is printed in Foxe, VII. Appendix 9.
9. Latimer had not been inhibited in his own diocese, which Browne incorrectly gives as Bath.
10. We know about Hilsey's letter from a subsequent letter. See below, pp. 90-91.
11. Wilkins, *Concilia*, III. 756.
12. Foxe, VII. 473. *Works*, II. 358.
13. Seyer, *Memoirs of Bristol*, II. 220.
14. For Powell, see *DNB* and Foster, *Alumni Oxonienses*, Early Series III. 1190.
15. For Hubberdin, see Foster, *op. cit.*, II. 688.
16. Letter to Morice. Foxe, VII. 476-477. *Works*, II. 365-366.
17. Foxe, VII. 477-478.
18. *LP*, VI. No.572 (SP 6/3/11) and *LP*, VI. No.596 (SP 1/76. p.183).

19. "Articles". Foxe, VII. 469. *Works*, II. 239-241.
20. *LP*, VI. No.433, Item 1 (SP6/1/19). This statement is in a letter signed "Tuus, L." No addressee is named. Gairdner supposes that the letter was written by Latimer. It is reprinted in Foxe, VII. Appendix IX, where the editor suggests that it was addressed *to* Latimer. Gairdner's guess seems the better, although it is difficult to know why he believed that it was addressed to Dr. Bagarde, the chancellor of Worcester.
21. Both sets of verses are in Strype, I (2). 180-182. I have been unable to find Strype's originals.
22. *LP*, VI. No.572 (SP 6/3/11). "Doctor Powell saying as followeth in the pulpit within the town of Bristol upon St. Marks day and on the Sunday following. Anno r.r. Henr. VIII, XXV." Printed in Foxe, VII. Appendix IX.
23. *LP*, VI. No.799. Items 2 and 3 (SP 2/0.f.11). Printed in Foxe, VII. Appendix IX.
24. *LP*, VI. No.433. Items 4 and 5 (SP 6/1/19). Reprinted in Foxe, VII. Appendix IX.
25. Cotton MS Cleopatra E.IV. 140, and *LP*, VI. No.433, Item 3 (SP 6/1/19). Reprinted in Foxe, VII. Appendix IX; and in Wright, *Letters Relating to the Suppression*, pp.11-13. Wright incorrectly describes it as being addressed to Cromwell.
26. *LP*, VI. No.596 (SP 1/76.p.183).
27. *LP*, VI. No.411 (SP 1/75.p.228). Gairdner dates the letter in April, 1533, but it must have been written after May 25th, since it refers to Latimer's preaching in Rogation Week.
28. *LP*, VII. No.722.
29. Letter from John Bartholomew to Cromwell. Cotton MS Cleopatra

E.IV. f.56. Reprinted in Foxe, VII, Appendix IX; and in Wright, *Letters Relating to the Suppression*, pp.7-10.
30. *ibid*.
31. *LP*, VI. No.799 (SP 2/0.f.11).
32. See above, note 29.
33. *ibid*.
34. *LP*, VI. No.796 (SP 1/77.p.207).
35. *LP*, VI. No.412 (SP 1/75.p.229).
36. *LP*, VI. No.873 (SP 1/78.p.21). A letter from one Richard Jones of Bristol to the mayor. The tone is

one of mockery at the unfortunate Hubberdin.
37. A list of prisoners in the Tower at that date is given in *LP*, XII, Part 2. No.181.
38. *LP*, VI. No.951.
39. *LP*, VIII. No.1001.
40. We learn these details from a letter from Archbishop Cranmer to Cromwell. Cranmer, *Miscellaneous Writings and Letters*, p.252. For the whole story of Hilsey's career, see *DNB*.

CHAPTER FOURTEEN

The Tide Turns

1. The account of Joye in the *DNB* is demonstrably inaccurate at several points.
2. *LP*, VI. No.402 (SP 1/75, f.210).
3. For Tyndale's part in this episode, see Mozley, *William Tyndale*, pp.271-272.
4. *LP*, VI. No.1255.
5. *LP*, X. No.346. This is dated 25 Feb. 1535/6, but the sermon to which Staunton alluded was evidently preached some years earlier.
6. *LP*, VI. No.1582.
7. *Calendar of State Papers . . . Venice*, IV. No.971.
8. *LP*, VI. No.1249. Chapuys does not name Latimer, but Gairdner has no doubt that the reference is to Latimer.
9. Frith was executed July 4, 1533. See Foxe, V. 1-16; and *DNB*.
10. *LP*, VI. No.1214. The inhibition, dated April 24, 1533, is printed in Foxe, VII. Appendix VIII.
11. *LP*, VI. No.1214. Printed in Foxe, VII. Appendix VIII. An English translation was printed by Foxe in the 1563 edition of the *Acts and Monuments*, p.507. This translation was reprinted in Wilkins, *Concilia*, III. 760, where it is misdated October 2nd.
12. Foxe, V. 62.
13. Foxe, VII. 477. *Works*, II. 366.
14. Harleian MS 6148, f.41. Cranmer, *Miscellaneous Writings and Letters*, p. 309.
15. *LP*, VII. No.32 (SP 1/82.p.47),
16. Cranmer, *loc. cit.*, p.308.
17. Sampson's letter to Cranmer. See note 15, above.
18. *LP*, VII. No.441. A letter of John Rokewood to Lord Lisle.

19. *LP*, VII. No.304. Rokewood to Lord Lisle.
20. See the account of Philips in *DNB*.
21. *LP*, VII. No.228. Sir William Kyngston to Lord Lisle.
22. More, *English Works*, p.1428, and Rogers, *Correspondence of Sir Thomas More*, pp.503-504.
23. In a letter of 1536 he refers to one Master Coots, a monk of Hayles, as being "Dunsly learned, Moorly affected." *Works*, II. 374.
24. Harte, *Gleanings from the Common Place Book of John Hooker*, pp.13-14. In 1534, Hooker was himself nine years old. His father, one of the leading citizens of Exeter, was present at the second of the two sermons which Hooker describes (Harte, pp.7-8). There is therefore good reason to accept the story as substantially accurate.
25. For Cardmaker, see *DNB*.
26. In the deed for the restoration of the temporalities of Worcester when he became bishop he is called "dilectum et fidelem capellanum nostrum." See below Chapter XV, Note 10.
27. Cranmer to Latimer. Harleian MS 6148, f.41. Cranmer, *Miscellaneous Writings and Letters*, pp.296-297.
28. *LP*, VII. No.578. (SP 1/83. f.193). *Works*, II. 367.
29. Muller, *Stephen Gardiner*, pp.54-55.
30. Trinity Coll. MS 613. It is described fully, with long extracts, by Janelle, "An Unpublished Poem on Bishop Stephen Gardiner." *Bull. Inst. of Hist. Research*, VI (1928-29). 12-25, 89-96, 167-174. The relevant stanzas are at ff.14b-15a

of the MS. This poem was evidently unknown to Muller.
31. Chapuys to Charles V. *Cal. of State Papers . . . Spain,* V. (1). pp.381-382. Also *LP,* VIII. No.48.
32. Letter of Robert Ward to Cromwell. *LP,* XIII, Pt.2. No. 571 (SP 1/137. f.149).
33. *LP,* VIII. No.253 (Cotton MS Vitellius B.XIV.127 and B.M. Addi-

tional MS 29,547, f.7).
34. Lisle to Cromwell. *LP,* VIII. No.279 (MS Vespasian F.XIII. 111).
35. Sandys to Cromwell. "Clotton by his writings had declared upon Latimer and I am supposed to be of his mind. I will never offend the king in such matters and it grieves me to be thus slandered." *LP,* Addenda, I. No.981.

CHAPTER FIFTEEN

Bishop of Worcester

1. On this subject see Mandell Creighton, "The Italian Bishops of Worcester", in his *Historical Essays and Reviews,* pp.202-234.
2. Chapuys to Charles V. *LP,* VIII, No.48.
3. See below, p.169.
4. *LP,* IX, No.151 (SP 1/95. ff.148-149).
5. *LP,* IX. Nos. 203, 252 (SP 1/96. ff.6, 71-72).
6. *LP,* IX. No.273 (SP 1/96 f.81).
7. *LP,* IX. No.272 (SP 1/96. f.80). *Works,* II. 368-369.
8. *LP,* X. No.1257 (ix); XI. No.117.
9. Stubbs, *Registrum Sacrum Anglicanum,* p.99. Actually there is no record of Latimer's consecration. But Fox's consecration is recorded in the Hereford register. Hilsey's in the Rochester. Since, as Stubbs points out, Latimer's precedence was between Fox and Hilsey, the conclusion is obvious that the three were consecrated on the same day and by the same consecrators.
10. This document reads as follows: "Rex Escaetori suo in comitatu Wigorniae salutem: Cum reverendissimus in Christo pater Thomas, Cantuarensis Archiepiscopus, totius Angliae Primas et Metropolitanus, vacante nuper episcopatu Wygorniensi, per deprivationem Jeronimi de Ghinuccis ultimi episcopi ibidem, Prior Ecclesiae Cathedralis Wygorniensis et ejusdem loci commanachi sive conventus, dilectum et fidelem capellanum nostrum Magistrum Hugonem Latymer sacrae Theologiae professorem, in eorum episcopum elegerint et nominaverint, cui quidem electioni et personae sic electae regium nostrum assensum adhibuimnus et favorem, confirmaverit, ac ipsum Hugonem Latymer

episcopum Wygorniensem consecraverit, ipsum que episcopalibus insignibus investiverit, sicuti per literas patentes ipsius reverendissimi in Christo patris nobis inde directas constat, Nos, confirmationem et consecrationem illas acceptantes, fidelitatem ipsius electi et confirmati nobis pro temporalibus episcopatus praedicti debitam cepimus, et temporalia praedicti prout moris est restituimus eidem: et ideo tibi praecipimus quod eidem electo temporalia praedicta sine delatione liberes: Teste rege apud Westmonasterium, quarto die Octobris. Anno 1535." Rymer, *Foedera,* XIV. 553. (*Syllabus,* II. 774).
11. *VCH, Worcestershire,* III. 381,431; IV. 254; and the references there cited.
12. *Valor Ecclesiasticus,* III. 219,220.
13. *LP,* XIII, Part 2. No.1133 (SP 1/140. f.176). *Works,* II. 412-413.
14. Foxe, VII. 517.
15. It is listed in *Warwickshire Historical Publications,* VIII. I have been unable to examine this register.
16. Stubbs, *Registrum Anglicanum,* p. 202.
17. *LP,* XI. No.1374 (SP 1/113/35). *Works,* II. 375. The appointment was partly due to Cromwell's good offices on Bagarde's behalf. *LP,* XII, Pt. 1. No.38.
18. For example, Peter Vannes, the distinguished diplomatist.
19. *LP,* X. No.56 (SP 1/101/47). *Works,* II. 371-373.
20. For Holbeach, see below, p.130, and *DNB.*
21. *LP,* X. No.1099 (SP 1/104. f.157).
22. *DNB, s.v.* Gerard, Thomas. He later became chaplain to Cranmer and rector of All Hallows, Honey Lane.
23. For Taylor, see *DNB:* for Brad-

ford, see above, pp.36-37, and Strype, I (1). 486-487.

24. *LP*, XI. No. 1374 (SP 1/113. f.35). *Works*, II. 375-377.

25. *Works*, II. 387.

26. Rymer, *Foedera*, XIV. 586 (*Syllabus*, II. 776). *LP*, XIII, Part 1. No. 646.

27. Stubbs, *Registrum*, p.101; and *DNB*.

28. See below, p.135.

29. Hooper, *Later Writings*, pp.130-151.

30. *LP*, XII, Pt.2, No.530, 534. XIII, Pt.1. No.715. (SP 1/130. f.64).

31. *LP*, XIII, Pt.1. No.1509 (Sp 1/134. f.298). See also *LP*, XIII, Pt.2. No. 194.

32. *LP*, XIII, Pt.1. No.545 (SP 1/130. f.85).

33. *LP*, XIII, Pt.1. No.1178 (SP 1/133. f.31). *Works*, II. 390-391.

34. *LP*, XIII, Pt.1. No.1258 (Sp 1/133. f.205). *Works*, II. 397-398.

35. See above, pp.88-89.

36. *LP*, XII, Pt.1. No.508. This long report supplies all the details included in this paragraph.

37. *LP*, XII, Pt.1. No.308 (SP 1/115. f.166).

38. *LP*, X. No.1099 (SP 1/104. f.157).

39. See below, pp.114-116.

40. He mentions by name the chaplains Bennett and Garrett, and also the following: "Sir" Saunders, parish priest of Winchecombe; John Ashe, parson of Staunton; Henry Marshall, not otherwise identified; and a Dominican nicknamed "Two-year Old."

41. See above, note 38.

42. *LP*, XII, Pt.1. No.308 (SP 1/115. f.166).

43. *ibid.* Also *LP*, XII, Pt.1. No.701 (SP 1/117. f.91) and *LP*, XII, Pt.1. No.831.

CHAPTER SIXTEEN

The Bishop of Worcester and the Progress of Doctrine

1. *LP*, X. No.371. Cranmer had entrusted to his brother, Edmund, archdeacon of Canterbury, and to Latimer the examination of Tristram Reuel's translation of François Lambert's *Farrago Rerum Theologicarum*. Latimer thought the work extreme at several points, but it was printed by Redman in 1536 (*STC*, 15179).

2. *LP*, X. No.462 (Cotton MS Cleopatra IV. f.110). Printed in Wright, *Letters Relating to the Suppression of the Monasteries*, pp.36-39.

3. *ibid.*

4. Bodleian MS Don. C.42.

5. The injunctions are printed in Strype I (1). 322-325. I (2). 218-219.

6. 27 Henry VIII, C.42. "An act concerning the exoneration of Oxford and Cambridge from payment of their first-fruits and tenths." *Statutes of the Realm*, III. 599-601.

7. *LP*, XII, Pt.2. No.258 (SP 1/122. f.254). *Works*, II. 377-379.

8. An account of Day will be found in the *DNB*. For Crayford and Swynbourne see Venn, *Alumni Cantabrigienses* and Cooper, *Athenae Cantabrigienses*.

9. *LP*, XII, Pt.2. No. 501 (SP 1/124.

f.16). *Works*, II. 381-382.

10. *LP*, XIII, Pt.1. No.1024 (SP 1/132. f.134). *Works*, II. 391-393.

11. Strype supposes that it was in connection with the reform of the universities that Latimer wrote a puzzling letter to young Matthew Parker the future archbishop of Canterbury. The pertinent part of the letter reads, "Mine own good Master Parker, *salutem*. And as I have devised nothing nor yet will till I have spoke with the king's grace, or have passed through the next Parliament. And thus what I shall alter or change, found or confound, you shall not be ignorant of." The remainder of the letter is in Latin; and briefly encourages Parker to "show himself to the world." C.C.C.C.MS and B.M. Additional MS 19,400, f.17. The letter was first printed in Strype, *Life and Acts of Matthew Parker*, I. 20-21.

12. Alexander Aless to Queen Elizabeth, Sept. 1, 1559. *Calendar of State Papers, Foreign Series, of the Reign of Queen Elizabeth*. I. 524.

13. *LP*, XII, Pt.2. No.947. *Works*, II. 385.

14. Wriothesley, *Chronicle*, I. 47.

15. The Latin Sermon is printed in

Works, II. 447-465, where it is misdated. The English version is in *Works,* I. 33-57.

16. *STC,* 15285. See Bibliography.
17. *STC,* 15286. See Bibliography. The unique copy is now at the Folger Library.
18. *Works,* I. 37.
19. This kind of personification was in the direct tradition of friarly preaching. Owst, *Literature and Pulpit,* Chapter 2.
20. For Tracy's story, see Foxe, V. 31-32.
21. *Works,* I. 46.
22. *Works,* I. 52-55. Only Canon Dixon seems to have recognized the full import of this short passage. *History of the Church of England,* I. 402.
23. *Works,* I. 56-57.
24. *LP,* XII, Pt.1. No.953. (Cotton MS Caligula E. I. 46).
25. "Erroneous opinions complained of in convocation." Wilkins, *Concilia,* III. 804-807. The list was first printed by Fuller, from the original which was subsequently destroyed by fire.
26. In the Sermon on the Ploughers. *Works,* I. 60.
27. The debates usually associated with this session of Convocation really belong to the discussions of the Bishops' Book a year later. This was pointed out by both Gairdner and Dixon. See below, pp.118-119, and Note 33 to this chapter.
28. Wilkins, *Concilia.* III. 825.
29. MS Cotton Cleopatra E.V.
30. *STC,* 10033. The texts of both the MS and the printed book are given in Charles Lloyd (ed.), *Formularies of Faith Put Forth by Authority during the Reign of Henry VIII.*
31. Lloyd, p.xxiii.
32. There is extant a document in which 14 bishops and other clergymen, including Latimer, affirm the divine institution of holy orders. I take this to be a memorandum prepared for the king about this time. Cotton MS Cleopatra E.V.f.45. Wilkins, *Concilia,* III. 832-835.
33. It is perhaps necessary to insist that this was not a session of Convocation, as is often said. An account of the debates is given in Foxe, V. 378-384. Foxe dated these debates in 1536. But Foxe was merely transcribing from Alexander

Alesius, *Of the auctorite of the word of God agaynst the bysshop of London,* n.p., n.d. (*STC,* 292), where it is expressly stated that the debates occurred in 1537 (Sig. A5r). Indeed, it is only in connection with debates on the Bishops' Book that the discussion makes sense. For convenience sake, I give the quoted passages below from Foxe, since Alesius' work has never been reprinted.

34. Foxe, V. 379.
35. Foxe, V. 380.
36. Foxe, V. 381-382.
37. Foxe, V. 382.
38. MS Cotton Cleopatra E.V. ff.130-133. Printed in Strype, I (2). 388; and *Works,* II. 245-249.
39. This particular remark is from a transcript, in the king's holograph, of part of Latimer's original. *LP,* XII, Pt.1. No. 1312; and Strype, I (2). 99.
40. *LP,* XII, Pt. 2. No.295 (SP 1/123. f.32). *Works,* II. 379-381. At the end of this letter Latimer recommends that Thomas Gibson be given the printing of the book. In 1535 Gibson had printed the first concordance to the English New Testament (*STC,* 3046).
41. *STC,* 5163. Reprinted in Lloyd, *op. cit.*
42. The Latin original and an English translation are printed in Pollard, *Records of the English Bible,* pp. 175-177.
43. Pollard, *Records,* pp.196-198.
44. *STC,* 10085. Reprinted in Frere, *Visitation Articles and Injunctions,* II. 1-11.
45. The best account of the English Bible in the 16th century is Butterworth, *The Literary Lineage of the King James Bible, 1340-1611.* See also the same author's "How Early Could English Scripture Be Printed in England?" [Univ. of Penna.] *Library Chronicle,* XIV (1947). 1-12.
46. See for example Pollard, *Thomas Cranmer,* p.111.
47. Cranmer's letter is printed in Pollard, *Records,* pp.214-215.
48. *ibid.,* p.216.
49. *ibid.,* pp.218-219.
50. *ibid.,* pp.219-222.
51. For a fuller account of the injunctions, see below pp.135-136.

CHAPTER SEVENTEEN

The Bishop of Worcester and the Dissolution of the Monastaries

1. For the visitation injunctions and articles see Burnet, *History of the Reformation*, I (2). 207-223.
2. The standard Protestant version will be found in Froude and Coulton. The opposing side can be read in Dixon and Gasquet. The best short modern summary is in Baskerville, *English Monks and the Suppression of the Monasteries*.
3. Second Sermon before King Edward VI. *Works*, I. 123.
4. Baskerville (p.142) offers the amazing argument that Latimer was not present, and that after the lapse of twelve years the memory can be depended upon to reconstruct only 15 percent of the truth.
5. *LP*, X. Nos.282, 283.
6. Thomas Dorset, curate of St. Margaret, Lothbury, to the mayor of Plymouth and others. Wright, *Letters Relating to the Suppression of the Monasteries*, pp.36-39. The original letter in MS Cotton Cleopatra E. IV. f.110.
7. *LP*, X. No.1201 (SP 1/104/222).
8. Hall, *Chronicle*, p.819; Grafton, *Chronicle*, II. p.454.
9. So, at any rate, says a late tradition. Spelman, *The History of Sacrilege*, ed.1698. p.183.
10. The best modern account of the Pilgrimage of Grace is Dodds, *The Pilgrimage of Grace 1536-37*.
11. *Works*, I. 25-32. See also Bibliography.
12. *ibid.*, 29-30.
13. The charge occurs in many documents pertaining to the rebellion. See especially *LP*, XI. Nos.585, 705, 853, 902, 1319.
14. On this, see my article, "The Authorship and Provenance of a Political Ballad of the Reign of Henry VIII." *Notes and Queries*, CXCV

15. (1950). 203-205; and the documents there cited.
15. Robert Aske, at his examination on April 11, 1537. *LP*, XII, Pt.1. No.901 (p.409).
16. Dixon, *History of the Church of England*, I. 468.
17. *LP*, XII, Pt.1. No. 1079 (MS Cotton Titus B.I. f.441).
18. Third Sermon before King Edward VI. *Works* I. 163.
19. *LP*, XII, Pt.2. No. 194 (SP 1/122. f.185).
20. Burnet, *loc. cit.*
21. *LP*, XI. No.67. *Works*, II. 417.
22. Bodleian MS Don. C. 42.
23. First Sermon before King Edward VI. *Works*, I. 93-94.
24. Richard Ingworth, suffragan bishop of Dover, was the visitor for the friaries in Worcestershire. He had some correspondence with Latimer on the subject which indicates his eagerness to remain in Latimer's good graces. *LP*, XIII, Pt.2. Nos.49, 170.
25. *Works*, II. 402,405.
26. *LP*, XIII, Pt.1. No.1179 (SP 1/103. f.33). *Works*, II. 417-418.
27. *LP*, XIII, Pt.2. No.543 (SP 1/137. f.111). *Works*, II. 402-404.
28. For an inventory of the Black Friars and Grey Friars at Worcester, see *LP*, XIII, Pt.1. No.1513.
29. Second Sermon before King Edward VI. *Works*, I. 123.
30. *LP*, XIII, Pt.2. No.646 (SP 1/137. f.32). *Works*, II. 405-406.
31. Although Great Malvern was geographically in the diocese of Worcester, it was subject to the abbot of Westminster.
32. *LP*, XIII, Pt.2. No.1036 (MS Cotton Cleopatra E. IV. f.264ff). *Works*, II. 410-411.

CHAPTER EIGHTEEN

The Bishop of Worcester and the Destruction of the Shrines

1. Article 7 of the royal injunctions of 1538 ("The Second Royal Injunctions") called for the removal of "feigned" images and relics from the churches. Frere, *Visitation Articles and Injunctions*, II. 38.

2. See his remarks in the Sermon on the Ploughers. *Works*, I. 75-77.
3. *LP*, XII, Pt.2. No.587 (SP 1/124. ff.10-12).
4. Of the numerous contemporary accounts of the "exposures" of the

relics and images in London the fullest and probably the most accurate is that in Wriothesley's *Chronicle*, I. 74 ff.

5. Wriothesley, I. 75-76. Also the letter of John Finch to Conrad Humpard. *Original Letters* ["Zurich Letters"], II. 606-607.

6. *Original Letters*, II. 707.

7. *LP*, XIII, Pt.1. No.1177 (SP 1/133. f.29). *Works*, II. 395.

8. Wriothesley, *Chronicle*, I. 83.

9. The *DNB* article on Forest is based on Hall and is quite unreliable. The account in Wriothesley, I. 78-81, is supported by the letter of Latimer quoted below. Wriothesley and Latimer were writing independently of each other and may therefore be presumed to be reliable. Accordingly, this paragraph is based upon Wriothesley and Latimer.

10. *LP*, XIII, Pt.1. No.1024 (SP 1/132. f.134). *Works*, II. 391-393.

11. Latimer's preaching on this occasion seems to have set a standard. In August 1538, the Bishop of Norwich was commissioned to preach "as was done by the Bishop of Worcester at Friar Forest's execution" at the burning of Anthony Browne, another of the Friars Observant. *LP*, XIII, Pt.2. No.34.

12. Hall, *Chronicle*, pp.825-826. The account in Holinshed is taken from Hall.

13. Hume, *Chronicle of King Henry VIII of England*, pp.77-81.

14. The Spaniard is demonstrably guilty of errors of fact. He asserts, for instance, that at the time of Forest's execution Cranmer was chaplain to Anne Boleyn's father, and that Forest was imprisoned in the Tower.

15. Wriothesley, *Chronicle*, I. 79-80.

16. Froude, for example, whose feeling for Latimer is just this side idolatry, speaks of it as an episode "which clouds the memory of the greatest of the Reformers." *History of England*, III. 270.

17. Fourth Sermon before King Edward VI. *Works*, I. 160.

18. The history of the abbey and of the relic will be found in Dugdale, *Monasticon Anglicanum*, V. 686-689.

19. See above, p.87.

20. The abbot's letter is given in full in Gasquet, *Henry VIII and the English Monasteries*, II. 536-537.

21. *LP*, XIII, Pt.2. No.710. The full text of the commission's report is printed by Corrie in the notes to *Works*, II. 407-408.

22. *LP*, XIII, Pt.2. No.709 (SP 1/138. f.48). *Works*, II. 407-408.

23. This canard seems to have originated in Hearne's *Benedict of Peterborough*, p.751.

24. Wriothesley, *Chronicle*, I. 90. Holinshed, *Chronicle*, III. 807.

CHAPTER NINETEEN
The Bishop in His Diocese

1. *LP*, XI. No.778. *Works*, II. 404-405. The letter is dated Oct. 18, without any year. Corrie assigned it to 1538. But the reference to the abbey of Tewkesbury, which had evidently not yet been suppressed, would seem to place it in 1536, since Tewkesbury fell early in 1537.

2. *LP*, XI. No.790 (MS Cotton Cleopatra E. IV. f.142). *Works*, II. 375. The prophecy is at f.143 of the same MS. It begins: "Sancta Sion filia, dudum in cruore, Dedicata Domine, languet in cruore."

3. See above, pp.106, 107.

4. The story is in Strype, II (1). 70-71, where it is assigned, without particular reason, to 1537 or 1538. Beyond the reference to Peter Martyr, Strype cites no authority.

5. *Works*, II. 380. See above, p.119.

6. *LP*, XII, Pt.2. No.258 (SP 1/122. f.254). *Works*, II. 378.

7. The earliest letter from Hartlebury in this year is dated July 25.

8. The Injunctions have been frequently reprinted. They may be found most conveniently in Wilkins, III. 832; *Works*, II. 240-244; Frere, *Visitation Articles and Injunctions*, II. 12-18.

9. Frere, *Visitation Articles and Injunctions*, II. 65-66.

10. For Bell, see *DNB* and above, p.110.

11. *V.C.H. Warwickshire*, II. 123-124.

12. *LP*, XII, Pt.2. No.909 (SP 1/125. ff.209-210). *Works*, II. 383-384.

13. *LP*, XIV, Pt.1. No.79 (SP 1/142. f.69). *Works*, II. 413-414.

14. What we know of the affair is set

N O T E S

forth in two documents: (1) A report sent by Thomas Lucy to Cromwell (*LP*, XII, Pt.2. No.303. SP 1/123. f.46 *et seq.*). This was printed in the *Atheneum* for April 18, 1857, and is summarized in Fripp, *Shakespeare's Haunts Near Stratford*, pp.108-112. (2) A long letter from Lucy to Latimer (*LP*, XII, Pt.2. No.302. SP 1/123. f.42 *et seq.*). This letter has apparently not been printed.

15. See preceding note, Item (2).
16. *LP*, XIII, Pt.1. No.1455 (SP 1/134. f.241). *Works*, II. 399, where it is assigned to the year 1538. But the contents clearly indicate that it belongs to the preceding year.
17. *LP*, XII, Pt.2. No.501 (SP 1/124. f.16). *Works*, II. 381-382.
18. *LP*, XII, Pt.2. No.840 (SP 1/125. f.142). *Works*, II. 382-383.
19. *LP*, XII, Pt.2. No.909 (SP 1/125. ff.209-210). *Works*, II. 383-384.
20. Foxe, V. 444.
21. *LP*, XII, Pt.2. No.1043 (MS Cotton Cleopatra E. IV. f.139). *Works*, II. 386-387.
22. He alludes to the Coventry appointment again in a letter dated Dec. 25, 1537. *LP*, XII, Pt.2. No.1259 (SP 1/127. f.141). *Works*, II. 388-389.
23. Wriothesley, *Chronicle*, I. 70-71.
24. *ibid.*, p.72.

25. The will is printed in Strype, I (2). 368. See also *LP*, XII, Pt.2. No. 1100.
26. See above, note 22. In transcribing this letter Canon Corrie misread "Winchester" for "Worcester" as the place of Barnes' sermon.
27. *LP*, XIII, Pt.2. No.1178 (SP 1/133. f.31). *Works*, II. 390-391.
28. *LP*, XIII, Pt.1. No.1202 (SP 1/133. f.55). *Works*, II. 396-397. See also *VCH Warwickshire*, II. 124-129.
29. *LP*, XIII, Pt.2. No.515 (SP 1/137. f.78). *Works*, II. 401-402.
30. *LP*, XIV, Pt.1. No.740 (SP 1/150. f.116). *Works*, II. 416. A letter from William Bennett, Latimer's chaplain, to Latimer indicates that Bennett was active in setting the affairs of the college in order. *LP*, XIV, Pt.1. No.638 (SP 1/144. f.199).
31. *LP*, XIII, Pt.1. No.1177 (SP 1/133. f.29). *Works*, II. 393-395.
32. *Works*, II. 391, 395, 397, 418.
33. Cranmer, *Miscellaneous Writings and Letters*, p.375.
34. See above, note 27.
35. *LP*, XIV, Pt.1. No.84 (SP 1/142. f.88). *Works*, II. 415-416.
36. See above, note 21 and *LP*, XIII, Pt.2. No.646. *Works*, II. 405.
37. *Works*, II. 393.
38. *VCH Worcester*, II. 173-175.
39. *LP*, XIII, Pt.1. No.1258 (SP 1/133, f.205). *Works*, II. 397-398.

CHAPTER TWENTY

The Six Articles

1. "And your lordship would have thanked the king's grace's highness for my stag, in my name, I had been much bounden to you. I have made many merry in these parts, for I eat not all myself. God save the king!" Latimer to Cromwell. *LP*, XIII, Pt.2. No.543 (SP 1/137. f.111). *Works*, II. 404.
2. George Joye, *A contrarye (to a certayne manis) consultacion: that adulterers ought to be punyshed wythe deathe*. (n.p.1549?) (*STC*, 14822). Joye's book is an attack on John Foxe's *De non plectendis morte adulteris consultatio*, 1548 (*STC*, 11235), which was re-issued in 1549 under the title *De lapsis in ecclesiam recipiendis*. The re-issue is not listed in *STC*. (For this refer-

ence I am indebted to Rev. J. F. Mozley.)
3. Third Sermon before King Edward VI. *Works*, I. 134-135.
4. Seventh Sermon before King Edward VI. *Works*, I. 231.
5. Many letters of this period indicate the close contact between the English and the Continental reformers. Thus in October of 1538 Martin Bucer wrote to Cranmer to say that the archbishop's "godly designs have prospered beyond expectation, assisted by the Latimers, the [Edward] Foxes, and others." (*Original Letters* ["Zurich Letters"] p.520). Another letter reports the English reformers' approval of a book by Henry Bullinger, the Swiss theologian (*LP*, XIII, Pt.2. No.373).

6. Cranmer, *Miscellaneous Writings and Letters*, p.375.
7. See above, pp.108-109.
8. See Foxe, V. 181-236, and *DNB*.
9. *STC*, 7790. Printed in Wilkins, III. 777; and in Strype's *Cranmer*, II. 685-691. See also Steele, *Tudor and Stuart Proclamations*, No.176.
10. Merriman (*Life and Letters of Thomas Cromwell*) minimizes the extent of his interest in the doctrinal aspects of the reformation.
11. See Muller, *Stephen Gardiner and the Tudor Reaction*, Chapter XIII.
12. *Lords' Journal*, I. 105.
13. Sermon on the Gospel for All Saints' Day. *Works*, I. 487.
14. Third Sermon before King Edward VI. *Works*, I. 136.
15. *LP*, XIV, Pt.1. No.1040 (Cotton MS Cleopatra E.V. f.129).

16. *LP*, XIV, Pt.1. No.1065.
17. *Statutes of the Realm*, III. 739-743.
18. Seventh Sermon before King Edward VI. *Works*, I. 231-232.
19. *State Papers, Henry VIII*, I. 848-851. Also *LP*, XXI, Pt.1. No.823.
20. *DNB*, *s.v.* Shaxton.
21. *LP*, XIV, Pt.1. No.1220 (SP 3/11. f.3).
22. Foxe, VII. 463.
23. Hist. MSS Comm. Calendar of Salisbury MSS, Part 2, p.121.
24. Foxe, VII. 463.
25. It may be noted that although Sir Thomas More disapproved the Act of Supremacy, he was *permitted* to resign the chancellorship on the grounds of poor health.
26. This is the view of A. F. Pollard in *Thomas Cranmer and the English Reformation*, pp.131-132.

CHAPTER TWENTY-ONE

The Silent Years

1. *LP*, XIV, Pt.1. No.1217 (SP 1/152. f.143).
2. *LP*, XIV, Pt.1. No.1228 (SP 3/4/19).
3. *LP*, XIV, Pt.1. No.1354 (item 30).
4. *LP*, XIV, Pt.2. No.113 (items 2 and 13).
5. Stubbs, *Registrum Sacrum Anglicanum*, p.101.
6. Third Sermon before King Edward VI. *Works*, I. 135-136.
7. *LP*, XIV, Pt.1. Nos.1219, 1227 (SP 3/8. f.41; SP 3/5. f.29).
8. See above, note 2.
9. Fourth Sermon before Edward VI. *Works*, I. 164.
10. *LP*, XIV, Pt.2. No.255.
11. *LP*, XIV, Pt.1. No.1260.
12. *LP*, XIV, Pt.2. No.41, items 2 and 3 (SP 1/153. f.27, 28).
13. *Calendar of State Papers Relating to Ireland*, pp.234-235.
14. See above, note 12.
15. *LP*, XIV, Pt.2. No.236 (p.73). Shaxton received the same amount.
16. *LP*, XV. p.541. *LP*, XVI. No.754, f.13. *LP*, XVII. No.258, f.17. *LP*, XVIII, Pt.1. No.436, f.65. *LP*, XVIII, Pt.2. No.231, p.122. *LP*, XIX, Pt.1. No.368, f.46. *LP*, XX, Pt.1. No.557, f.44. *LP*, XXI, Pt.1. No.643, f.54. *LP*, XXI, Pt.2. No.775, f.71.
17. *LP*, XIV, Pt.2. No.400. The letter was first printed in *Archaeologia*, XXIII. p.56.
18. *LP*, XIV, Pt.2. No.423.

19. *LP*, XIV, Pt.2. No.444. A translation of the Latin original is in Foxe V. 350-358.
20. See especially Muller, *Stephen Gardiner and the Tudor Reaction*, pp.83-89, and Rupp, *Studies in the Making of the English Protestant Tradition*, pp.44-46.
21. *LP*, XV. No.719.
22. *LP*, XV. No.737.
23. There is no official record of this prohibition. Richard Hilles, writing to Bullinger, said that Latimer and Shaxton were forbidden to come within "two or three german miles of our two universities, the city of London, or their own dioceses." *Original Letters* ["Zurich Letters"], I. 215. A "German mile" was equal to between four and five English miles.
24. *Original Letters* ["Zurich Letters"], I. 203-204.
25. Demaus, pp.367-368.
26. For the Glovers, see Richings, *Narrative of the Sufferings of Mr. Robert Glover of Mancetter*.
27. Becon, *The Jewel of Joy*. In *The Catechism of Thomas Becon . . . with Other Pieces*, p.426.
28. See Olde's preface to the Duchess of Somerset in the second part of the translation of Erasmus' *Paraphrase*.
29. John Olde, *A Confession of the*

Most Ancient Christian Catholic Old Belief (STC, 18798). Sig. A 2v.

30. *ibid.*, E 7r.
31. Mozley, *John Foxe and His Book*, pp.26-27.
32. For a more recent theory as to the model for Justice Shallow, see Hotson, *Shakespeare versus Shallow.*
33. Foxe, V. 553-561. The alleged words of the King are at p.555.
34. *STC*, 5168. Reprinted in Lloyd's *Formularies of Faith.*
35. Cranmer, *Miscellaneous Writings and Letters*, pp.83-114.
36. Foxe, VII. 463.
37. *LP*, XXI, Pt.1. No.810.
38. From the Council's account of Latimer's examination on May 13, 1546. *LP*, XXI, Pt.1. No.823. The document is printed in full in *State Papers, Henry VIII.* I. 848-851. The whole of what follows is drawn from this report.

39. *Works*, II. 249. See above, p.119.
40. Last Sermon before King Edward VI. *Works* I. 276.
41. In the Fourth Sermon Preached before King Edward VI, Latimer spoke of his having once been a prisoner in the Tower. *Works*, I. 162. Again, when he entered the Tower in 1553 he is said to have greeted one of the wardens with, "What, my old friend, how do you? I am now come to be your neighbor again." (See below, p.198). These passages can refer only to his imprisonment in the Tower at this time, since there is nothing in the record to indicate that he had previously been confined there.
42. *LP*, XXI, Pt.1. No.1086. Dasent, *Acts of the Privy Council*, n.s. I. 458.
43. For Anne Askew's story, see Foxe, V. 537-550; and *DNB.*
44. Pollard, *Thomas Cranmer*, p.181.

CHAPTER TWENTY-TWO

Return to the Pulpit

1. For Somerset's career as Protector, see Pollard, *England under Protector Somerset.*
2. 1 Edward VI. C.12. *Statues of the Realm*, IV. 18. See also Pollard, *op. cit.*, p.61.
3. *Calendar of State Papers, Domestic Series . . . 1547-1580.* p.5.
4. Stow, *Annals*, p.1002.
5. *STC*, 10088. They are reprinted in Frere, *Visitation Articles and Injunctions*, II. 114-130.
6. Article 6.
7. Article 21.
8. Article 32.
9. *STC*, 13639 ff.
10. Article 15.
11. Article 35.
12. Articles 11,23,27,28.
13. *STC*, 7812. See also Steele, *Tudor and Stuart Proclamations*, No. 318, where it is erroneously stated that no printed copy is extant.
14. *Annals*, p.1002.
15. *ibid.*
16. The date is given on the title page of the printed sermon. See below, pp.164-165.
17. *Works*, I. 61.
18. *ibid.*, pp.64-65,69.

19. *ibid.*, pp.70-71.
20. *ibid.*, p.71.
21. *ibid.*, pp.72-75.
22. *ibid.*, p.70.
23. *ibid.*, pp.66-69. He seems to refer especially to Cuthbert Tunstall, bishop of Durham, who was also president of the Council of the North.
24. *ibid.*, pp.66-67.
25. *ibid.*, p.74.
26. *ibid.*, p.70.
27. Stow, *Annals*, p.1002.
28. Last Sermon before Edward VI. *Works*, I. 262.
29. For Bradford, see Foxe, VII. 143-287, and *DNB.*
30. For Harington, see *DNB.*
31. *Works*, I. 262.
32. The relevant letters are printed in Foxe, VII. 277-280, where they are evidently mis-dated.
33. *Works*, I. 262.
34. Dasent, *Acts of the Privy Council*, n.s. II. 266,409,410.
35. Strype, *Memorials of Cranmer*, I. 254.
36. *Original Letters* ["Zurich Letters"], I. 320.
37. *ibid.*, p.322.

38. See above, pp.160-161.
39. Disputation at Oxford. *Works,* II. 265.
40. Cranmer himself, however, was said to have been strongly influenced by Bishop Ridley. See below, p.206. For a recent study of Cranmer's Eucharistic opinions, see Smyth, *Cranmer and the Reformation under Edward VI,* Chapter 2.

CHAPTER TWENTY-THREE

Apostle to the English

1. Nichols, *Illustrations of Antient Times,* p.13.
2. Rymer, *Foedera,* XV. 181. Pollard, *Thomas Cranmer,* pp.261-263.
3. *Journals of the House of Commons,* I. 6.
4. Dedication to the Duchess of Suffolk, *Works,* I. 82.
5. See Bibliography. There survives a MS copy of a Latin translation of the First Sermon—C.C.C. MS 104. This has been printed by Elizabeth T. Hastings, "A Sixteenth Century Manuscript Translation of Latimer's *First Sermon before Edward*". *PMLA,* LX (1945). 959-1002. Miss Hastings' careful comparison of the Latin with the printed English text leads her to the conclusion that the English text is pretty close to Latimer's original.
6. It is interesting to compare them with the sermons which Thomas Lever preached at court this same Lent. Lever's sermons are the more coherent, Latimer's the more effective. See Lever, *Three Fruitful Sermons* (*STC,* 15551) and *Sermons, 1550* (ed. Arber.).
7. On this question see Tawney, *The Agrarian Problem in the Sixteenth Century.*
8. Pollard, *England under Protector Somerset,* p.217.
9. On this topic in its larger aspects see White, *Social Criticism in Popular Religious Literature of the Sixteenth Century.* Also, with respect to the relation of Latimer's thought to the main currents of his day, see the suggestive essay by Charles M. Gray, *Hugh Latimer and the Sixteenth Century.*
10. For Lever see *DNB* and his printed sermons as listed in *STC.*
11. The best account of Hales is in Miss Lamond's introduction to *A Discourse of the Common Weal of this Realm of England.*
12. Lansdowne MS 238. Quoted in Pollard, *England Under Protector Somerset,* p.216.
13. Pollard, *loc. cit.*
14. Strype, II (1). 147.
15. The letter is printed in Russell, *Kett's Rebellion in Norfolk,* pp.202-203.
16. *A Discourse of the Common Weal.* Introduction, pp.xxii-xxiv.
17. *Works,* I. 88-93.
18. *ibid.,* pp.85-86.
19. *ibid.,* p.97.
20. *ibid.,* pp.93-94.
21. *ibid.,* pp.99-101.
22. *ibid.,* p.98.
23. *ibid.,* pp.126-127,142.
24. *ibid.,* p.152.
25. *ibid.,* pp.125,133.
26. *ibid.,* pp.86-88.
27. See the Last Sermon before King Edward VI. *ibid.,* pp.265-266. Also the Lincolnshire sermons. See below, pp.190-191.
28. *ibid.,* pp.137-139.
29. *ibid.,* pp.98-99.
30. *ibid.,* pp.101-102.
31. *ibid.,* pp.99-100.
32. *ibid.,* p.134.
33. *ibid.,* pp.188-189.
34. *ibid.,* pp.190-191.
35. *ibid.,* p.139.
36. *ibid.,* pp.185-186.
37. *ibid.,* pp.186-187.
38. Pollard, *England under Protector Somerset,* pp.126-128.
39. *Works,* I. 126-128.
40. *ibid.,* p.134.
41. *ibid.,* p.133.
42. *ibid.,* p.196.
43. *ibid.,* pp.169-170.
44. *ibid.,* p.95.
45. Pollard, *England under Protector Somerset,* pp.108-109.
46. *ibid.,* p.108, note 1.
47. See Tawney, *Religion and the Rise of Capitalism,* and White, *Social Criticism in Popular Religious Literature of the Sixteenth Century.*
48. *Works,* I. 123,178,200.
49. *ibid.,* pp.121-122.
50. *ibid.,* pp.123-124.
51. *ibid.,* p.176.

52. *ibid.,* p.152.
53. *ibid.* p.272.
54. *ibid.,* p.207.
55. *ibid.,* p.154.
56. *ibid.,* p.122. See especially Canon Corrie's note 3 for the identification of Smith as the person alluded to by Latimer.
57. *ibid.,* p.201.
58. *ibid.,* p.208. The complaint that the people preferred "Robin Hood to God's word" was not original with Latimer. It occurs in *Piers Ploughman* and in a sermon of John Purvey quoted by Miss Deanesley, *The Lollard Bible,* p.274. There, however, the protest is against the preference for the "merry tales of Guy of Warwick, Bevis of Hampton, or of Robin Hood."
59. 1 Edward VI. C.14. *Statutes of the Realm,* IV. 24-33.
60. Pollard, *England under Protector Somerset,* pp.121-129. See also Leach, *English Schools at the Reformation,* Chapters 11 and 12.
61. *Works,* I. 69.
62. It will be remembered that it was the proposal to unite Clare to Trinity at this time that inspired Bishop Ridley to write the letter in which Latimer is praised as one of Clare's most distinguished sons. See p.5 of the present work.
63. See p.2.
64. *Works,* I. 178-179.
65. *ibid.,* p.121.
66. *ibid.,* pp.199-200, 209-210.
67. *ibid.,* pp.168,172.
68. *ibid.,* p.225.
69. *ibid.,* pp.121,129-130,167.
70. *Journal of the House of Commons,* I. 5.
71. *Works,* I. 118.
72. *ibid.,* p.117.
73. *ibid.,* pp.88-92.
74. *ibid.,* pp.117-118.
75. By this time the negotiations for the marriage of the king to Mary Stuart had collapsed.
76. *Works,* I. 94-97.
77. *ibid.,* pp.91-92.
78. *ibid,* p.91.
79. For Thomas Seymour, see *DNB* and Pollard, *England under Protector Somerset,* Chapter 7.
80. John Fowler to Seymour. *Calendar of State Papers, Domestic Series, 1547-1580.* p.9. (SP 10/4/31).
81. *Works,* I. 148. This and all the other passages pertaining to the Lord Admiral were deleted from all editions of Latimer's sermons after the first edition (1549) of the Edward VI sermons.
82. *ibid.,* pp.160-162.
83. *ibid.,* p.164.
84. *ibid.,* pp.181-183.
85. *ibid.,* pp. 228-229.
86. *ibid.,* p.204.
87. *ibid.,* pp.183-184.
88. We learn of this in Latimer's court sermon of the following year. *A Moste faithfull Sermon,* etc. Sig. A7v-A8r. This passage is not included by Corrie in his edition of the sermon.
89. Foxe, VI. 283.
90. *Works,* I. 183-184.
91. *A Moste faithfull Sermon,* Sig. A8r.
92. *Works,* I. 184.
93. This view was not shared by John Milton, who attacked Latimer in the tract *Of Reformation Touching Church Discipline in England (The Works of John Milton,* Columbia Edition. Vol.III, Pt.1. pp.9-10). Elsewhere I have tried to show that Milton's knowledge of Latimer's attacks on the Lord Admiral was based partly upon a reading of Latimer's sermons, and that Milton deliberately suppressed the fact that Latimer had denied the charges that he had lied or had been suborned. "Milton, Latimer, and the Lord Admiral." *Modern Language Quarterly",* XIV (1953). 15-20.

CHAPTER TWENTY-FOUR

The Last Sermons

1. *Works,* I. 82.
2. *ibid.,* p.111.
3. John Stumphius to Bullinger. *Original Letters* ["Zurich Letters"], II. 465.
4. See Russell, *Kett's Rebellion in Norfolk.*
5. *Works,* I. 246.
6. *ibid.,* p.252.
7. As printed in 1550 it was called *A Moste faithful Sermō preached before the Kynges most excellente Maiestye . . . Anno Domi. M.D.L.*
8. *Works,* I. 239.

9. Two manuscript copies of this sermon are extant—Royal MS 18 B. XX, and Sloane MS 1460. Both are fair copies and seem to have been made from the printed text. The latter has a title page which gives the date of the sermon—March 2, 1550—and includes a dedication to King Edward by John Douglas, presumably the scribe.
10. *Works*, I. 247-248.
11. *ibid.*, p.249.
12. In the *Dialogue Concerning Heresies*.
13. *Works*, I. 249-252.
14. *ibid.*, p.268.
15. *ibid.*, pp.273-275.
16. *ibid.*, p.243.
17. *ibid.*, pp.374-381.
18. On November 9, 1550, preaching at Stamford, he speaks as if at this time his customary residence was still in London. *Works*, I. 307.
19. Strype, II (1). 385; II (2). 200.
20. Foxe, V. 704.
21. Dasent, *Acts of the Privy Council*, n.s. III. 382.
22. Strype, II (2). 205.
23. North, *Chronicle of the Church of St. Martin, Leicester*.
24. North, "Churchwardens' Accounts of Melton Mowbray". *Trans. Leicestershire Archaeological Soc.*, where the entry is misdated October 1553. The year was 1552. I owe this information to the kindness of Mr. J. F. Mozley and Mr. C. H. Thompson, Leicester County Archivist.
25. Foxe, VII. 285.
26. For the Duchess of Suffolk, see Cecelie Goff, *A Woman of the Tudor Age*.
27. Sermon preached at Grimsthorpe on St. John Evangelist's Day. *Works*, II. 123.
28. Sermon Preached at Baxterly [but more likely at Grimsthorpe] on Christmas Day. *Works*, II. 92.
29. Quoted in Goff, *op. cit.*, pp.237-238.
30. *Calendar of State Papers, Domestic, 1547-1580*, p.41 (SP 10/14/57).
31. The latest extant sermon which can be dated was preached at Grimsthorpe on January 6, 1553.
32. Goff, *op cit.*, p.215.
33. Foxe, VIII. 558-559.
34. Strype, III (1). 227-229.
35. I have already cited the evidence for doubting the accuracy of this statement about Latimer's age. See above, pp.2-3.

36. *Works*, I. 320-321. Foxe (VII. 463-464) gives the same details, which he evidently took from Bernher.
37. See p.200.
38. *STC*, 15276.
39. Demaus, p.470, n.3.
40. *STC*, 15277, 15284. See Bibliography.
41. This was first pointed out by Demaus, p.470, n.2.
42. *STC*, 15278-83.
43. *STC*, 15279.
44. For example, in the Third Sermon on the Lord's Prayer. *Works*, I. 355-357.
45. *Works*, I. 282-308.
46. Sermon for St. Stephen's Day. *Works*, II. 96-97.
47. Sermon for the 23rd Sunday after Trinity. *Works*, I. 511-513.
48. Fourth Sermon on the Lord's Prayer. *Works*, I. 371.
49. *Works*, I. 376,410-411; II. 17,81,82-83.
50. Sermon for Christmas Day. *Works*, II. 86.
51. Fifth Sermon on the Lord's Prayer. *Works*, I. 394-396.
52. Second Sermon on the Lord's Prayer. *ibid.*, pp.349-351.
53. This is the central theme of the Sermon for St. Andrew's Day. *Works*, II. 23-43.
54. Third Sermon on the Lord's Prayer. *Works*, I. 363-364. Sermon on the 23rd Sunday after Trinity. *Works*, I. 531-532.
55. As Latimer indicates at the beginning of the First Sermon. *Works*, I. 326.
56. *Works*, I. 307-308.
57. See especially the Sixth and Seventh Sermons.
58. For characteristic passages see *Works*, I. 383-384,474. II. 137.
59. See *Works*, I. 495-496; II. 114, 209-210.
60. Sermon for Twelfth-day. *Works*, II. 137-138. See also the passages in the Sixth Sermon on the Lord's Prayer (*Works*, I. 419-420) and the Sermon for St. Simon and St. Jude's Day (*Works*, I. 449).
61. Sermon for the 3rd Sunday after Epiphany. *Works*, II. 175-176.
62. *ibid.*, p.175. See also the passage in the Sermon for Septuagesima, *ibid.*, pp.204-208.
63. Melanchthon to Cranmer. Quoted in Browne, *An Exposition of the Thirty-nine Articles*, p.422, from

Melanchthon, *Epist.*, Lib. III, Epist.
44.
64. *Works*, II. 127.
65. See above, p.184.
66. Second Sermon on the Lord's

Prayer. *Works*, I. 341.
67. Sermon for the 23rd Sunday after
Trinity. *Works*, I. 524.
68. Fourth Sermon before King Edward VI. *Works*, I. 155.

CHAPTER TWENTY-FIVE

The Debate on the Sacrament of the Altar

1. Foxe, VI. 592, 645.
2. Dasent, *Acts of the Privy Council*,
n.s. IV. 340.
3. Foxe, VII. 464. Bernher's Dedication to the Duchess of Suffolk in
Works, I. 321.
4. Foxe and Bernher, *loc. cit.*
5. Foxe, VII. 464.
6. Foxe, *loc. cit.*
7. *Certain Godly, Learned, and Comfortable Conferences between . . .
D. Nicholas Ridley . . . and M.
Hugh Latimer.* In Ridley, *Works*,
p.121.
8. Nichols, *Chronicle of Queen Jane*,
pp.26-27.
9. *ibid.*, p.27.
10. Coverdale, *Certain Godly Letters*
and Ridley, *Works*, p.370.
11. Ridley, *Works*, p.390.
12. Foxe, VII. 464.
13. *STC*, 21046.
14. *STC*, 21048-9. Another edition was
published in London by John
Awdeley in 1574 (*STC*, 21050). A
garbled version appears in Foxe.
The text of the first edition is reprinted in Ridley's *Works*, pp.97-
151.
15. Ridley, *Works*, p.112.
16. *ibid.*, p.116.
17. *ibid.*, p.117.
18. *ibid.*, pp.146-147.
19. *ibid.*, p.119.
20. *ibid.*, p.118.
21. For Grimald, see *DNB* and L. R.
Merrill, *The Life and Poems of
Nicholas Grimald.*
22. We learn these details from a letter written by Ridley to Latimer
and Cranmer while the three were
confined separately in the Tower.
23. Ridley to Bradford. Ridley, *Works*,
p.372.
24. Turner, *Hunting of the Romish
Wolf*, Sig. E4r.
25. Ridley to Edmund Grindall. Ridley, *Works*, p.390.
26. Disputation at Oxford. *Works*, II.
259.

27. Dasent, *Acts of the Privy, Council*,
n.s. IV. 406.
28. Foxe, VI. 439.
29. Ridley, *Works*, p.390. The date
given in the *Chronicle of Queen
Jane* (p.27) is March 12th.
30. Marginal note to a letter from
Ridley to Bradford. Ridley, *Works*,
p.359.
31. Ridley, *Works*, p.360.
32. Ridley to Grindall. Ridley, *Works*,
p.390.
33. We learn of all these details from
a letter written by Ridley to Bradford. Ridley, *Works*, pp.358-360.
34. Two of the letters are subscribed
from Bocardo. The third is subscribed "Written by Mr. Latimer,
being in captivity."
35. Foxe so describes her in the edition of 1563, p.1356. There are
numerous references to her in the
letters of Ridley and some of the
other martyrs.
36. Foxe, VII. 517. *Works*, II. 444.
37. Strype, III (2). 296-302. *Works*,
II. 429-434.
38. *Works*, II. 430.
39. Strype, III (2). 302-310. *Works*,
II. 435-444.
40. *Works*, II. 435.
41. The names of the delegates are
given in Strype, *Memorials of
Cranmer.* Appendices 77 and 78.
42. The details which follow are given
in Foxe, VI. 440-441.
43. The account of the first appearance
of Cranmer, Ridley and Latimer
before the divines is from Foxe,
VI. 441-443.
44. This is the English version of the
articles as given in Foxe, VI. 445.
The Latin version, from the official
copy in Harleian MS 3642, is
printed in the Appendix to Foxe,
VI. p.761.
45. Foxe, VI. 443.
46. Foxe, VI. 443-469.
47. Foxe, VI. 469-500.
48. See above, p.135.
49. Foxe, VI. 500-501.

50. The most readily available report of Latimer's disputation is in Foxe, VI. 500-511. This varies in some details from the official record in Harleian MS 3642. There are other accounts in Strype, I (2). 288-295 (from a Foxe MS now lost) and in MSS at Caius and Emanuel Colleges, Cambridge. Canon Corrie (*Works*, II. 251-288) reproduces Strype's version, collated with the two Cambridge MSS.
51. *Works*, II. 251-254.
52. Foxe, VII. 538.
53. That is, you hold your doctrine in feoff from Cranmer. A little earlier Weston had said, "Your learning is let out to farm and shut up in my lord of Canterbury's book."
54. *Works*, II. 278.
55. What follows is based on Foxe, VI. 533-534.

CHAPTER TWENTY-SIX

The Martyrdom

1. Dasent, *Acts of the Privy Council*, n.s. V.17. Cranmer had been attainted of treason for his alleged share in Warwick's plot to make Lady Jane Grey queen.
2. *ibid.*, pp.77,233.
3. Strype, *Memorials of Cranmer*, I. 562-563.
4. Ridley to Bradford. Ridley, *Works*, p.365.
5. Glover to Bernher. B.M. Add. MS 19,400. No.38.
6. Ridley to Bradford. Ridley, *Works*, p.379.
7. Ridley to Bradford. Ridley, *Works*, pp.363-366.
8. *ibid.*, p.366.
9. Demaus, pp.515-516, and Christmas, the editor of the Parker Society's edition of Ridley.
10. Pollard (*Thomas Cranmer*, p.371) argues that Cranmer *was* more sensitive than Latimer and Ridley because he had a broader intellect and a more open mind. But how can we be sure?
11. Foxe, VII. 465. Bernher, Dedication to the Duchess of Suffolk. *Works*, I. 322-323.
12. See Gairdner's article on Bonner in the *DNB;* Muller, *Stephen Gardiner and the Tudor Reaction*, pp.269-285; Schenk, *Reginald Pole, Cardinal of England*, pp.149-155.
13. Foxe, VII. 217.
14. Foxe, VI. 620.
15. Coverdale, *Certain Godly Letters*, Sig. M6r. Of about this same date is a letter written to Latimer by John Careless, the Coventry weaver, who in 1553 had warned Latimer of his approaching arrest. Careless, now a prisoner for religion, wrote to comfort Latimer and added, "And, dear father, I beseech you to remember me when you talk with your good God, that He may give me the strength of His Spirit, that I manfully yielding my life for His truth may do you some honesty, who have put me into His service to be a soldier in His camp." Careless was not burned; he died in the King's Bench in 1556. The letter to Latimer is printed in Foxe VIII. Appendix IV.
16. This account of the examination of Latimer and Ridley is from Foxe, VII. 518-542.
17. Both the Latin and English texts are given in Foxe VII. 525-526.
18. Foxe, VII. 529.
19. *ibid.*, p.530.
20. *ibid.*, p.531.
21. *ibid.*, p.532.
22. *ibid.*, p.534.
23. *ibid.*, p.538.
24. *ibid.*, p.540.
25. *ibid.*, p.540-541.
26. *ibid.*, p.542.
27. Ridley, *Works*, pp.395-418.
28. So at least says Froude, *History of England*, VI. 367. De Soto's sessions with Cranmer are well attested, but I know of no contemporary evidence that he also exerted himself with Latimer and Ridley.
29. Foxe, VII. 542-545.
30. Strype, *Memorials of Cranmer*, I. 563.
31. Foxe (VII. 547-551) gives us our only contemporary account of the execution. It is the most famous passage in the *Acts and Monuments*.
32. Ten years later Thomas Dorman, a Roman Catholic, in the course of

a battle of the books with Dean Alexander Nowell of St. Paul's, charged that the use of gunpowder would not have been approved by the early Christian martyrs. In rebuttal Nowell cited St. Ignatius, who said that he "would provoke and anger the beasts, that they might the more speedily tear him in pieces." The books in this controversy were Dorman's *A proof of certain articles in religion* (*STC*, 7062); Nowell's *A reproof of a certain book entitled, A proof of certain articles* (*STC*, 18740); Dorman's *A Disproof of M. Nowell's reproof* (*STC*, 7061); and Nowell's *A Confutation of M. Dorman's last book* (*STC*, 18739). The passages relative to the use of gunpowder are reprinted in Strype, III (1). 387-388.

33. Foxe, VIII. 266.

34. *ibid.*, p.289.

BIBLIOGRAPHY

Alesius, Alexander. *Of the auctorite of the word of God agaynst the bisshop of London.* [Leipsic? 1537?] (*STC*, 292).

Allen, J. W. *A History of Political Thought in the Sixteenth Century.* London, 1928.

Articles Devised by the King's Highness Majesty to Stablish Christian Quietness and Unity Among us, and to Avoid Contentious Opinions, etc. ("The Ten Articles".) [London], 1536. (*STC*, 10033).

Aubrey, John. *Wiltshire: The Topographical Collections of John Aubrey . . . Corrected and Enlarged* by John Edward Jackson. Devizes, 1862.

Bailey, Derrick S. *Thomas Becon and the Reformation of the Church of England.* Edinburgh, 1952.

Barnes, Robert. *A supplicatyon made by Robert Barnes doctoure in divinite unto the most excellent and redoubted king henrye the eyght.* [1534?]. (*STC*, 1470).

Baskerville, Geoffrey. *English Monks and the Suppression of the Monasteries.* London, 1937.

Bateson, Mary (ed.). [Cambridge University] *Grace Book B. Parts I and II* (Luard Memorial Series, Volumes II and III). Cambridge, 1903, 1905.

Becon, Thomas. *The Catechism of Thomas Becon, S.T.P., Chaplain to Archbishop Cranmer, Prebendary of Canterbury, & C. With Other Pieces Written by Him in the Reign of King Edward the Sixth.* Edited by Rev. John Ayre, M. A. Cambridge, The Parker Society, 1844. (Volume II of the Parker Society edition of Becon's *Works.*)

Bridgett, Thomas E. *The Life of Blessed John Fisher, Bishop of Rochester, Cardinal of the Holy Roman Church, and Martyr under Henry VIII.* 5th ed. London [1935].

Browne, Edward H. *An Exposition of the Thirty-nine Articles, Historical and Doctrinal.* First American edition, edited by J. Williams. New York, 1865.

Burnet, Gilbert. *The History of the Reformation of the Church of England.* 3 volumes in 6 parts. [Oxford Edition]. Oxford, 1829.

Butterworth, Charles C. *The English Primers (1529-1545). Their Publication and Connection with the English Bible and the Reformation in England.* Philadelphia, 1953.

Butterworth, Charles C. "How Early Could English Scripture Be Printed in England?" [University of Pennsylvania] *Library Chronicle,* XIV (1947). 1-12.

Butterworth, Charles C. *The Literary Lineage of the King James Bible, 1340-1611.* Philadelphia, 1941.

Calendar of Letters, Despatches, and State Papers, Relating to the Negotiations between England and Spain (1485-1553). Edited by G. A. Bergenroth *et al.* 11 volumes. London, 1862-1916.

Calendar of State Papers, Domestic Series, of the Reigns of Edward VI, Mary, Elizabeth, 1547-1580. Edited by Robert Lemon. London, 1856.

Calendar of the State Papers Relating to Ireland, of the Reigns of Henry VIII, Edward VI, Mary and Elizabeth, 1509-1573. Edited by H. C. Hamilton. London, 1860.

Calendar of State Papers, Venetian. Edited by Rawdan Brown, Cavendish Betinck, and Horatio Brown. 9 volumes. London, 1864-1898.

Calendar of Wills Proved in the Vice-Chancellor's Court at Cambridge, 1501-1765. Cambridge, 1907.

Carlyle, R. M. and A. J. *Hugh Latimer.* London, 1899.

Certain Sermons or Homilies Appointed to be Read in Churches in the Time of Queen Elizabeth. ("The Book of Homilies."). 3rd American ed. Philadelphia, 1844.

Chambers, R. W. *Thomas More* (Bedford Historical Series, Vol. II). London, 1938.

Chester, Allan G. "The Authorship and Provenance of a Political Ballad of the Reign of Henry VIII." *Notes and Queries,* CXCV (1950). 203-205.

Chester, Allan G. "Hugh Latimer at Cambridge." *Crozer Quarterly,* XXVIII (1951). 306-318.

Chester Allan G. "Milton, Latimer, and the Lord Admiral." *Modern Language Quarterly,* XIV (1953). 15-20.

BIBLIOGRAPHY

Chester, Allan G. "A Note on the Burning of Lutheran Books in England." [Univ. of Pennsylvania] *Library Chronicle,* XVIII (1952). 68-71.

Chester, Allan G. "Robert Barnes and the Burning of the Books." *Huntington Library Quarterly,* XIV (1951). 211-221.

The Chronicle of Queen Jane, and of Two Years of Queen Mary, and Especially of the Rebellion of Sir Thomas Wyat. Written by a Resident in the Tower of London. Edited by John G. Nichols (Camden Society Publications, Vol. XLVIII). London, 1850.

Cooke, Frances E. *Three Great Lives* [Savonarola, Latimer, More]. London, 1884.

Cooper, Charles Henry. *Annals of Cambridge.* 3 volumes. 1842-45.

Cooper, Charles Henry, and Thompson Cooper. *Athenae Cantabrigienses.* 2 volumes. Cambridge, 1858, 1861. Vol. 3, *Additions and Corrections . . . with an Index* by George J. Gray, Cambridge, 1913.

Coulton, G. G. *Five Centuries of Religion.* 4 volumes. Cambridge, 1929-1950.

Coulton, G. G. *Medieval Panorama.* Cambridge and New York, 1938.

Coverdale, Miles. *Certain Most Godly, Fruitful, and Comfortable Letters of Such True Saints and Holy Martyrs of God, as in the Late Bloody Persecution Here within This Realm, Gave Their Lives for the Defense of Christ's Holy Gospel.* London, 1564. (*STC,* 5886).

Cranmer, Thomas. *A defence of the true and catholike doctrine of the Sacrament.* London, 1550. (*STC,* 6000).

Cranmer, Thomas. *Miscellaneous Writings and Letters of Thomas Cranmer.* Edited by John Edmund Cox. The Parker Society. Cambridge, 1846.

Cranmer, Thomas. *The Remains of Thomas Cranmer, D.D., Archbishop of Canterbury.* Edited by Henry Jenkyns. 4 volumes. Oxford, 1833.

Creighton, Mandell. "The Italian Bishops of Worcester." In *Historical Essays and Reviews.* London, 1902. 202-234.

Dasent, John R. (ed.). *Acts of the Privy Council of England.* New Series, Volumes 1-5. London, 1890-1892.

Deanesly, Margaret. *The Lollard Bible and Other Medieval Biblical Versions.* Cambridge, 1920.

Demaus, Robert. *Hugh Latimer, A Biography.* London, 1869. Revised 1881. Reprinted 1904, 1927.

A Discourse of the Common Weal of this Realm of England. First printed in 1581 and commonly attributed to W. S. Edited by Elizabeth Lamond. Cambridge, 1893, 1929.

Dixon, Richard W. *History of the Church of England from the Abolition of the Roman Jurisdiction.* 3rd edition, revised and enlarged. 6 volumes. Oxford, 1895.

Dodds, M. H. and R. *The Pilgrimage of Grace 1536-37 and the Exeter Conspiracy 1538.* 2 volumes. Cambridge, 1915.

Dugdale, William. *The Antiquities of Warwickshire . . . revised, augmented, and continued by William Thomas, D.D.* 2 volumes. London, 1730.

Dugdale, Sir William. *Monasticon Anglicanum,* edited by John Caley, Sir Henry Ellis, and Bulkeley Bandinel. 6 volumes. London, 1849.

Duyckinck, George L. *The Life of Hugh Latimer.* New York, 1861.

Echard, Laurence. *History of England . . . to the Establishment of King William and Queen Mary upon the Throne in the Year 1688.* 3rd edition. London, 1720.

Ellis, Sir Henry (ed.). *Original Letters Illustrative of English History.* Series I, 3 vols. Series II, 4 vols. Series III, 4 vols. London, 1825-1946.

Fisher, Herbert A. A. *The History of England from the Accession of Henry VII to the Death of Henry VIII.* (*The Political History of England,* edited by W. Hunt and R. L. Poole, Vol. V). London and New York, 1906.

Forbes, Mansfield D. *Clare College 1326-1926.* 2 volumes. Cambridge, 1928.

Foster, Joseph. *Alumni Oxonienses: the Members of Oxford University, 1500-1714.* 4 volumes. Oxford, 1892.

Foxe, John. *Actes and Monuments of these latter and perillous dayes, touching matters of the Church.* London, 1563. (*STC,* 11222).

Foxe, John. *The Acts and Monuments* [Edited by R. R. Mendham and Josiah Pratt]. 4th edition, revised and corrected by Josiah Pratt. 8 volumes. London [1875].

Frere, Walter H., with the assistance of William McClure Kennedy. *Visitation Articles and Injunctions of the Period of the Reformation.* 2 volumes. (Alcuin Club Collections, XIV, XV) London, 1910.

Fripp, Edgar I. *Shakespeare's Haunts Near Stratford.* London, 1929.

Froude, James A. *History of England from the Fall of Wolsey to the Death of Elizabeth.* 12 volumes. New York, 1865-1870.

Gairdner, James. *The English Church in the Sixteenth Century from the Accession of Henry VIII to the Death of Mary. (A History of the English Church,* edited by W. R. W. Stephens and William Hunt, Vol. IV). London, 1902.

Gairdner, James. *Lollardy and the Reformation.* 4 volumes. London, 1908-1913.

Gasquet, Francis A. *Henry VIII and the English Monasteries.* 2 volumes. 2nd ed., London, 1888-89.

Gilpin, William. *The Life of Hugh Latimer, Bishop of Worcester.* London, 1755.

Goff, Cecilie. *A Woman of the Tudor Age* [Katherine Willoughby, Duchess of Suffolk]. London, 1930.

Grace Book A. See below, *s. v.* Leathes.

Grace Book B. See above, *s. v.* Bateson.

Grace Book Gamma. See below, *s. v.* Searle.

Grafton, Richard. *Chronicle; or the History of England.* Edited by Henry Ellis. 2 volumes. London, 1809.

Gray, Charles M. *Hugh Latimer and the Sixteenth Century. An Essay in Interpretation.* (Harvard Phi Beta Kappa Prize Essay). Cambridge, Mass., 1950.

Green, John Richard. *Short History of the English People.* 4 volumes. London, 1892-1894.

Hall, Edward. *Chronicle Containing the History of England,* etc. Edited by Henry Ellis. London, 1809.

Harte, Walter J. *Gleanings from the Common Place Book of John Hooker, relating to the City of Exeter (1485-1590).* Exeter, n.d.

Hastings, Elizabeth T. "A Sixteenth Century Manuscript Translation of Latimer's First Sermon before Edward." *Publications of the Modern Language Association,* LX (1945). 959-1002.

Holinshed, Raphael. *Chronicles of England, Scotland, and Ireland.* Edited by Henry Ellis. 6 volumes. London, 1807-1808.

Hooper, John. *The Later Writings of Bishop Hooper.* Edited by Charles Nevinson. The Parker Society. Cambridge, 1852.

Hotson, Leslie. *Shakespeare versus Shallow.* London, 1931.

Hume, Martin A. S. (ed. and trans.) *Chronicle of King Henry VIII of England. Being a Contemporary Record of Some of the Principal Events of the Reigns of Henry VIII and Edward VI. Written in Spanish by an Unknown Hand.* London, 1889. (For the identification of the Spanish Chronicler as Antonio de Guaras, see Hume's *Year After the Armada, and Other Essays* [London, 1896], p.77.)

The Institution of a Christian Man, Containing the Exposition or Interpretation of the Common Creed, of the Seven Sacraments, of the Ten Commandments, and of the Pater Noster and the Ave Maria, Justification and Purgatory. ("The Bishop's Book.") London, 1537. (*STC,* 5163).

Janelle, Pierre. "An Unpublished Poem on Bishop Stephen Gardiner." *Bulletin of the Institute of Historical Research,* VI (1928-29). pp. 12-25, 89-96, 167-174.

Journals of the House of Commons. Vol. I. n.p., n.d.

Journals of the House of Lords. Vols. I and II. n.p., n.d.

Joye, George. *A contrarye (to a certayne manis) consultacion: that adulterers ought to be punyshed wythe deathe.* n.p. 1549 [?] (*STC,* 14822).

Joye, George. *The refutation of the byshop of Winchesters derke declaration of his false articles.* London, 1546 (*STC,* No. 14827)

Lamb, John. *A Collection of Letters, Statutes, and Other Documents from the MS. Library of Corpus Christi College, Illustrative of the History of the University of Cambridge during the Period of the Reformation, from A.D. M.D. to MDLXXII.* London, 1838.

Latimer, Hugh.
(a) "Sermons on the Card." First printed, in summary, in John Foxe, *Acts*

BIBLIOGRAPHY

and Monuments, 1563 (*STC,* 11222). pp. 1298-1307.

(b) Convocation Sermon, 1536.

Concio quam habuit Reuerendiss. in Christopater Hugo Latimer', epūs Worcestrię in cōuētu spiritualiū, nono Iunii, ante inchoatiōnē Parliamenti celebrate Anno. 28. *īuictiss. Regis Henrici octaui.* 8°. Southwark: James Nicolas for John Gough, [1537]. *STC,* 15285. (Reprinted, 1592. *STC,* 15288).

The Sermon That The Reuerende Father in Christ, Hugh Latimer, byshop of Wercester, made to the clergie, in the cōuocatiō, before the Parlyament began, the 9. day of Iune, the .28. yere of the reigne of our Souerayne lorde kyng Henry the VIII. nowe translated out of latyne into englyshe to the intēt, that thingis well said to a fewe may be understande of many, and do good to al thē that desyre to be better. 8°. London: Thomas Berthelet, 23 November, 1537. *STC,* 15286. (Another issue is dated 24 March, 1537. *STC,* 15287).

(c) Sermon on the Ploughers.

A notable Sermō of yᵉ reuerende father Maister Hughe Latemer, whiche he preached in yᵉ Shrouds at paules churche in Londō, on the .XVIII. daye of Ianuarie. 1548. 8°. London: John Daye and William Seres, 1548. *STC,* 15291. (Two other issues were printed in the same year. *STC,* 15292-2ᵃ).

(d) Court Sermons, 1549-50.

The fyrste Sermon of Mayster Hughe Latimer, which he preached before the Kynges Maiestie wythin his graces palayce at Westmynster M.D. XLIX. the viii of Marche. 8°. London: John Daye and William Seres, [1549]. *STC,* 15271. (Two other issues were printed in the same year. *STC,* 15272-3.)

The seconde Sermon of Master Hughe Latemer whych he preached before the Kynges maiestie, within hys graces Palayce at Westminster the .XV. day of Marche. M.ccccc.xlix. 8°. London: John Daye and William Seres, [1549]. *STC,* 15274. (This volume contains also the second, third, fourth, fifth, sixth, and seventh sermons preached before Edward VI. Another edition was printed by John Daye in 1562. *STC,* 15275.)

A Moste faithfull Sermō preached before the Kynges most excellente Maiestye, and hys most honorable Councell, in hys Courte at Westminster, by the reuerend Father Master Hughe Latimer. Anno Domi. M.D.L. 8°. London: John Daye, [1550]. *STC,* 15289-90.

(e) Sermons at Stamford, 1550.

A Sermon of Master Latimer, preached at Stamford the .ix. day of October. Anno. M.ccccc. and fyftie. 8°. London: John Daye, [1550]. *STC,* 15293.

(f) Collected editions of the sermons.

27 Sermons Preached by the ryght Reuerende father in God and constant Matir of Iesus Christe, Maister Hugh Latimer, as well such as in tymes past haue bene printed, as certayne other commyng to our handes of late, whych were yet neuer set forth in print. Faithfully perused & allowed accordyng to the order appoynted in the Quenes Maiesties Iniunctions. 4°. In two parts, with separate title-pages. London: John Daye, 1562. *STC,* 15276. (Part I contains the Convocation Sermon, the Court Sermons of 1549-50, and the Stamford sermons. Part II contains the seven sermons on the Lord's Prayer, the sermons for the 20ᵗʰ—24ᵗʰ Sundays after Trinity, All Saints Day, St. Andrew's Day, and the 1ˢᵗ—3ʳᵈ Sundays in Advent).

Frutefull Sermons Preached by the right reuerend father, and constant Martyr of Iesus Christ M. Hugh Latymer newly Imprinted: with others, not heretofore set forth in print, to the edifying of all which will dispose themselues to the readyng of the same.

4⁰. In three parts. London: John Daye, 1571-2. *STC*, 15277, 15284. (Part I, with contents as for Part I of *27 Sermons,* was issued in 1571 [*STC*, 15277]. Parts II and III were issued in 1572, with title-page reading *Seven Sermons, made upon the Lordes Prayer . . . . Whereunto are annexed certaine other Sermons* [*STC*, 15284, which fails to indicate the relationship to 15277]. The contents of Part II correspond to Part II of *27 Sermons.* Part III contains twelve sermons not previously printed—the sermons for SS. Simon and Jude's Day, Christmas, St. Stephen's Day, St. John Evangelist's Day, Twelfth Day, the 1ˢᵗ—5ᵗʰ Sundays after Epiphany, Septuagesima Sunday, Sexagesima Sunday. The *STC* records seven editions of *Frutefull Sermons* between 1571 and 1635 [*STC*, 15277-83]. The 1536 sermons on the Rebellion in the North was added in the edition of 1578 [*STC*, 15279]).

The Works of Hugh Latimer, Sometime Bishop of Worcester, Martyr, 1555. Edited by George E. Corrie. 2 volumes. The Parker Society. Cambridge, 1844, 1845.

Latimer, Hugh and Nicholas Ridley. *Certayne godly, learned, and comfortable conferences. Betwene the two reuerende Fathers and holy Martyrs of Christ D. Nicolas Rydley late Bishop of London, and M. Hugh Latimer, sometyme Bishop of Worcester, during the tyme of their imprisonments.* 8⁰. [Zurich: C. Froschauer, 1556.] Reprinted, London: John Awdeley, 1574. *STC*, 21048-50.

Leach, Arthur F. *English Schools at the Reformation, 1546-8.* London 1896.

Leathes, Stanley M. (ed.) [Cambridge University] *Grace Book A* (Luard Memorial Series, Vol. I). Cambridge, 1897.

Letters and Papers, Foreign and Domestic, of the Reign of Henry VIII. Arranged and catalogued by J. S. Brewer and James Gairdner. 21 vols. and addenda. London, 1862-1910.

Lever, Thomas. *Three fruitfull sermōs made by Thomas Lever 1550, Now newlie perused by the aucthour.* London, 1572. (*STC*, 15551).

Lever, Thomas. *Sermons, 1550.* Edited by Edward Arber. (English Reprints). London, 1870.

Lloyd, Charles. (ed.) *Formularies of Faith Put Forth by Authority during the Reign of Henry VIII.* Oxford, 1856.

Lupton, J. H. *A Life of John Colet, D.D., Dean of St. Paul's and Founder of St. Paul's School, with an Appendix of Some of His English Writings.* New edition. London, 1909.

Madan, Falconer. "The Day-Book of John Dorne, Bookseller in Oxford, A.D. 1520." In *Collectanea, First Series,* edited by C. R. L. Fletcher. (Oxford Historical Society Publications, Vol. V). Oxford, 1885, pp.71-177.

Maitland, S. R. *Essays on Subjects Connected with the Reformation in England.* London, 1849.

Merrill, L. R. *The Life and Poems of Nicholas Grimald.* (*Yale Studies in English,* Vol. LXIX). New Haven, 1925.

Merriman, Roger B. *Life and Letters of Thomas Cromwell.* 2 volumes. Oxford. 1902.

Milton, John. *Of Reformation Touching Church Discipline in England.* (*The Works of John Milton,* Columbia edition. Volume III, Part I). New York, 1931.

More, Sir Thomas. *The Correspondence of Sir Thomas More,* Edited by Elizabeth Frances Rogers. Princeton, N. J. 1947.

More, Sir Thomas. *A dyaloge of Syr Thomas More knyghte.* (*STC*, 18084). [Reprinted in volume II of *The English Works of Sir Thomas More,* edited by W. E. Campbell and A. W. Reed, London and New York, 1927 and 1931.]

Mozley, J. F. *John Foxe and His Book.* New York [1940].

Mozley, J. F. *William Tyndale.* London and New York, 1937.

Muller, James A. *Stephen Gardiner and the Tudor Reaction.* New York, 1926.

Mullinger, James Bass. *The University of Cambridge from the Earliest Times to the Royal Injunctions of 1535.* Cambridge, 1873.

Narratives of the Days of the Reformation, Chiefly from the Manuscripts of John Foxe the Martyrologist; with Two Contemporary Biographies of Arch-

bishop Cranmer. Edited by John Gough Nichols. (Camden Society Publications, Vol. LXXVIII). London, 1849.

Nichols, John. *The History and Antiquities of the County of Leicester.* 4 volumes. London, 1795.

Nichols, John. *Illustrations of the Manners and Expences of Antient Times in England, in the Fifteenth, Sixteenth, and Seventeenth Centuries. Deduced from the Accompts of Church-wardens and Other Authentic Documents.* London, 1797.

Ogle, Arthur. *The Tragedy of the Lollards' Tower.* Oxford, [1949].

Olde, John. *A Confession of the most auncient Christen catholike olde belefe.* Southwark [Zurich?], 1556. (*STC*, 18798).

Original Letters Relative to the English Reformation, Written during the Reigns of King Henry VIII, King Edward VI, and Queen Mary: Chiefy from the Archives of Zurich. Translated and edited by Hastings Robinson. The Parker Society. 2 volumes. Cambridge, 1846, 1847.

Owst, G. R. *Literature and Pulpit in Medieval England. A Neglected Chapter in the History of English Letters and of the English People.* Cambridge, 1933.

Pollard, A. F. *England under Protector Somerset. An Essay.* London, 1900.

Pollard, A. F. *Henry VIII.* New edition. London, 1902.

Pollard, A. F. *Thomas Cranmer and the English Reformation, 1489-1556.* New York and London, 1904.

Pollard, A. F. *Wolsey.* London, 1929.

Pollard, Alfred W. (ed.) *Records of the English Bible. The Documents Relating to the Translation and Publication of the Bible in English, 1525-1611.* London, 1911.

Read, Conyers, *Bibliography of British History—Tudor Period.* Oxford, 1933.

Read, Conyers. *The Tudors. Personalities and Practical Politics in Sixteenth Century England.* New York, 1937.

Richings, B. *A Narrative of the Sufferings and Martyrdom of Mr. Robert Glover of Mancetter, a Protestant Gentlemen Burnt at Coventry A. D. 1555,* etc. London, 1833.

Ridley, Nicholas. *The Works of Nicholas Ridley, D.D., Sometime Lord Bishop of London, Martyr, 1555.* Edited by Henry Christmas. The Parker Society. Cambridge, 1843.

Rupp, E. G. *Studies in the Making of the English Protestant Tradition (Mainly in the Reign of Henry VIII).* Cambridge, 1947.

Russell, Frederic W. *Kett's Rebellion in Norfolk; Being a History of the Great Civil Commotion that Occurred at the Time of the Reformation, in the Reign of Edward VI.* London, 1859.

Rymer, Thomas *et al.* (edd.) *Foedera, Conventiones, Litterae,* etc. 20 volumes. London, 1704-1735.

[Rymer, Thomas.] *Syllabus (in English) of the Documents Relating to England and Other Kingdoms Contained in the Collection Known as Rymer's Foedera.* Compiled by Thomas Duffus Hardy. 3 volumes. London, 1869-1885.

Savine, Alexander. *English Monasteries on the Eve of the Reformation (Oxford Studies in Social and Legal History,* Vol. I). Oxford, 1911.

Schenk, Wilhelm. *Reginald Pole, Cardinal of England.* London, 1950.

Searle, William G. (ed.) [Cambridge University] *Grace Book Gamma,* Cambridge, 1908.

Seebohm, Frederic. *The Oxford Reformers, John Colet, Erasmus and Thomas More. Being a History of Their Fellow-Work.* 3rd edition. London, 1887.

Seyer, Samuel. *Memoirs Historical and Topographical of Bristol and its Neighbourhood.* 2 volumes. Bristol, 1821.

Smith, H. Maynard. *Henry VIII and the Reformation.* London, 1948.

Smith, H. Maynard. *Pre-Reformation England.* London, 1938.

Smyth, C. H. *Cranmer and the Reformation under Edward VI.* Cambridge, 1926.

Smyth, Charles. *The Art of Preaching. A Practical Survey of Preaching in the Church of England, 749-1939.* London, 1940.

State Papers, Henry VIII. 11 volumes. London, 1830-1852.

Statutes of the Realm. Edited by A. Luders, T. E. Tomlins, J. Raithby, *et al.* 11 volumes. London, 1810-1828.

Steele, Robert. *Tudor and Stuart Proclamations, 1485-1714. Volume I. England and Wales.* Oxford, 1910.

Stokes, H. P. *The Chaplains and the Chapel of the University of Cambridge, 1256-1568.* (Cambridge Antiquarian Society, Octavo Series, Vol. XLI.). London, 1906.

Stow, John. *The Annales of England, from the first inhabitation until 1600.* London, 1600 *(STC, 23335).*

Strype, John. *Ecclesiastical Memorials, Relating Chiefly to Religion and the Reformation of It and the Emergencies of the Church of England under King Henry VIII, King Edward VI, and Queen Mary I.* Clarendon Edition. 3 volumes in 6 parts. Oxford, 1822.

Strype, John. *The Life and Acts of Matthew Parker.* Clarendon Edition. 2 volumes. Oxford, 1821.

Strype, John. *Memorials of the Most Reverend Father in God Thomas Cranmer, Sometime Lord Archbishop of Canterbury.* New edition. 2 volumes. Oxford, 1840.

Stubbs, William. *Registrum Sacrum Anglicanum. An Attempt to Exhibit the Course of Episcopal Succession in England from the Records and Chronicles of the Church.* 2nd edition. Oxford, 1897.

Sturge, Charles. *Cuthbert Tunstall, Churchman, Scholar, Statesman, Administrator.* London and New York, [1938].

Tawney, R. H. *The Agrarian Problem in the Sixteenth Century.* London, 1912.

Tawney, R. H. *Religion and the Rise of Capitalism.* N. Y., 1926.

Turner, William. *The huntyng of the Romyshe Wolfe.* [Zurich, 1554]. *(STC, 24356).*

Valor Ecclesiasticus Temp. Henr. VIII. Edited by John Caley. 6 volumes. London, 1810-1834.

Venn, John and J. A. *Alumni Cantabrigienses. A Biographical List of All Known Students, Graduates and Holders of Office at the University of Cambridge from Earliest Times to 1900. Part I, From the Earliest Times to 1751.* 4 volumes. Cambridge, 1922-27.

The Victoria History of the Counties of England: Warwickshire. 6 volumes. London, 1904-1951.

The Victoria History of the Counties of England: Worcester. 4 volumes. 1901-1924.

White, Helen C. *Social Criticism in Popular Religious Literature of the Sixteenth Century.* New York, 1944.

Wilkins, David (ed.) *Concilia Magnae Britanniae et Hiberniae.* 4 volumes. London, 1737.

Wing, John. *"The Candle Not Put Out." An Account of the Tercentenary Commemoration of the Martyrdom of Latimer and Ridley, Holden at Thurcaston ... on the 16th Day of October, 1855.* London, 1856.

Wordsworth, Christopher. *Ecclesiastical Biography; or Lives of Eminent Men Connected with the History of Religion in England from the Commencement of the Reformation to the Revolution.* 4th edition. 4 volumes. London, 1863.

Wright, Thomas (ed.) *Leters Relating to the Suppression of the Monasteries. Edited from the Originals in the British Museum.* (Camden Society Publications, Vol. XXVI). London, 1843.

Wriothesley, Charles. *A Chronicle of England during the Reigns of the Tudors.* Edited . . . by William Douglas Hamilton. 2 volumes. (Camden Society Publications, New Series, Vols. XI and XX). London, 1875, 1877.

INDEX

251

INDEX

Designed by: Guenther K. Wehrhan
Printed and Serviced by: Kutztown Publishing Company, Kutztown, Pa.
Bound by: Arnold Bindery, Reading, Pa.